ALSO BY THOMAS C. HOLT

*Black over White: Negro Political Leadership
in South Carolina During Reconstruction*

*The Problem of Freedom: Race, Labor, and Politics
in Jamaica and Britain, 1832–1938*

*The Problem of Race in the Twenty-first Century:
The Nathan I. Huggins Lectures*

CHILDREN OF FIRE

CHILDREN OF FIRE

A History of African Americans

THOMAS C. HOLT

Hill and Wang

A division of Farrar, Straus and Giroux

New York

Hill and Wang
A division of Farrar, Straus and Giroux
18 West 18th Street, New York 10011

Copyright © 2010 by Thomas C. Holt
Distributed in Canada by D&M Publishers, Inc.
Printed in the United States of America
First edition, 2010

Library of Congress Cataloging-in-Publication Data
Holt, Thomas C. (Thomas Cleveland), 1942–
  Children of fire : a history of African Americans / Thomas C. Holt. — 1st ed.
    p. cm.
  Includes bibliographical references and index.
  ISBN: 978-0-8090-6713-8 (alk. paper)
  1. African Americans—History. I. Title.

E185.H57 2010
973'.0496073—dc22

                                                                    2010026595

Designed by Jonathan D. Lippincott

www.fsgbooks.com

1   3   5   7   9   10   8   6   4   2

For

Leora

and

in memory of
Grover Cleveland Holt (1917–2000)
and
John Hope Franklin (1915–2009)

CONTENTS

ILLUSTRATIONS

IN INSERT

the HEW offices. Courtesy of the *Washington Post Star* photographic archives, copyright *The Washington Post*, reprinted by permission of the District of Columbia Public Library.

12. Malcolm X in Chicago, 1961. By Eve Arnold. Used by permission of Magnum Photos.

PREFACE

[You] are the brothers of God's preparation and the children of God's fire. The children of God's fire of the present transmigration of slavery, because in this condition God's fire impressed the mark of slavery upon you; and, granted that this is the mark of oppression, it has also, like fire, illuminated you . . .

 —"Sermões," Padre Antônio Vieira, seventeenth-century Brazil

[E]verything shines by perishing. I am told that the sun is burning itself out at a rapid rate of speed. It's shining by perishing. Light a candle . . . and it shines by perishing. And even you and me in this Albany Movement, if we are to be a significant part, we got to shine! We got to give of ourselves! We are shining not only in Albany but to the world around. Saying that the Negro can do without! The Negro can stand together! The Negro can protest together for the things that are right and justly his.

 —"The Eagle Stirreth Her Nest," Rev. Ben Gay, Albany, Georgia, 1961

I first heard Rev. Ben Gay's powerful sermon of redemption through suffering in the summer of 1963, when Avon Rollins, a fellow civil rights activist working for the Student Nonviolent Coordinating Committee (SNCC), generously gave me a phonograph recording that documented the Albany Movement. Albany's was the first of the broad-based mass street demonstrations that rocked America in the early 1960s. Drawing support across a wide spectrum of classes, professions, and generations, its leaders sought not only an end to racial discrimination in public life but political and economic equality. Most of all they sought their fellow white citizens' recognition of black people's humanity. They sought, as Reverend Gay put it: "Just to be like everybody else. To walk the streets with dignity and pride." Achieving those goals might require making "the supreme sacrifice," he declared solemnly, "for no doubt [God was] using the Negro to save this nation."

Albany's momentum would eventually falter, but Gay's message of self-sacrifice for a higher cause would echo through similar campaigns in scores of other cities during that amazing decade. This was true, no doubt, because his message resonated with a long tradition in black American thought. Recognition of one's humanity and access to democratic citizenship were demands even those most alienated from the nation could endorse. The notion, moreover, that an oppressed people would one day redeem the nation's democratic promise was not only deeply embedded in African Americans' interpretation of the Judeo-Christian faith but part of their folk wisdom and of their secular intellectual tradition. Being black in America was to live an unresolved paradox: to be intimately a part of, yet starkly apart from, American opportunity, aspirations, and identity. From that liminal position, however, one might achieve what W.E.B. Du Bois called "second sight," a special appreciation, honed by a history of oppression, for how "the greater ideals of the American Republic" might be made to conform to and make real the broader "ideal of human brotherhood." Black Americans aspired simply to be "co-workers in the kingdom of culture," wrote Du Bois at the dawn of the twentieth century, and their cultural creativity and genius had yet survived and triumphed over public mockery and contempt. Having endured and outlasted a slaveholding republic and the nightmare of searing racial violence that followed, they had learned that "the harsh discipline of Negro life," as the writer Ralph Ellison called it, could be a source of strength as well as peril. Thus black intellectuals and ordinary folk alike believed that their historical experience mattered, that it made them who they were.

During my studies of the black historical experience in the Americas, I came across Father Antônio Vieira's remarkable sermon to a congregation of Brazilian slaves and their masters in the early seventeenth century. Father Vieira was a Jesuit priest, a diplomat, and sometime adviser to the Portuguese Crown. He was, I later learned, also of partial African descent and had for a while served as the official "Protector" of enslaved Native Americans. Although Vieira's metaphor of God's fire—one that illuminates even as it immolates—was strikingly reminiscent of Gay's "shining by perishing," his was a different message, for a different audience. While acknowledging the manifest inequality of slavery and scolding the slave masters for their cruelty, Vieira urged slaves to accept rather than resist their lot. Their masters controlled their bodies, but not their souls; slavery in this world was temporary, freedom in the next eternal.

Notwithstanding their fundamentally different political messages, the moral framing of each sermon was strikingly similar. Both Vieira and Gay were trying to make sense of the violent oppression and injustice that saturates the histories of Africa's descendants in the Americas. Both urged their audiences to accept that one is more than the sum of one's treatment and condition. Their message was that each person possesses an inner light that shines bright against the dark and that somewhere in the darkest night there is the light of redemption. It was a message that resonates with one of the most popular songs of the Civil Rights Movement, "This Little Light of Mine." It was a faith that Martin Luther King, Jr., expressed movingly in one of his last great speeches, "the arc of the moral universe is long but it bends toward justice."

Invoking such cosmic framing for ordinary people's everyday reality is potentially dangerous terrain for a historian. If some children were illuminated by God's fire, some just as surely were consumed. King's cosmic arc provides a better fit than older, more secular visions of a linear, upward sweep—"progress," some might say—though even it is not entirely congruent with narrative plotlines that were more likely to resemble an undulating wave pushing forward but not always upward. I find myself drawn to the latter image, because it better captures the complexity, tension, and contingence of the black experience as revealed in these pages.

I discovered inspiration for the shape of this narrative in my own lived experience, or more precisely in the interplay of my father's lifeline with my own. My academic training had taught me to frame the broad sweep of African American history in neat chronological boxes, each congruent with a phase of "official" history—wars, presidential administrations, and occasionally broad social transformations like industrialization and urbanization. The slave trade, slavery, emancipation, Jim Crow, the Great Migration, the Civil Rights Movement—all were self-contained and clearly delineated. My father's death led me to question this organization, however. Born in 1917, he lived through some of Jim Crow's most virulent years and the Civil Rights Movement that ended it. His childhood was enmeshed in the southern agrarian economy, and as an adult he witnessed its demise. Beginning life in the wake of the crusade to save the world from democracy's enemies, he would later fight in the Pacific to secure that democracy a second time. Returning home to the same Jim Crow nation he had left, he would fight to save democracy once again. In the end, he would leave a very different world than the one he had been born into.

What my father's life suggested to me was that ordinary people don't live history as it is taught by historians. They live across our chronological divides. And if historians' conventional divisions of historical time failed to capture the life he had lived, then what of people like Richard Allen, born into slavery, then spiritually reborn during social and political revolutions at the turn of the nineteenth century, and finally ending his days leading a fierce challenge to the slave power? What of Frederick Douglass, also born into slavery and leading the successful struggle to destroy it, only sadly to witness its virtual rebirth during the last decades of the nineteenth century? What of W.E.B. Du Bois, who would spend most of his life carrying on Douglass's struggle for full citizenship in his native land, but end his days as a citizen of an African nation, on the very eve of that struggle's triumph? As with my father and me, these were not stories of discreet generational cohorts moving independently through time, but of overlapping intergenerational experiences.

Thus, the story I tell here unfolds through roughly generational units of time. It is not intended to be encyclopedic—everything that ever happened to black people in America or every black person who did something important—but hopefully it provides a comprehensible perspective on that history as it was experienced by the subjects who people and animate this narrative. What could be known and thought? What was the world like as a living being experienced it, and within timeframes that he or she could comprehend? It's a history that also reflects the intergenerational transfers—of memories, values, and deficits—all of which can make the past a force in the present.

As a consequence, the break points of my narrative often fall in different places than in more conventional histories. For example, there is no break between the Civil War destruction of slavery and the Reconstruction that followed, because in the lived experience of many of the principal actors there was a continuation—the same people, the same basic struggle, although fought under radically different conditions and with different resources. This is not, then, an argument about continuity versus discontinuity (in the ways historians have argued over it), but rather an attempt to understand how a contemporary actor would have encountered and responded to both the continuities and the discontinuities, each of which is constitutive of any given moment.

The contingencies that shape individual lives matter, but so do broader structural relations and seemingly abstract forces. People were and are the agents of their own destinies, but they are not free to shape those destinies in any way they choose. No history illustrates the truth of Karl Marx's pithy dictum more starkly than that of African Americans. One cannot make sense of a generation's lived experience without attending to the broad shifts in the political and economic contexts in which they made their way, and for African Americans that context was very often international as well as national. The slave trade and slavery were obvious forces impinging on black life in America, but so were the international pressures that destroyed those institutions and provided precedents for U.S. emancipation. Foreign wars often reshaped the terrain of domestic politics, but so did mass migrations and immigration. I have tried to render this complex history through the stories of people, not only because their stories might make these developments more immediate and accessible, but because they make history's complexity palpable. Hopefully, I have captured the jagged edges of real human experience, of people ordinary and extraordinary, who lived through contradictions and complexities, and struggled with life's nuances and ironies.

I also hope the history narrated here succeeds in showing that even ordinary people can recognize the larger meaning of their local and everyday struggles. People, such as those to whom Reverend Gay spoke, knew that their claims to American citizenship were also claims to a common humanity and a universal striving. With cries of "Amen," they affirmed Gay's message and acknowledged thereby the cumulative wisdom of a people's history almost three and a half centuries old. Suffering could demean the body, crush the spirit, and even destroy the soul—but it could also be a source of enlightenment and insight and, perhaps on some distant shore, redemption.

CHILDREN OF FIRE

1

MIDDLE PASSAGES, MIDDLEMEN
Europe, Africa, America, and the Slave Trade

In his *Generall Historie of Virginia*, published in 1624, Captain John Smith documented the difficult early years of settling the Virginia colony at James-town, the first permanent English settlement in North America, an achieve-ment generally taken to be one of the seminal moments in American history. Tucked almost inauspiciously among Smith's long descriptions of Indian wars and friendships, physical hardships and the eventual successes that defined this southern version of what the Puritans would later call an "errand in the wilderness," was the following brief passage quoted from a letter from John Rolfe. "About the last of August [1619]," Rolfe wrote, "came in a dutch man of warre that sold us twenty Negars."

The passage John Smith quoted with merely a passing glance would prove to be a momentous development. Momentous not because these were the very first Africans in North America; they weren't. Others had come almost a century before, with the Spanish conquistadores exploring the Southwest. There were probably some accompanying the expedition of Ponce de León to Florida, and certainly some among the aborted at-tempt to establish an early settlement in the Carolinas in the sixteenth century. In fact, these were not even the first Africans in Virginia; a mus-ter roll for March 1619 shows that there were already about thirty-two African slaves in the colony when that Dutch warship Rolfe mentioned laid anchor. Nonetheless, arriving scarcely twelve years after Jamestown itself was founded, these Africans were clearly the pioneers among those Ira Berlin has called the founding or "charter" generation of African Americans and certainly the first to receive written acknowledgment of their presence by one of the colony's founding fathers. Indeed, it was an acknowledgment not simply of their presence but of the character of that presence and of its provenance. Twenty Negroes . . . from a Dutch man-of-war . . . *sold*.

And it is their provenance—vague and emblematic though it may be— that catches our attention here. Embedded in Smith's cryptic notation are the complex and multilayered beginnings of the history of African Americans on the North American continent. Now, less than a decade away from marking the fourth century of that presence, we are struck by the fact that for more than half that time (two and a half centuries), the great majority of black Americans were slaves. How and why that came to be is the first question that must be answered in beginning a history of those four centuries. How is it, *why* is it, that when that Dutch warship laid anchor in Jamestown's harbor, Africans were in the hold and Europeans were on the deck? Why is it that the Africans were the ones in the position to be *sold*. It is a simple question; the answer, however, is very complex and far-ranging.

Of course, it may not seem so, or certainly it hasn't seemed so in the past to many historians and non-historians. Africans were the slaves and Europeans the captors because Africans were an inferior people, fit for or vulnerable to enslavement by a superior force. Others, anxious to redeem the reputation, or at least the moral superiority, of the Africans, turn that interpretation on its head: Africans were actually culturally superior to Europeans, but the Europeans were so thoroughly evil and rapacious that they subdued and enslaved the Africans. Despite their apparent opposition, both answers embrace a racial premise—virtue or evil, superiority or inferiority are racial properties. Such answers effectively foreclose further examination, for by their logic, biology or culture or morality is determinative and historical narratives emerge out of the innate qualities of peoples rather than out of the give-and-take, the contingencies, the larger social forces that condition or shape the possibility for one historical outcome rather than another.

Given the latter, more contingent, view of historical process, one must seek answers to this question—why Africans in the hold and Europeans on deck—in the complex unfolding of a long history of European and African contact that predated that landing at Jamestown by almost two centuries. What we must ask is, what social forces and historical developments brought this conjuncture to pass? Racial interpretations to the contrary, the more we learn of that earlier history, of Europe and of Africa,

"Landing Negroes at Jamestown from Dutch Man-of-War, 1619." This artistic rendering of the historic landing at Jamestown was drawn for the January 1901 issue of *Harper's Monthly Magazine*.

the less obvious it is that Africans were *necessarily*, and certainly not always, the social or political inferiors in that encounter. But, more important, we stand to gain from this approach some tentative insight into not only the forces that put those twenty Africans into the hold of that Dutch ship, but also who they were, or at least what the broad collection of Africans at that time and place were likely to be.

Although much of their history is likely to remain enigmatic, we can be fairly certain that the twenty Africans on that Dutch man-of-war were at the apex of a triangle formed by Europe, Africa, and America. At that moment in particular, three European powers—England, the Netherlands, and Spain, struggling for supremacy in Europe—were pushing the boundaries of their conflict into Africa and the Americas. There is strong, though not conclusive, evidence that the twenty Africans landed at Jamestown were part of a cargo of slaves on a Portuguese ship, the *São João Bautista*, that left São Paulo de Luanda—then the Portuguese stronghold in what would become Angola—bound for Vera Cruz, Mexico. It is "extremely likely" that the *São João Bautista* was the ship attacked in Caribbean waters by an English warship, the *Treasurer*, and a Dutch privateer. Although 1619 was the tenth year of a twelve-year truce, this attack appears to have been part of an ongoing civil war between the Dutch and the Spanish, the then-dominant European power that had occupied the Netherlands for several decades. For their part, the English, seeking to defend their still-fragile Protestant state against Spanish Catholicism, had formed a temporary alliance with the Dutch.

The forces propelling this particular narrative, then, were European social and political conflicts into whose vortex these African men and women became almost incidentally drawn. The Dutch ship was not a slave trader, but a ship of war bent on disrupting Spanish shipping and weakening the Iberian empire, of which Portugal was then a reluctant junior partner. It just happened that the prize carried by the *São João Bautista* on this day was slaves rather than the preferred silver or gold. At Jamestown, an English frontier outpost only recently discovering a growing need for servile labor, these captives were promptly exchanged for "victualle," that is, food and provisions.

But there is necessarily another side to this triangle: the supplier for this momentous exchange at Jamestown. Although we know little for certain about the twenty Africans who landed at Jamestown, we do know that unlike most of the African slaves and servants they found there, these people had come directly from Africa, rather than via the interregional trade with the Caribbean. Moreover, scholars have made a fairly educated guess that they were probably captives seized in Portuguese-sponsored warfare in central Africa during the years 1618 to 1620. Luis Mendes de Vasconçelos, newly appointed governor of the Portuguese enclave at Luanda and veteran of the Spanish campaign against the Dutch rebellion in Flanders, forged an alliance with an African warring band called the Imbangalas, or Jagas, to attack the kingdom of Ndongo (site of modern-day Angola). Ndongo was particularly vulnerable at this point because of a palace coup and succession crisis. No doubt Vasconçelos also sought revenge for a humiliating defeat that the Portuguese had suffered at the hands of the Ndongo in 1589, just thirty years earlier. The more immediate motivation for him and his Imbangala allies, however, was slaves. As in other African wars of that era, the line between military campaign and slave raiding was fine. Certainly one outcome of this war was that thousands of slaves were crammed into the port of Luanda awaiting shipment to the Americas—so many that the chances are considerable that the *São João Bautista*'s cargo was drawn from this provenance.

Those twenty Africans did not end up in the hold of that man-of-war, then, because they came from an inferior people—whether one defines that inferiority in cultural or racial terms—but because they were the losers, the pawns in a multinational struggle in which ruling elites of Africa, Europe, and the Americas competed for resources and power. In other words, their fateful subjugation arose out of very ordinary historical processes and developments, shaped by social, economic, and political forces. Indeed, more fortunate and opportunistic Africans participated in that slave trade—in its earliest years at least—more nearly as equal partners than as victims. It is true that, from a long-term perspective, they made a bad bargain, for in time the slave trade would render them, as a people, vulnerable to European penetration and overrule. Meanwhile, some European states would grow stronger as a result of that trade and the slave systems in the Americas it supported. By the eighteenth and nineteenth centuries, Africans would indeed be "inferior" to Europeans in the economic and military power at their disposal and, in some ways, in their material culture. By the end of the nineteenth century the African continent would be carved up and colonized by European imperialists. But one should not fall into the anachronistic fallacy of reading the later relationship back into the fifteenth, sixteenth, and seventeenth centuries. In 1619—and for at least a half century thereafter—the relationship between Africa and Europe was far more complex.

Out of those complex interactions—commercial, technological, social, and political—that characterized European-African relations in these earlier centuries, there developed new worlds, new experiences, and often entirely new peoples. Although in some ways many of the Africans who landed in North America were in the back channels rather than in the vanguard of these developments, they, too, were its legatees and they followed a course of cultural and social development first pioneered by a generation of African Americans whom Ira Berlin has called "Atlantic creoles." The development of American slavery and its eventual racialization must be understood against this complex historical backdrop. That history begins with another question haunting that moment in Jamestown harbor: What brought Europeans to the western coast of Africa in the first place?

Europe

If one takes the question at its most literal level—why were Europeans launching explorations of Africa and the Americas and not the other way around?—the answers are fairly straightforward and relate to physical geography and technological innovation. Although Europeans had extensive experience with sea travel, navigating the South Atlantic had long posed major problems, because well-defined systems of currents and winds limited the possible voyages that could be safely undertaken. The Canary Current, running north to south, sped ships down the West African coast but blocked their return. Arab sailors may have found ways to negotiate these currents, but if so, they left no enduring legacy, except possibly the geographical knowledge that eventually made its way to Portuguese mariners. Obviously the same current that so long held Europeans at bay had to have been an equally forbidding obstacle preventing Africans from sailing north, assuming they wanted to try.

Meanwhile, southern Europeans gained experience navigating two inland seas—the Mediterranean and, by the late thirteenth century, the Baltic—from which technical and geographical skills accumulated that enabled them eventually to master the open seas of the Atlantic. The

Mediterranean-Baltic connection shifted long-distance trade from primarily luxury goods to bulk commerce, especially grain, preparing the way for the movement of sugar, tobacco, and slaves that would later propel the Atlantic trade. As the volume of trade along this axis grew, fortuitous geographical discoveries became almost inevitable. Thus, in 1312, a Genoese sailor, Lanzaroto Malocello, accidentally rediscovered the Canary Islands. Just sixty miles off Africa's northeast coast, the Canaries would become a principal way station for voyages from Europe to the Americas and from Africa to Europe.

Though a necessary part of the story, these material and technical factors are ultimately inadequate to fully explain these developments. Some African groups also had very skilled boatmen; in fact, their skills at navigating inland waterways were put to effective use by slaveholders in the Americas. An equatorial current runs from Senegambia, on the west coast of Africa, to the Caribbean; indeed, it would later become an important route in the slave trade. Thus it was, technically, as plausible for Africans to sail west toward the Americas as for the Iberians. One scholar, Ivan van Sertima, has offered a controversial interpretation of archeological evidence from Central America to argue that Africans did in fact make such a journey long before Columbus. Even if some Africans made the journey, however, obviously they never established a continuing relationship or contact there; consequently, they did not—in this way at least—shape the history of the Atlantic world that unfolded.

West African waterways were full of falls and land blockages that prevented navigation by oceangoing vessels, but they were accessible to smaller craft with head porterage at critical junctures—which sustained a thriving African *inland* commerce along a riverine system that would later be integrally linked to the Atlantic slave trade, especially along the Central African coast. Faced on one side with such formidable barriers in navigating the South Atlantic, and on the other with ample opportunities for trade along coastal and inland rivers, Africans concentrated on the latter. In this choice, they resembled the Chinese sailors during the Ming dynasty who undertook seven voyages into the Indian Ocean between 1405 and 1433, led by the eunuch-admiral Cheng Ho. The Chinese flotilla made contact with Ceylon, Calcutta, the Persian Gulf, and Mogadishu in East Africa, but despite possessing the technological skills for further exploration and discovery, they simply showed the flag and sailed home—never to return. Like the Africans, perhaps, they, too, were content—or compelled—to apply their skills and knowledge to other tasks, developing commercial and cultural contacts closer to home.

The crux of the issue, then, is what was the social, cultural, economic, or political impetus behind the European push to solve the daunting technical problems, to make the necessary investments, to take the physical and financial risks? And here, too, we need to pause to make certain we do not fall into a typical anachronism that so often bedevils such analyses. What do we mean when we say "Europe"? In the fifteenth and sixteenth centuries, when these voyages unfolded, not only was there not a single cultural entity called "a European," but neither were there the nation-states we typically conjure up in our minds when we speak of *the* Spanish, *the* French, or *the* Dutch. When the *Genoese* admiral Columbus made his first landfall in the Caribbean, Italy was a bunch of warring city-states. The formation of the Dutch republic was still almost a hundred years in the future, and Spain—having only recently freed itself from centuries of Muslim rule—still confronted the problem of integrating its several provinces with a then-dominant Castile. For much of the slave trade era, Portugal went through alternating periods of independence from and absorption into the Spanish realm. England and France occasionally turned from civil wars at home to fight each other over territorial and dynastic claims. But even more important, our current vision of a state system, one that can command and direct resources from a centralized government, does not conform to the political formations we find it convenient to call "nations" in this earlier period. It would be more accurate to say that the causal arrow points the other way: that the development of the transatlantic slave trade was among the proximate causes, rather than the effect, of these powerful, modern nation-state systems' formations. Perhaps "Europe" was born of this expansionist project.

Much more important to this question of why European exploration—or, more accurately, why certain polities within Europe undertook exploration—were social transformations within key sectors that created new socioeconomic and political entities capable of and motivated to engage in innovation. The innovation in this instance was not just technical, but social, political, and economic. Not only did wind power have to be harnessed to move boats where one directed, but so did human effort, capital, and will. No one nation or group was responsible for this innovation; no one group held all the keys or talents. Instead the torch of change moved from one to another, leapfrogging over time and space—first the Portuguese, then the Spanish, then the Dutch, who landed those twenty Africans at Jamestown. Each of these had their moment of world dominance and then faded back into relative obscurity. Eventually, at the height of the slave trade in the eighteenth century, the lesser of the Northern European powers, the English and the French, would spill blood in a series of protracted conflicts that raged across Europe, America, and sometimes Asia to gain the upper hand—a fight the British eventually won.

Drawing adventurers and investors from across Europe to Iberian ports, the initial explorations were strikingly multinational, in any event. Indeed, it was nations from the Mediterranean world, which nurtured those multinational spaces, that took the lead in developing the Atlantic trade and modern slavery during its first two centuries. Their world, evoked in such vivid detail by Fernand Braudel, was a crossroads of cultural as well as economic traffic from Europe, China, India, and Africa. Across its eastern borders flowed the silks and spices that would motivate expeditions throughout most of the early modern era in search of a sea route to their sources in India and China. On its southwestern shores lay the northern gateways to an ancient trans-Saharan trade that drew from West Africa the bulk of Europe's gold well into the sixteenth century.

"Charlemagne, without Mahomet, would be inconceivable" was medieval historian Henri Pirenne's pithy summary of the process by which the European subcontinent was transformed politically and culturally through its engagement with the peoples, cultures, and trade goods of the Eastern world. His remark underscores the fact that the Mediterranean was not simply a crossroad of trade, but also the contested terrain of two militant and expansionist religious systems, Catholicism and Islam. Crucial to their engagement and Europe's transformation were the Christian Crusades, which by mobilizing Europe's diverse cultures and polities in a common cause, gave substance to a nascent cross-national identity, notably the idea of belonging to "Christendom." This arguably was the beginning of the concept of Europe and the West.

The Church, moreover, could mobilize not only military forces to battle Islam, but also work forces to build great cathedrals and monasteries, whose massive ruins remind us even today of the tremendous power of religion at a time when modern state systems were barely in their infancy. Nurtured by the Crusades, a cross-national Christian identity would continue to be proselytized, at home and abroad, through the international religious orders (Benedictine, Cistercian, and, later, the Dominicans and Franciscans) that were one of the First Crusade's institutional legacies. Orders such as the Knights Templar and Knights Hospitaller remained quasi-military in their organization and raisons d'être, and were incorporated into various expeditionary projects later, including many in northern and western Africa. The subsequent projects of exploration were inspired and enabled by these modes of thought and social infrastructures; they would provide both motivation and means.

Thus, Portuguese efforts to solve the problem of navigating the West African coast were motivated by religious injunctions to defend the Church against Islam as well as by materialist desires for greater access to the Far Eastern luxury trade. In the near term, gold and slaves attracted adventurers to sail and capitalists to invest. In the long term, the search for a sea path to the East added a strategic objective that could and did join the interests of the merchant and political classes. As always, however, religious enthusiasm lent material self-interest an aura of divine approval, bringing with it the transnational power and influence of the Church, which could be crucial in protecting and holding whatever gains such expeditions might bring. The crusading mission often took form, for example, with the idea that the Islamic world could be outflanked by establishing contact with a legendary African Christian kingdom led by a fabled chief named Prester John. Portuguese diplomatic missions to Christian Ethiopia in the early sixteenth century suggest a possible source for this myth and something of its enduring power.

Of all the European powers, Portugal was especially well situated to pursue these twin objectives—certainly better situated than her Iberian neighbor. For although Spain was moved by similar material and religious forces, and would in fact assume the lead in Atlantic exploration and colonization by the sixteenth century, Portugal was better positioned to undertake the earlier expeditions into West African waters. Both countries had similar geographical advantages: ports that were close to the Atlantic currents and to Africa, and that were convenient stops on the Mediterranean-Baltic trade route. But having recaptured its territory from Muslim invaders in 1253—almost two and a half centuries before Spain achieved the same feat—Portugal was the first to seize upon these advantages. Perhaps even more important, it was enjoying a period of peace in the early fifteenth century while most of the other future seagoing powers in Europe were busy cutting one anothers' throats in various dynastic and religious conflicts. Perhaps one of the "peace dividends" Portugal reaped was its relatively greater capacity to consolidate its emerging nation-state well in advance of other European powers. This is not to say that fifteenth-century Portugal was yet a nation in the modern sense, but as Braudel aptly puts it, "all things considered, it was already halfway there." It was one of the earliest state systems able to command the surpluses that would support exploration, settlement, and exploitation. In the years following their respective *Reconquista*, both Spain and Portugal evolved monarchies that succeeded in taming the powers of their nobility; but owing its victory in this dynastic struggle to bourgeois classes, Portugal's ruling House of Aviz strongly favored the commercial-entrepreneurial sector over the landed aristocracy, thus giving an early boost to its explorations.

Although the money and initiative behind fifteenth-century explorations came largely from private sources, the backing of strong unified state systems was not irrelevant to the success of these undertakings, because only states could sustain and consolidate such ventures in the long run. Private initiatives and investments were reassured by the mobilization of military and naval resources and the deploying of the diplomatic connections necessary to protect one's discoveries, at court or at the Vatican. Such general policies and state actions characterize the efforts of Prince Henry, the third son of João I.

The moniker "Navigator" given to Prince Henry by an enthusiastic British historian is at best an overstatement; he had no special talents at navigation and ventured out to sea rarely and for very short distances. Descended from the English Plantagenets on his mother's side, Henry was named for his maternal uncle, the English duke of Lancaster. Not being in the immediate line of succession to the throne, he deployed the independent household and income his father allotted him to make his mark and fortune in seagoing enterprises. Although the notion that Henry set up a special maritime school at Cape Sagres turns out to be a myth, he did gather about him a consort of merchants and sea captains whom he cajoled to undertake risky naval expeditions, and he brokered the finances to pay for them. The idea, moreover, that Henry's efforts enabled major technological developments is also considerably overstated. The replacement of the square-rigged with the triangular lateen sail—which gave more maneuverability when sailing into the wind—was probably the only significant new development directly relevant to navigating the African coast. For the most part, Portuguese seamen simply gained the confidence and skills to push ahead as they leapfrogged from one port to another along the coast and among the Atlantic Islands. And here Henry's role was perhaps crucial, as he supplied the exhortations and brokered the means to forge ahead.

In that latter role, it was important that Henry was "Prince Henry," even if his initiatives were often private and any profitable returns they generated flowed into his personal coffers. In 1415, at about the same time as his English cousin Henry V was urging his "brave few" on to victory at Agincourt, Prince Henry persuaded his father to mount a naval expedition to capture Ceuta, a Muslim stronghold on the North African coast across from Gibraltar that would give Portugal an African foothold from which to launch future expeditions. Five years later, at his father's request, the Pope made Henry head of a Christian military order modeled on the Knights Templar, a resource that could be applied in future swashbuckling ventures. Henry mobilized efforts to pacify and exploit the Atlantic Islands, the Canaries and Madeira, both of which became important sites for slave-based plantation cultivation. For Henry, the religious mission to convert pagans usually meant enslaving them.

Indeed, slavery was an early and persistent feature of the heroic expeditions undertaken under Henry's auspices. In 1444, Captain Lançarote da Ilha, tax collector and member of Henry's household, undertook the first slaving expedition. In a tragicomic scene, after landing on the Mauritanian coast, Lançarote managed to drag 240 slaves—many of whom were light-skinned Tuareg—onto his boats and bring them back to the slave market in Lagos. Watching the auction from astride his horse, Henry made certain that 46 of the best slaves were set aside as his share. Lançarote was knighted on the spot for his troubles.

For *his* troubles, the Pope granted Henry his blessing in 1455, authorizing him to conquer and convert sub-Saharan Africa. As many as twenty thousand slaves were probably imported during Henry's lifetime, a small number compared to what was to come. With four thousand or more being brought in each year overland via the ancient caravan trade route across the Sahara, African slaves soon became a common sight on the streets of Lisbon and other Portuguese cities.

As one parses Prince Henry's role in stimulating and encouraging the Atlantic explorations and the slave trade, however, it becomes clear that he stood at the nexus of broader social and historical developments. In the long history of slavery, it was fractional, often marginal groups within and between nations—including African nations—that made the critical moves to push and unfold this phenomenal development in world history. It is axiomatic, as Philip Curtin aptly put it some years ago, that "long-distance trade required *someone* to go abroad and become a foreigner." The omnipresence of such people—truly "middlemen," dislocated in time and space—provided essential resources for the crucial operations and innovations of the slave trade. The remarkable character of these and similar merchant cohorts is captured by Fernand Braudel's eloquent descriptors: adaptable, versatile, and "weightless." The last adjective especially conveys a sense of how social marginality—the ability to thrive in liminal spaces— actually enabled the odious innovations that would make the Atlantic slave trade possible. Living in enclaves in foreign lands, forging new social and economic ties, procreating offspring who emblematized new cultural-political linkages, such men pushed the boundaries of physical exploration, provided the capital for risky ventures, created intersecting communities that formed the nodes of a system of global infrastructure that, in the absence of modern financial systems, ensured that a deal was indeed a deal. The Mediterranean city-states produced the first exemplars of the breed and a model for others found later in trading entrepôts along the West African coast and in the slaving emporiums of the western Atlantic.

The earliest of these merchant cohorts emerged in the fifteenth century among traders from the Italian city-state Genoa. Genoese traders were a ubiquitous presence in the western Mediterranean: not only in Seville and Lagos, from which they managed the trade to Northern Europe, but in Ceuta, where they greeted Prince Henry's invaders—having probably provided material support to both the defenders and the attackers. Their presence in the western Mediterranean was the result of their being closed out of the lucrative Eastern trade. Facing east across the Adriatic, Venice already possessed geographical advantages in the Eastern trade that its political and diplomatic skills turned to economic dominance. Between 1353 and 1433, Genoa fought and lost three wars to Venice, and with the fall of Constantinople to the Turks in 1475, it was practically shut out of Eastern markets. Thus Genoa was forced to look west, exploiting existing markets and developing new ones. Genoese were the first Italian traders in the Northern European markets, beating the Venetians by almost fifty years. They were at the intersection of the exchange of Sicilian grain for West African gold brought by caravan across the Sahara. Winning trade concessions from royal houses in Spain and Portugal, the Genoese colonies were the most prominent among the merchant settlements established in Seville and Lisbon. Indeed, the Genoese were foremost among the Italian merchants who pioneered the protected, segregated enclaves of foreign traders throughout Europe and the Mediterranean. Either as private investors or through loans to the state, they financed an undetermined but significant share of the cost of the earliest Portuguese explorations of the Atlantic Islands and West Africa. It is clear that they were major investors in the settling and cultivation of the Canaries, Madeira, and São Tomé, all crucial staging grounds for initial explorations of the West African coast and voyages to the Americas. Genoese traders provided initiative, capital, and techniques (milling and irrigation) for the introduction of sugar cultivation into the Azores and Madeira. Indeed, Genoese merchants in Seville would continue to be major financiers of American trade ventures until the mid-sixteenth century.

Middlemen need not be, or remain, marginal, however. Genoese and other Italian merchants established marriage alliances with Portuguese families and became landed aristocrats. The Lomellini, moneylenders to the Portuguese nobility and the Crown, were exemplary of the transformation from marginal status to elite. The first of the clan, Bartolomeo, appear in Lisbon in 1424, along with other Genoese compatriots, supplying Sicilian and Castilian corn to the African fortified city of Ceuta. From there the family trading network spread as far as Nantes, in France, and to London. Other Lomellini established themselves in the Madeira sugar trade, and by the late fifteenth century they controlled the trade of wines, sugar, honey, and preserves to Flanders, Genoa, Venice, and even India. Through intermarriage with the Portuguese, the Lomellini became part of the landed aristocracy, and by the sixteenth century they had gained official recognition as nationals. Many of the fifteenth-century voyages along the West African coast and the exploitation of the Atlantic Islands that proved crucial to early slaving expeditions were funded by the Lomellini. Moreover, their activities illustrate the fact that these trading ventures faced two directions, toward the bulk trade in the Baltic Sea and toward the trans-Saharan trade in gold and precious stones from western Africa.

Aided by such middlemen, the Portuguese made slow but steady progress down the West African coast. Prince Henry's campaign in 1415 to capture Ceuta had provided a port of entry into Africa and shifted attention decisively southward. By 1434, after Henry's persistent urging, Gil Eannes had rounded Cape Bojador, the westernmost promontory on the Saharan coast. Thereafter, exploration of the Atlantic Islands mitigated the anxiety about the possibility of making a return voyage from Africa, since it was now clear that one had only to sail west and pick up winds and currents that eventually would bring one home. After an initial foray onto the Mauritanian coast by Lançarote da Ilha, the Portuguese made contact with Senegambia, the Gold Coast, and the Niger Delta. By 1483, twenty-three years after Henry's death, brief contact was made with the Kongo of West Central Africa, leaving only the voyage around the Horn of Africa to open the way to the Indian Ocean. In 1482, to consolidate their position on the West African coast, the Portuguese built a fortress near the mouth of the Volta River, São Jorge da Mina, known later as simply Elmina ("the mine"), a name reflecting Portugal's initial goal of gaining access to the mineral wealth of the Gold Coast. One of Africa's most legendary and earliest slave factories, Elmina was designed not only to keep African traders a safe distance away but also, with its cannons all pointed out to sea, to ward off European competitors, an aim replicated by numerous fortifications built along the West African coast thereafter. By 1493, they had established themselves on the island of São Tomé, just off the Gold Coast, at first as an entrepôt for the coastal trade and later as a sugar plantation. From there, during the early years of the trade, reversing the usual pattern, they actually supplied slave laborers to African miners in exchange for gold.

Over time Portuguese exploration and settlement evolved from state-supported but essentially private commercial ventures to expeditions, in the last decades of the fifteenth century, that involved more direct state sponsorship and management, especially once the trade in slaves had become a central part of American and European economies and institutional life. Thus when Bartolemeu Dias and Vasco da Gama set sail to circumnavigate the world in 1487 and 1498, respectively, their missions reflected broader geopolitical and commercial goals than even Prince

Henry had managed. However, the mixture of state sponsorship and private commercial initiative that Henry had perfected would long endure as a model for all such enterprises, as reflected later in the joint-stock companies of the English and the French, the Royal African Company and La Compagnie des Indes Occidentales, respectively.

By the beginning of the sixteenth century, then, the Portuguese—propelled equally by the quest for gold and slaves; for a shorter, safer trade route to the wealth of the Indies; and for contact with the fabled Prester John—had virtually mapped the main areas of the West African coast that would feed the subsequent Atlantic slave trade. The Treaty of Tordesillas with Spain, mediated by the Pope, consigned Africa, and thus the slave trade, to those two nations. Subsequently, though Spain succeeded in creating an American empire in the sixteenth century, it was dependent on Portugal to supply it with African slave labor. No other European power was prepared to compete with either of them at that time.

Africa

In much the same way Europeans were not yet "Europeans," Africans in the fifteenth century were not yet "Africans." In fact, to some extent, both of those more global identities would be forged in part from the dialectic of their relations with each other. Altogether Portugal's trade and political influence in West Africa ranged along a 26,000-kilometer coastline (16,100 miles) that would eventually embrace the principal slave-producing regions of the Atlantic trade, a space that encompassed a cultural and demographic array even greater than Europe's. The Africans spoke fifty different languages, worshipped an incalculable number of gods, traced their family lineages through fathers or mothers or both, and withal comprised a diverse array of ethnicities and social systems. Some lived under centralized hierarchical states similar to the monarchies Europeans were familiar with. Others—about one quarter, by one estimate—lived in small decentralized societies governed by systems bearing some similarity to the local democracies Puritans would inaugurate in New England towns some two centuries later. Certainly the Europeans and Americans most intimately engaged with African labor recognized the differences among them. American planters, for example, were well aware that the Igbo were of a different character than the Akan, or that Akan and Senegambians possessed different skills and training, even if such observations were often grounded in racist and highly suspect assumptions. The cultural, economic, and political backgrounds of Africans transported to the Americas varied tremendously, therefore, as did the historical experience out of which their travail took shape.

Nonetheless, Africans from different ethnic groups often shared a common cultural template, especially those living near the regional contact zones created by intense trading relationships. The African peoples of the Niger Delta, for example, were perforce either multilingual or had to create a lingua franca to facilitate the communications necessary to trade with one another. Living at such crossroads of human contact fostered both difference and affinity; indeed, their cultures as well as their languages were likely to have been dialectically related, like two sides of the same coin.

After years of lively, sometimes bitter debate, historians now generally agree on the broad aggregate numbers and overall patterns of the Atlantic slave trade, including the captives' ethnic origins. Although pinpointing the ethnic origins of the slaves carried to particular American locations remains difficult and contentious, it is much less relevant if one does *not* assume that African identities could be transferred to the Americas whole cloth and thereafter remain unchanged. On the contrary, if one understands that Africans were vulnerable to ordinary social-historical processes much like other people, and thus not immune to the political and social transformations those processes wrought, then it is likely that cultural change had already begun before the slaves even left the African continent. Part of a trade spanning four centuries, Africans were very much at the vortex of internally and externally driven historical transformations from the time they encountered Europeans on their western coasts—and, for some, even before.

In any event, we can determine geographical origins much more precisely than ethnic origins, and without conflating the two, one can depict the different historical conjunctures that produced slaves for American plantations, if not their specific ethnicities. Historian Michael Gomez suggests that six cultural-geopolitical regions—Senegambia, Sierra Leone, the Gold Coast, the Bight of Benin, the Bight of Biafra, and West Central Africa—were the principal venues for North American slaves, and these seem useful for our purposes. Gomez defines the Senegambia region as the area bracketed by the Senegal River in the north and the Casamance in the south, its principal ethnicities being Wolof and Mande, both heirs of the ancient kingdoms that bestride the trans-Saharan trade and home to Muslim centers of learning and religion. The "Sierra Leone" region embraces the modern country of that name plus Liberia and the Ivory Coast. "Gold Coast" roughly conforms to the area of contemporary Ghana; and the Bight of Benin corresponds with contemporary Benin and western Nigeria. The Bight of Biafra encompasses eastern Nigeria and much of the Niger Delta, while West Central Africa refers to the area encompassed by the contemporary Congo and parts of Angola. Very few slaves from Africa's southeastern coast landed in North America.

Data drawn from extant shipping records provide useful estimates of the relative proportions of slaves drawn from the principal regions that Gomez identifies. These estimates conform with others indicating that the Bight of Biafra, Senegambia, and West Central Africa were the principal sources for slaves who landed in North America, altogether supplying more than 60 percent of the whole. The Gold Coast and Sierra Leone supplied a little more than 20 percent, and Benin and the Windward Coast less than 10 percent. Not only were Biafra and West Central Africa among the principal suppliers of slaves to North America—roughly 43 percent according to these shipping records but closer to half by some estimates—they also frame the diverse patterns of European-African trading relations and the ethnic and cultural roots of North American slaves. Moreover, in contrast with most other areas, the flow of slaves from Biafra and Central Africa was fairly constant over the peak trading years of the eighteenth century, when most North American slaves arrived. In some ways, then, these two zones of African-European contact might serve as useful counterpoints for our inquiry, for together they embraced the opposite poles of the slave trade experience and thus bracket its diverse and complex history.

"I was born, in the year 1745, situated in a charming vale, named Essaka," wrote Olaudah Equiano. These words begin one of the more remarkable personal accounts of the experience of African enslavement that has come down to us. Written in the late eighteenth century, it tells the story of an Igbo kidnapped by African slave dealers from his village somewhere in what is now southeastern Nigeria. Six months after his

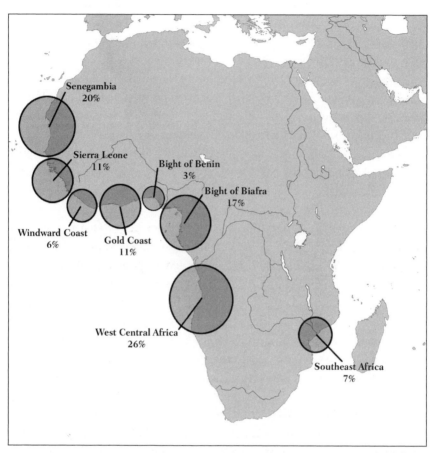

This schematic map drawn from data in extant records of slave voyages provides good estimates of the geographical origins of Africans landed in North America from 1619 to 1808.

capture, Equiano finally reached Calabar, from whence he embarked on a ship for the Americas. Though written for the benefit of the early campaigns for the abolition of the slave trade, with many of its narrative details proving difficult to confirm, Equiano's story, by turns harrowing and heroic, stands nonetheless as one of the compelling documents of the passage from freedom to slavery in the peak years of the slave trade.

Nearly a century earlier, in 1643, Garcia II, ruler of the kingdom of the Kongo, sent three envoys to Recife to meet with Johan Maurits, the Dutch governor of northern Brazil. One of them, identified later as most likely Dom Miguel de Castro, had his portrait painted by Albert Eckhout, which, by way of the Dutch, eventually passed into a collection in the National Museum of Denmark, where it now hangs. For the occasion, the Kongolese envoy donned clothing he had received as gifts from Maurits; gifts of clothing appearing to have been a standard diplomatic practice at the time. For this portrait, therefore, he wore a black velvet coat trimmed in gold and silver and a plumed, beaver felt hat with a gold and silver band; he carried a silver-plated saber. Dom Miguel's portrait carries no hint of the condescension and obeisance such gifts and "dressing up" might have suggested in the Atlantic world Equiano inhabited a hundred years later. Rather, he looks out at us with the self-confident bearing of one venturing into a world not entirely unfamiliar or threatening. In fact, he was but one of a veritable ambassadorial corps dispatched over the preceding century by successive Kongolese kings to various European powers, including the Vatican.

The experiences of these two men mark the outer boundaries of the three-and-a-half-century Atlantic slave trade. On the one hand is the youthful Equiano, ripped from his village and family and propelled on a harrowing journey into slavery somewhere in the Americas; on the other, the confident Kongolese envoy negotiating as an equal with the Dutch governor, possibly over some aspect of that very same trade that would ensnare Equiano a century later. Between the two lie worlds of time and space that shaped European-African relations in radically different ways. This Africa was not the seemingly homogenous space and timeless pool of later imaginings into which Europeans dipped their lines fishing for human gold. Rather, time and place matter very much in tracing the history of that trade and how it reshaped the fates of three continents and the destinies of Africans in the Americas.

Dom Miguel de Castro, circa 1643–44. One of three Kongolese emissaries to the
Dutch governor in Brazil, who was painted by the seventeenth-century Dutch artist
Albert Eckhout. African ambassadors to European capitals and the Vatican were fairly
common in the sixteenth and seventeenth centuries.

• • •

Portuguese explorers had reached the Kongo in 1483, almost a decade before the mission to find a water route to Asia took Columbus in the opposite direction. Diogo Cão had set out with something similar in mind, but like Lançarote had done fifty years earlier, he settled for seizing hostages for display in Portugal. But a measure of how much had changed in the intervening years was when he returned with those captives two years later, having heard from them of the wealth and power of the mani Kongo (king) and hoping perhaps to impress him with the wonders and power of the new world beyond the sea. Thus Cão bore presents (fabric, clothes, ornaments, instruments, horses) and people (priests, stonemasons, carpenters, and women to instruct the Kongolese in housekeeping Portuguese-style).

Even before Cão's party reached the capital, they received a warm welcome in one of the outer provinces. An impressive spectacle unfolded before them: dancers of a *nkimba* cult, naked to the waist and painted white, with palm cloth wrapped around their waists and feathers in their hair, performed their ritual movements. A regional leader and his son were baptized, and old fetishes were burned. The welcome was repeated at the capital, where Nzinga a Nkuwu, the current mani Kongo, and members of his court were baptized, and where he took the name of the king of Portugal, João, and his courtiers the names of members of the Portuguese royal household.

None of this should be interpreted as acts of obeisance or submission, however. Rather, as historian Anne Hilton suggests, for the natives, these gestures were meant to deflect and master this outside power—like some form of sympathetic magic perhaps. Kongolese cosmology divided the world in twain, that of the living and that of the dead, and much of the people's ritual attention was devoted to mediating that divide. Since the ocean represented one physical manifestation of this abstract principle, the Portuguese, having breached it, arrived wrapped in an aura of death—as suggested by the name the Kongolese gave to Portugal, *Mwene Puto*, the Land of the Dead.

The Kongolese rulers undoubtedly deduced nonspiritual reasons to treat their visitors with diplomacy rather than hostility, notwithstanding the latter's association with death. The Portuguese were obviously a formidable people and possibly useful allies, with their sailing ships and guns and trade goods. One of the mani Kongo's first acts was to dispatch his personal ambassador to João I bearing gifts to reciprocate those he had received. Meanwhile, the European masons set about immediately building a church.

The rapid, perhaps even precipitous, conversion of the ruling group to Catholicism probably reflected their view that the newcomers' spiritual-ritual powers had something to do with their manifest earthly powers. Such conversions were more calculating than fearful, however. Richard White's masterful dissection of the very similar relations between French missionaries and Algonquins of the North American Great Lakes region in the seventeenth century is suggestive of how such relationships might unfold. Much like the French-Canadian missionaries, the Portuguese met their African hosts on what White calls a cultural "middle ground"—that is, a political and social space where each party needs or wants something from the other but neither has the power to completely subdue the other. What follows, argues White, is "a process of mutual creation" in which differences are negotiated as each attempts, in their fashion, to understand the world in the other's terms, or at least just enough to achieve their ends. When the differences become too great, however, each party is just as likely to translate the stranger's actions according to their own cultural rules and move on. Such "creative misunderstanding"—most notably in religious beliefs—sometimes allows both sides to move past irreconcilable differences. On the middle ground, one lives in "a realm of constant invention," White suggests, which ultimately becomes a new "convention."

White's idea provides a supple framework for thinking about not only the making of African American peoples in the New World, but also the nature of their roots in the Old. He reminds us of an obvious fact too often forgotten: "roots" are either living, growing things or they are simply dead. Or, as the anthropologist James Clifford has written, an identity should be thought of not "as [a] boundary to be maintained but as a nexus of relations and transactions [to be] actively engaged." Perhaps nowhere are these ideas more useful than in trying to humanize the experience of Africans in the era of the slave trade, especially since their experience is so often depicted as frozen and static—mere stick figures of another's imagining. The image becomes more dynamic if we think of Africans moving through a kind of *cultural* Middle Passage, first in Africa, then in America, prologue and sequel to the physical Middle Passage. Each of these passages was brutal in its own way, but each was also a moment of profound creativity. In each instance the boundary of new contact was not simply with Europeans, but with other Africans—who often were strangers, too. Each of these passages moved Africans into a new world where physical and psychological survival often hinged precisely on their ability to turn spontaneous inventions into new conventions.

From this perspective we might better understand why and how the Kongolese conversion to Catholicism was neither insincere nor merely expedient. The African historian John Thornton has demonstrated persuasively both the institutional depth and the sincerity of their conversions. By all accounts, the Kongolese acceptance of Catholicism was a syncretic process. As often happens in such conversion experiences, there were familiar elements in the new religion, making it comprehensible even if revolutionary. Many of those elements centered on the key doctrines of death and resurrection, facilitating the melding of the two conceptual orders. As in contact situations elsewhere, the new converts merged Catholic saints with indigenous deities.

The Portuguese may well have thought of this mission much like many others before it, the bringing of a heathen people under the earthly and spiritual suzerainty of the Catholic Church, but this was not Mexico or Peru, where Spanish missionaries arrived in the wake of conquerors. If they sometimes forgot that they came as invited guests and stayed only at the sufferance of their hosts, the Kongolese rulers did not hesitate to remind them of this by expelling those who offended them.

To be sure, this embrace of Catholicism, whether for diplomatic or spiritual reasons, was not unanimously approved by all members of the African ruling group. There was disaffection with this new cult; some thought it witchcraft. The missionaries' insistence that the mani Kongo abandon all but one of his wives lent credence to the doubters, since this suggestion threatened to incite a political crisis. By tradition, political balance was maintained among the central lineage groups constituting the kingdom by naming a successor from precisely the offspring of this group of secondary wives. Such conflict was not unfamiliar to European royalty of that era; their royal households often had to negotiate conflicts between the peculiar sexual morality dictated by the Church in Rome and the political-biological requirements for keeping a given lineage in power— England's King Henry VIII being one of the more spectacular failures at reaching such an accommodation. In the Kongo, the matter was more skillfully finessed: the king simply married the first wife and, following European practice, called the others his concubines.

As is often the case on the middle ground of early cultural contact situations, the tensions prompted by European contact and cultural influence were not always about Europeans as such. Afonso, as the mani Kongo's son by his principal wife, looked favorably upon the Christians' novel insistence on monogamy and primogeniture, since otherwise he would not have been in the traditional line of succession. In the conflict precipitated by his seizure of the throne after João's death in 1506, therefore, his alliance with the Portuguese was instrumental in both a cultural and political-military sense. Prefiguring the Christian justifications for conquest and colonization of three centuries later, Afonso chose to represent this particular succession crisis as a struggle between Christians (his allies) and heathens (his opponents).

From the last decade of the fifteenth century and well into the mid-seventeenth, this transatlantic relation held both promise and peril, exhibiting synergies and schisms in the relations between the Portuguese and the Kongolese. Relations were initially between sovereign states, as reflected in the exchange of ambassadors, the Kongolese requests for "foreign aid," and the education of the Kongolese elite. In 1526, when Afonso concluded that the Portuguese had supplied a surplus of priests but not enough master teachers of grammar, he demanded more of the latter. In other cases, children were sent to be educated in Europe, with a number of them becoming fluent in European languages and ordained as priests to assume leadership positions in the indigenous church. Manuel Robrerdo, a Luso-African Kongolese trained by the Jesuits and ordained in 1637, was a prominent example of this phenomenon. The remarkable Robrerdo, who entered the Capuchin Order in 1653, became fluent in Latin and several other European languages and produced a grammar for his native tongue, Kikongo. Since the Church had designated the Kongo an Episcopal see in 1596, many similarly talented Africans rose in the Church hierarchy.

This moment of European contact was simultaneous with Kongolese imperial expansion, and Kongo's alliance with Christian Portugal often ensured victory in secular struggles within the kingdom and against enemies without. Occupying approximately 80,000 square miles of territory, the Kongo kingdom was only a medium-size African state (fifteenth-century

Songhay was estimated at between 300,000 and 600,000 square miles, by contrast), but considerably larger than Portugal (90,000 square kilometers) and only slightly smaller than England (150,000 square kilometers). Indeed, his initial monopoly on access to European products enabled Afonso to draw many neighboring groups into tribute relations, creating thereby "a greater Kongo" far larger than the late-fifteenth-century entity he had inherited.

A trading relation that had begun with the export of copper and ivory soon turned insistently to human beings, however, and the growing Portuguese demand for slaves thereafter became a source of political instability as well as political strength. Initially slaves had been drawn from groups such as the Tio, deep in the interior, beyond the treacherous falls that cut

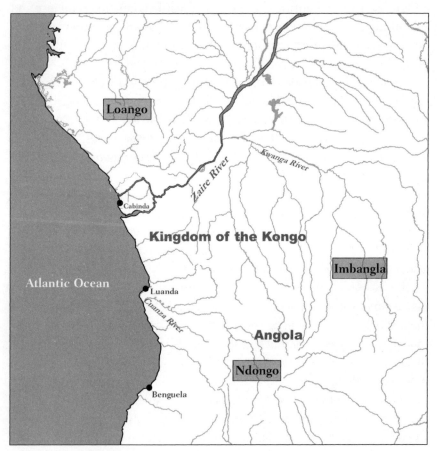

The port of Luanda provided a key embarkation point for slaves from West Central Africa, many of whom had been transported from the interior along the Kongo and other rivers.

the Zaire River, but the growing demand soon drew more and more from inhabitants of the kingdom itself. As in most African societies, misfortune might reduce members of one's own group to slavery, but normally one's own people were not sold abroad. There were even different words to mark the status distinction among slaves acquired by different means and subject to different treatment. Among the Bonbangi in Central Africa, slaves were all those deprived of the protection of kinspeople, but their traders distinguished those liable to sale to outsiders, *montamba*, from those who were not, *montonge*. Similar distinctions were found among other groups.

While it may be, as John Thornton argues, that increased warfare was only coincidental with the increased slave trading rather than causally related to it, there can be little doubt that that trade was in one way or another deeply implicated in the internal power struggles and the general political-military effects of the Portuguese connection. In Africa, slave raiding and war were but two sides of the same coin. As such, it can be very difficult to untangle cause from effect in gauging the impact of the slave trade, or to neatly separate the general impact of economic and social intercourse with Europeans from the effects of slave trading in particular. Some broader societal transformations appear to have been spurred by the demands of the trade, while other changes intensified and expanded that trade. Whichever direction the causal arrow points, however, slave trading and societal change seem to have been interdependent.

Alliance with the Portuguese gave the Kongolese a military edge at certain moments in their ongoing expansionist project. When the Jagas invaded Kongo in 1568—probably in an effort to break its monopoly over the slave trade—Portuguese guns and soldiers aided in repelling the invaders. In the aftermath of that victory, the ruling elite gained strength and independence from the traditional lineage groups that hitherto had been their social and economic base. Victory brought augmented trade revenue, which the Kongolese invested in slaves, who were used as soldiers and cultivators. Thus, as in Europe, a process began by which the monarchy became increasingly independent of the aristocracy and the traditional lineages that underpinned them.

Other transformative processes were subtler, and ranged far beyond those affecting the elite sector. As trade increased in volume and value, for example, former fishing villages became trading posts and traders wrested power from traditional chiefs. With developments in river transport came vastly improved communications, as fleets of large canoes, manned by sixty to seventy paddlers, doubled the speed of personal transport and quadrupled the range of royal messengers. There was also a greater reliance on communicating those messages in written text, which was enabled by the expanded literacy made possible, in turn, by missionary schools and the efforts to build an indigenous clergy. Written text favored rule by precedents rather than oral traditions; thus Christianity focused and legitimized central authority. As an inevitable corollary of this growing political inequality, the gap between rich and poor widened. The people ending up on slave ships were, almost by definition, likely to be the losers of such struggles: the poor, the vulnerable, the unlucky who found themselves on the short end of either wars or internal power struggles within their own societies.

As in any relations between sovereign states, tensions and intrigue developed between the Kongolese and their Portuguese allies. For example, Garcia II (who ruled the Kongo from 1641 until 1661) sought to make an alliance with Dutch newcomers in Luanda against the Portuguese, with whom relations had cooled as they switched their attention to Angola and threatened Kongolese sovereignty. Indeed, it may have been that the three envoys sent to Brazil were on some such related mission. Be that as it may, the strategem failed when the Dutch and Portuguese made peace in 1641. Thus Garcia II turned to the Pope, with whom the Kongo also maintained diplomatic relations, seeking to use the Vatican as a counterweight to the Portuguese Crown. Spanish and Italian Capuchin missionaries were invited to come to the Kongo in an effort to gain greater independence from Portuguese missionaries. But, of course, two could play that game: as Africans often set one European nation against another, Europeans encouraged what were essentially proxy wars among African nations to gain trade advantages.

By the seventeenth century, European conflicts—as that between Protestant Netherlands and Catholic Spain—gripped West Central Africa in their bloody embrace. As noted earlier, it was one such conflict that likely produced the twenty Africans landed at Jamestown in 1619. And, indeed, the political history of the Kongo for most of the seventeenth century played out within a triangle of intrigue between the Portuguese, the Dutch, and various African allies and enemies. From long experience, the Kongolese rulers were usually able to turn these intrigues either in their favor or at least to a stalemate, until two events undermined and weakened the rulers' internal coherence and hegemony. First, in 1648, a Portuguese attack, ironically initiated from Brazil under the leadership of a New World colonist, Salvador de Sá, defeated the Dutch decisively at Luanda and limited their field for maneuver in west central Africa more generally, thus depriving the mani Kongo of a counterweight to the Portuguese. Although the Kongo itself was not overrun, the Brazilians intensified the slave trade and made repeated incursions over the border. Second, in 1665, came the climactic Battle of Mbwila, where a formidable Kongolese army was defeated decisively by a Portuguese-led army of Angolans and Jagas. Although this victory was again not followed up by invasion of the kingdom proper, the royal household was so weakened as to be vulnerable to internal factionalism and soon fragmented in a quarter century of civil wars. Many of the African slaves landed in the Americas during this period could trace their misfortune to that internecine warfare.

The years of almost constant civil wars took their toll. By the first decade of the eighteenth century, various efforts had been made to secure a permanent peace and reunite the Kongo. These efforts eventually succeeded in 1709, when the Kongolese king Pedro IV was able, through a combination of skillful peace negotiations and military success over his rivals, to forge a new Kongo. In the process, he also had to contend with a different kind of threat from a remarkable indigenous religious movement, "the Antonians," led by an equally remarkable woman, Dona Beatrice Kimpa Vita. Originally descended from a noble household, Dona Beatrice was a local priestess who claimed to be possessed by Saint Anthony's spirit. She prophesied the establishment of a new royal household that would reunite the Kongo and bring an end to the civil wars. The prophecy was appealing to the Kongolese country folk, who had suffered greatly from the constant warfare and the threat of transatlantic enslavement it entailed; so they flocked to her side. Though neither anticlerical nor wholly opposed to the Kongolese ruling class, Dona Beatrice and her followers, the Antonians, articulated ideas, religious practices, and conventions that departed from standard Catholic doctrine, while depicting a political future that threatened the ambitions of particular leaders and claimants. It was a potent mix of religious enthusiasm and political salvation that in another era might have produced a proto-nationalist movement. However, the seed of its demise lay in its success: its sudden surge to power attracted some powerful enemies. Eventually, Dona Beatrice threw her support to a rival of Pedro's, which brought war rather than peace. She was captured and burned at the stake as a heretic.

One could read this episode, and other internal disputes, as a purely indigenous and self-contained event in Kongolese history. And yet, the internal antinomies of the Antonian movement are striking. Beatrice burned the Christian cross as a fetish and questioned the limits of the authority of the Pope. Her obvious purpose, however, was not to topple Christianity but restate it in Kongolese terms, as when she reinterpreted the birth of Christ as a Kongolese event that took place on Kongolese territory. Most notably, it was in the moral habiliment of a Catholic saint that she cloaked her own authority, and in her prophesy, it was the Christian God that authorized a new political order for the Kongo. Her story, then, was emblematic of how even indigenous fights were now thoroughly saturated with meanings and signs accrued from a now-two-centuries-old contact with Europeans.

Not just war and intrigue, then, but broader changes in the political-economic terrain changed the Africans' world. One of the principal motivations for reunifying and pacifying the Kongo, for example, was to establish the basis for a steadier and thus more profitable exploitation of slaves transshipped across its borders and channeled through its ports. Other African states along the West African coast would face similar political problems in calibrating their dealings with the European powers and with one another. Many of them also began, like the mani Kongos, bargaining as equals, but ended prostrate before European powers or, at best, as junior partners in a trade relation they could no longer control.

Although the overall pattern described for the Kongo-Angola coast—contact, transformation, and declension—may hold in some sense for every African people ensnared by the slave trade, the world of the eighteenth-century Igbo was very different from that of the seventeenth-century Kongolese. The people American planters knew as "Ibos" were drawn from the densely populated region formed by the Niger Delta and its hinterland. It was a world bounded by the Benin River on the west and the Cross River in the east, with its southern boundary formed by the Niger Delta, which extends about 270 miles along the Atlantic coast and thrusts 120 miles inland. Here the Niger River stretches watery fingers to the southern Atlantic. Together with four other major rivers—the Benin, the Brass, the Bonny, and the Cross—all interlaced with creeks and lagoons, it forms a vast and complex network of navigable waterways. The area has been dubbed "the Venice of West Africa," and it is claimed that in earlier times a canoe could maneuver from one end to the other and never go into the open sea. As in Venice, the inhabitants were a trading people, and the vast and vibrant trade networks they constructed formed the template for extraordinarily complex interethnic social and political relations, a dense human crossroads.

This area had been settled, just decades before European contact, by successive waves of migrants from the eastern interior, some set in motion

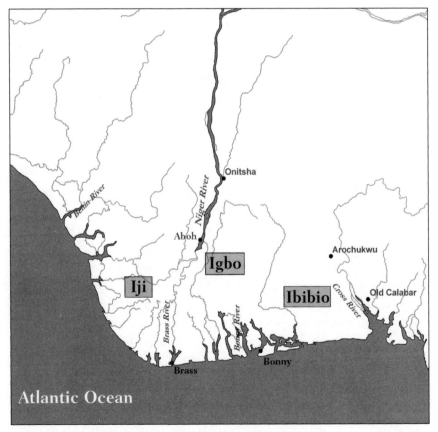

Niger Delta waterways, which some called "the Venice of West Africa," provided ideal embarkation ports to feed the transatlantic slave trade.

by population pressures, others attempting to slip the control of the empire of Benin, whose eastern boundary lay at the Bonny River while its western edge abutted contemporary Lagos. Later, the prospect of trading with the Portuguese drew yet more migrants, until this became one of the most densely populated regions in Africa and a shifting terrain of human traffic and fusion.

Like all such migrations perhaps, these engendered conflict between groups who regarded themselves as ethnically distinct—Igbo, Ibibio, Efik, and many smaller groups. Little wonder, then, that the youthful Olaudah Equiano was awestruck by the strange appearances and cultural habits of the many people he encountered as he was moved to the coast. Though productive of conflict and differentiation, however, these migrations also encouraged co-residence and intermarriage, a sharp reminder of the problem of retrospectively imposing static categories of identity on a people in the midst of rapid social transformation. Here, a socially and often physically mixed population emerged, especially in the urban trading communities of the delta city-states, but this in turn may have opened a cultural gap between these city-dwellers and those remaining in rural villages. As a mark of this sense of differentiation, inland Igbo referred to inhabitants of the delta city-states as "the saltwater people," a phrase that would echo on the other side of the Atlantic ironically as a term of derision Creole slaves hurled at African newcomers. But, in fact, this constant east-to-west movement, this ubiquitous ethnic transformation, formed a common template of lived experience. In many cases those African newcomers to the Americas may well have emerged from a kind of African melting pot that prefigured the very world they would later inhabit.

Unlike the Kongolese, or for that matter many of their neighbors to the west and north, these peoples inhabited highly decentralized and diverse social formations, politically as well as culturally. In contrast with the powerful monarchy evolving in seventeenth-century Kongo, for example, Equiano describes a form of governance centered on the local village, where respected elders and men with "titles," that is, honors recognizing their achievements, had political and judicial authority. He recalled that his own village, Essaka—which was probably located east of the Niger River in the Onitsha region of modern Nigeria, an area of hilly terrain and savannah grasslands—had only a loose, tributary relationship with the empire of Benin. An oft-quoted Igbo popular proverb goes, *"Igbo enwegh*

eze" (the Igbo have [or make] no king). This is, in fact, an overgeneraliza-
tion, since some Igbo groups did have kingship, especially those claiming
direct descent from Benin, where monarchy was a highly developed mode
of governance. That caveat notwithstanding, even in the most centralized
traditional polities, an Igbo's identity centered on his or her local village.
Like Equiano, most Igbo became aware of themselves as part of a broader,
"imagined" ethnicity only when away from home.

Decentralized should not be read as disorganized, however. These
societies fostered dense networks of associations and institutions that mediated practically every aspect of social interaction. The most important of
these were the formal age cohorts into which boys and girls were inducted
at puberty and the secret societies that adults joined, some of which resembled professional guilds, much like the *compagnonnages* formed by
French artisans during roughly the same period. Moreover, Equiano's nostalgic recollections of a blissfully isolated and provincial childhood should
be credited only so far. In his own account one finds telltale signs of links
to the burgeoning trade activity in the Niger Delta, which clearly had already connected his village to the larger Atlantic world. For example, his
fond memories of Igbo cooking included not only the traditional savory
stews flavored with pepper and spices but also a New World legume: corn.
Despite his preadolescent ignorance of the world beyond his village, the
Atlantic trading network soon brought his village, like many others, within
the grasp of the slave trade.

In many ways, decentralized societies such as Equiano's village were
better able to resist the slave trade than were peoples subject to the
large-scale, hierarchically ordered kingdoms and empires found elsewhere
in West and West Central Africa—at least initially. There were, of course,
small-scale inter-village wars that produced slaves in decentralized societies, but these were much less important in the delta than in places such
as the Kongo, where large centralized states were bent on conquest. The
small populations of scattered villages were simply less inviting to large-
scale military attack. Villagers also developed a number of effective coun-
ters to slave raiding. The Balanta of Central Africa built fortified hamlets,
while the Diola lived in widely dispersed settlements. Others built walled
compounds with a single entryway and no windows opening to the exterior. When threatened by slave traders, the Kabe of northern Togo retreated to mountainous terrain and developed more intensive cultivation

methods to compensate for the poor soil. As in Equiano's case, violent enslavement for any of these groups was more likely to come at the hands of kidnappers than soldiers.

Given that a significant portion of the estimated ten million or more slaves landed in the Americas were from decentralized communities, however, it seems unlikely that random kidnapping could account for more than a small minority of them. It is not too much of an exaggeration, perhaps, to say that in decentralized societies such as those found in the Niger Delta, the other side of slave trading was not war or kidnapping but trade. Or, to put the matter more precisely, both kidnapping and war were part of larger, more complex political and social developments that engendered novel social formations within African communities. It is very likely that Equiano's fate, like that of so many other African youth, was sealed miles away by one such novelty: the Aro cult.

The Aro cult phenomenon demonstrates not only the modes of operation through which the slave trade could penetrate decentralized communities, but also how the slave trade prompted changes in traditional systems of governance and social values more generally. The Aro transformed a subsistence agricultural community into the hub of a long-distance trading network, with slave trading becoming its central component and its raison d'être. In the process they perfected a supra-village organization that effectively provided a substitute for large-scale political organization. Strategically located west of the Cross River between the coast and the interior of the hinterland northeast of Old Calabar, the Aro eventually developed a network of 150 colonies throughout Igbo and Ibibio areas.

According to traditional accounts, their power was consolidated and sustained through manipulation of the Aro Chuku Oracle, a powerful deity the Aro had appropriated from the Ibibio. In fact, various local traditions seem to agree that the Aro Chukwu somehow emerged from the successful resolution of tensions between the Igbo and Ibibio, two West African ethnic groups with a history of both cooperation and conflict. According to one oral tradition, sometime in the seventeenth century, the Akpa, led by Akuma, intervened in a conflict between the Igbo and Ibibio. The Akpa were already a trading people and had acquired a limited number of firearms, which were not abundant in this area until the nineteenth century, and this apparently gave them advantages in their bid to mediate.

African historian Kenneth Dike has proposed an intriguing hypothesis that the subsequent Aro cult was spurred by migration into a malarial environment, which we now know stimulates adaptive traits that in turn can lead to outbreaks of sickle cell anemia. The mysterious deaths of otherwise healthy children that would inevitably follow may well have produced social tensions and encouraged an increased use of oracles and diviners—all providing the social basis for the development of the Aro cult.

The Aro cult is credited with controlling much of the slave trade from at least the mid-eighteenth century onward. Indeed, the Aro were so focused on trade that they actually imported food from neighboring groups. They committed their youth to a long trading apprenticeship, and sons or trusted members of a trading household were often sent out to establish new settlements, a practice reminiscent of some Europeans' use of familial and religious connections to facilitate trade. From these strategic outposts, they became the sole middlemen dominating the movement of goods from the hinterland to the coast. Emblematic of the Aro's intermediary status, such trading settlements were typically located at the crossing of rivers and the intersections of roads.

Long-distance trade was dangerous, and Aro traders flourished because they developed a variety of techniques to make it safe. Traveling in convoys, a privilege for which one paid a fee, the traders' caravans could include as many as thirty to forty merchants, who along with their apprentices and porters would add up to several hundred people. They also hired mercenaries to protect the convoys, built up a transport network, and sponsored or controlled the location of trade fairs, all of which gave them influence over a vast area not under their direct political control. Moreover, they were very skilled in diplomacy as well as war, and sought to make alliances with potential competitors. Advantageous marriages were contracted with families of leading traders in other towns to cement relationships of mutual interest. Traditional blood covenants, such as that of the Igbanu, which originally applied only to kin, were adapted to create fictive kin ties between merchants. They incorporated foreigners and slaves into their communities through formal adoptions. Thus many Africans were already familiar with multiethnic, heterogeneous societies even before being thrust into slave ships and onto American plantations.

Through their commercial and clientage linkages, the Aro mobilized agents within decentralized societies to act on their behalf and against the normal tendencies of those societies. The Aro traders gathered slaves not through wars or raids, but by means that were, on the surface at least, nominally consensual. Normally they did not themselves engage in kidnapping or slave raiding, but rather introduced systems of exchange whose incentives and penalties prompted others to do the dirty work for them. For those within their orbit, a system of taxation encouraged households not otherwise committed to slaving to participate, because each household was obligated to pay taxes or fines in the form of slaves, by some accounts as many as four slaves per person. By such means, the Aro system stimulated independent, small-scale raiding and exchanges.

This thriving market for slaves came to mediate otherwise unrelated tensions in decentralized West African societies, which probably accounts for its reach beyond even the specific activities of groups such as the Aro. Polygeneous societies, for example, in which prestige and social and political power rested with the male heads of household left many young men frustrated and impatient under the control of their elders, a problem exacerbated by an inheritance system that favored older siblings. Kidnapping and selling slaves provided quick access to the cloth, guns, or wherewithal to buy cattle or similar "capital" goods that would enable these young men to marry and establish a household. Indeed, one scholar argues that "generational conflict was probably the most important force opening [such] societies to the action of the market." There was no other way in these societies to prosper and secure the dependents and titles that provided security in old age. A scenario such as this may well account for the raiders—two men and a woman working alone—who captured Equiano. After his capture, Equiano was not transported via a larger trading party or sold at a fair, as were many other slaves similarly abducted. Rather, he was sold by these apparently independent operators and then passed along from hand to hand, until he was drawn inexorably to the sea.

The Aro were not alone in corrupting extant indigenous political and social institutions to generate ever more slaves for sale. As Walter Rodney argued many years ago, the desire of elite classes to gain advantage from the subjugation of those less powerful was as compelling a motivation among Africans as among the Europeans they encountered on their shores. Throughout West Africa in this period of heightened social tension, new laws were made and old laws reinterpreted to the advantage of the ruling groups. As with the Aro, in a number of West African societies, enslavement became the punishment meted out for a host of social infractions, such as adultery and theft, that had previously been punished by the restitution of goods or by fines. Prisoners, heretofore held until ransomed by their kinsmen, were now sold as slaves.

In numerous instances, groups threatened by slave raids were drawn reluctantly into the trade themselves. What began as a form of self-protection was often soon sustained by greed for profit. Thus some West Africans, such as the king of Bonny, made common cause with American slave masters in opposing the abolition of the slave trade in 1807. The former's intransigence throughout the nineteenth century would help foster the myth of the "dark continent," a place where Africans enslaved their kinspeople. This myth was fashioned, of course, in the very nations that had been these African slave traders' avid partners for four and a half centuries.

The willing participation of some Africans in the slave trade, combined with the fact that the institution was indigenous to Africa, would later become a key argument in the defense of North American slavery. Indeed, even in the early twentieth century, a prominent white southern historian continued to argue that bondage on New World plantations was in fact a rescue from barbarism, a gift of civilization. Such transparently specious and self-serving justifications need not distract us here, but it is necessary to reckon with the very real impact that indigenous African slavery may have had on the development of the Atlantic slave trade, if for no other reason than its importance for understanding the impact the trade had on Africa as a whole.

Slavery appears in Equiano's account as a common social institution. Though defensive, Equiano's distinction between the slavery he knew at home and what he encountered in America, with respect to status and treatment, is generally correct, even if his overly benign portrait of the former is not. In no society are slaves the true equals of non-slaves, regardless of how well they are treated or whatever opportunities for social advancement are open to them. As Orlando Patterson's exhaustive survey of slave systems demonstrates, even when slaves were vested with impressive social or political authority—and slaves in Africa and Asia often were so invested—they were still marked as socially degraded by whatever measures their particular society reckoned human worth. In Africa, as elsewhere, therefore, slaves were a socially subordinated and "dishonored" people.

In traditional African societies, however, slavery was motivated by broader social purposes than simply satisfying labor needs, and this shaped the nature of the slave experience. In contrast with Europeans, who built security and power hierarchies on the possession of land, Africans found their security in gathering around them people whose fates or needs were somehow tied to their own, either through kinship or dependency. Given

the fearful threats of natural hazards and the social and structural limitations on amassing adequate wealth or even food surpluses, Africans relied
on human ties and obligations, on kin and dependents, for security. These
were societies for which kinship was the principal idiom through which
social relations were sorted out and understood. It is revealing, then, that
slaves were sometimes literally adopted. Kenneth Dike's description of the
initiation of a slave into an Aro household suggests the social meanings
that could attach to the institution more generally.

> His hair was shaven off, his nails clipped, and he was given a ritual
> bath at the sacred stone. The initiate jumped up and down seven
> times and was knocked on his head by the head of the household.
> The head, *nna ulo*, then chanted a ritual address to the god of the
> household, informing it and the ancestors of the increase in the
> family members. Subsequently, the initiate was given a new name
> and a ritual meal by the new mother, often one of the wives of the
> household head.

Thus separated from home and all those who could protect them, slaves
tended to become the loyal subjects of their new households, which offered them protection and often real potential for social and material advancement. As in many other slave systems, the bond relation could shade
off into something more like patron and client than master and slave, and
was couched in the language and idiom of kinship. Cloaking the inherent
brutality of bondage in the language of kinship is something that even
slaveholders in the nineteenth-century American South would well understand, however. And, as with other indigenous institutions, the slave trade
eventually corroded the more benign features of African slavery as well.
At roughly the same moment that Equiano was experiencing relatively
gentle treatment in the household of one of his African owners, American-
style slave plantations were being founded in the kingdom of Dahomey, a
slave-trading empire that had itself been spawned by the growing Atlantic
demand for slaves.

Whatever effects slavery may have wrought on African societies as a
whole, it clearly had a demonstrable impact on the creation of new social
entities and phenomena, which have clear parallels with and links to sim-

ilar developments in Europe. If a long-distance trade requires, as Philip Curtin put it, "someone to go abroad" to act as a middleman, long-distance slave trading seems to have been peculiarly dependent on complexly elaborated and novel social arrangements, at the center of which stood a new type of middleman. As we have seen, the middlemen who facilitated long-distance trade often occupied an anomalous social position within the European societies in which they resided. Although the wealthiest might merge into the local nobility, such as the Lomellini in Portugal, more often they formed physically and culturally separate enclaves within the host society, as with most other Italians in Spain or Portugal. Indeed, such enclaves were often legally defined and protected.

The Europeans who manned the ports and slave "factories" of the West African coast formed separate enclaves as well. Some mated with African women, producing children who formed yet a different kind of middling group from their fathers, and whose national and social position was even more anomalous. As aliens within traditional African societies—much as Jews and New Christians were in Europe, for example—such people tended to follow in their fathers' footsteps and become traders themselves. Much like the Aro, they devoted themselves exclusively to trade, and thus became good at it, often trumping both European and African competitors with their maneuvers and single-mindedness.

Mixed-race communities were formed largely through concubinage, though sometimes through legal marriage, especially among the French and Portuguese. European communities also appear to have instituted the practice of fostering African children. Historian Walter Rodney describes rituals associated with this practice that are strongly reminiscent of how Kenneth Dike depicted the initiation of a slave into an Aro household. "Permission was obtained from the father or paternal uncle, the child was baptized (or at least given a saint's name), and upon passing into the home of its adopted parents the child automatically became 'Christian', 'white', and 'Portuguese.'"

Boubacar Barry argues that intra-European wars during the late eighteenth century actually reduced the number of resident European traders, thus opening the way for Euro-Africans to emerge as dominant actors. On the Upper Guinea Coast these traders forged links with indigenous trade networks, forming "a trading diaspora" from Saint-Louis and Gorée, and Fort Saint James down to the southern rivers. Describing a similar group on the Upper Guinea coast as "a comprador class," Rodney suggests that by straddling two worlds, they felt constrained by the traditions and rules of neither.

In a somewhat less judgmental analysis one might simply note that, as in similar cases, the cultural middle ground that formed owed more to syncretism than to a complete assimilation to European norms. Although flaunting the outward signs of Europeanization—swords, muskets, and dress—these communities more often spoke a Creolized version of Portuguese or French and adopted a syncretized form of Catholicism. To the Portuguese they were *filhos da terra* (sons of the soil), but they were not only sons. One of the most powerful of them was Senhora Bibiana Vaz, the widow of a Portuguese captain, who had been one of the richest men on the coast in the late seventeenth century. The widow Vaz probably inherited her two-mast sailing vessel from her husband, along with other boats, but the key sources of her power were her extended mulatto family and her kinship ties with African clans among the Papel and Banhun, all of which gave her unusual muscle in bending competitors to her will. Claiming a similar power base in the first half of the eighteenth century was another dominant figure, Senhor José Lopez de Moura, who was reputedly the grandson of a Mane emperor. By no means, therefore, should these people be imagined as occupying some cultural and social no-man's-land. Rather, it was their multiple connectedness, their familiarity with two worlds—in a word, their hybridity—that gave them power in the Atlantic ports and Creole communities that the slave trade had fostered and depended upon.

Although mulatto traders were conspicuous, attracting the bulk of the attention of both their contemporaries and historians, they were but one species of a broader social type. *Cultural* intermixture actually produced a much larger and even more powerful community than biological. Other Africans found it advantageous to adopt European religion, dress, language, and housing. Indeed, traditional Africans appear not to have made much distinction between those who were culturally white and the phenotypically white. Both were regarded as "a people apart." Behavior rather than ancestry appears to have marked the dividing line between indigenes and European communities. Language, dress, and religion were the principal markers that identified individuals and communities as having a different social purpose, if not a different racial heritage, from indigenous Africans. Thus some Africans extended the Portuguese term *grumetes*, which designated the foot soldiers of the slave trader's retinue, to *all*

Africans closely associated with the Portuguese in religion or cultural be-havior. A striking example of the type was an eighteenth-century African native, Captain Francisco Correia, who commanded a trading vessel and had traveled to Lisbon and Santiago. Literate and propertied, he spoke good Portuguese and wore European clothing. Africans considered him "white" and "Portuguese."

Among some English traders, the relations with interior chiefs appear to have been mediated by debts rather than kinship. Somewhat reminiscent of the Aro, these traders extended credit to inland chiefs and then demanded payment in slaves. Henry Tucker and James Cleveland, eighteenth-century traders in what would become Sierra Leone, were prominent examples of this technique. But even the less avaricious of these merchant princes, such as John Kabes in Komenda and John Konny, relied upon the ma-nipulation of differences among Europeans as well as those among Afri-cans to sustain their influence over the trade. Kabes, who acted as a kind of cultural and economic broker, was respected and feared; opposition to him could and did lead to dismissal (as in the case of one English colonial agent), and the Dutch once tried to assassinate him.

In some sense, then, capturing and selling slaves to Europeans may be regarded as an extension of a preexisting set of social relations and in-stitutions, but it also reflected the growing power of European partners to turn the trading relation to their own needs and ends over time. Either way, it soon created the social basis for its own perpetuation. Supplies of African slaves were available to meet European demand because proce-dures of capture, enslavement, and sale were already well established, but the modes by which slaves were supplied were no less vulnerable to con-tingent historical developments than were the markets generating the de-mand for them. Neither the powerful state system of the Kongolese nor the crafty evasions of the decentralized Igbo could long deflect the ever-swelling appetites, for profits and staples, of their voracious European and American contemporaries.

America

"It is not possible to accomplish anything in Brazil without slaves," de-clared Prince Johan Maurits of Nassau, the Dutch governor in Recife,

Brazil, in the late 1630s. Writing during the initial, abortive effort at Dutch colonization, Governor Maurits expressed what would soon be taken as a truism in both the temperate and tropical zones of the New World. The forced labor of indigenous people had been crucial to sustaining Spain's foothold in the Americas from the beginning, and King Ferdinand authorized the transport of African slaves from the Iberian Peninsula and the Atlantic Islands to the Caribbean in 1510, just seventeen years after Columbus's first landfall. Eight years later, Charles V approved imports directly from Africa, establishing in the process a precedent and method of operation—the asiento, or royal license—that would endure for almost three centuries.

Although these decisions would in time prove fateful, the first century of European settlement did not witness a dramatic infusion of African slave laborers. A century after Columbus sighted Hispaniola, there were still fewer than 40,000 African slaves in the Americas, a distinct minority among the 118,000 Europeans and the 192,000 people of mixed European, African, or Native American origin, and certainly a far cry from the millions who would eventually re-people the Western Hemisphere, devastating Africa in the process. For the bulk of their labor needs, the Spanish conquerors still relied on the more than eight million native peoples within their dominion. A half century later this demographic profile underwent a radical change, one causally linked to social and political transformations in both Africa and Europe and crucial to the formation of a new Atlantic world.

During the first fifty years of the seventeenth century, Spain licensed the import of three times as many Africans as during the entire previous century, and Portugal's Brazilian settlements brought in about two hundred thousand more. By mid-century, Father António Vieira would echo Governor Maurits's observations on the necessity of slave labor, but he drew the lines of causation much more starkly: "without Negroes there is no Pernambuco, and without Angola there are no Negroes." The growth of sugar cultivation in the Americas set this change in motion, but even that was dependent on a series of linked events there and in Europe. As long as the Habsburg dynasty of Spain dominated both Europe and America, as it did until the late sixteenth century, the pace of American economic development in general and slavery in particular, outside Santo Domingo, was sluggish. With its Habsburg rulers determined to consolidate and hold on to their European empire, Spain's efforts to exploit America's bounty were focused on extracting and transporting the windfall of gold and silver discovered in its central highlands. Although some African labor was used for this purpose, Spain relied mostly on the mainland native populations.

Historian Robin Blackburn has characterized this first century of slavery in the Americas, and the crucial transitions slavery underwent during the century that followed, as reflecting a movement from a baroque to a modern age. Ill defined—or perhaps just impossible to define with precision because it is invoked to label multiple domains of consciousness and temporality—the word *baroque* has roots in both a Portuguese adjective describing a misshapen pearl and an Italian term for an obstacle in schematic logic. In the fine arts, it generally refers to the sensibilities and aesthetic tastes current in much of Europe in the late sixteenth and early seventeenth centuries. For social historians, it can evoke the ways people of that era sought to adjust to and account for a world they often perceived to be radically disordered and incoherent. Perhaps the most useful definitions take its disorder, irregularity, and even its ostensible "chaos" as the very essence of baroque sensibility. The baroque was a style of living rather than merely an aesthetic form, argues the esteemed Spanish historian José Antonio Maravall, in which one sought psychic control of a world turned upside down by accommodating to its very contradictoriness, its astonishing instability, its vital dynamism. In short, one made virtues of the very qualities later critics would see as illegitimate departures from accepted rules of balance and proportion, or simply as bizarre and exotic.

Although religious conflicts may have formed the baroque template, secular and political lifeworlds also resonated to its themes, which are most commonly recognized in the architectural traditions of Europe's absolutist monarchs (such as Versailles) and in the musical genius of Scarlatti, Handel, and Bach. The most striking examples of the period's baroque architecture were found in north-central Brazil, however. The sense of grandeur, sensuousness, vitality, and tension generally associated with the baroque temperament found ready inspiration in the Americas. Contemporaneous with the disorders and reaction unleashed after Luther tacked his theses on a Wittenberg church door, Europeans' certitude about a divinely ordered and contained universe were being profoundly challenged by the "marvelous possessions" in the Americas, where a sense of infinitude, diversity, and complexity was inescapable. The new peoples discovered

there, and the new mixtures of peoples that arose in the course of settlement, inspired fascination and wonder. American Indians were transported thousands of miles to perform elaborate pageants in royal courts,
as were the Tupinambá, whom French colonists brought to Rouen in
1550 to entertain Henri II and Catherine de Médicis. Meanwhile, the
New World progeny of mestizos and mulattos were sketched, painted, and
rendered in word pictures for popular consumption. Numerically dominant among the non-indigenous population, mixed-blood peoples challenged conventional ways of ordering and managing social relations, giving
rise to many interstitial spaces within the European-dominated social order. Similarly, the world of ordinary laborers was rendered seemingly chaotic as a mixed labor force—European, African, and Native American;
free, slave, and something in between—emerged to dredge wealth from
the plantations and mines of the New World. The more "modern" slave
societies of later centuries would be governed by very different social and
political ideals, would attempt (though often unsuccessfully) to establish
a more sharply delineated racial order, and most important, would initiate
a rationalization of productive processes that drove the slave trade to heretofore unimaginable heights. It was in the Americas, then, that the baroque world of the Kongolese envoy Dom Miguel de Castro was transformed
into the modern world of Olaudah Equiano.

The radical refashioning of America—and with it, Africa—was contingent on equally radical changes in Europe. Specifically, the global hegemony of Spain, the epitome of the baroque cultural aesthetic, had to be
broken. Many Europeans were not especially enthusiastic about perma-
nently settling the world "beyond the line," their term for the American
wilderness. Indeed, from a much smaller population, Portugal sent more
emigrants across the seas than Spain. The Spanish conquered and managed a breathtaking expanse of the Caribbean and South America through
their skillful manipulation of the cross and the sword, neither of which
relied on numerical superiority. Moreover, Spain relied on Portugal to
supply the African slaves necessary to exploit some parts of its vast territory. Indeed, before 1620, Portugal supplied the bulk of all slaves brought
to the Americas. When the rapid acceleration of the slave trade took place,
however, Portugal's monopoly quickly began to slip, and Northern European powers replaced it as the main carriers of slaves to the Americas.
Meanwhile, Spain, too, would soon face aggressive challenges from com-

peting European powers, eventually diminishing its preeminence in American trade and development, all of which opened the way for new economic and social innovations that would transform the Atlantic world and alter the course of human history.

Leading the attack on Spain's hegemony were the people of the United Provinces of the Netherlands, who fought an eighty-year war to free themselves from Spanish rule. Their rebellion was dictated by religious and economic motives more than incipient nationalism, and these led them to fashion a society relatively tolerant of religious and cultural differences. Amsterdam became a magnet both for political thinkers, such as Descartes and Locke, and for religious minorities of all kinds—Calvinists from Belgium, Sephardic Jews from Spain and Portugal, Puritans from England, and after 1685, French Huguenots. With this diversity came talented innovators who stoked Dutch enterprise and enlivened its cultural life. The veritable "Golden Age" that followed rivaled that of their Spanish antagonists in its breadth and depth, though theirs was as decidedly bourgeois as Spain's tended toward the aristocratic.

As with many bourgeois societies, piety and profit formed an odd but potent amalgam, one soon reflected in the evolving Dutch role in the slave trade. In 1596, on the eve of the Netherlands' Golden Age, Pieter van der Haagen, a Rotterdam ship captain, brought 130 Africans to Middleburg, the capital of Zeeland. In contrast to the reception he might have expected in any other port in the then known world, van der Haagen's moral right to hold or sell such cargo was sharply challenged. After a heated debate about the morality of slavery—perhaps prefiguring antislavery rhetoric two centuries later—the city fathers decreed slave trading to be immoral and forced the captives' release.

Aside from their moral proclivities, the Dutch often appear simply not to have recognized the economic value of slaves. In 1606, for example, Captain Pieter van den Broecke seized a ship with ninety slaves, but seeing no economic value in them, he sold them to an English captain for mere "victuals," just as the famous "dutch man of warre" sold its twenty Africans at Jamestown thirteen years later. Indeed, the principal instrument of Dutch economic and political intervention in the Americas, the Dutch West India Company (De West-Indische Compagnie, or WIC), initially refused to participate in the slave trade, having consulted religious authorities on its moral justification and found none.

It seems unlikely that the religious authorities consulted were from the Dutch Calvinist majority, however, since its clergymen were inclined to cite the curse of Ham as ample biblical justification for African enslavement. Aggressively bourgeois but grounded in an equally militant Protestant, anti-Spanish oligarchy, the WIC sought to wrap its program in high moral claims; but these, in turn, reflected a complex mixture of attitudes about blacks, slavery, and conspicuous consumption. Thus, upon closer inspection, its refusal to participate in slave trading seems much more like the early Kongolese opposition than a precursor to nineteenth-century abolitionism—an opposition premised on strategic or local considerations, or simply their moral ambivalence about slavery.

In any event, the geopolitical competition in which Holland was engaged soon turned opposition or ambivalence toward slave trading into an avid embrace. Indeed, the WIC was modeled on the East India Company (Vereenigde Oost-Indische Compagnie, or VOC), which had engaged in slave trading since its founding in 1602. Like the VOC, the WIC was a private, commercial corporation invested with quasi-state powers, including war-making powers. Setting out to achieve in the Atlantic what the VOC had done in the Pacific, the WIC launched a global assault on the Spanish and Portuguese commercial and colonial system. In 1628 their fleet captured the entire Spanish silver fleet, which reportedly led Genoese bankers to cut off credit to the Spanish Crown. Central to this maritime guerrilla warfare was the policy of seizing Spanish slave cargoes, amounting to some 2,336 slaves between 1623 and 1637. These seizures seemed motivated by the determination to pillage Spanish commerce rather than plunder its goods, however. As late as 1626, a WIC captain, having seized a Spanish slave ship, let it go without confiscating the 600 slaves on board.

Once the company's mission shifted from maritime warfare to colonization, so did its attitude toward slavery. In 1629, the WIC launched seventy-seven ships to attack the Portuguese colony in Brazil; by 1630 it had managed to seize a portion of the northeastern region, Pernambuco. Now in possession of a colony whose development—if not survival, as Johan Maurits pointed out—depended on slavery, the WIC did not bother to consult theologians further about the morality of slave trading. They dispatched traders to Angola and began a series of incursions into Portugal's African entrepôts, a competition that fostered proxy wars among African nations from Benin to Angola. Forty years later, Spain granted the

WIC its asiento, the exclusive right to supply its colonies' slaves. Although the WIC would fold in 1673, the Dutch would hold this trading monopoly until 1730. Thus a company and a people who had explicitly repudiated slavery ended up enmeshed in the slave trade as their principal business.

For much of the seventeenth century and well into the eighteenth, however, Dutch involvement in the slave trade could not be grounded in either American colonial possessions or African outposts. In 1645, Portuguese planters joined together with free blacks and Native Americans, who made up a quarter of their strength, rose up in revolt, and drove the Dutch out of their last strongholds in Brazil nine years later. Meanwhile, Portugal, now independent of Spain, regained most of its commercial outposts in Africa and the Pacific.

The significance of the Netherlands' role in the development of the slave trade, therefore, lies in neither its brief hold on Brazil nor its African incursions. Indeed, one authority argues that the Dutch were actually not very good at either colonization or slave trading, and that both the Brazilian sugar trade and the slave trade receded under Dutch stewardship. In contrast to their hesitant and brief tenure as slave traders, however, the Dutch had long been integral to the commercial activities linked to that trade. Brazil had provided a direct source of American dyestuffs for the Dutch textile industry, and long before its conquests in Brazil, the Netherlands had provided capital investment, shipping, and a market for Brazil's slave-grown sugar. By 1622, Holland's twenty-nine sugar refineries (up from three in 1598) were providing the main European market with sugar, and Dutch shipyards were constructing fifteen ships annually for the Brazil trade alone. It was not, then, principally as owners or even traders of Africans that the Dutch drove the Atlantic system dramatically forward. Rather, their crucial contributions lay first in breaking Spain's hegemony in the Atlantic and thereafter in indirectly promoting French and British colonial development in the Caribbean. Even as many of its leading citizens pondered the morality of engaging in slave trading, therefore, the Netherlands helped mediate the political and economic transformations that made the vast expansion of that trade and of the Atlantic system possible.

After years of desultory growth, sugar cultivation finally took off in Brazil in the last decades of the sixteenth century. Brazilian planters separated cane growing from milling, promoted innovations in grinding mechanisms, and benefited from fertile soil to boost production. In some cases, they also enjoyed shorter times and safer sailing to and from their sources of slaves in Africa. All of which enabled seventeenth-century Brazilian sugar planters to outstrip their more established competitors in the Atlantic and Mediterranean islands. A magnet for new investors, northeast Brazil soon acquired a multiethnic mercantile class that mirrored its multiethnic work force.

The system of production that Brazilian planters perfected Dutch interlopers transmitted to other auspicious sites for sugar production. Dutch refugees from Pernambuco scattered throughout the Caribbean, carrying with them Brazilian sugar technology and the capacity to finance and organize the movement of that produce to European markets. The several hundred Sephardim in Brazil and the Netherlands, most of them originally from Portugal, were key participants in these developments, and their role in this process further illustrates the complex forces shaping and pushing forward the Atlantic system, and with it the slave trade. Unfortunately, honest discussion of that role has been complicated in recent years by debates over the extent of Jewish involvement in the slave trade. One side of that debate, eager to score political points against contemporary Jews by casting them as historical villains, argues for their substantial "responsibility" for the slave trade. The other side responds reasonably enough that the small number of Jews involved cannot possibly support such extravagant claims. Moreover, among that small number the principal participants were "New Christians," whom some might arguably exclude from the count as no longer really Jewish.

This debate, if one might call it that, has proved to be more a distraction from than a useful way of understanding the complex dynamics in the development of the slave trade. Certainly focusing on the small numbers of Jews involved in the slave trade is misleading and vacuous. At the same time, the focus on the quantitative aspect of their role rather than its nature is also misdirected and even somewhat disingenuous. It is certainly arguable that although numerically small, Jewish converts to Christianity played important roles in promoting the slave trade, and that the ambiguities of their social position as converts likely enabled their role. More often than not the Iberian Jew's forced conversion to Christianity, especially in Portugal, was pragmatic and strategic; certainly many of the New Christians who immigrated to the Netherlands did not sever their cultural and institutional ties to Judaism or, even more germane, to the powerful Sephardic network that facilitated commercial relations between Portugal and Holland even during times of war. As close studies of this group have shown, many of these men clearly identified themselves as Jews, building synagogues and supporting similar cultural institutions in their new homeland. This was a wealthy and successful community, several members of whom would become shareholders of the WIC, but their most important contribution to Atlantic slavery was not as traders but as investors and sometimes settlers and planters, first in Brazil and then in the Caribbean. As such, the transformation of the New World economy, and thus of the slave trade, cannot be told without reference to their role.

Including these New Christians in our assessment of slavery's development does not substantially inflate Jewish numerical involvement in the slave trade, therefore, but excluding them does distract attention from developments that are historically compelling. The Dutch Sephardic community occupied a social and economic position strikingly similar to that of the earlier Genoese enclaves in Seville and Lagos, and not unlike some of the African Creole communities along the West African coast. They were all men, and sometimes women, occupying interstitial positions in the social order. They were crucial intermediaries, the middlemen, and one might say the midwives who facilitated the birth of new social mores and practices. Their networks and strategies illuminate the means by which the Atlantic slave trade emerged not as a continuation of Old World patterns, but as part of the social and commercial innovations of modernity. Throughout its long history, outsider-insider figures—African as well as European—freed of traditional constraints and thus strategically positioned to support political and commercial innovation, enabled the radical transformations that propelled the slave trade to new heights. These "middlemen" shaped "the Middle Passage," in the broadest sense of that term, through which African slaves, often themselves already Creolized, passed from Old World to New.

Both Dom Miguel de Castro and Olaudah Equiano were formed in this moral-material nexus, but the worlds they inhabited would probably have been mutually incomprehensible. We have no reliable measures of the American sugar crop for the year de Castro set sail for Brazil, but we know it had to have been minuscule compared with the annual marketable product a century later, when Caribbean plantations rushed to satisfy a growing European sweet tooth. The American sugar crop had reached

80,000 tons by 1720. The year Equiano was packed into the hold of a slave ship, annual output stood at 206,964 tons. In little over a century, practically every major European nation had come into possession of colonies engaged in growing sugar—all with slave labor. England, a laggard in the slave trade in the early seventeenth century, was the clear leader by the end of the eighteenth. Importing 175 million tons of sugar each year, England was both the principal carrier of slaves to the New World and the primary consumer of the Americas' premier slave crop, sugar. Sugar fueled its growing proletarian work force and supplied fancy confections and desserts to their "betters," all adding up to roughly twenty-three pounds per person per year (six times the consumption of England's nearest competitor, the French). By 1763, having defeated in succession the Dutch, the Spanish, and the French, Britain was poised to become the new dominant world power.

By the middle of the eighteenth century, the fates of Africa and African America were more than ever linked to the destiny of Europe. The seventeenth-century world of Dom Miguel de Castro may have briefly offered the promise of a more positive destiny arising from that link, one of roughly equal exchanges of knowledge, goods, and people that might have enriched both. Olaudah Equiano's voyage framed a very different European-African encounter, a world of unequal exchanges that blighted the hopes of whole peoples. Notwithstanding that fateful outcome, Equiano's story does not end in the hold of that slaver en route for Virginia. Desperate as his plight might have been, his voyage was not an ending but a beginning.

2

MANY THOUSANDS BORN

The Roots of African America

The individual life stories of the twenty Africans who disembarked from the Dutch man-of-war at Jamestown in 1619 remain a mystery to us. We have only informed guesses as to their origins and know little of their ultimate fates. But we do know that as a group, then and for many decades to follow, Africans constituted only a small portion of the newcomers to North America, which was itself scarcely more than a frontier outpost in the still-emerging British Empire. There were about 1,200 whites in the Chesapeake when the Africans arrived. Some forty years later there would still be fewer than 34,000 whites, and blacks numbered just 1,708. There were fewer still in the Massachusetts Bay colony (22,062 whites and 422 blacks), the Carolinas had not yet been settled, and what would soon become New York was still Dutch New Amsterdam. In contrast with the hemisphere as a whole, where African settlers outnumbered Europeans three to two, the population ratio of British North America was roughly twenty-five whites for every one black. Before 1675, the average number of Africans disembarking annually at seaports in mainland North America scarcely exceeded the stray Dutch cargo of 1619. Even as late as 1685, there were by one estimate roughly 2,600 Africans in Virginia, out of a population of almost 44,000 (including 38,100 Europeans and 2,900 Indians, by then already decimated by disease and war). Nonetheless, these men and women formed the center of the black world in North America, and as the founding, or "charter," generation of African Americans, as Ira Berlin has called them, they would live lives that both framed and sharply deviated from those of their descendants.

The Baroque World of Anthony Johnson and Its Demise

Much of what we know about that founding generation emerges from a small number of African American families who managed to gain their freedom, and thus left individual marks on the public record. One of the most thoroughly documented of these was the brood of Anthony Johnson, a black landowner and slaveholder on Virginia's Eastern Shore. Johnson probably arrived in Jamestown in 1621, just two years after the first recorded landing of Africans there. He was likely one of the two men identified in colonial records as "Antonio, the Negro," a name hinting at a recent sojourn in the Iberian world, possibly even in one of the Portuguese slave depots or cities along the west coast of Angola that provided the cargo seized by the Dutch ship in 1619. We cannot be certain whether Johnson spent his first years in America as an indentured servant or a slave, although chances are that he, like most blacks during this period, was legally bound for life. In any event, some of the first direct evidence of his status and condition emerges, ironically, from court records detailing his assertions that another black man, John Casar, was *his* slave. Those claims were but emblematic of the multiple ironies and anomalies of his life, and of black life generally in seventeenth-century America.

In many ways, no doubt, Anthony Johnson's story was clearly unusual among the three hundred or so black inhabitants of Virginia's Eastern Shore at mid-century. Indeed, the civil status and modest economic successes that free blacks like him enjoyed in British North America's first century have often puzzled historians who have tried to decipher the connection between the evolving racial system and the slave system. And yet the broad contours of Johnson's world illustrate what many other African newcomers encountered in the early seventeenth century. Like Johnson, a significant number of that first generation—about one of seven—was able to purchase their freedom by mid-century and live relatively secure lives. One of his contemporaries, Francis Payne, known formerly as "Francisco, the Negroe" and later as Frank Paine, began purchasing his freedom in 1649, a task he completed in 1656. Another, Emanuel Driggus (or Rodriggus), who, like Anthony Johnson, appears to have arrived on Virginia's Eastern Shore sometime during the 1620s or 1630s, gained his freedom in the early 1660s. Like the bulk of the white indentured servants who arrived in the Chesapeake, however, most of these men lived and died landless and poor.

Anthony and Mary Johnson were among the exceptions, having acquired the extra hands of John Casar sometime during the 1640s, by which time they had also managed to secure not only their own freedom but that of their four children. Freedom came at an optimal moment for the Johnsons. With Europeans' growing addiction to tobacco, Virginians finally discovered a staple crop on which to ground their economy. The final defeat of the Algonquins in 1646 opened virgin land to an orgy of speculation and subsequently fueled a dramatic economic expansion. The newly manumitted Johnsons must have been among the beneficiaries of these boom times. If they had indeed borne the costs of John Casar's transportation to Virginia, they would have received a 50-acre land grant. In any event, they went on to amass a freehold totaling 250 acres by 1651, which along with some cattle constituted a substantial estate, one that excited the envy of some of their white neighbors. Given their relative prosperity, the Johnsons left a substantial footprint on the public record. Indeed, much of our knowledge of this family comes *grace* their time in court, defending their property, often against the frequent harassment of neighbors. For example, John Casar's suit, claiming he was actually an indentured servant rather than a slave, appears to have been instigated at the behest of the Parker brothers, George and Robert, who had several run-ins with the Johnsons over the years. Given Casar's seventeen years of service in the Johnson household, there is reason to doubt the veracity of his claims to a *limited* term of service. Nonetheless, Johnson lost the case on the initial suit, but he won at a second trial, a scenario suggesting both the possibility of a black man of property sustaining his claims before the law and the precariousness of a black man's hold on his possessions. Indeed, success often depended on not only official acknowledgment of one's civil rights but also patronage and support—in Johnson's case, from his former owners the Bennetts and allies such as Edmund Scarburgh, the wealthy and politically powerful surveyor for the Eastern Shore, who appears to have aided Johnson on several occasions. Such patron-client relationships were hardly unusual among Johnson's contemporaries, whether white or black, in either England or America.

Presiding over his extended family, Johnson himself must have cut the figure of a minor patriarch by the mid-1650s, with his two married sons supporting their own households and likely looking to him for an inheritance out of the hundreds of acres he had patented by then. His son John had married a free black woman named Susan, while Richard had wed a white woman, also named Susan. This white daughter-in-law suggests at least something of the differences between Anthony Johnson's world and that which his grandchildren would have to negotiate. Whatever other troubles they might have encountered, Richard and Susan remained lifelong residents of Accomack County on Virginia's Eastern Shore peninsula, and their marriage endured until Richard's death parted them in 1689. Two years after Richard's death, however, Virginia enacted a statute to discourage such marriages—an ominous sign of the world to come.

Virginia's restraints on interracial marriages were but one of a series of steps to curtail the basic civil rights that free blacks like the Johnsons had previously enjoyed. Indeed, the increasingly ominous threats to the legal status of blacks and the continued harassment by some of his neighbors, coupled perhaps with declining tobacco prices, may be what led Anthony Johnson to sell most of his Virginia property in the spring of 1665 and move his family, except for Richard and Susan, to the Maryland side of the Eastern Shore. Their destination, Somerset County, appears to have been something of a haven for political and religious mavericks at the time, among them an Anglican Nonconformist, Stephen Horsey, from whom Anthony leased a three-hundred-acre tract of land. When Anthony died in 1670, leaving his Maryland land-lease to his second wife, some property in Virginia to Richard, and the cattle to be divided among his sons, the world he had inhabited was already rapidly changing.

As a consequence, like most other descendants of that founding generation, Anthony Johnson's sons do not appear to have fared as well as he. The fifty acres he left to Richard in Accomack County were immediately seized by his old nemesis George Parker, on the novel and insidious ground that since Richard was a Negro he was an alien and thus not eligible to own land. While Richard, who was trained as a carpenter, accumulated enough money to purchase another tract, his brother John did not have such good fortune. A tenant farmer for most of his life, he became a landowner only when he purchased a forty-four-acre tract in Somerset County during the last decade of his life. Moreover, he found himself in trouble with the law, suffering indignities his father never countenanced. He was prosecuted for sexual relations with a white servant girl, escaping a jail term only thanks to the efforts of his wife, who bailed him out with the help of a white neighbor. In 1670, the very year his father died and Richard's inheritance was stolen, further indignities were heaped upon John when his testimony was disallowed in court until he could produce proof of baptism and that he understood the meaning of an oath. Seven years later, he purchased a homestead in Somerset County, which he called "Angola." Perhaps this was, as many historians have suggested, a gesture toward his ancestral origins; it was almost certainly an act of defiance toward his and his brother's palpable alienation from the world they now inhabited. Literally without a place in the world of his birth, John moved several times before ending his days in a Delaware settlement. Echoing his father's fate, his only son became a fugitive. His daughter stayed on in Somerset County, where she married John Puckham, an Indian. One historian has speculated that the Johnsons may have left traces among Indian survivors on the Eastern Shore, including their surname and, in at least two places, an odd place name, "Angola."

Unlike the Johnsons, most of the five children that Emanuel Driggus and his wife, Francis, bore were never freed. Indeed, the Driggus family illustrates how much freedom was confounded with slavery in the lives of many of these early African settlers and their descendants. The man from whom Emanuel purchased his freedom, William Kendall, also became his landlord, leasing him 145 acres. Meanwhile, Kendall continued to hold Emanuel's son Thomas and his daughter Ann as slaves. We can only guess at the stresses, intergenerational and familial, that such an arrangement produced. Most free blacks were manumitted only after years of installment payments, gaining freedom well into their mature years, implying a complex, perhaps tense, patron-client relationship not only with their former masters but with the larger white world.

Clearly the stresses on free African American families increasingly came to be the rule rather than the exception as their civil status declined. In numerous cases children were bound out without their parents' consent. In 1661, the Virginia Assembly passed a law that determined the slave or free status of black children according to the condition of their mother. A common response of black men was to marry a free woman, black or white. The resulting labor force, made up of slaves and indentures, of black, red, and white, was not simply segmented by civil status and race but, joined by co-residency and a common work regime, encouraged liaisons and marriages across those same racial and civil divides.

Thus Emanuel's slave son Thomas, who would spend his entire life on Kendall's plantation, married Sarah King, a sixteen-year-old free black woman. Motivated by similar logic, perhaps, the young couple entrusted their first child to be raised by a free black family—and thus out of Kendall's reach. Even so, the strain of living in a slave household led Sarah herself to move out just a few years later, apparently to escape the complaints of her husband and his master about her independent ways.

Like the second generation of Johnson children, Emanuel Driggus's offspring had much less success than he in forging a decent life. Sarah Driggus fled the Chesapeake for Delaware in 1688, after hearing a rumor spread by a white neighbor that free blacks would soon be reenslaved. The rumor turned out to be false, just a ruse to seize her abandoned property, but the fact that she found it credible suggests a profound shift in circumstances. Although one of Emanuel's grandsons, Azaricum, who had been apprenticed to a carpenter, parlayed his skills into a modest fortune, most of his descendants died poor, no more able than their white landless neighbors to compete with the growing pool of slave labor, which by the middle of the next century would make up more than 70 percent of the total labor force on the Chesapeake's Eastern Shore. By then the idea that a black man would vote or take a white wife or go abroad armed for self-defense was but a distant memory.

Historians have long debated how and why Anthony Johnson's world changed so dramatically. Indeed, some have even cast doubt on its very existence, insisting that from the start, racial differentiation overrode all other factors shaping social relations. In its pithiest form, this debate can be summarized as the "chicken or egg" question: Which came first, the degraded social standing that was codified into racist laws by the early eighteenth century, or an innate and primordial white racism that required from the outset that blacks be degraded and enslaved? What one makes of that debate really depends on whether one insists that racial prejudice exists as a discrete, even autonomous, force shaping human social relations and institutions, or can itself be a contingent and thus variable phenomenon shaped by other social forces unfolding over time. There is probably no way to *prove* either viewpoint conclusively. Certainly there is ample evidence that Englishmen brought long-standing racial prejudices to America, and even more evidence that they treated people with black skin differently from whites at the outset of their errand in the American wilderness. On the other hand, there is equally compelling evidence that it was less the ideas and attitudes they brought with them from England than the environment and opportunities they found in Virginia that decisively shaped the racist social regime that emerged.

Whatever their personal prejudices, Anthony Johnson's white neighbors possessed only a limited capacity or even ambition to fashion a social order in which one's race, economic role, and civil status were absolutely congruent. As in most frontier societies, even the most pretentious could not stand long on ceremony when confronted with the demands of preserving their lives and livelihoods. This was most evident, for example, when European settlements were under attack by Indians. Whatever their reservations about arming black inhabitants—and after 1640 there were explicit legal prohibitions against doing so—necessity demanded otherwise. Theirs was, moreover, a triracial world in which Indians, blacks, and whites were all intensely engaged and interactive. All three groups were numbered among the servants or slaves on plantations, but, significantly, before the turn of the century the majority of those workers were white. The evolving demography of the labor force may have been as much the cause as the result of an evolving racial regime.

Anthony Johnson's seventeenth-century world more closely resembled the Iberian colonies in the previous century than British colonies in the next: a baroque world in which mixed labor forces encouraged a more complex interplay between color and civil status. And like the misshapen pearls that form one of the etymological roots of the word, the baroque societies formed out of laws and customs in this seventeenth-century world confound efforts to neatly sort out the role race played in their making and unmaking. Those seeking a pre-racial Camelot are bound to be disappointed, since racial distinctions were evident in law and practice well before that first generation of free black families emerged. For example, by the early 1640s, the women in households such as Anthony's were liable for tithes, the special taxes levied on productive labor, while white serving women were not. The logic behind the distinction was consistent with the racial segmentation of the work force: black women worked in the fields, white women did not. More than symbolism was at stake here; such exactions amounted to a discriminatory tax that could well make the difference between a successful crop season and financial hardship for a black family. In both material and symbolic terms, the law degraded blacks.

One should not imagine, therefore, that the world Johnson and his black neighbors negotiated was free of racial prejudice or antipathy, but neither should one assume a fully formed racialized social order. What is striking, from the perspective of their descendants, was how often this pioneer generation of African Americans *assumed* their entitlement to civil rights and equal status, and how often those assumptions were confirmed. Over time the laws governing social and labor relations would be rationalized—or we might say "modernized"—as greater efforts would be made to align racial origin with labor service and roles in the polity. As the law became more thoroughly consistent with an evolving system of black slave labor, summary judgments were rendered at lower judicial levels. These judges or their immediate neighbors were more likely to be the interested parties in the cases, which led to increasingly arbitrary and unjust decisions. For much of the seventeenth century, however, the treatment of African slaves tracked closely the treatment of white indentured servants, who still made up a majority of the work force and often shared their work and living quarters with blacks. It was hardly the case that white planters could not tell the difference between black and white, but the demographic and social profile of their work force made any effort to structure their behavior and laws according to those differences hardly worth the bother. On the other hand, slaves, like indentured servants, enjoyed fairly liberal access to the courts, and thus issues of slavery, freedom, and the appropriate status of Africans were constantly being raised and adjudicated. The ruling elite was forced, therefore, to address issues explicitly that they might otherwise have left to the vagaries of an individual planter's decisions.

The numerous freedom suits filed by black people contesting the inaccuracy of their assigned civil status suggests that being black and being a slave were not yet the same thing, even as the fact that they felt compelled to file these suits indicates the growing precariousness of their status. A striking illustration of both the ambiguities of their status and its erosion is found in the legal case instigated by one of Anthony Johnson's contemporaries, Elizabeth Key. One of the earliest extant freedom suits, Key's case also tracks closely the adoption of explicit statutes that attempted to address the myriad issues raised by black bondage. The illegitimate daughter of an unnamed slave woman and Thomas Key, a member of the Virginia House of Burgesses, Elizabeth had been indentured after her father died in 1636, to her godfather, Humphrey Higginson, another prominent political figure. Somehow her indentured status later morphed into outright enslavement to John Mottram, a magistrate in Northumberland County. When Mottram died in 1655, Key sued his estate for her freedom. She contested her slave status on three principal grounds: first, that she was actually an indentured servant and not a slave; second, that since her father was English, her civil status was governed, under English law, by his condition; and finally, that she was a Christian. Local jurors found in her favor, and although she lost on appeal to the General Court, the General Assembly, which acted as the highest court of appeal until the 1680s, eventually confirmed her freedom. Like Anthony Johnson, therefore, whose successful defense of his right to hold John Casar as a slave transpired at roughly the same time, Key exemplifies the ambiguities of race and class relations in the middle of the seventeenth century. Shortly after the case was settled, Key married her white lawyer, yet another indication of the fluidity of racial relations in that protean moment.

The eventual responses that her case provoked, though, reveal a hardening of racial boundaries and a changing social order. The grounds on which Key claimed her freedom exposed the anachronisms of a legal system now grown incongruent with the evolving labor regime. Even if unsuccessful, such suits would amount to an expensive nuisance to owners of slave property. The same Assembly that apparently felt compelled to grant Key's suit, therefore, closed the door to further litigation on similar grounds. In 1662, following the precedents of English law on bastardy, Virginia legislators concluded that like bastards, a mulatto's paternity was likely to be unknown, and thus the fate of "children gott by any Englishman upon a negro woman" would henceforth be determined by the *mother's* civil status, not the father's. In practice, however, it soon ceased to matter whether paternity was known or not.

With the same statute legislators took a somewhat timid initial step toward discouraging the reproduction of more people like Elizabeth Key, one of its clauses providing that "any Christian" who fornicated with a black man or woman would be liable to double the usual fine for such violations. The numerous cases of interracial fornication that made their way to court dockets thereafter suggest that such differential fines had limited effect, however. Sometime later the law was broadened to prohibit "intermarriage" as well as casual sex. This law, passed in 1691, targeted indentured white women in particular, fining them fifteen pounds or five years additional service for birthing bastard children of Indian or African origin. Notwithstanding that such children should have been free by the legal logic privileging their maternal origins, they were bound out to service until thirty years old, which, given prevailing mortality rates, could effectively be for a lifetime. These 1691 provisions were part of a law entitled "An act for suppressing outlying Slaves," suggesting that overall security concerns motivated these efforts to regulate sexual relations and the offspring who blurred both civil boundaries and existing hierarchies of control.

Five years after Key won her suit, the Assembly eliminated the remaining argument justifying her freedom, her Christian conversion. Given ancient justifications of slavery based on religious apostasy, claims of free status by virtue of being a Christian and not a heathen were fairly common in the Americas. Indeed, the Assembly may well have been prompted to act by another freedom suit filed that year in the Norfolk County court. Armed with documents in Portuguese attesting to his earlier conversion, a slave named Fernando sought his freedom. Since no one could read Portuguese, Fernando's suit came to naught, but it may well have set off alarms among the legislators. When convened a month later, they solemnly declared that "baptisme doth not alter the condition of the person as to his bondage or freedome."

The notion of writing laws on such matters, much less enforcing them, depended on a political climate and infrastructure in which such lawmaking made sense. It is notable that this veritable flurry of legislation from the 1660s onward corresponded with the cessation of hostilities in England's civil war, the restoration of royal authority there and in the colonies, and the quickened pace and intensity of colonial territorial and commercial expansion. One of Charles II's first acts upon his succession was to grant letters patent to the Royal African Company—followed three years later by a charter—to monopolize the slave trade. Indeed, throughout the British colonial system, the systematic regulation of the relations between the races was increasingly tied to the emergence of a political economy in which labor recruitment and its reproduction depended on racial differentiation. Ultimately, it is within this complex and evolving material-political context, therefore, that one must understand both how Anthony Johnson could have lived the life he did and why his grandchildren could not.

North American Slavery in the Atlantic World

The social transformation of labor in the Chesapeake was not an isolated development, a fact too often neglected in historical accounts of slavery in North America. Somewhere between 240,000 and 295,000 people left the British Isles during the first sixty years of the seventeenth century, but most of them ended up in Ireland or the Caribbean, not North America. Indeed, as late as 1660, only about 50,000 had set out for the Chesapeake. The expansion and consolidation of Britain's American settlements depended first on the delicate interplay between labor supply and demand on both sides of the Atlantic and was further complicated by a half century of political turmoil at home. After an aborted effort in Guyana, the English put down stakes in St. Kitts and Barbados during the early 1620s. Following pretty much the same script and at roughly the same time as in the Chesapeake, those colonists struggled to find a staple crop that would sustain permanent communities, turning eventually to tobacco, which they cultivated with a mixed labor force of free white settlers and white indentured laborers, leavened with small numbers of African and, where available, Indian slaves. By the second quarter of the seventeenth century, however, the Caribbean colonies departed from this script, shifting to sugar cultivation on large plantations worked by hundreds of African slaves. The impetus for this change lay farther south, where Portuguese success in expelling Dutch settlers from Brazil sent tremors throughout the Atlantic world. In the far-flung maritime conflicts that ensued, the Dutch broke Spain's sea power and commercial monopoly, opening up the whole Atlantic trade to all comers, but especially to the British and French. A secondary effect of that war was the transfer of Portuguese skills in large-scale sugar cultivation with slave labor to the Caribbean, as Brazil's erstwhile Dutch settlers scattered throughout the Americas. Barbados was among the principal beneficiaries of this diaspora, and by 1643 it had made its first sugar crop. Within a couple of decades its labor force had shifted from mostly white indentured servants to African slaves. Between

1601 and 1650, Barbados brought in more than 25,000 African slaves; by contrast, for all of North America, the number reached just 1,400.

In time the intensification of staple production and the turn to slave labor would unfold in the southern colonies of British North America as well, but at a much slower pace and with a different crop. By the early 1630s, Virginia had become the dominant producer of tobacco, which reflects a number of natural advantages as well as its poor terrain for sugar cultivation. More than most other crops, tobacco leaches the soil of its nutrients, which means that fields have to be rotated frequently. Given its larger land mass, therefore, Virginia could produce the crop more cheaply. It also gained a market advantage with a reputation for the superior mild taste of the sweet-scented tobacco produced in the most fertile regions of the tidewater.

Tobacco was always a roller-coaster crop, however, subject to sharp cycles of prosperity and depression as European demand waxed and waned. Thanks to greater efficiencies in production and shipping during the middle decades of the seventeenth century, tobacco's secular trend was largely bullish, with bumper crops and good markets for several decades. It is probably no accident that it was during these years that Anthony Johnson and some others of his generation made the successful transition from slavery or indentured servitude to freedom, with some of them achieving a measure of well-being. It is also clear, however, that this same tobacco boom fastened the chains on other Africans all the more tightly.

In sharp contrast with the rest of the hemisphere, given its relatively slower development, the Chesapeake had not hitherto provided a particularly good market for slaves. In fact, it was not until late in the seventeenth century that it began to receive substantial and regular cargoes directly from Africa rather than the leftovers from saturated Caribbean markets fed by the sugar boom. Consequently, while their countrymen elsewhere were turning to slaves, the planters of the Chesapeake still relied heavily on indentured white laborers, who at times made up 80 to 90 percent of their labor force.

Indentured labor had developed in England as a nationally regulated system of labor recruitment and control some eighty years earlier. Legally, the indenture contract was a personal covenant that bound household workers and tradesmen for a limited term of service. In the Americas, such servants served terms ranging from four to seven years, depending partly on age, but ultimately on the prevailing political and economic context that conditioned their initial negotiations. Such laborers lost their personal freedom, including the right to marry, and their contracts were commercial property. For the duration of their contracts they had the legal status of chattel, and thus, like livestock, household furniture, and slaves, they could be bought, sold, inherited, or put up as security for debts. Indeed, the fact that there could be any possibility of confusing the status of a slave and an indentured worker—as in Anthony Johnson's dispute with John Casar—owes a great deal to the similarity of their actual life circumstances. They were like slaves in all but the length of their service and the civil status of their offspring. Of course, in those two exceptions—as both John Casar and Anthony Johnson well knew—lay a world of difference.

These seventeenth-century white settlers of the Chesapeake were drawn largely from the hinterlands of England's three principal ports, Bristol, Liverpool, and London. Not surprisingly, they were mostly young farm boys and unskilled laborers or tradesmen. That they came at all suggests that terrible conditions must have ravaged their places of origins. Their fate in America was often horrific. Many of Anthony Johnson's white neighbors lived short, brutish lives in a rude, masculine world where men outnumbered women by three to one and families were slow to form. At times, three of every ten surviving the sea voyage might not live to see a second year in America. Low life expectancy contributed to slow population growth in North America for most of the century, but even more important were the host of other factors that disfavored family formation and reduced opportunities for bearing children. Not only were women, white or black, scarce, but their years of procreation were abbreviated because indentured servants had to delay marriage until their terms expired, and sexual relations outside of marriage were severely punished. In pointed contrast with slaves, the children of indentured laborers were a burden to the planter rather than an asset.

The fearful rate of mortality began to moderate by the 1660s, although it still remained at a level experienced in Britain only during epidemics. By the last decades of the seventeenth century, the white population had begun to reproduce itself, as Creoles lived longer, married earlier, and bore more children, who themselves survived into adulthood. A similar pattern unfolded among the black population. These developments promoted the increased use of African slave labor. Indeed, favorable political, social,

and demographic developments for Englishmen on both sides of the Atlantic encouraged the turn to a mostly African slave labor force. Recover-
ing from almost a decade of civil war, England saw its political and economic
conditions improve, which produced much less incentive for English
workers to risk their lives and liberties as indentured laborers in the still-
treacherous environment of North America, especially as rising land prices
in settled areas made the economic rewards of such a venture increasingly
precarious. From the planter's point of view, the declining mortality rate
made it more attractive to buy slaves, who served for life, rather than purchase the contracts of increasingly reticent and fractious servants who
served for only limited terms. Heretofore having the *right* to hold someone
for life didn't mean much, if no one could be counted on to live very long
anyway. Moreover, the unbalanced sex ratio among slaves, together with
the high child mortality rate, meant that the right to a slave woman's offspring was not worth a lot, either. Applying this same mode of calculation,
however, by the late seventeenth century, the planters had reasonable expectations of a self-reproducing labor force. Thus the theoretical value of
a slave woman's increase became a real, living asset, which it could not be
as long as mortality continued at epidemic levels. Thus as more and more
children of slave women lived to adulthood, slavery proved a better investment than indentured labor. Such actuarial calculations would become
the ordinary folk wisdom of slaveholders in the next century, especially as
it became evident that black Creole women were much more fertile than
their African mothers.

An index of these demographic changes is the inflation of land prices
and labor costs by the turn of the eighteenth century. Of course, as white
parents lived long enough to see their children launched into maturity, the
resulting population increase boosted the demand by former indentured
laborers for landed property. The distinguished colonial historian Edmund
Morgan once ventured the controversial suggestion that such developments elevated class tensions to dangerous levels by the late 1670s because such demands could not be easily satisfied, and that this encouraged
the planter elite not only to switch to slave labor as an alternative but also
to foster legalized racial distinctions. Morgan argued that it became *politically* advantageous for the white elite to distinguish between the elevated
civil status of landless whites and that of slaves. In short, whatever their
problems, landless whites could be comforted by the fact that they were

"white" and, as such, a cut above the black slaves they or their fathers had once worked beside.

Whatever their motivation, it is indisputable that Chesapeake lawmakers in this period began to etch sharp legal distinctions between both slave and free labor, and blacks and whites more generally. By 1691, Virginia had consolidated its disparate slave laws into a unified code regulating race and labor relations. Likened to slaves, free black men (such as the sons of Anthony Johnson and Emanuel Driggis) were denied the civil status their fathers had routinely enjoyed. Not only could they no longer bear arms or vote, both important signs of citizenship, but they could not even defend themselves, legally or physically, from white aggression. A black man's testimony was no longer acceptable in courts of law, and striking a white man was a felony for which a black man could be severely punished. Interracial sexual relations, like Johnson's son's marriage to a white woman, were legally prohibited. Such relations did not end, of course, but they were driven underground. They could not be lived openly and without fear. In the southern colonies, slavery had come, directly or indirectly, to dominate the lives of all African Americans, whether enslaved or free.

The New World of African Americans

In the early summer of 1754, some eighty-four years after Anthony Johnson's death, a slave ship bearing the preadolescent Olaudah Equiano made its way up the Chesapeake Bay into the York River. There, on one of the region's many private landings, Equiano was sold to a planter named Campbell, on whose property he would spend his brief time in North America. Before the summer's end he would find himself on another ship, bound for England, now the property of its captain, Michael Henry Pascal. On the opposite side of the Chesapeake Bay, roughly fifty miles from the York River environs where Equiano spent his brief sojourn in Virginia, lay the stomping grounds of the Johnson family a century earlier. The world Equiano encountered, however, was one the Johnsons would have found unimaginable. Slaves now constituted the overwhelming bulk of the labor force, and white indentured laborers had all but disappeared, as indeed had almost all white employment in menial labor positions on plantations. The Native American population that had leavened relations between black and white was practically invisible, as were the Indians themselves in the heart of the principal slave colonies. Indeed, the progeny of many of the Indians who remained were now as much African as indigenous.

The faint beginnings of these trends could have been discerned during the last twenty years of Anthony Johnson's life, when the numbers of African slaves brought into British North America increased dramatically, although they still counted in the dozens for any given year and totaled a mere 900 souls over the quarter century between 1651 and 1675. Johnson's grandchildren would see more than ten times that number over the thirty years following his death, when another 9,800 slaves entered North America. The pace would quicken yet again during the eighteenth century, doubling during the first decade, leaping sevenfold the next, and tripling again over the three decades leading up to the American Revolution.

Some of the impetus for this accelerated pace came from the slave-trading monopoly granted to the Royal African Company in 1663 and renewed in 1672, just one of many acts of state patronage taken by the restored monarchy, intent on consolidating its post–civil war regime. Despite its early inefficiencies, the company can be credited with jump-starting a trade that Britain would soon come to dominate. It quickly faded into irrelevance, however, as independent traders came to monopolize 90 percent of the business by the turn of century. With the market spurred by their greedy enterprise, British ships would carry more than four of every ten slaves landed in the Americas over the next century and a half, a fact that surely must have furthered the shift to slave labor in Britain's American colonies.

In these years colonists forged a new political economy in North America, one that transformed once more the lives of its inhabitants of African descent, much as the sugar revolution had already transformed the southern half of the Western Hemisphere. From 1700 to 1780, reversing the earlier pattern, about twice as many Africans as Europeans crossed the Atlantic to North America, and an increasing share of the total wealth created there now derived from slave-produced commodities. Between 1768 and 1772, the very eve of the American Revolution, Virginia and South Carolina—the principal sites for the development of North American slavery in this period and still home to all but a small fraction of the slaves on the continent—generated about two thirds of the average annual value of the mainland's commodity exports, a regional pattern that would not change dramatically until well into the nineteenth century, when agricultural and industrial production in the North and Midwest would move into high gear.

These changes sprang partly from the civil war and postwar restoration in England, which laid much of the political, social, and institutional groundwork for the emergence of a planter class in the Chesapeake. By the middle of the eighteenth century, roughly 125 great planters controlled half the tobacco crop and most of the slaves in Virginia. It is not clear whether the Mr. Campbell who purchased Equiano was among them, but, like him, they controlled frontage on the deep rivers—the James, York, Rappahannock, and Potomac—that served the Virginia Tidewater and thus gave privileged access to the ships that came to buy tobacco and sell slaves. The founding fathers of many of these families were of the generation born in the middle of the previous century who had immigrated to Virginia either during the civil war or the thirty-year Restoration period that followed. William Fitzhugh, the first William Byrd, Robert "King" Carter, and Lewis Burwell II were exemplary of the rise of this new elite class. Hard-driven men, mostly descended from the middling English gentry, they seized opportunities offered by political, economic, or domestic connections and founded Virginia dynasties. Beginning with modest holdings in most cases, they expanded these through advantageous marriages into the established first families of Virginia (such as the Tuckers, the Filmers, and the Bacons), which staked them to even larger landed estates, slave-enriched dowries, and political and social influence. The social influence was perhaps most important, since it could be parlayed into officeholding, which further positioned them to seize huge windfalls of real property. Class inequality and stratification among whites were augmented proportionately. Thus, for example, a survey of Virginia's five best tobacco-growing counties in this period (Charles City, James City, Henrico, King and Queen, and Middlesex) shows 25 percent of landholders engrossing 70 percent of the land.

Located on the James River about ten miles from both Williamsburg and the historic settlement at Jamestown, Carter's Grove reveals something of the meaning of the new world fashioned by this planter elite, and its implications for the world their slaves were able to make. Although a residence had been established on the property in 1738, the main house at Carter's Grove was not built until the 1750s, at the tail end of a two-decade building boom that refashioned the tidewater's landscape and sought to inscribe the new social order into its built environment. The estate's origins, however, were embedded in the genealogy of the great planter elite that had emerged during the previous half century. Carter Burwell (1716–1756), the Grove's first occupant, was a grandson of Lewis Burwell II (c. 1646–1710), one of the great planter founding fathers, who had parlayed land rights inherited from his own father into a considerable fortune. As was typical of this group, his wealth had been amassed through a combination of political influence, economic savvy, and social prowess. He accumulated slave property from diverse sources—a few had been purchased from the Royal African Company, some seized for debt, a few more purchased from neighbors, but the bulk came from his marriage to Abigail Smith, an heiress to her uncle Nathaniel Bacon (a cousin and namesake of the famous rebel). Carter's father, Nathaniel Burwell (1680–1721), had married well in his turn, an alliance with a daughter of Robert "King" Carter (1663–1732). It was this maternal grandfather—reputedly the second richest man in North America after a Dutch noble in New York—who purchased for his grandson Carter Burwell the property that became Carter's Grove.

Both the purchase and renaming of the property emblematized the pretensions and ambitions typical of the eighteenth-century planter elite. By mid-century, the great planters had succeeded in clothing their ill-gotten economic and political power in the ideological raiment of a refined patriarchalism that justified their elite status and control over the lives of their social inferiors, black and white, male and female. As Rhys Isaac has shown, their social vision was replicated and reinforced by the built environment, which was carefully fashioned to display the social power and authority of the gentry in the columns and formal gardens of the great houses, in the organization of the pews of Anglican churches, and through lavish displays and entertainments.

The social power on display, however, was that of dynasties as well as individuals. In 1705, following a precedent established by Barbados during the consolidation of its planter class in the previous century, Virginia defined slaves as real estate instead of chattel, in an effort to prevent valuable estates from being dismantled in probate settlements among competing heirs. Thereafter both slaves and land could be entailed, which limited the rights to their inheritance to direct male heirs. A later act, in 1727, went further, enabling slaves to be attached to particular plantations. The consolidation of the Burwell-Bacon holdings benefited from these legal changes.

So did their slaves. The more typical practice, especially among small and middling planters, was to apportion slaves equally among the heirs, a practice also followed by courts when an owner died intestate. Thus slave families were likely to be broken up upon the death of their owner, if not already sold to cover his debts or to raise capital. An unintended consequence of the law of entail, therefore, was that slave families on the larger properties—which were mainly in the tidewater and controlled a disproportionate share of the enslaved population initially—confronted much less risk of physical separation than other slaves.

With the consolidation of the great tidewater estates, it fell to the smaller properties, together with the offshoots from the large plantations in the Piedmont, to fuel the enormous demand for slaves that had developed by mid-century. This surge in slave imports first had to overcome entrenched resistance from the established planter elite in the tidewater, however—an illustration of how internal class conflicts and international economics shaped slavery from the outset. Once they had adequate hands on their own estates and/or as their labor forces reproduced by natural means, the great planters had sought to raise tobacco prices by reducing production, which was best achieved by starving smaller planters of slave labor. Small planters were also forced to make slave purchases with cash rather than financing their debts through bills of exchange like the big men. Moreover, these big men, who controlled the local political machinery, imposed onerous duties on the importation of Africans.

Such measures ran contrary to some metropolitan interests, however, leading to a tacit alliance of small and middling planters with a new group of merchants and slave traders operating out of secondary ports such as Bristol and Glasgow. Frozen out of the lucrative Eastern trade by the gigantic trading monopolists in London, these men were anxious to finance an expanded slave and tobacco trade in North America. Since their income rose with the volume of the export trade and the debts they underwrote for slave purchases, their interests lay with an expansion of tobacco production and slaveholding. The great planters soon ran afoul of the British government as well, especially as duties became an increasing source of income to pay the escalating costs of colonial defense. During the 1720s and 1730s, Sir Robert Walpole's ministry deliberately sought to exploit the class conflict among the colonists and to shift the economic burden of colonial support from merchants to planters. With the support of their merchant and slave trader allies and the tacit backing of the Crown, then, smaller property owners began to buy slaves. As a result, the annual slave imports to Virginia, which had been counted in the hundreds in the early 1720s, exceeded three thousand by 1736. Notwithstanding a brief contraction in the 1740s, the slave trade grew even more dramatically during the third quarter of the eighteenth century, in tandem with the vast social and geographical expansion of tobacco cultivation. Thus the ship that brought Equiano to Virginia was one of scores docking at North American ports that year bearing thousands of slaves, many of them from Bonny or Old Calabar.

The rhythms of the slave trade were uneven and the spatial distribution of its cargoes shifted over time, structuring a complex and varied social environment for relations within slave communities. Both the vastly increased numbers of slaves and their provenance had a transformative impact on the North American slave experience. The greater or lesser presence of Africans could profoundly shape the health of a given community, leaving settled slave communities ever vulnerable to demographic and cultural disruptions by a sudden influx of newcomers. The timing and number of these infusions and their cessation might determine the physical and social character of a slave community in a given locale at a given time. As a consequence, a profound structural tension was built into the very fabric of colonial black communities.

Whether a substantial number of a community's members were African- or American-born might well determine its patterns of mortality and family formation and thus the fundamental conditions of possibility for a more "normal" life. Mortality, especially infant mortality, remained fearsome in the eighteenth century, but as with most settler populations, native-born women lived longer and were healthier and more fertile than the newcomers. They began childbearing earlier (in their teens) and had more children (about one every other year). Given a full reproductive cycle, one historian estimates that a woman might bear eight or nine children. This did not escape the notice of slave owners. As a young Thomas Jefferson informed his overseer: "a woman who brings a child every two years is more valuable than the best man on the farm." So, even as the slave trade accelerated, the native-born population grew faster. Sometime during the second decade of the eighteenth century, Virginia became the first slave colony in the New World to achieve population growth through natural increase.

Nonetheless, the influx of African newcomers not only upset the demographic balance but shifted the social dynamic in other ways. Africans with fresh memories of the Middle Passage knew and had experienced the world differently from Creoles born and reared in America, and each shipment disgorged in southern ports renewed the collective memory of otherwise unimaginable worlds, experiences, and ways of being. This was especially true in the last half of the eighteenth century, when the horrific images of the slave trade would be etched into the imaginations of contemporaries and subsequent generations: human bodies reduced to objects of commerce, shorn of all recognizable human relationships; ships tightly packed and crews morally oblivious to the awesome suffering and death that these voyages produced; bodies thrown overboard like so much offal so that ship owners could collect the insurance. Thus, the Atlantic trade had a profound influence on the formation of African American communities; it became part of the material and conscious negotiation of their everyday lives. Even those born in America, the Creoles, must have been affected by those memories' palpable presence.

Beyond raw statistics, we know the human toll of the Middle Passage mainly through the graphic testimony of survivors, such as Equiano, whose wrenching narrative provides insight into how that harrowing experience not only devastated its victims but transformed them. Embarking from ports in the Bight of Biafra, Equiano's Igbo compatriots and Ibibio neighbors constituted the largest ethnic cohorts landed in Virginia during the mid-eighteenth century. In sharp contrast with the transatlantic trade as a whole, they were almost evenly divided between men and women, and like Equiano, substantially larger numbers of them were mere boys and girls less than fifteen years old. They would come of age aboard those slave ships bound for America, with new identities, collective and individual, forged in the horrors of the passage. No longer fully African or entirely American, either, they likely brought to the American scene a consciousness and repertoire of survival skills very different from those of the Creole slaves they found there.

Their transformative process began on the west coast of Africa, in slave coffles to the coast, or even earlier, in villages threatened by slaving predators. Equiano describes his astonishment at the first sight of a slave ship and his growing terror as his body was poked, handled, and humiliated to determine his potential worth in the American slave markets. Given European slavers' intense curiosity about their captives' bodies, as they sought to determine whether they could endure the deprivations of the long sea journey to come, it is little wonder that many slaves shared young Equiano's fear that he was destined to be eaten by these men of such "horrible looks, red faces, and loose hair." Having fainted from fear, he describes being calmed, ironically, only when some of the slave traders' black henchmen reassured him that he was destined *merely* for forced labor rather than a white cannibal's stomach.

Equiano's temporary reconciliation with that fate soon turned once more to terror, however, when the ship raised its anchor and set out across the Atlantic, a six-week journey that could take two months if winds and tides were unfavorable. The living death of this so-called Middle Passage was, he tells us, "a scene of horror almost inconceivable." Certainly, after witnessing the death and unceremonious dumping into the sea of one of the white crewmen following a vicious, "unmerciful" whipping, he had little doubt of what these savage white spirits were capable. Entering this world of chilling, seemingly senseless violence and brutality, he could explain what he saw and heard only in terms of enchantment and magic.

By mid-century, the seemingly insatiable demand of American plantations had turned slave ships into virtual storage silos of human flesh. Parliamentary inquiries into insurance frauds turned up evidence that ships designed to carry 451 people were found to hold more than 600, tightly packed into every possible recess of the vessel. To ensure security upon setting out into the open seas, the captives were confined for weeks on end below deck, "so crowded that each had scarcely room to turn himself." Thus immobilized, they found themselves floating into a veritable hell. All their senses were assaulted by pain and degradation: manacles rubbed skin raw; the air grew foul with sweating bodies and oppressive heat; the shrieks and groans of suffering humanity were ever more inescapable and unrelenting.

The dominant trope in Equiano's description of his voyage is suffocation, the sensation of being unable to breathe or of breathing at one's very peril. The intolerable stench of human excrement was everywhere, as the captives relieved themselves in "the necessary tubs." These were large cone-shaped buckets standing more than two feet high and tapering from a one-foot top to a two-foot bottom—just large enough, Equiano tells us, for small unattended children to occasionally slip into them and suffocate. On those small boats, tossed and rolled by the rough Atlantic waves, the tubs must have overturned on more than one occasion, leaving the captives to eat and sleep immersed in their contents, living and dying in their own filth. Little wonder that residents of seaports throughout the Americas described the stench pervading slave ships as arriving like heralds announcing their approach.

Under these circumstances, being allowed above deck was a signal privilege. It was normal practice to bring the slaves outside for air and exercise at some point during the day, but since captives regularly seized upon such opportunities to jump to their certain deaths in the sea, the privilege was sometimes limited to those judged too sick, too weak, or too young to cause trouble. From time to time, slaves found opportunities to rebel and seize control of the ship, but very few such efforts were successful. Much more frequently, the sick and despondent slipped silently behind shrouded eyes into the release of a welcome death.

The Middle Passage was not simply about physical suffering, rebellion, and death, however. One of the principal themes running through Equiano's account of his experience is the ordeal of losing and regaining human communication and community. Perhaps the possibility of speech looms so large among his concerns because it represented the lost capacity to establish or reestablish human relationships. From the beginning of his captivity he had moved in and out of zones where cultural and linguistic communication was possible or voided, and this pattern continued throughout the Middle Passage and his brief stay in North America. He repeatedly describes the inability to speak or to be understood as a circumstance that filled him with despair. During the voyage to America this alienation was overcome by adopting the pidgin dialects that had grown up in trading ports of the Atlantic littoral and forging new social bonds with the "shipmates" passing through this man-made storm. However deeply felt, such relations were necessarily fragile and destined to be disrupted once ships docked in the Americas and their cargoes were auctioned off. Upon his separation from the last of his shipmates in Virginia,

Equiano found himself once again locked in silence, unable to speak to or be understood by an uncomprehending and incomprehensible slave community—despite the fact that most of them were likely to have been of Biafran ancestral origins like him. The sense of loss was profound; he describes it as having left him "wishing for death," a measure of both the powerful kinship the young Equiano had forged with shipmates during the Middle Passage and his emotional distance from the Creole slaves who peopled Campbell's plantation.

In Virginia at mid-century, Equiano would have found only one African among every four slaves he met. By contrast, had he been in South Carolina, the ratio would have been very different, since Africans still predominated there at mid-century. Even Virginia's Creole majority had been temporarily reversed in the Piedmont and Southside regions, however, following a surge in African imports after 1745, again most of them from Biafra. Equiano's alienation, therefore, reflects the domestic effects of the rapidly changing regional demography of the slave trade and its cultural consequences. In that aspect, at least, his story is that of African America.

We know very little about the Campbell property to which Equiano was sold in 1754, but its history probably resembled that of its neighbor, Carter's Grove. Situated in the York River naval district to which Equiano was taken, the Carter-Burwells built their fortunes cultivating the sweet-scented tobacco Europe most coveted. Like most of their neighbors, they imported the bulk of their work force before 1740 and were able thereafter to rely on its natural increase to sustain their holdings. As early as 1738, the slave population at the Grove was composed of two roughly equal-size groups of African-descended peoples, those who had arrived from Africa during the recent resurgence of the trade in the early eighteenth century and a Creole group descended from those arriving during the previous century. Constituting what was possibly an exceptionally closed and stable community that experienced very few additions for years thereafter, the slaves on the Carter's Grove properties nonetheless illuminate the varying trajectories for the evolution of Virginia's slave communities.

The slave management practices of the Carter-Burwells and their neighbors might have eventually softened Equiano's poignant isolation

had his Virginia sojourn lasted longer. African workers struggling to survive in that alien environment confronted a number of possible scenarios.
Initially, most new arrivals were likely to have found themselves among
other slaves who differed from them in practically everything but the color
of their skin. On many properties they would have found themselves eventually placed under the tutelage of an experienced Creole worker to learn
the ropes. Not only was the period of isolation and "seasoning," as it was
called, more abbreviated in such circumstance, but their cultural reeducation and integration were probably quite rapid, given their minority ethnic status and relative youth. On the other hand, the large planters in the
Virginia Tidewater, owning multiple cultivation sites, or "quarters," were
just as likely to scatter the newcomers among them rather than employing
them on the home plantation among their Creole slaves. Indeed, by the
late eighteenth century, they were deploying most new arrivals onto frontier settlements in the Piedmont, rarely visited by whites and often under
the management of a trusted slave. Given the limited makeup of the slave
cargoes from which Virginia planters had to make their purchases, Africans on these quarters might well have found themselves among people
who were culturally familiar, if not of the same ethnic group. And given
their relative isolation not only from the Creole black population but from
whites as well, the possibility of re-creating aspects of their African past
would have been greatly enhanced. They almost certainly would have
shared the harrowing experience of the Middle Passage, even if they did
not have a common African cultural origin. Experiences of capture may
have differed, but the horror of the sea passage to the Americas was pain-
fully similar, while the evolving repertoire of resistance fashioned new
connections and new identities. In such an environment, acculturation to
Creole norms was likely to have been retarded, and the reliance upon
African cultural resources prolonged. It may well be that in these quarters
a generic "African" identity replaced an ethnic one.

Some slave memoirs suggest that the Africans' alien ways sometimes
drew ridicule from Creole members of their own families, especially when
they fell into nostalgic chants and dances from "the old country," but other
evidence suggests that African knowledge was also venerated. The older,
predominantly male African cohort in any given community possessed
personal resources and worldly knowledge that undoubtedly lent them
authority. Throughout the Americas, for example, Africans or Creoles

claiming supernatural powers associated with the old country took the
lead in organizing rebellions against their enslavement. In everyday life,
slaves drew on ritual knowledge, their understandings of pharmacopeia,
and various other skills to reshape their lived environment. African culture emerged and long endured as a kind of undervoice of African American consciousness, evidenced in folktales, herbal medicinal practices, and
dreams of magical liberation. The African memory offered means of fic-
tively re-creating an alternative existence, or a dual nationality; it could
also serve as a prophylactic to racial degradation, stanching the living death
of bondage.

Where slaves were densely concentrated, as on the large estates of the
southern Carolina lowlands, the potential for retaining discernibly African ways of knowing and doing would have been even more enhanced.
After a belated start, the slave trade quickened there in the late eighteenth century, spurred by the growing European market for rice and indigo. Organizing their labor forces along lines similar to the Caribbean
plantations from which many of them hailed, Carolina planters created a
world that was almost entirely black, and slave communities that were
tantamount to small villages.

Wherever one fell along this continuum of North American experience, however, the ultimate trajectory was toward cultural Creolization—
that is, the social interactions and historical transformations by which
Africans, under pressure and by choice, became African Americans, endowed with new modes of behavior, new ways of thinking, and new structures of feeling. All this was synthesized from the cultural materials
brought from Africa, from strategic adaptations to the constraints imposed by Europeans, and from the knowledge and skills freely borrowed
from Native Americans. Changes in the social and physical character of
each colony's slave population were inexorable, notwithstanding different
demographic and work environments. Scarified bodies with ritual mark-
ings became rarer. Housing evolved from barracks or quarters in the out-
back to family cabins in slave villages adjacent to the plantation. Despite
a physically more hostile work environment and a high African-to-Creole
ratio, therefore, even South Carolina witnessed an overall pattern of increasing numbers of slaves living in families—by one historian's reckoning, from 52 percent in the 1730s to 79 percent by the 1790s. Meanwhile,
the number of slaves living alone declined from about half to one fifth.

Ironically, despite their more favorable African-to-Creole ratios, plantations in Virginia and Maryland were less conducive to nuclear households because slaves were often forced to form families across smaller units belonging to different owners, or in the still geographically scattered quarters of the large planters.

In all regions, nonetheless, what slaves ate, how they were housed, what they knew of their physical environs, and how they spoke all bore the marks of a synthetic process. The syntheses, moreover, were not simply African European but African Indian, and not just unilineal but reciprocal. Native Americans taught African Americans to extract medicines from American plant life, while African Americans taught Native Americans their folktales about trickster figures such as "Brer Rabbit."

Still, Native Americans were not the only cultural interlocutors of African and Creole slaves. Eighteenth-century planters may well have enjoyed much greater and more intimate physical and social contact with their slaves than their nineteenth-century descendants. Given the similarities in the early modern worldviews of Europeans and Africans, especially their sense of time and causation, Mechal Sobel imagines that an "interpenetration of values" facilitated cultural familiarity and transfer. The consequences of such cultural openings were especially manifest during the religious revivals of the century's last decades, when "racial closeness and interaction . . . left an African impress on Southern perceptions and values, and both Southern whites and Southern blacks were heirs to a new cultural mix." This cultural fusion, arising from the surprisingly easy melding of African-influenced ideas and practices with evangelical religious beliefs, enabled some Africans to emerge as "role models and practical guides" to whites in a mutually intelligible world. A startling example of this were the black preachers who held white audiences spellbound by their discourses on damnation and salvation.

Contrary to notions of a cultural memory wiped clean, therefore, Africans in America found diverse and creative ways to hold on to a familiar cultural repertoire, possibly by privileging the African legacy in quiet intergenerational transfers, but far more often by boldly implanting it within the broader southern culture. Such cultural transfers were never a matter of simply transporting African practices and values to America like the contents of a stuffed suitcase, but rather bending the American environment to an African rhythm and beat. The evidence for this complex, dialectical process—of a culture simultaneously surviving and transforming itself—can be found in widely different art forms. In music, housing, basketry, and textiles, Africans and African Americans worked with the materials at hand and/or in their few spaces of relative autonomy to fashion complex *new* creations. Unable to bring the tools of their trade through the Middle Passage and confronting inadvertent or deliberate constraints on their ability to practice a craft, Africans fashioned objects of work and everyday life that were new but bore the marks of their places of origin. Planters bent on maximizing production and security often tolerated such activities because they conformed with their own interests. African-style basketmaking, for example, proved especially useful for fanning rice or carrying cotton, a tradition that took hold and endured well into the twentieth century. Slave ironworkers embedded African-influenced designs into the metalwork decorating southern mansions. African aesthetic influences are found not only in the housing that slaves built for themselves but those they constructed for their masters. In any case, the master's surveillance was never so total and his control never so absolute that slaves could not find space and time for creative independence; and with it they fashioned a material world, an environment of sound, sight, and motion that better conformed to their own aesthetic tastes. In their joyful embrace of asymmetry, unpredictability, and contradiction—what art historian Robert Thompson has called "the off-beat"—they cultivated tastes that were and remain strikingly reminiscent of Africa.

These aesthetic preferences have endured and can be discerned in a wide array of creative domains. African American quilting, for example, provides a visually powerful expression of these themes. Here in a mundane, everyday activity, ordinary people etched in cloth the aesthetic foundations of a living culture, showcasing the dexterity that enabled a people's enduring sense of self and group solidarity. Thus the deep influence of African strip-weaving is readily evident in the African American quilting traditions, but so is its adaptation to American influences, materials, and conditions of labor. Working with textiles, a male-dominated craft in Africa, became the province of women in America. Anglo-American quilting practices, which also deployed striped patterns, influenced their work, too. For white quilters, however, these patterns connoted order and regularity, while for blacks the basic structure provided a platform for improvisation and playfulness. Just as slaves turned Wesleyan hymns into

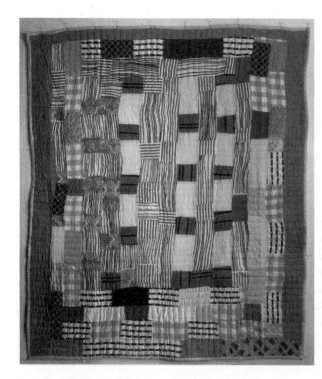

With its irregular
patterns and
counterpoints, this
twentieth-century
strip quilt illustrates a
centuries-old African
aesthetic tradition.

spirituals, black quilters improvised on Anglo-American patterns, varying
the size, arrangement, and color combinations of cloth strips to create
wholly different designs. Linear notions of mere survival and cultural borrowing fail to capture the vital essence of these creative acts. Prefiguring
the celebrated and easily recognized aesthetics of twentieth-century blues
and jazz, quilters played on the tensions between freedom and constraint,
individual creativity and solidarity within a community. Their symbolic
repertoire sometimes literally embodied familial ties and histories. Passed
along from generation to generation, these humble heirlooms sublimated
the tension between past and future. A people in the act of becoming
must change, they seemed to say even while drawing on the group's past
experiences to fashion that new collective self.

The strength of African cultural retentions in the colonial period, therefore, did not long deflect the inexorable trajectory of peoples of African descent as they moved toward a distinctly American identity, toward a culture
at once new and old, synthetic and authentic. By the time Hector St. John
de Crevecoeur composed his famous *Letters from an American Farmer* in

1782, celebrating the "new man, this American," there was no group more representative of his portrayal of the melding of diverse ethnicities into a new nation than Americans of African descent. Arising in response to the everyday challenges of living, cultural syncretism proved a potent, even if unconscious, strategy for surviving the pressures of a brutal and alien environment, while creatively preserving at least some core ancestral values. Cultural synthesis was not a moral choice for African Americans, but an imperative, a creative response to the problem of survival and life.

A Creole People in a Revolutionary Age

By any measures, the resistance of Africa's progeny in the New World was fiercest and longest lived to European religious beliefs and the worldview they fostered, but once that resistance was overcome, the Christian faith would profoundly reshape African Americans' cultural and political identity. Initially religion was the cultural domain over which slaves exercised the most control, possibly because their preferences coincided with their master's. During American slavery's first century, planters had opposed the conversion of their slaves to the Christian faith, fearing that it would open the door to their manumission. Despite Parliament's encouragement, the Anglican Church's early conversion efforts had been fairly minimal and limited. Some Anglican clergymen owned slave laborers themselves, and all of them depended on the goodwill of the planter elite. They were not inclined to ignore any objections the latter might make to proselytizing their slaves. Over time, the planters' resistance to religious conversion relaxed, and for some of the same reasons that they had grown more enthusiastic about family formation: security and productivity. Just as many of them had come to recognize that the formation of families might keep slave men close to home and at work, they slowly became convinced that religion might keep them docile. In this instance, however, their interests were not necessarily congruent with those of their slaves. Africans' resistance to their masters' god remained strong. Consequently, Christians remained a minority among the slave population long after planters' objections had softened, indeed, well into next century.

Nonetheless, a substantial and ultimately influential cohort of Christian slaves had emerged by the latter half of the eighteenth century, especially among the American-born youth, which suggests the close correlation between Christianity and the growth of the Creole population. Given that the plurality of North American slaves still resided in Virginia and that the overwhelming majority of these were American-born, that state became the principal site for the ultimate fashioning of black Creole culture. A typical parish in the tidewater is illustrative of this process. With less than 2 percent of its slaves converted before 1720, St. Peter's Parish counted 14 percent of its total population and half its slave children among the church's converts by 1740.

Conversions accelerated even more during the final decades of the century as an evangelical revival rolled through the Upper South. This new "awakening" was, in some ways, a continuation of the pre–Revolutionary War religious movements, but one much more radical and egalitarian than anything seen before. Baptists and Methodists brought a very different religious vision to converts, and their numbers swelled dramatically, including far greater numbers of blacks who were generally treated more nearly as equal participants in church governance and practice than had been the case before or later. Once the slaves' religious conversion was linked with these white religious insurgencies, an explosive mixture was produced that briefly challenged the entire social-political order. It would soon become clear that the planters' original fears were well founded. Christianity could indeed render slaves docile, but it could also provide them new rationales for resistance.

In contrast with the dry catechisms of the more hierarchical Anglicans, the Baptists seemed more like a community of religious equals through which one might find not only salvation in the afterlife but also a rich communal life in this world. To some extent that egalitarianism embraced blacks as well. Indeed, the racial character of the southern awakening was striking, with blacks making up 40 percent of all Methodists by 1794, as well as an unspecified, but obviously large, proportion of the Baptists. Although the number of black converts was still probably less than 10 percent of the total African American population, the psychic and political impact of their presence was profound. In the Baptist practice of total immersion, black members might have found echoes of African rituals. Meanwhile, in African religious beliefs and practices, such as spirit possession and styles of worshipping, white Baptists might find resonances with, if not models for, their own spiritual lives.

Most important, however, was the decentralized nature of Baptist congregations and their governance, which rendered them responsive to local conditions and preoccupations. As the church came to envelop every aspect of a member's life, the slaveholder's treatment of his or her slave became church business, and thus fell under the jurisdiction of the church's informal courts, which adjudicated disputes and grievances among the members and sanctioned their ungodly behavior. Thus slaves could and often did bring complaints against their masters to the church congregation. Indeed, some slaveholders resorted to these same church assemblies to discipline slaves, which was an unexpected—indeed, quite astonishing—concession of authority to an external body. It was a concession that can be understood, perhaps, only in the context of this multiracial religious community, in which the slave might be more likely to internalize the invocation to obedience, rendering church sanctions even more effective than ordinary corporal punishment.

Extant records suggest that these assemblies were often preoccupied with issues of sexual morality, which probably worked to the benefit of the slaves as well. At the very least, interdictions against white sexual immorality might offer a modicum of protection to vulnerable slave women. But equally important was the encouragement Baptists gave to marriage and their insistence that slaves, no less than whites, take seriously its sacraments mandating chastity and enduring bonds, all of which challenged the logic of slavery, wherein one was the disposable property of another. Consequently, these same church minutes reveal solemn injunctions barring masters from separating married slaves by sale. A catechism of a church in Upper King and Queen Parish in Virginia, for example, read, "Query: Is it agreeable to scripture for any member to part man & wife? Answer: No. And any member who Shall be guilty of such crimes shall be dealt with by the church for such ~~crimes~~ [sic] misconduct."

That the exercise of the slaveholder's legal prerogatives might even fleetingly be labeled "a crime" is telling. That the word was quickly crossed out in favor of the less damning *misconduct* is equally so. The moment of egalitarianism was short-lived, slackening under pressure from planters loath to surrender either their property or their authority and the "maturing" of the religious insurgencies as the revolutionary moment passed. Indeed, some historians have argued that the evangelicals in Virginia made an explicit choice to soften their antislavery commitments in exchange for the religious disestablishment offered by ruling elites, such as Jefferson and Madison. Whatever the cause, antislavery attitudes among the evangelicals weakened as their denominational strength grew in the 1790s, and were soon to be renounced altogether. Thus the Methodist Conference, which had explicitly condemned slaveholding as a sin in 1780, reversed itself the very next year. The Baptists denounced slavery in 1789, but thought better of it by 1793, when after some debate they decided to leave the matter to the law and individual conscience. In 1802, anxious to reconcile God's hierarchy with Caesar's, the Dover Baptist Association issued the following response to the question of blacks' role within the church: "No person is entitled to exercize [sic] authority in the church, whose situation in social life, renders it his duty to be under obedience to the authority of another, such as minor sons, and servants."

Richard Allen was born and reared on the slave South's northern boundary, came of age as social and political revolutions shook that world to its foundations, and lived to see their retrenchment. Born in 1760, six years after Equiano's brief sojourn in Virginia, Allen, along with his family, was the property of Benjamin Chew, a wealthy lawyer and politician then resident in Philadelphia, who owned a one-thousand-acre plantation and scores of slaves in Kent County, Delaware. In 1768, Chew sold Allen and his family to a neighboring Delaware planter, Stokeley Sturgis, who was struggling to make ends meet on a two-hundred-acre farm about six miles northeast of Dover. Young Allen grew into manhood on Sturgis's farm, but his mother and three siblings were sold by the financially pressed small farmer sometime before 1780, possibly in 1776. Confronting this traumatic personal loss even as he witnessed the political world around him turn upside down, sixteen-year-old Richard—like many of his white and black contemporaries—found solace in religion. Fortunately for him, Stokeley Sturgis, who had hosted a number of Methodist luminaries to preach on his farm, was also drawn to Methodism and inspired by it to strike a deal by which Richard and his brother could purchase their freedom. Of course, as with so many other manumissions during the Revolutionary era, Sturgis's decision clearly involved economic as well as religious motives; he gained sixty pounds hard currency with this act of idealism. But, then, it might also be said that conversion had secular utility for Allen, too, since it was the means by which he bargained for his freedom. Fearful that the sixty-year-old Sturgis might expire before the deal could be consummated, Allen worked feverishly chopping wood and hauling salt to accumulate the full sum within little more than three years, receiving his free papers in 1783, the year Britain recognized America's independence. In an act of extraordinary magnanimity, Allen accompanied his "freedom dues" with a valuable gift of salt to his former master.

Drawing on the metaphors in Charles Wesley's hymn, Allen described his conversion experience as a shaking of dungeons and falling of chains, but as a recently freed slave he knew the dungeons and chains were hardly metaphorical. If conversion to Methodism was, as historian Gary Nash writes, "a spiritual rebirth" for the individual, then so, too, might it be for an enslaved people. Although couched in the otherwordly cadences of evangelical rhetoric, therefore, from the first, Allen's theology was firmly grounded in a commitment to a moral reform that had secular and social consequences. His God was a present reality.

Shortly thereafter, the twenty-year-old Allen forsook worldly pursuits and devoted himself full time to five years of itinerant preaching, traveling up and down the Atlantic Coast from New Jersey to South Carolina—at his own expense initially—preaching to mostly white congregations. Early in 1785, he focused his efforts on the Baltimore circuit (which included Virginia and the Carolinas) and later that year moved to Radnor, a town west of Philadelphia. From there he was called by the presiding elder of the Philadelphia circuit to minister to a small group of black Methodists connected with St. George's Church in Philadelphia. Allen would remain in Philadelphia for the rest of his long life, where he arguably became the most important leader of the African American freedom struggle of his generation.

Fifteen years older than Allen, Olaudah Equiano lay similar claims to the mantel of generational leadership among black émigrés in London. Although he lived a very different life from Richard Allen's, Equiano's fundamental trajectory was much the same. After being purchased by Lieutenant Pascal, he lived a charmed life befitting his name, "the fortunate one." He spent almost twenty years at sea, first as a slave seaman on Royal Navy vessels during the Seven Years' War and then as a freeman embroiled in various picaresque adventures from the Caribbean to the Arctic Sea. Having purchased his own freedom in 1766, he was for a brief time entangled in business dealings from which he earned profits from slave labor. Settling in England in 1773, he was drawn to Christianity and converted in late 1774, six years before Richard Allen. Over the next fifteen years Equiano would be drawn into the growing antislavery controversy, joining other African émigrés adding their voices to the protests against the slave trade. In 1787, when a scheme was devised to settle American slave fugitives in the newly founded Sierra Leone colony, Equiano served as a kind of bursar for the company. After a bitter dispute with the principal officer in charge of the settlement, however, he resigned his post. With that decision he also gave up the prospect of returning to Africa and any direct involvement in its Christian redemption. His lasting contribution to the struggle against slavery would be the publication in 1789 of his own life story, *The Interesting Narrative of the Life of Olaudah Equiano*. The book would reach nine editions within his brief lifetime.

Both Equiano and Richard Allen passed their adult lives in a world in ferment, as opening salvos were being fired in the struggle against slavery in the Atlantic world. They both underwent religious conversion during this period of revolutionary upheaval, through the prosyletizing of early Methodist dissenters from the Anglican Church. They both came to view their respective conversion experiences and lives as paradigmatic for the destiny and life course of their race. To be converted was to pass from the ignorance of slavery to the enlightenment of freedom, to be reborn, to be *re-created*. Thus, what formerly would have been merely manumission— an individual's liberation from slavery (which mirrored the convert's personal liberation from sin)—now became much more. In each man's case, his personal freedom came as social and political transformations unfolded that would change the conditions of possibility for the collective re-creation of Africans in the Americas as a free people. As a consequence, both men exemplified the new lives that were possible in this revolutionary age. In contrast with Anthony Johnson, who had been a full participant in the slave labor regime of his day and for whom there is no indication that the church played any role in promoting a new consciousness, both Allen and Equiano would, as adults, grow committed to Christianity and to antislavery, as interdependent phenomena. Deeply implicated in and conscious of the sweeping developments in the Atlantic world, therefore, these men were truly newborn with the spirit of the age and anticipated further revolutionary changes in that world.

Equiano's autobiography was a calculated protest, couched in the language of European morality and turning the Christianity that it proselytized back upon its adherents. His very image embodied the future abolitionist challenge: "Am I Not a Man and Brother?" Although his experiences were in many ways more provincial, Richard Allen might be taken as Equiano's American double. He would build a church that, like Equiano's autobiography, provided a virtual script for turning Christianity into a weapon of liberation. His associates, and no doubt some of his church congregation, were drawn from that same milieu; their lives, too, were profoundly shaped by the transatlantic evangelical and political revolutions. Consistent with that consciousness, the Philadelphia Free African Society that Allen and Absalom Jones had founded actively explored the possibility of African emigration in the 1790s. A Rhode Island offshoot of their organization, the Free African Society in Newport, organized in 1787, endorsed the African settlement scheme with which Equiano had been briefly associated, sending an agent to Sierra Leone to investigate a possible site and to make arrangements with the British for settlement there. Although the situation was later judged unsatisfactory and no action taken, their declaration of intent captured the spirit of the moment and would echo down the centuries: In the very year a new American nation was born, they anticipated a key theme of Equiano's memoir, boldly declaring, "Every pious man is a citizen of the world."

"Citizen of the world" could have easily been the epitaph for Equiano's remarkable life. He had rendered the notion of a cosmopolitan identity and belonging palpable and real. Richard Allen lived a very different life, one extending several decades beyond that revolutionary moment. Although different, Allen's life resonated to the same cosmopolitan spirit as Equiano's, as demonstrated by the work his church would engage in in later decades. Having witnessed amazing progress and devastating setbacks, however, Allen sought to ground his identity in the terra firma of America, indeed, in its then-premier black urban community, Philadelphia. There he would fashion his generation's claim to the patrimony of the land of their birth. There he would spend his remaining years seeking simply to be known as a "citizen."

3

SLAVES AND CITIZENS

African America in the Age of Revolution

In the twilight hours of April 20, 1793, several hundred slaves near Trois-Rivières, a small village in the French West Indian colony of Guadeloupe, rose in revolt against their masters, killing twenty-two of them. After laying waste to several of the properties, the rebels paused to deliberate on their next steps. Organizing under the leadership of one Jean-Baptiste, they formed themselves into quasi-military units, posted sentries to secure the estates they had seized, and sent a detachment marching in order toward Basse-Terre, the island capital. As they approached the town, they encountered French soldiers who, having been alerted to the revolt, had set out to put it down. When the two groups came within firing range of each other, a soldier called out, "Who goes there?" To which one of the rebels responded, "Citizens and friends!" A squad of French soldiers approached the slave rebels and began questioning them: Are you citizens? Are you patriots, they asked? "We are friends," a rebel replied. "We have come to save you, and hate only those aristocrats who want to kill you . . . We want to fight for the Republic, the law, the nation, order." Then followed an extraordinary scene, in which black slave rebels and French soldiers marched into town as comrades in arms, shouting, "Vive la République." Even more extraordinary, perhaps, some of the capital's white inhabitants turned out to welcome them with cheers.

These extraordinary events at Trois-Rivières, as described in local newspapers sympathetic to the French Revolution, were interpreted very differently in the bitter recollections of Victor Collot, governor of the island during the revolt, who had fled to Philadelphia along with thousands of other refugees uprooted by the revolution. From his North American refuge, Collot—who had tried mightily as governor to see that the slave rebels were treated as savage insurrectionists rather than brave patriots— passionately disputed accusations that he was responsible for losing Guadeloupe to the British the following year. His principal defense it seems was that he had been the victim of deluded Jacobins, black and white. As Laurent Dubois has argued persuasively, however, the revolt at Trois-Rivières encapsulates in local detail the larger political and social transformations that were unfolding in the French Caribbean in the last decade of the eighteenth century, not least of which was that enslaved blacks armed themselves to defend revolutionary ideals, becoming in the process, and however fleetingly, "citizens."

Ironically, Collot composed his account from his exile in Philadelphia, a city in the eye of the revolutionary storms that had swept North America just decades earlier, which had raised in their wake very similar questions about the legitimacy of slavery and the citizenship claims of former slaves. The peak of the American revolutionary moment had now passed, and with it much of the optimism about how it might transform the civil status of peoples of African descent in the new republic. In fact, little more than two months before the extraordinary events at Trois-Rivières, the newly constituted American Congress enacted legislation to ensure that escaped slaves were returned to their masters. Just months later, Eli Whitney perfected a machine to gin cotton that would eventually raise the demand for those slaves to unprecedented levels. Nonetheless, throughout its first decade, internecine turmoil throughout the French Antilles sent waves of refugees to North American port cities, keeping open the question of what civil status peoples of African descent might have in the Americas' "first new nation."

Four years after the storming of the Bastille, news of radical transformations in the French social order roiled American politics, enlarging the factional splits among the Founding Fathers. There was no way to shield slaves, much less free people of color, from the image of a world turned upside down. Consequently, throughout the Caribbean, and in parts of North America as well, slaves and free people of African descent seized the moment, their actions both mirroring and moving beyond what they had heard about events unfolding on the streets of Paris. In the spring of 1793, Toussaint Louverture took command of a slave army in Saint-Domingue that would eventually make that island, renamed Haiti, the first independent black republic in the Americas just over a decade later—a development that sent shockwaves throughout the Western Hemisphere. The rebels at Trois-Rivières had felt these shocks, and there would be scattered echoes resounding elsewhere in rebellions and conspiracies throughout the Caribbean basin and in North America.

As in Collot's account, many observers could not imagine that the blacks around them might possibly be independent agents; they sought instead to relegate them to secondary roles, the pawns of whites, mere deluded masses, and so forth. Many of these black insurgents seized the still-evolving republican language of human rights and made it their own, however, sometimes recasting it into more familiar terms and accents. Thus was the incident at Trois-Rivières, and scores more like it throughout the Americas, neither a simple story of a revolutionary contagion spreading from Europe nor a purely indigenous uprising; rather, it was a complex mixture of both. A long tradition of slave resistance that had evolved in plantation societies throughout the Americas during the previous three centuries provided the modus vivendi for realizing long-standing desires for freedom from slavery, but were now inflected by a revolutionary ethos that provided new content and form to those aspirations.

Thus with his characteristic boldness, François-Dominique Toussaint Bréda adopted the surname "Louverture" sometime after he had ridden off to join slave rebels in the hills of northern Saint-Domingue. Precisely why or when Bréda chose his new name, or whether he intended it to convey a political message remains a mystery. It is clear, however, that his choice was strikingly appropriate to the historic moment, simultaneously rejecting his former slave identity and announcing his rebirth. *Louverture* literally seized upon the dominant motif of his era, a moment pregnant with seemingly infinite possibilities—"openings." Indeed, his own renaming suggests his keen grasp of the political and social currents then moving through the Atlantic world, a world suddenly *opened* to the possibility of forming entirely new social and political arrangements. Old hierarchies—monarchial, religious, and economic—all seemed, if not yet faltering, at least vulnerable to challenge from below. What else could one make of bold cries for "liberty, equality, and fraternity," of unblushing declarations that "all men are created equal"?

If the Revolutionary era created an opening for the freedom demands of free people of color and slaves, however, the reaction that followed

closed those openings, consolidating in the process a more intensely po-
liced social order rooted in slavery. At the cost of tens of thousands dead
in their wars of liberation and decades of economic isolation, Haitians were
the exceptions to this reactionary trend, having won both freedom and a
nation. After Napoleon seized power and redirected France's revolutionary ardor into wars of national expansion, however, slavery was reinstated
in Guadeloupe and the rest of the French Antilles. A similar pattern could
be observed in North America, where after an all-too-brief challenge,
slavery also became more entrenched. The acquisition of the Louisiana
Territory in 1803, for example—a sale forced upon Napoleon by the financial exigencies of continued war in Europe and his failure to recapture
Saint-Domingue—strengthened slavery's hold in the United States, just
as it had seemed to waver.

    In both the challenge to and the consolidation of slavery, therefore,
the fate of African Americans in this period was powerfully shaped by
events in the broader Atlantic world. Refugees and ideas made their way
north from the war-torn Caribbean, arriving just as Americans were fashioning their own postcolonial social and political order. The role of slaves
and free people of color in the new republic would be hotly debated. Over
the decades that followed, events such as that at Trois-Rivières and elsewhere resonated with these transformations and influenced their course,
sometimes subtly, sometimes overtly. In North America as well as in the
French Antilles, therefore, former slaves looked to be citizens of nations
forged in wars fought under banners touting liberty and equality, wars in
which black soldiers were counted among the fallen.

Openings: Contesting Slavery in an Age of Revolution

Young James Forten's experience growing up amid the political turmoil of
revolutionary Philadelphia, within earshot of Patriots' cries for liberty and
equality, captures the potential impact that these revolutionary decades
held for black Americans. Forten was keenly aware of the initial faint tremors of the movement that would shake Toussaint from his watchful waiting three decades later, transforming the Atlantic world's political order in
the process. The signs of a revolutionary opening had been much more
uncertain then, of course. The whispered possibility of a new world coming

was sufficient, nonetheless, to encourage young James and thousands of others like him to seize the time. The Philadelphia of Forten's youth was one of the epicenters of revolutionary agitation. Indeed, many of the era's watershed events took place within blocks of Forten's home, such as the first meeting of the Continental Congress in 1774 and the first public reading of the Declaration of Independence on July 8, 1776. Forten recalled witnessing the latter event, and no doubt its soaring idealism led him to later cast his lot with the rebel cause. Being only ten years old, however, he had to wait five years more, until 1781, the decisive final year of fighting, before shipping out as a powder boy on Stephen Decatur's privateer, the *Royal Louis*. After one triumphant voyage, the *Royal Louis* was captured, and Forten spent the rest of the war on a British prison ship. From this brief youthful exposure to war and defeat, he emerged in later years an indomitable champion of the cause of freedom and of the struggle against slavery.

Many, if not most, of the roughly five thousand blacks who eventually cast their lot with the Patriots' cause were no doubt much less idealistically motivated than young James Forten, who was of the third generation of a family that traced its Philadelphia roots to the days of William Penn. Certainly, as they weighed the relative benefits of joining the British or the Patriot forces, the "freedom" in question was quite literal: an exchange of military service for freedom from bondage. Northern blacks, slave and free, were more likely to be English-speaking Creoles, living in the towns and villages where the prewar agitation was most intense. They may well have been more immediately receptive to the evolving egalitarian ideology of the Revolution, especially in New England, and to have joined the Patriots' cause. The overwhelming majority of North American blacks, however, were slaves residing in the South—indeed, nearly half in Virginia alone—so it was there that the most intense battle for their hearts and minds would be fought. For the most part, they placed their bet on a British victory, which appeared to offer them the best prospects for gaining freedom, especially since the early tide of battle favored that side. Thus slaves in the mid-Atlantic states, where most of the first battles were fought, immediately sought refuge within British lines, flocking to the advancing Redcoats as Washington retreated. In time, they discovered that both sides actually sought to preserve slavery and pursued policies toward the blacks in their ranks that were at best ambivalent. As with slave insurgents in the French Antilles two decades later, however, it was not their hosts' intentionality that most mattered, but the breach in slavery's hegemony that a conflict among white folks inevitably opened up.

No doubt, even in the South the slaves' choices were already primed by the prewar agitation. A decade before the first shots were fired, there were signs that the colonists' dispute with Britain had already aroused expectations in slave quarters. South Carolina whites, for example, were alarmed to hear their vehement protests against the Stamp Act echoed by slaves chanting, "Liberty," through the streets of Charleston. At about the same time, new maroon colonies of slave fugitives were being formed throughout the Low Country, which did not reassure increasingly nervous authorities. Eventually they enlisted the aid of the Catawba Indians to hunt down one such installation in Georgia that for four years had successfully repulsed repeated attacks by the white militia.

Indeed, contemporaries were always surprised at how well informed presumably isolated and ignorant slaves were about the flow of current events, even as they failed to appreciate that slave intelligence was also keenly sensitive when those currents appeared to be running against their masters. Just a year before the shootout at Lexington, for example, a pamphlet had been published in America detailing the antislavery arguments of Granville Sharp on behalf of James Somerset, an American slave who had been taken from Boston to England in 1769 by his master, Charles Stewart, a customs officer. Somerset filed suit against Stewart to avoid being sold to Jamaica as punishment for his attempted escape while in London. In 1772, Lord Chief Justice Mansfield granted his suit, albeit on narrow, carefully delineated grounds. But Sharp's bold argument on behalf of his client that slavery was incompatible with British liberty provided more compelling reading and soon came to stand in for the more circumspect official decision. No doubt its ringing phrases soon became familiar to colonial slaves, especially in America's major port cities.

Even those slaves who never heard of Somerset could sense opportunity in these turbulent times. Often their own masters' incautious ranting against the British unwittingly made the case for them. After overhearing just such an anti-British tirade in 1774, for example, a Virginia house slave named Bacchus gathered up his clothes, changed his name to John Christian, and took off. Weighed down by his heavy baggage, Christian was caught before he could make good his escape. Five years later, Boston

King had better luck. Traveling light, he made the arduous and dangerous journey through enemy lines from South Carolina to temporary refuge in New York and eventually joined the British evacuation to Nova Scotia at the end of the war.

In 1775, the first year of the war, the insurrection scares that had long rippled through the Lower South reached a fever pitch, as rumors of slave conspiracies gave way to actual revolt. In December 1774, six men and two women on a Georgia slave plantation killed their overseer and left several other whites dead or wounded before they could be intercepted and killed. The fact that most of the slaves involved in this outbreak were new arrivals from Africa—long feared as a restive element in the labor mix—did not assuage the colonists' suspicion that Britain might yet attempt to turn their slaves against them. It is likely that those fears were only heightened a month later when a member of the House of Commons introduced a measure suggesting that the threat of emancipation be deployed against the anticipated colonial insurgency. Five months later rumors were rife that South Carolina slaves were awaiting the arrival of a new governor who would bring such an emancipation decree with him, which would signal the moment for a general uprising. In August, Thomas Jeremiah, a free black fisherman and pilot was hanged for allegedly plotting to assist the British fleet's entry into Charleston's difficult harbor. Similar fears surfaced regarding the movement of the British fleet from St. Augustine to Norfolk in July. Indeed, fears of slave uprisings in support of a British invasion also occupied discussions of the Provincial Congress that summer. Although some of these plots may have been only the product of white hysteria, their mere anticipation, the detailed exposition of how they might unfold, and the trials and executions of the alleged conspirators could not have been lost on slave onlookers. At the very least, they suggested that a British invasion might alter their circumstances for the better.

The British hardly deserved their liberator's image, however, and by the end of the year, events would expose just how shallow and misleading that image was. The anvil finally dropped on November 7, 1775, when Governor John Murray, the fourth earl of Dunmore, declared martial law in Virginia and included in that proclamation a provision granting freedom in exchange for military service to any slaves or white indentured servants owned by those in rebellion against the Crown. Lord Dunmore, who himself owned a slave plantation at Berkeley, Virginia, worded his promise of freedom carefully, however, limiting it to those "able and willing to bear Arms." Indeed, he even returned fugitives whose masters later recanted their disloyalty and swore allegiance to the Crown, and he disarmed and abandoned black soldiers who later became unfit for service.

Still, Dunmore's duplicity does not appear to have slowed the flow of refugees to his lines. While some estimates put Dunmore's black army at no more than eight hundred, that figure ignores the heavy casualties, mostly from disease, that blacks endured and thus grossly underestimates the total number. Moreover, such estimates do not come close to accounting for the thousands of men, women, and children uprooted by this mobilization. Thomas Jefferson's estimate that Virginia lost thirty thousand bondsmen is no doubt greatly exaggerated, but even more conservative accounts suggest that ten thousand or more blacks were freed, died in their efforts to escape, or were removed from the American slave labor force by Loyalists seeking refuge elsewhere in the Empire.

Many of the newly enlisted men were placed on boats and barges and folded into the small, interracial bands that raided the tidewater plantations arrayed along the inland waterways of the Chesapeake. Knifing through the most densely settled slave population in North America, the impact of these raiding parties clearly agitated the rebel colony. No matter Lord Dunmore's carefully worded proclamation and its cynical application. His caution would not have consoled John Willoughby, for example. He lost all of his eighty-seven slaves—men, women, and children—during the tumultuous months of the British invasion.

A similar scenario unfolded farther south that spring, when General Henry Clinton conducted a waterborne invasion in North Carolina's Cape Fear region, prompting a wave of slave desertions. Among the fugitives was Thomas Peters, an African-born slave who had been captured by French slave traders in the Niger Delta in the 1760s and eventually sold to William Campbell, a leader of the Sons of Liberty in Wilmington, North Carolina. Like thousands of his fellow slaves, Peters intuited that the enemy of his enemy offered a better chance of his escaping bondage, so he was among those sworn into the Black Pioneers, which General Clinton formed to support his operations. Later he would be among the British forces occupying the Patriot capital, Philadelphia, in 1777.

Once British strategic objectives shifted north, the intensity of the operations in southern theaters subsided. By August 1776, the Earl of

Dunmore had been forced out of Virginia, although the bleeding of that state's slave population would continue as the British kept up hit-and-run raids in the tidewater. Scarcely a hundred of Dunmore's black soldiers were left when he marched into New York City at the end of that historic second summer of the war. Nonetheless, despite all the suffering and betrayal they had endured or witnessed, these men proudly wore the literal marks of their transformed selves: A patch on their uniformed shoulders declared, "Liberty to Slaves." The words hung like a sword over American slavery.

The point of that sword had been blunted by the very British forces that raised it, however. Headquartered at New York City throughout the war, British forces contended for political and military control of the surrounding counties, producing what historian Graham Russell Hodges has called a "neutral zone." General Clinton folded into his Black Pioneers some of the male refugees making their way to his lines from the New York–New Jersey countryside. By early 1777, however, the military role of the Pioneers had been adjusted to accommodate the racial tensions aroused by arming blacks in a revolutionary war. In March of that year, Clinton separated the Pioneers from the Provincial Forces, that is, the Loyalists organized under the regular army as opposed to the many irregular units that had been commissioned. His motive, according to the preamble of the proclamation, was to put the all-white regular units "on the most respectable Footing" by excluding "all Negroes, Mollatoes, and other Improper Persons." Thereafter, the primary function of the reorganized Black Pioneers was to provide field support for Clinton's regular troops in the form of labor and foraging. Thus when Thomas Peters's unit was moved to Philadelphia in the winter of 1777–78, they were employed mostly at cleaning that city's streets.

Among the irregular vigilante bands that emerged in the neutral zone around New York–New Jersey and in the Carolinas and Georgia, however, blacks continued to have a combat role. Guerrilla bands were commissioned by both sides in the Carolinas and Georgia, although the white working class favored the British side more often than their elite neighbors. Indeed, the southern struggle often resembled a continuation of earlier class conflicts, a virtual civil war. As in the North, some of the southern guerrilla bands were racially mixed—including Indians as well as blacks— while others were all white. Indeed, unlike the Pioneers, at least a couple of the bands in the middle-Atlantic states were led by black officers, such as "Colonel" Tye, a former slave, who terrorized rebel enclaves in New Jersey throughout the war. Loyalist slaveholders, no less than Patriots, were unnerved by these bands, which often did not trouble themselves about exactly whose property they were "liberating."

In December 1778, the British resumed in earnest their southern strategy, which aimed to split the presumably more vulnerable plantation South from the rebellious colonies in the North, and the tension between their antislavery means and their support for the status quo was exposed even more. To a far greater degree than in other theaters of the war, slaves captured in guerrilla raids or in battles between regular troops, whether by the British or the Patriots, faced the danger of being sold to the profitable slave markets in the West Indies. Indeed, partisans on the American side charged that such slave trading occurred frequently. Although historians have been unable to confirm those charges, there is some circumstantial evidence to sustain their suspicions. In any case, it is incontrovertible that British actions reinforced slavery in the Americas at the same time as their invasion undermined it. Indeed, General Clinton confirmed as much with his general order of June 30, 1779, issued from his headquarters in Phillipsburg, New York, which effectively extended to other theaters Dunmore's earlier proclamation of freedom to physically able slaves who voluntarily joined the British. It also declared, however, that slaves captured from rebels could be sold "for the benefit of their captors." Since dividing the spoils of war among British officers was a common practice, and since slaves were not exempt from that policy, it would hardly be surprising—indeed it was very likely—that some of this captured "property" was redeemed in Caribbean slave markets, especially since the war itself had disrupted the Atlantic trade and driven up slave prices.

Nothing in either Dunmore's or Clinton's policy, moreover, challenged the notion that blacks were fit mainly for menial labor and to serve whites. With the notable exception of those on the waterborne gunboats, blacks in British uniforms were more often deployed as military laborers than in combat. Indeed, many of the blacks in His Majesty's service were literally the servants of British officers. In the days preceding his defeat at Yorktown, General Cornwallis took time to clarify the allocation of black servants to his officers: two for each field-grade officer and one to those of lower grade. Later, surrounded and facing a slow starvation as the Franco-American siege tightened, Cornwallis ordered the expulsion of thousands of blacks from his camp. Outside, many of their erstwhile masters awaited them.

Even Britain's first act in the peace was double-edged. By early July 1782, British convoys laden with refugees were already embarking from Savannah, Charleston, St. Augustine, and New York City. Although the precise number of evacuees is disputed, clearly there were enough to raise sustained protests from American slaveholders and roil British-American diplomatic disputes over compensation claims for many years thereafter. British treaty negotiators in Paris and commanders in the field stood firm against American demands to return the slaves who had sought and received refuge within British lines. Despite General Washington's last-minute efforts to stop them, therefore, thousands of black Americans, most of them former slaves, pushed their way onto British ships, just ahead of masters rushing to retrieve their lost "property." Among the 2,775 leaving New York was Thomas Peters, along with his wife and two children. Bound for Nova Scotia, which had been acquired by Britain at the end of the Seven Years' War, they sought to take advantage of the land and three years of rations the government offered both to the black refugees and to decommissioned white soldiers in an effort to populate the colony. Some of the black Nova Scotia settlers eventually moved on to Sierra Leone, West Africa, while other black refugees from the Carolinas and Georgia settled in Jamaica, where they founded Baptist congregations that profoundly shaped that island's history and culture.

The fate of some of the slave soldiers who had belonged to American Loyalists was less clear, however. Echoing the ambiguity of their role in the Revolution, many of these soldiers were sent to the West Indies, where they formed the nucleus of the black regiments that the British created shortly after the American war. Signing up to serve nine-year terms, these "Black Pioneers" eventually received certificates of freedom and lifetime pensions at half-pay. Their purpose, however, was to help defend Britain's slave colonies in the West Indies from enemies foreign and domestic, that is, from their European competitors and from the colonists' own slaves.

The authors of the American Revolution were confounded no less than the British by the difficulty of preserving the racial status quo in the middle of a revolution. They, too, vacillated and temporized on whether to

involve black people in what most regarded as a white man's fight. Some
states welcomed black recruits at first, only to reverse themselves later. As
with the British, the Americans' ambivalence did not stop blacks from
finding their way into Patriot ranks, especially in the northern colonies,
where slavery, freedom, and the road to revolution had evolved very differently than in the South.

Blacks had been among the first casualties of the struggle in New
England, even before independence was formally declared. Present in disproportionate numbers on American seagoing vessels and thus among the
floating populations of port cities, blacks had been conspicuous in the urban unrest and rioting that preceded the general outbreak of armed conflict. Those who joined the Minutemen on Lexington's green to harass
Major Pitcairn on April 19, 1775, were of a different sort still. Many of the
slave or ex-slave Minutemen whom we can identify were recruited from
local towns, where hostility to British rule crested early on. The "shot
heard 'round the world" at Lexington might well have been fired by Pompy
from Braintree or Prince from Brookline or Cato Wood from Arlington or
Prince Estabrook of Lexington, who in fact was wounded in that firefight.
Many, like Peter Salem, formerly enslaved in Framingham, were freed
and armed for the express purpose of fighting for the rebels.

These black Patriots were artisans, watermen, farm laborers, or domestics. Before the war they might have worked side by side with some of
the white men now in their ranks, notwithstanding the broad racial divide
that otherwise fragmented everyday life in northern as in southern communities. The fundamental difference from the South, however, is that
they did not live in societies where the enslavement of blacks constituted
the raison d'être and modus vivendi of the entire social order. In that
sense their place in society differed greatly from that of the plantation
slaves of the southern colonies. The most visible difference: they had
guns. Various reports on their marksmanship suggest that they knew how
to use them.

The American Revolutionary leadership soon lost its nerve for an interracial struggle for freedom, however. Notwithstanding the Patriots'
moral victory at Bunker Hill one month earlier—a battle in which many
blacks had served with distinction—upon his arrival to take command of
the Continental Army, George Washington, a substantial Virginia planter
and slaveholder, ordered an end to the recruitment of these "slaves and

Vagabonds," echoing British general Clinton's justification for segregating the Pioneers. The Continental Congress confirmed his order four months later, and a number of states stopped taking any more blacks into their militias. South Carolina's Edward Rutledge offered legislation to cashier those blacks already serving, but it failed to pass, and many of the now-veteran black troops continued to be found in most of the major battles of the war that followed. Peter Salem would add Sarasota and White Plains to his service record. Twenty-eight-year-old Salem Poor of Andover, cited for gallantry at Bunker Hill, would winter with Washington at Valley Forge. Barzillai Lew of Chelmsford, a veteran of the French and Indian War, was reputed to have later formed a band of black guerrillas.

Within three years of Washington's interdiction of new black soldiers, Congress reversed its position, approving in March 1779 a general mobilization of slave recruits. The following year, Virginia followed suit—at least to the extent of accepting free blacks—which left only the lower South states of South Carolina and Georgia, which were holding out against incorporating blacks, free or slave, into their regular troops. But even there, blacks continued to be among the irregular forces. As with most future wars in the American hemisphere, black recruitment had become an unavoidable military necessity and was recognized as such by military leaders on all sides of the conflict. Indeed, George Washington would certainly not be the last slaveholder to recruit slave soldiers in a revolutionary struggle.

There were very practical advantages favoring black recruitment. Most white enlistees in the Revolutionary army not only served extremely short terms—ninety days was standard in the militia—but pressed to serve only in theaters close to their homes, which exacerbated the chronic manpower problem of the American forces. Although about four hundred thousand white men fought for the Patriot cause, therefore, only about thirty-five thousand did so at any one time. Otherwise, according to some military historians, they might easily have outmanned British forces that never exceeded forty-two thousand men. Within two years of the outbreak of formal hostilities, by which time the pressure to accept black recruits had become inexorable, all of the New England states were once again looking for black soldiers, despite the congressional ban. Well served by its major catchment of slaves on the large plantations of the South Kingston area, Rhode Island saw in its recruitment the most dramatic and earliest example of the war's impact on northern slavery. When Colonel Christopher Greene, a Quaker who had abandoned his pacifism to fight in the war, assumed command of the First Rhode Island Battalion in the summer of 1778, he confronted a force made up principally of slaves who had been promised their own freedom if they fought for the nation. Many of them, like the African-born Richard Rhodes, who had come to Rhode Island as a child, served for the duration of the war, including at the climactic battle at Yorktown. Such recruitment need not have been motivated by any general abolitionist sentiment. New York and Connecticut, for instance, both authorized the substitution of slaves to serve in place of their masters.

The military careers of Cato Howe, Quomony Quash, and Plato Turner are suggestive, if not representative, of the complex forces that drew many northern blacks to the Patriot cause rather than to the British. A nineteen-year-old slave from Plymouth, Massachusetts, and veteran of the Battle of Bunker Hill, Cato Howe enlisted in the Continental Army in the spring of 1775, more than a year before the Declaration of Independence, and notwithstanding the "official" Massachusetts policy at the time not to accept black enlistments, slave or free. Neither did the ambiguity of the situation stop another Plymouth man, sixteen-year-old Quomony Quash, who accompanied his master to war in 1775. Upon reenlistment, however, Quash extracted an explicit, written promise from his master, Theophilus Cotton, that in exchange for his service he would receive freedom papers. "In Consideration of my Negro Quomminy having inlisted himself at my request into the Service of the Continant for three years," Cotton wrote shortly before his death in 1781,

> and upon his faithfully Serving the full time without departing therefrom, and my receiving the one half of the wages due for said Service, together with the bounty Given by the Town, do at his commencing twenty-one years of age, quit all pretentions to him as a Slave . . . And I do allow said Quomminy out of the bounty Three hundred paper Dollars—old Emission, and five hard ones, with half of his Wages.

Cotton's frank detailing of the pecuniary benefits to him of Quash's enlistment is suggestive of how motives other than idealism might have moved many northern slaveholders as well as their slaves. At stake for Cotton, however, was merely the loss of a manservant, not an entire system of production and the social order it supported.

Joining Colonel John Bailey's Second Plymouth Regiment in the spring of 1776, Plato Turner, a thirty-two-year-old mariner, helped fill Plymouth's quota during one of the frequent lulls in the flow of white recruits— another common factor favoring black recruitment. Turner would also serve until the end of the war, again illustrating a key difference in the typical service of blacks as contrasted with the well-known resistance white veterans exhibited toward serving multiple enlistments. As with Quash and many others, pecuniary considerations may have influenced Turner's commitment. The bounty money earned when he reenlisted in 1779 enabled him to buy a house in what had once been the sheep's pasture for the town of Plymouth. Aptly named Parting Ways, this settlement became one of the many all-black communities free people established after the war. Among Turner's neighbors were none other than Cato Howe and Quomony Quash.

A complex mix of idealism and practicality, therefore, shaped the black experience in the American Revolution. Black Americans' clear and compelling goal was freedom from slavery and its stigma, whether they cast their lot with British or American forces. As historian Gary Nash has so aptly put it, the American Revolution was in effect "the first large-scale rebellion of slaves in North America." Many white Americans also recognized that more than the change of a colonial relationship was involved in this struggle. However much their leaders vacillated over the question, some slaveholders had seen immediately the incompatibility of wagering one's life and fortune for personal liberty while holding other human beings in bondage. Like the Connecticut man who freed his slaves as he marched off to join the Continental Army, they recognized that they could not do both.

As the British army surrendered at Yorktown, the American military band played "The World Turned Upside Down," no doubt oblivious to the irony of their selection. Certainly the double meaning of those words would not have escaped the notice of the slaves and free black people who witnessed the ceremony. Much like old Toussaint Bréda two decades later, they must have sensed an unprecedented historic opening, beyond which might lay liberty and justice for all. Some managed to walk through that opening; most did not. And it would not last.

America's First Emancipation and Its Legacies

Whatever the intentionality of its partisans, the Revolution disrupted the slaveholders' hegemony. For the American rebels, a bold affirmation that "all men are created equal" seemed necessary justification for waging a fratricidal war against their sovereign, little realizing apparently that those words would come back to haunt the nation ever after. Keen to the demands of personal honor as well perhaps, some of the most gifted orators of the independence movement had raised the rhetorical stakes of the conflict to befit the boldness of the step they now championed, seemingly oblivious all the while to the ironies of their personal situation as owners of property in human beings. The contradiction had been glaringly evident, often embarrassingly so, to almost everyone else. As Abigail Adams bluntly put it to her husband, John, "It always seemed a most iniquitous scheme to me to fight ourselves for what we are daily robbing and plundering from those who have as good a right to freedom as we have." Her thoughts echoed the black poet Phillis Wheatley, who had written in 1774 that "in every human Breast, God had implanted a Principle which we call love of freedom; it is impatient of Oppression, and pants for Deliverance; and by the leave of our modern Egyptians, I will assert, that the same principle lives in us." Future president James Madison recalled that much the same sentiments had been expressed by his own slave Billey, who declared that he "merely [coveted] that liberty for which we have paid the price of so much blood, and have proclaimed so often to be the right . . . of every human being." Meanwhile, British pundits and press had a field day, seizing upon the blatant contradictions and ridiculing the fire-eating Patriots' overheated rhetorical flourishes: with one hand they held resolutions of freedom, while the other grasped a slaver's lash.

Surrounded by slaves, most southern whites could not permit themselves the luxury of dwelling for long on the contradiction, however blatant. They simply changed the subject. Although he found it impossible to summon intellectual or moral justifications for the continuance of slavery itself, for example, Thomas Jefferson declared to his European interlocutors in 1785 that black people were not like white men and could not live as equals in the same society. Despite his affirmation of racial justifications for human inequality and his advocacy of separation, Jefferson never managed to act on those convictions and separate himself from his own slaves. Such moral paralysis did not stop some of the "lesser" men of his generation from doing precisely that, however. Robert Carter III, a fellow Virginian and an heir to the Carter-Burwell fortune, devised a plan to free fifty of his five hundred slaves each year over a ten-year period. Carter's abolitionism was motivated by a seamless mixture of the political ideals of the Revolution and the religious convictions gained from his recent conversion to the Baptist Church. This was not an uncommon mixture in the immediate postwar period, and it is not surprising therefore that most of the voluntary manumissions occurred then.

Where it had existed at all, southern antislavery enthusiasm faded quickly, whether motivated by a political or a religious faith. Rather than seeking a general emancipation, many antislavery advocates took aim at the slave trade. In this they sometimes found surprising allies among the established planters, who were well stocked with slaves already and increasingly anxious about the security risks of bringing in more. Unmentioned was the fact that any limitation on new supplies would also increase the value of their current assets. This same incongruous alliance of the wealthiest slave owners and antislavery advocates eventually enabled passage of a federal law terminating the legal slave trade after January 1, 1808.

More germane to the fates of slavery in the upper Chesapeake, broad transformations took hold in the agricultural economy as planters switched from labor-intensive tobacco to grains. When the Seven Years' War disrupted foreign trade, many planters in the Chesapeake, such as the Carter-Burwells, had begun experimenting with grain crops, which required much less labor and benefited from rising European demand. The disruption of trade during the Revolutionary War, coming just ten years later, confirmed the wisdom of many of these planters' earlier decision to switch. Although there was a postwar rebound in tobacco prices, the French Revolution brought further trade disruptions in the 1790s, by which time Virginia's tobacco crop was scarcely half of what it had been. In time, many of the great planters found it cheaper and more efficient in periods of increased labor needs to supplement a smaller slave labor force with free wage workers. Thus while many planters in the Chesapeake responded to reduced labor needs by simply selling surplus slaves farther south, others added their emancipated workers to the rapidly expanding rural free black population, forming in the process the useful reserve army of labor their new economy required. Through a combination of strong patron-client relations and repressive laws, the white elite enjoyed the benefits of labor control without the fixed costs of maintaining an inflexible work force. By this fiendish alliance the hard-won freedoms of many recently emancipated slaves were vitiated.

In sharp contrast with the South, slaves and free blacks in the northern states were able to harness the egalitarian sentiments intrinsic to revolutionary ideology more directly and forcefully. Clearly there was no way to convince slaves that the freedom their masters' held dear was not for them. But just as important, the war itself undermined and sometimes disrupted the system of controls on which slaveholders relied. Tellingly, nearly eight hundred advertisements for escaped slaves in the New York–New Jersey area were recorded between 1716 and 1783, of which about forty per year were placed during the war—more than doubling the average annual rate for the preceding fifteen years. This was a war unlike earlier wars.

Ultimately, however, this first American emancipation and its aftereffects were grounded in the character of northern slavery, which would in turn shape the evolution of the free black urban communities emerging after emancipation. Although the fact is perhaps obscured by a national memory fixated on the indelible image of slaves toiling on antebellum southern plantations, slavery touched every colony in North America during the first two centuries of European settlement. Slaves had landed in Dutch New Amsterdam seven years after they were put ashore at Jamestown, and by the time Holland's North American colony was seized by the Duke of York and renamed in his honor, it had become the leading slave market on the continent. Indeed, before century's end, slaves would be at work in practically every northern colony, and by 1715, one of every five slaves in North America belonged to a northern master. Although their share of the continent's total enslaved population declined thereafter, the concentrations in particular areas in the North created vested interests in the institution's continued existence among powerful political and economic elites. During the institution's peak years, slaves were owned by more than half the families in Kings County, New York, by one in four Connecticut households, and by many of Rhode Island's cultural elite. At times the density of these concentrations rivaled southern slave strongholds. As late as 1790, for example, New York City still had as many slaves as Charleston.

It is not surprising, therefore, that New York and New Jersey had fashioned comprehensive slave codes in 1702, roughly about the same time as Virginia. They had good reason. African-born slaves led a bloody revolt in New York City just ten years later—and notably twenty-seven years before an Angolan-led outbreak at Stono, South Carolina. Having withstood this attack, the city would again be terrified by rumors of a threatened slave rebellion in 1741. The brutality that countered this slave unrest was as savage and unpitying as any southern riposte: eighteen hanged and fourteen burned at the stake in 1741, one roasting ten hours over the fire.

In later years, during the run-up to Civil War, southerners were quick to remind their northern critics that it was they who had taken the leading role in promoting the Atlantic slave trade, and they owed the fortunes of many prominent northern families and institutions to its profits. Even newspapers, such as Ben Franklin's *Pennsylvania Gazette*, drew a substantial share of their revenues from advertising slave sales and runaways. The best, the brightest, and the most pious often owned a slave or two, or had made a killing in the slave trade to fund more respectable pursuits.

Northerners turned to slave labor for much the same reason as elsewhere: the abundance of cheap land and thus their inability to get free laborers to work it at prices employers were willing to pay. Consequently, huge landed estates emerged in New York's Hudson Valley, Rhode Island's Narrangansett region, and in eastern Connecticut that were very reminiscent of slave plantations elsewhere: devoted to large-scale agriculture, dairy farming, or cattle rearing and worked by scores of slaves who were housed in quarters separate from their owners. The employment of slave labor proved useful also in the great commercial centers such as New York City, Philadelphia, and Boston, and in smaller but vital Atlantic port cities such as New London, Newport, Portsmouth, and Perth Amboy. Lightly taxed, slaves were useful in every northern enterprise, being sought after by artisans, merchants, maritime traders, and small farmers. For a booming economy lacking sufficient wage labor, slaves offered a relatively flexible work force, being available for hire as well as through purchase.

Although northern slavery had developed during the first half-century or so, much as it had in the southern colonies, by the mid-eighteenth century the economies of the two regions had begun to deviate sharply. While southern colonies perfected a system of monocultural production and marketing that relied almost exclusively on slave laborers *and* on the natural reproduction of that human property, the economies of northern colonies were increasingly based on small farms, home manufacturing, artisanal and maritime trades, and Atlantic commerce. Slaves were an important resource for all of these enterprises in the early stages of their development, but they were just one segment of a larger, mixed labor force in which slaves often worked alongside indentured and wage workers—much as they had in southern colonies in the previous century.

Perhaps the most critical difference in the character of northern and southern slave systems, however, was that the smallholders in the North never perceived a slave woman's reproductive capacity as an economic asset. Women of childbearing age were disfavored in northern slave markets, and small-scale ownership was not conducive to family formation. Thus the sex ratio among northern slaves remained highly skewed much longer than in the South: by mid-eighteenth century it was still 2 males to 1 female in Massachusetts, 4 to 3 in New Hampshire, 3 to 2 in Connecticut, and 125 for every 100 in New York. One historian's survey finds that children in New York made up 40 percent of the slave population, but few of those over six years old lived with their parents. By the early eighteenth century, southern planters had come to regard children as precious investments, but northern masters still regarded them as an expensive nuisance. Indeed, many owners responded to the prospect of abolition by attempting to unload this nonremunerative property. Pennsylvania had to amend its abolition law in 1788 to prevent owners from selling children and pregnant women out of state.

Although slaves were much less important to the reproductive than to the productive economies of the North, their presence was critical nonetheless to the growing articulation of the North's market economy. As home and work emerged as separate spheres, historian Joanne Pope Melish has suggested that slaves, by performing still-critical domestic labor tasks, freed white males to pursue other non-household, market-oriented activity. Domestic labor in this case refers not simply to housework in its contemporary sense, of course, but to the heavy labor that sustained a colonial household economy: the harvesting and preparation of grains, rough processing of cloths, tending animal stocks, and various home manufactures (e.g., candle and soap making, and spinning). Ironically, the more the market economy enticed production out of the household and into the shop and factory, the more the incentive for slave labor weakened. Or, at least, it did so as soon as there were enough wage laborers to satisfy the labor demands, at acceptable prices, of an expanding economy.

Thus, indentured labor declined from more than 40 percent of Philadelphia's work force in the mid-eighteenth century to virtually none by 1800, which suggests that a re-articulation of the labor force might well have been under way in some urban areas even before the Revolution. If so, the transformation was temporarily stalled at mid-century by the Seven Years' War. The importation of slaves into northern colonies increased dramatically during that war in response to a labor shortage created by Britain's recruitment of white men to fight the French. Philadelphia imported thirteen hundred slaves between 1757 and 1766, for example. This pattern reversed during the brief interlude of peace but continued during the Revolutionary era, recasting in the process the character of the slave population and of slave ownership in some major urban centers. The demographic importance of slaves declined in relative and sometimes absolute numbers, and the character of their employment changed. Manumissions, which had been insignificant in the prewar period, increased, and the in-migration of freed slaves from rural areas added significant numbers of free blacks to urban populations. There were also broad shifts in northern economies that produced changes in their labor mix. Artisans, who had been a major employer of slave labor, turned increasingly to free wage workers for help, a choice that the postwar depression may well have accelerated. Consequently, merchants and professionals looking for household laborers superseded artisans as the main employers of the remaining slave laborers in some cities.

With the economic rationale for slave labor steadily eroding, slaves and freed people eagerly seized upon the revolutionary rhetoric of freedom and equality to challenge it. Mounting a determined, inexorable campaign for abolition, they inundated American courts with petitions for freedom. Such petitions were practically as old as slavery itself in British North America, and their formulas had become quite familiar. Usually the plaintiffs seized upon the ambiguities inherent in the rationalization for holding property in human beings and their offspring, finding grounds for their freedom claims, for example, when the master or his heirs reneged on manumission promises, when mixed-race children could claim descent from a free mother, or, more rarely, when technical registration requirements were violated as slaves were moved from one jurisdiction to another. These were not frontal attacks on the right to hold humans as property but charges of having done so illegally or improperly. For example, Virginia's attempt to prohibit the importation of African and West Indian slaves after 1778 required owners moving into the state to file affidavits certifying the origins of their slave property. Failure to do so made them liable to suits by those slaves.

To this traditional arsenal, the Revolution added the ideal of a divinely ordained, "inherent and inalienable" mandate of freedom for all. In those areas where slavery's hold was weakest or greatly attenuated, the mere exposure of this contradiction might result in a swift legal victory, perhaps adding to the seeming inevitability of freedom's progress. In 1777, with the Revolution barely two years' running, Vermont wrote general emancipation into its new constitution, a number of local municipal bodies barred the slave trade from their jurisdictions, and a few Massachusetts towns simply declared slavery and the Revolutionary cause to be incompatible. In 1783, the year Britain conceded American independence in the Treaty of Paris, Quock Walker brought a freedom suit against Nathaniel Jennison that ended with the Massachusetts Supreme Court declaring slavery to be inconsistent with the state's new constitution, the preamble of which declared all men to be created equal. Notwithstanding the fact that this decision—and most other legislative decrees of the sort—required the slaves themselves to take the initiative to secure their freedom, within five years of the war's end all of the New England states had taken some step to eradicate slavery, and by the first decade of the new century there were little more than a thousand left in the region.

Emancipation in the middle Atlantic progressed much more gradually and faced greater resistance. High-sounding declarations of principle gave way to arguments appealing to self-interests and pragmatic compromises. The moral challenge to slavery had begun early in the eighteenth century, with Quakers often in the lead. Despite their deep involvement in commercial activities in which slave trading figured heavily, Quaker reformers had largely succeeded in purging slaveholders from their own ranks by the eve of the Revolution, at which point the Pennsylvania brethren set their sights on general emancipation. By that time, however, the state's Quakers had lost their accustomed hold on public offices because of their pacifism in an era of almost continuous warfare. Consequently, new voices shaped by the revolutionary experience emerged to lead the abolition debate in the state legislature, where control had passed from the Quakers to an unlikely coalition of Philadelphia radicals and backcountry Scots-Irish. On March 1, 1780, a year before the victory at Yorktown, the Pennsylvania legislature abolished the institution of slavery. Though a landmark achievement, no living slaves were actually freed under this law, because it applied only to children born *after* the law's passage. In a formula that would be repeated by many other slave societies in the Americas, this "law of the free womb," as Brazilians would later call it, eliminated property rights in children yet to be born while leaving the existing slaves to complete their life sentence to bondage. Moreover, as in Pennsylvania, most such laws obliged even the newborn children to serve their mother's master until adulthood, the definition of which ranged between eighteen years for females to twenty-eight years for males. In most cases, slaveholders received not only compensation indirectly through continued labor service but by direct cash payments as well.

Every northern state with a substantial slave labor force adopted some version of the Pennsylvania "free womb" model. Rhode Island and Connecticut did so a year after the Treaty of Paris was signed, and New York came within a few votes of doing so the following year. In that case, slavery's defenders outfoxed the abolitionists by loading the proposed law with amendments that took away existing civil and political rights from free blacks, thus leading the governor to veto the entire bill. Eventually, after protracted political struggles, both New York (in 1799) and New Jersey (in 1804), the two states that held the majority of northern slaves, embraced gradual abolition schemes. Indeed, the emancipation process often proved so gradual that some nominally free states continued to have slaves well into the nineteenth century: five hundred could still be found in New York as late as 1820, and some were entered onto the New Jersey census rolls in 1860. There were no longer any slaves in Connecticut in 1860, but that state did not get around to abolishing the institution as a legal category until 1848, the same year as did Guadeloupe in the French West Indies.

More than seventy years after the signing of the Declaration of Independence, therefore, one northern state still retained slavery as a legal status in its law code while another still enumerated slaves among its population. These facts are but emblematic of the protracted process of ending bound labor in the so-called free states, and they underscore the profound shadows menacing the emergence of northern black communities. Although thrown into a netherworld between servitude and freedom, these communities would nonetheless become the principal loci of the continuing struggle against slavery. Their very existence challenged the moral and ideological rationales for the enslavement of other blacks, and they produced leaders and institutions to press the case that America should live up to the ideals of its founding.

These developments indicate a growing internal differentiation within emerging black urban communities. Like Richard Allen, some members of those communities were part of the huge in-migration from places such as the Delaware and Hudson valleys, where former slaves had been freed, either at their master's volition, during the war, by self-purchase, or by some combination of these. A small group perhaps were urban artisans who exploited the manifest uncertainties of the Revolutionary era— the postwar depression and imminent abolition legislation—to negotiate the end of their bondage. Voluntary, uncompensated manumissions spiked upward during economic downturns, suggesting that, in contrast with the South, northern slaveholders might have been very open to such transactions.

Left in limbo, then, were those whose status the first emancipation laws did not address, and those who were freed juridically but remained subject to their former masters' control as so-called apprentices. Those in the first group, all born in the eighteenth century, remained legally enslaved for at least four decades after the Revolution. Those in the second group, being indentured workers, could still be bought and sold—that is, their "contracts" could be—making them vulnerable to separation from family and kin at their masters' necessity or whim. Though nominally emancipated, the first cohort of these people, required to serve their mothers' owner until twenty-eight years old, would not become unconditionally free in Pennsylvania, for example, until March 1, 1808. There were several thousand such people in the state of New York when it finally mandated an end to their ordeal in 1827. In 1790, half of the free blacks in Philadelphia lived in white households; a fourth of them were indentured workers and children.

The indentured labor of juridically free children helped buy the slave owners' assent to abolition, despite being inconsistent with their reputed disdain for such underage workers. Their sudden, otherwise inexplicable, popularity might be explained by a provision that both New York and New Jersey inserted into their abolition laws allowing masters to abandon these free-born children to the "Overseer of the Poor," who reimbursed their ostensible expense. Effectively, this procedure became a ruse disguising the extraction of additional compensation, since slave masters first abandoned and then apprenticed the children, collecting fees from the state for the transactions. Indeed, the rapidly rising costs of such schemes created a scandal, leading to its abandonment in New York in 1804. New York's scandal did not prevent New Jersey from adopting a similar clause in its law, however, which ended up consuming 40 percent of the state's budget. It, too, was eventually repealed, once it was calculated that the per capita cost to the state exceeded the lifetime services of a slave.

Their conjugal relations discouraged during slavery, northern slaves first and most frequently responded to emancipation by marrying, but many of them soon discovered that their new freedom did not mean the establishment of households independent of their masters' direct control and surveillance. In freedom, too, they confronted a rapidly changing economy, which led some to choose, if they had any choice at all, to remain in the jobs in which they had been employed as slaves. As many as a third in New York City, for example, were live-in domestics, working mainly for board and lodging.

Those slaves who had managed to negotiate private deals with their masters—gaining their freedom in return for cash or trouble-free service for a number of years—were often more fortunately situated in the new economy. Such negotiations favored the skilled, the industrious, and the tenacious, and for such people this was likely a period of optimism and hope. Many of them made the best of it. Slave artisans and skilled workers stood to benefit from the rapid economic transformations in northern economies in the early nineteenth century. With a third of the new nation's trade passing through the port of New York and much of the rest through Philadelphia, there was a lot of work for mariners and dockworkers in both places. Of those workers, substantial proportions—as many as a fifth of Philadelphia's dockworkers, for example—were black. Occupational directories also show free blacks employed in a wide range

of skilled trades in these cities: carpenters, coopers, cabinetmakers, uphol-
sterers, sailmakers, butchers, and bakers. Among them was Richard Allen,
who supported himself as a shoemaker in his early years in Philadelphia,
while biding his time before establishing a church that would anchor that
city's black community and profoundly shape the emerging struggle against
southern slavery.

In general, however, whether working in shops or households, worshipping in churches, meeting in lodges, or just moving through their daily
routine at home among their kinfolk, the newly emancipated found themselves in the company of other blacks who were still enslaved or bound to
abolition law indentures. Their social relations, conversations, and experiences were undoubtedly complex, and perhaps marred by collective and
personal tensions. And yet those relations may also have endowed these
free people with a certain insight and empathy for those still in bondage.
Certainly the legatees of America's first revolution and emancipation identified with their still-enslaved brethren and became militant opponents of
slave regimes to a far greater extent than communities of free people of
color elsewhere in the Americas, where more often than not, they identified with slavery's defenders.

Living Between Freedom and Slavery

At mid-century, of all cities in America, Frederick Douglass declared,
Philadelphia "holds the destiny of our people." And, indeed, the city does
best exemplify the rise of free black communities in the Revolutionary era
and the wellsprings of their enduring militancy. For three decades following the American Revolution, Philadelphia had the largest concentration
of free people of color in the Americas, being superseded by New York
City sometime after the War of 1812. Ballooning to two thousand by 1790,
their numbers were boosted an additional 25 percent when several hundred slave fugitives and free colored refugees started arriving from Saint-
Domingue following the fall of one of its principal cities, Cap François, to
Toussaint Louverture's army in 1793. These free-born people of color were
not just a polyglot collection of humanity, however, but the beginning of a
perhaps unique social formation that would sustain diverse social movements over the decades that followed.

The lives and careers of James Forten and Richard Allen, both of whom had returned to Philadelphia shortly after the war, map the interconnectedness and the vitality of that community's dense networks. Sometimes allies, sometimes antagonists, these men represent the seemingly diametric poles of black experience and the intimate interactions that would shape a common consciousness. As such, they exemplify the diverse forces that shaped the destiny of the whole community. Scion of a family that traced its roots to the city's seventeenth-century origins when his great-grandfather arrived in chains, James Forten would earn a fortune in postwar Philadelphia, would lead the fight against slavery and for black civil rights, and would found a family that would carry those struggles deep into the next century. Allen, by contrast, descended from a slavery-broken family, but he would soon create its institutional alternative, a church family that would ground the consolidation of a substantial portion of the city's and the nation's black community, also enabling the struggle for black liberation for decades to come.

Having spent most of his service in the Revolutionary War on a British prison ship, where he narrowly escaped being sold into West Indian slavery, James Forten passed some time at sea and in London before rejoining his mother and two siblings in postwar Philadelphia. Upon his return, he confronted the responsibility of providing for their support, because his father had died when James was just seven years old, leaving the boy's mother, Margaret, in dire financial straits with three small children to rear. The elder Forten left a legacy of career and religious choices that appear to have decisively shaped the young Forten's destiny. James became a common laborer in the loft of Robert Bridges, a descendant of Irish immigrants now risen to the city's mercantile elite. From Bridges, James's father, Thomas, had learned the sailmaker's craft. Thomas also appears to have passed down to James his Anglican faith, to which the elder Forten had most likely converted during the first great revival inspired by George Whitefield's visits to Philadelphia in the 1740s. The shop and the church would ground the Forten family's social activism thereafter.

James soon proved himself very adept at both the craft and business of sailmaking. Lacking an heir willing to take over his business upon his retirement in 1798, Bridges left James this thriving loft with its two dozen mostly white laborers, together with contracts with some of the biggest merchants in the city. Fortunately for Forten, he entered the business while Philadelphia was still a booming port, before the embargoes and recessions in later years undercut its competitive position on the Northeast Coast vis-à-vis New York. By that time, however, Forten had deftly parlayed his workshop into a substantial fortune, supplemented by real estate speculations and moneylending.

During this time, he also emerged as one of the anchors of Philadelphia's free black community, and his life maps crucial elements of that city's social formation. Black Philadelphia was the crucial hub for a broad network among free people of color stretching from Boston to Charleston. The connective tissue of that network formed most immediately and initially around the common civil status and political predicament of people who had to contest their right to life and the pursuit of happiness in a new nation still half-slave and half-free. Those bonds grew into the institutional sinews of churches and mutual aid societies through which free people of color organized their religious and social life and, occasionally, their political protests. Marriages promoted more extensive kinship ties that connected many of these prominent families, reinforcing relations that sustained undertakings both private and political.

With its long-standing commercial ties to the Caribbean and New Orleans, Philadelphia stood out as a natural destination for immigrants across the Atlantic world and, for the blacks among them at least, a true ethnic melting pot. The black population concentrated in Moyamensing and Southwark, where Forten had his shop, neighborhoods attracting a rich mixture of native-born migrants, African and West Indian immigrants, and black fugitives from former slave regimes in the Delaware Valley, New Jersey, and the Chesapeake. The ties with the French West Indies were particularly strong. Since the late eighteenth century, Saint-Domingue had been second only to Great Britain as an American trading partner. Those ties grew once France relaxed earlier trade restrictions and American traders moved in to profit from the disruptions caused by the Haitian Revolution. By one estimate as many as 848 Haitians of color made their way to Philadelphia in the 1790s, most of them women and adolescents, and some the offspring of planter fathers who'd left them bequests in their wills. Conflicts over their status ensued as some masters sought to exempt their slaves from Pennsylvania's recently passed abolition law's requirement that they be given indenture contracts instead. With the assistance of white and black antislavery forces, a few of them filed law-suits, others exploited the legal confusion to extract manumission agree-ments from their masters or mistresses, and still others simply slipped away into the growing free black community. Desiré, a thirty-three-year-old free man of color from Jacmel, who had stowed away on a ship bound for Philadelphia in 1797, registered himself as a resident alien. Meanwhile, thousands of native-born blacks continued to pour in from the Delaware Valley and the Chesapeake as restrictions on manumission there were re-laxed and the shift to cereals production accelerated.

Many of Forten's friends and associates were drawn from this dynamic mélange of former slaves and free colored refugees. One close friend, Shandy Yard, grocer and occasional mariner, was African-born. Others, such as the confectioners Jean and Ann Appo, were wealthy free colored refugees from war-torn Saint-Domingue. The Purvis family, with whom the Fortens became indelibly linked by marriage and political comrade-ship, arrived via Charleston and other southern ports, but traced their roots to the British West Indies.

Forten worshipped with many of these people at St. Thomas African Episcopal Church, which had been founded in 1794 by Absalom Jones, who would become a close friend as well as his minister. Present at its dedi-cation in 1794 and one of its vestryman by 1796, James soon became one of St. Thomas's strongest supporters. It was there, in 1803, that he wed his first wife, Martha Beatte, and, after her death, his second wife, Charlotte Vandine, a young woman of Native American, European, and African heritage. It was within this church community, too, that they would raise their nine children. And through his activism in St. Thomas, James Forten would occasionally join forces with Richard Allen.

Many members of Forten's generation had inherited the Christian faith of their parents, who had converted in the latter half of the previous century, often during the Revolution. During the decades bracketing the turn of the nineteenth century, they built on that faith the institutional structures of a distinctly black Christianity. Forten's minister, Absalom Jones, and his sometime collaborator Richard Allen were major actors in forging those institutions.

Like Allen, Absalom Jones was a former slave from the Delaware Val-ley who had managed to purchase his freedom. Born and reared a slave in Sussex, Delaware, Jones had been brought to Philadelphia in 1762, when he was sixteen years old. Working as a handyman and clerk in his master's store, he attended the school set up by the Quaker abolitionist Anthony Benezet. Through that connection, perhaps, he secured his freedom a year after the war ended, when Quakers bought his and his wife's liberty. In 1786 he joined St. George's Methodist Church, where he met Richard Allen, who had only recently arrived in Philadelphia following his stint as an itinerant preacher in Delaware and Maryland. Allen had traveled there with Bishop Asbury, who now ministered at St. George's. Asbury asked Allen to minister to the blacks in that congregation, much as he had been doing in the Maryland and Delaware camp meetings. Jones joined the younger man in forming a black prayer group of about forty persons. Tensions developed as some whites objected to the growing autonomy of the group, leading Jones and Allen to begin laying plans to form an independent congregation, an African church, even as they continued to worship at St. George's. They began, in May 1787, by forming a mutual aid organization, the Free African Society, which was nondenominational, but adopted a Quaker-style worship service. Meanwhile, St. George's launched a building program to accommodate its growing membership, to which its black members made significant contributions of money and labor. When the refurbished space opened later that November, black worshippers were mistakenly ushered to the new galleries instead of their usual section at the rear of the main floor. As they knelt in prayer, Absalom Jones was pulled roughly to his feet and ordered to leave the section, which was supposed to have been reserved for whites. Once prayers were finished, the blacks left as a group, with Allen and Jones vowing never to return.

Following the withdrawal from St. George's, the Free African Society filled the religious vacuum and sparked a social revolution in which this postwar generation turned the Christian faith they had inherited from their parents into an autonomous institution. Within a couple of years, Allen grew restive with its Quaker-style meetings and nondenominational stance, however, and withdrew to form his own church. By the summer of 1794, both he and Jones had established "African" churches: Bethel African Methodist and St. Thomas African Episcopal, respectively. Within a year of their openings, the two churches together embraced one third of the black adults in the city. With scenarios of secession unfolding in other cities almost identical to that at St. George's, most notably in Baltimore and New York, a broad social and religious movement took root. In 1816 these diverse congregations, stretching from Charleston, South Carolina, to Salem, New Jersey, all spawned by similar oppositions and desires, joined together to found the African Methodist Episcopal Church (AME), a profound expression of the growing urban free black communities. Of its 6,748 members in 1818, 6,225 lived in just three cities—Philadelphia, Baltimore, and Charleston.

Although originally a Methodist as well, Jones joined the Episcopal denomination, perhaps in deference to the preferences of his parishioners or in response to the preferred faith of St. Thomas's benefactors and financial supporters. He was ordained an Episcopal priest in 1804. Meanwhile, Allen struggled to raise funds to build his church, with considerably less financial assistance from whites, especially given the active opposition of the Methodist hierarchy and, after 1793, the shift of philanthropic attention to the Saint-Domingue refugee problem. Drawing substantially on his artisanal earnings, Allen purchased a blacksmith's shop, hitched a team of horses to it, and dragged it to Sixth and Lombard streets to serve as a temporary church. Given his strong commitment to the Methodist faith, however, he remained loosely tethered to St. George's for another two decades. Bishop Asbury officiated at Bethel's dedication, but Allen continued to be harassed by Methodist officials as they sought control of the property and its worship services, demanding the deed to Bethel's land in 1796 and the keys to the building in 1805, and even suing to gain access to the pulpit in 1816.

Like Jones, Allen was not ordained during the early years of this struggle and consequently remained dependent on white ministers, usually Asbury, to officiate over various sacramental services. The conflict at St. George's, therefore, was not about segregated worship per se. Allen had from the start been responsible for gathering blacks into separate services; and blacks had long accepted their assigned seats at St. George's. As they would inform Bishop Asbury in 1807, the worshippers at Bethel simply wanted to regulate their own secular and spiritual affairs, "the same as if we were white people." The issue was their presumption of equal standing—of being "citizens and friends"—in a house of worship that in multiple ways they had helped to build. In many ways, then, this fight mirrored their larger claims on the new nation—which they also had helped build.

Allen's crowded church gave his members more than inspirational preaching in a familiar call-response pattern. For their children he established a school within the church in 1804 and otherwise ministered to the parents' secular as well as religious needs. Reflecting the heterogeneity of its members and their families, Bethel became a haven for runaway slaves, work in which Allen's wife, Sarah, played a leading role. Bethel's God was a god of liberation.

Aside from the church—though sometimes organized under its auspices—the mutual aid societies that flourished in postwar black communities also formed a unifying framework for African Americans in the urban North. Allen, Forten, Jones, and several other men joined to form a Philadelphia lodge of Freemasons in 1797, which undertook the promotion of education and antislavery among its causes. They were likely influenced by the first such lodge founded by Prince Hall, a Barbadian-born leatherworker who had secured education and property after his immigration to prewar Boston and had become an activist for abolition and civil rights during the Revolution. Rejected by the American Masons, Hall had secured a charter from a lodge of British soldiers and eventually, in 1787, the endorsement of the British Grand Lodge in London. Because these organizations were both nonsectarian and international, they provided powerful vehicles of communication and mobilization for black urban elites.

As their bylaws made clear, membership demanded not simply mutual financial support but also active participation in funeral rites, and public behavior and dress that reflected well on the group as a whole. The Free African Society sought to foster social discipline—meaning sobriety, mutual aid, and protection of family life. Drinking, gambling, and marital infidelity were punished. Dues provided a form of collective social savings that could be drawn on to pay burial expenses and served as a form of insurance for the sick and financial support for widows and orphans. Under the leadership of Allen and Jones, the Philadelphia society organized the free black community to staff a temporary hospital and to nurse those (mostly white since many blacks were immune) felled by the yellow fever epidemic during the summer and fall of 1793.

During the decades bracketing the turn of the nineteenth century, such groups could be found in many cities along the Atlantic coast—Boston, Newport, Rhode Island, and New York City—as well as in Philadelphia.

These societies reflected the poignant self-consciousness of a generation not only just emerging from slavery to an uncertain freedom but also increasingly conscious of and insistent on its entitlement to citizenship. Appropriately, this was a moment of testing, which was conducive both to plaintiveness and militancy. The same Newport society that once embraced the idea of a cosmopolitan citizenship now lamented their feeling of being "strangers in a strange land."

Notwithstanding this poignant echo of a biblical plaint, what is perhaps most striking about this group and postwar generation as a whole is the revelation that two facets of black political activism, later deemed antagonistic, did in fact cohere. On the one hand, there was their public posture of protest and demand for respect from the white world. On the other was the mostly inward-looking face, one that demanded self-respect from and moral uplift of their fellow blacks, sometimes in excoriating terms. The second was a much more defensive posture, deeply self-conscious and animated by the fear that black people were on trial and that the behavior of even a few could have dire repercussions on the fate of the whole. Thus could their discourse merge seamlessly the ideas of self-critique and self-help, American identity and racial solidarity, the right to stay in the nation they had helped give life to and the right to emigrate. They did not feel the slightest contradiction or conflict among these positions, as some later generations would. Perhaps it was that they lived in a world that was matter-of-factly cosmopolitan in its everyday existence, a still-novel nation struggling to give form and content to itself. But most of all, perhaps, they lived in a still-revolutionary world, in which new national entities were being formed, not least of them the black nation of Haiti. Theirs was, as Elizabeth Rauh Bethel has called it, "a translocal moral community." Perhaps it was that special sense of community that led Forten—in some ways the ultimate assimilationist—to speak frequently of Haitian independence as offering the greatest hope for African Americans and for the uplift of the race elsewhere.

Forten's personal, political, and business relations with Paul Cuffee, a fellow seafarer, reflect some of the complex interactions within this translocal community. Forten took on Cuffee's grandsons as apprentices in his shop, while the sea captain undertook some of the earliest voyages to Africa to fulfill his dream of repatriating African Americans "home." While we do not know what conversations passed between these two men, clearly Forten and Cuffee recognized the latter's voyages as consistent with the freedoms they both sought. In 1815, Cuffee sailed on one of his ships, *Traveller*, along with thirty-one other prospective African American settlers, to Sierra Leone. For much of the early nineteenth century while he plotted his course, Cuffee's project found support among normally anti-separatists such as Forten. All this would change with the appearance in 1816 of the American Colonization Society and southern slaveholders' embrace of African emigration as their own. By that time, Forten's closest friend, Robert Purvis, would be numbered among the bitterest opponents of "Back to Africa" and other separatist schemes.

In the early postwar decades, however, as the northern free black communities took shape, the dense interplay of political, business, and religious relations bound a heterogenous people into a common front. Early in 1797, Jones, Allen, and Forten petitioned Congress to end slavery and repeal the 1793 Fugitive Slave Act. When Congress finally did pass such a ban on March 2, 1807, with the law taking effect on New Year's Day 1808, blacks launched the first of the many emancipation celebrations that would become part of the moral architecture of their communities. Fittingly, the first of these was held at Absalom Jones's St. Thomas's African Episcopal Church in Philadelphia.

Founding the New Nation, Closing Old Frontiers

Gale-force winds and rain swept through the Virginia Tidewater on the last Saturday of August 1800. As rising creeks washed away bridges and disrupted communications and travel, however, few white Virginians realized that another, even more violent storm had been narrowly averted. Several hundred slaves had planned to rendezvous that evening, at either Brook Bridge or the woods nearby, form into three columns, and march on the capital in Richmond, just six miles away. There they were to have seized four thousand unguarded muskets, placed Governor James Monroe under guard, and held the city until co-conspirators arrived from surrounding counties to reinforce them. With the city and the state's governor held hostage, they would calmly have negotiated the abolition of slavery and equal rights for blacks as citizens.

At the center of this audacious plot was an extraordinary twenty-four-year-old blacksmith named Gabriel, a former playmate and now the property of young Thomas Henry Prosser, who had just recently inherited Brookfield Plantation and its fifty-odd slaves upon the death of his father. All who met Gabriel, white as well as black, were awed by this six-foot-tall man with the piercing eyes. An incident two years earlier should have warned of the rebellious spirit behind that gaze. When he and his older brother, Solomon, had been discovered stealing hogs by a neighboring planter, Absalom Johnson, a fierce scuffle ensued during which Gabriel bit off half of Johnson's left ear. Indicative perhaps of the ambivalence of white authority in this still unsettled period, Gabriel did not suffer any of the usual penalties for his assault on white manhood. Instead, being literate, he was allowed to take advantage of a 1792 law permitting slaves to claim "benefit of clergy." Consequently, rather than being jailed, sold out of state, or killed, the future rebel leader was simply branded on his left thumb and freed. The lowly class status of his victim, a former overseer now aspiring to move up by renting land and slaves, might have swayed the judgment of a court made up of substantial planters. Perhaps Prosser reminded them, or they appreciated without prompting, that the skills of a good blacksmith were more valuable to them than racial solidarity with upstart competitors such as Johnson, especially in a new boomtown like Richmond. In any event, by earlier as well as later standards of southern racial justice, the disposition of Gabriel's case was extraordinary. For his role in the affair, brother Solomon, also a blacksmith, was acquitted altogether.

Obviously Gabriel did not interpret the public humiliation of being branded like an animal as leniency, because soon thereafter he set to plotting what would have been the largest slave rebellion in Anglophone North America to date. It may well be that some personal grudge triggered his outrage, since both his young master and the now-disfigured Johnson were, by all accounts, targeted to be killed at the outset of a revolt that was otherwise calculated to minimize bloodshed. The rebels were to seize Richmond, hold hostages, and negotiate, not rampage across the countryside.

Be that as it may, it is clear that their motivation and strategy were also shaped decisively by the prevailing political climate, domestic and international. The year 1800 was one of extraordinary tension for the still-infant republic. Reasonable observers might well have anticipated that the intense political warfare between John Adams's Federalists and Thomas

Jefferson's Democratic-Republicans might yet descend into internecine violence. Certainly slaves cognizant of the opportunities opened by the last quarrel they had witnessed among white folks might have sensed another such moment in the offing. Gabriel was born in the historic year 1776 and had grown to adulthood during nearly two decades of revolutionary turmoil. He and his fellow conspirators knew very well that somewhere down south, at that very moment, an army of slaves had just fought the best armies of Europe to a standstill. Likely they had heard as well about the thousands of slaves who had risen at Pointe Coupee in French Louisiana five years earlier. One might reasonably view with skepticism the stories about two shadowy Frenchmen being parties to Gabriel's plot, but it was by no means entirely implausible. Perhaps one of the French veterans of the Battle of Yorktown, some of whom were known to have settled in Virginia, was indeed ready to organize and train the rebel force. Even if the rumored French allies were fictitious, their prominence in the rebels' discourse is telling: theirs was a fight formed and informed by the revolutionary political currents of their day.

Like so many other North American slave plots—some real, some figments of white fear—Gabriel's was betrayed. Eventually he and his comrades were captured and either hanged or sold south. His bold plot lived on in popular memory, however, and it may well have inspired rebel aspirants of the next generation, one of whom, Nat Turner, was born within weeks of Gabriel's capture and execution. In the thirty-year interval between Gabriel's conspiracy and Turner's rebellion, another alleged conspiracy was exposed in South Carolina. Its leader, Denmark Vesey, evidenced a strategic consciousness about the broader Atlantic world strikingly similar to Gabriel's. Vesey and his co-conspirators also "died silent," leaving an ambiguous historical record and debates as to whether their resistance was merely the product of white hysteria.

Whatever efficacy Gabriel's legend may have had for subsequent generations of slaves, the revolutionary climate that nurtured his rebellion quickly passed, leaving entirely different conditions for any future imitators. The three decades that separated Gabriel's conspiracy and Nat Turner's insurrection in 1831 witnessed a fundamental transformation of the southern slave regime, including a vast geographical expansion, economic intensification, and political consolidation. Even during Gabriel's lifetime, national independence had opened to settlement and development of the vast western tracts the British had sought to preserve exclusively for Native American habitation. Although slavery was forbidden in the northern half of this western reserve, its southern counterpart would enter the Union as the slave state of Tennessee in 1796, and just over two decades later, two more slave states—Mississippi in 1817 and Alabama in 1819—would be formed out of what remained of the southwestern region. Once Eli Whitney's newly devised machine for separating cotton lint from its seed became widely available—which allowed short staple cotton to be cultivated more profitably—these lands grew immensely in value, as did the hilly upland areas of the older states. Meanwhile, technical breakthroughs, together with a tremendous social revolution in the mobilization of labor, greatly expanded England's industrial production of cotton cloth, creating a voracious appetite for the American crop. By 1825, the South had become the world's dominant cotton producer, and its cotton crop doubled every decade thereafter.

The expanding English textile industry also spurred renewed production of indigo, the source of textile dyestuff. A burgeoning European urban work force in need of cheap, calorie-rich foodstuffs on one side of the Atlantic spurred in turn a greater demand for slave labor on the other, as the recently acquired Louisiana sugar plantations went into high gear, reorganized and revitalized in large measure by the Haitian émigrés who poured into that territory during the century's second decade.

While this rapid transformation of the southern plantation economy snuffed out any reticence or ambivalence about the continued use of slave labor in the South, the dramatic changes in North America's political geography enhanced the security of that slave property. One by one the major European powers that had long contested for supremacy in North America abandoned their claims there. With the purchase of Louisiana in 1803, France ceased to be a factor on the mainland, a fact underscored by Napoleon's final defeat in 1815. In the Westphalian world order established after the Napoleonic threat was extinguished, Britain's potential challenge to America's hemispheric ambitions also greatly diminished. The threat Spain had once posed vanished, too, as that country emerged from the Napoleonic Wars fatally weakened in Europe and in America, having lost most of its colonies there. Within a short time—by 1819—the once proud mistress of the New World finally ceded West Florida and East Florida, its remaining North American possessions east of the Mississippi River.

Four years after American independence, the only remaining sanctuary for slaves challenging their bondage were a few Native American groups, mostly in Florida or scattered among inaccessible enclaves in other southeastern states and territories. Since the seventeenth century, southeastern Indians had formed complex bonds with African Americans. Although decimated early on in the Chesapeake region, Indians had at times made up as much as one fourth of the slave population in the Carolinas. These Indian slaves had been disproportionately female and the Africans male, which fostered biological intermixture and political alliances. Some Indian clans, moreover, adopted fugitive blacks into their communities, with full citizenship rights. Indians proved to be adversaries for blacks as well. A principal feature of the many treaties they concluded with southern whites called upon them to serve as slave catchers, a task some undertook with enthusiasm.

By and large, however, the Indian presence had constituted a kind of internal frontier, within which blacks found havens and occasional allies. The surviving Indian populations were themselves enduring tremendous pressure from the same land-hungry plantation complex, and most of them would soon be killed or moved to reserves in the trans-Mississippi West. The diminished European presence in North America had also deprived Indians of a counterweight to the American settlers, to whom some tribes now grew closer. Adopting sedentary agriculture, private landholding, and slaveholding after the Revolution, many of the so-called civilized tribes became increasingly hostile to the black population. Increasingly slaves could look for allies only among the dissident clans that splintered from these dominant groups, such as the Florida Seminoles, who had split off from the Cherokee. Not only did the Seminoles continue to offer black fugitives refuge and even military alliances against their common white planter enemies, but blacks also merged seamlessly into their communities. American military officers often noted their prominent role in Indian resistance, and at least one black man became a chief. The Seminoles, black and Native American, continued their resistance to the slave regime well into America's fifth decade, and many held out in Florida's inaccessible swamplands well after that.

Made keenly aware of the dangers confronting the slaveholder's hegemony, President James Monroe urged Congress to move the southeastern Indians into the new wilderness west of the Mississippi that his friend

Jefferson had acquired from France. Once the removal was completed in the 1830s, the Indian threat was neutralized in the principal areas of plantation cultivation. No future Gabriel would find allies, European or indigenous, to aid in a rebellion against the growing Slave Power.

Gabriel did not live to see this transformation, but one of his contemporaries, Charles Ball, did, and he left behind disturbing vignettes of what these changes might have meant to the slaves of his generation—the first to be born and reared in the young American nation. Born on the western shore of the Chesapeake in Calvert County, Maryland, three years before the British surrendered at Yorktown, Ball went on to have adult slave experiences that prefigured a labor regime in the making rather than the more relaxed order Gabriel had known. His mother and siblings were essentially unknown to him, the family having been auctioned to slave traders anxious to profit from the growing demand for labor farther south. Ball was just four years old at the time, and sometime later he lost his emotionally broken father as well, who escaped just ahead of being sold south. Charles grew up with his eighty-year-old African-born grandfather as his only kinsman. Having arrived in Maryland in 1730, Old Ben, as he was known, linked Charles not only to a rapidly fading African past—the religious rites of which Ben still practiced—but to the golden age of Chesapeake's founding fathers. Charles Ball's autobiography is laced with searing, invidious comparisons between that supposedly genteel world and the one he encountered on the new southern frontier, the emerging new South that had scattered his parents and siblings and eventually drawn him into its vortex.

Like many slaves, Ball found his fate determined by the debts or frugality, the health or mortality, of his owners. When he was twelve years old he was sold to a man who put him to work in the Washington Navy Yard. Like Gabriel, he experienced the relative freedom of being an urban slave who hired his time, and it was there that he first dreamed of freedom. In Ball's case, however, the dreams were of escape rather than rebellion, stimulated by his chance meeting with a free black sailor from Philadelphia. The idea and image of that city of black freedom and autonomy would continue to animate his imagination for years after. It was there, in his twilight years, that he settled to narrate an account of his life, one that embraced the profound transformation of slavery during the first three decades of the nineteenth century.

In the nation's capital of his youth, Ball witnessed the quickening pulse of the postrevolutionary slave economy, with its thriving slave market and the coffles of slaves being marched or shipped south. Before he could make good his own plan to escape by ship to Philadelphia, he was sold to a new master, who put him to work on a Maryland plantation. A few years later he was sold again and, shackled by an iron collar to a coffle of fifty-one other slaves, marched overland to South Carolina. His new owner was a former Atlantic slave trader who had turned to the domestic traffic, intent on quickly amassing the capital to purchase a plantation. The trader's ambitions were fully realized, Ball later learned, as he rose rapidly into Georgia's planter elite, a success replicated by other men on the make on the cotton frontiers of the Deep South. Meanwhile, Ball found himself first among the revived rice and long-staple cotton fields of the South Carolina Lowlands and then clearing virgin fields on Georgia's western frontier. He witnessed the raw abuse of a new slave empire, where men seeking to make or repair their fortunes were bent on extracting the last ounce of value from the soil and human labor.

Ball's enslavement came at the beginning stages of the concentration of land and slaves that greatly sharpened class distinctions among southern whites during the first decades of the nineteenth century. He offers acerbic sketches of the tensions and pretensions of the new social order. He describes land pushed to exhaustion and abandoned, slaves worked and beaten into a sense of hopeless submission, all decisions guided by a brutally rational calculus. Some planters found it cheaper to buy food for their slaves than divert their labor to grow it. Some found women "breeders" a better investment than men because their "produce" found a readier market. Even modes of discipline reflected this rational and brutal efficiency. Ball describes a sadistic array of punishments, all designed to inflict "the greatest degree of pain" without rendering the victim unable to work. Caught stealing food, he was strung up by his thumbs and lashed with a whip that lacerated the skin but did not bruise it, leaving him in agony after his wounds were washed with "pepper-tea"—but able to work. To avoid debilitating injuries to wrists or hands, slaveholders had women whipped while they lay spread-eagle on the ground. A young slave mother expressed relief that her dead child had escaped the living death of this new regime; an old man resigned himself to passive suffering, declaring escape attempts or resistance to be useless.

Ball did manage to escape, overcoming daunting obstacles and enduring a harrowing journey overland from deep in southwest Georgia. Later he was swept up into the war against the British in 1813–14, after which he moved and worked among the free black communities of Baltimore and Annapolis. In June 1830, he fell into the hands of the brother of his former mistress and was enslaved once more. His first escape attempt failed, but he finally managed to stow away in the hold of a ship carrying cotton to Philadelphia. He returned home, however, to discover that his wife and children had been kidnapped by slave catchers and sold to a southern plantation. In the end, therefore, both his family and most of his own adult life had been consumed by the voracious demands of the cotton kingdom that had come to dominate the American economy. Ball moved just outside Philadelphia and quietly struggled to resume the life of a freeman, but was forever fearful of recapture. The final words of his autobiography echoed the feelings he had expressed upon being taken by the slave trader twenty years earlier: his heart once more had "died away within me."

The year Charles Ball managed his second escape might be seen as a turning point in the struggle against slavery, however, notwithstanding the apparent strengthening of the system's political and economic position. Although the main geographical and systemic contours of the mature American slave regime had emerged—its organization of labor, its instruments of financial exchange, its social and political controls—the system's consolidation actually concealed the seeds of its eventual destruction. By 1831, a new, more aggressively militant abolitionist movement had emerged, inspired by the recent success of antislavery forces in Great Britain and armed with timely support from free black communities in the North. Just before the New Year, James Forten wrote to William Lloyd Garrison offering moral and financial support to his effort to found a new antislavery newspaper. In 1831, just weeks after Ball's final escape from Georgia, a charismatic slave preacher with a millennialist vision of justice, led a seventy-two-hour rebellion that devastated the Virginia Tidewater and evoked terror in the white South for a generation, reviving the long-standing Haitian nightmare.

Located in Virginia's historic southeastern corner roughly eighty miles east of Norfolk, by the 1830s Southampton County made a sharp contrast with the booming Lower South. Its population was almost evenly divided between whites and blacks. The ease with which the conspirators met and plotted the revolt suggests a far more relaxed security regime than Ball had endured in South Carolina and Georgia two decades earlier. The revolt Nat Turner led was also very different from some of those of the preceding generation, such as the one Gabriel had planned just thirty years earlier, or that the rebels at Trois-Rivières had undertaken. Only Turner's original target date, the Fourth of July, suggests anything like a mature political consciousness behind his plot. Otherwise, the military and political objectives of the shifting band of seventy-odd rebels are obscured by Turner's religious rhetoric and symbolism. Unlike Gabriel's, this was not to be a surgical strike aimed at eventual negotiations about political demands, but a spontaneous uprising guided by righteous anger and divine vengeance. Turner's was a revolt driven by otherworldly revelations rather than contemporary political opportunities and prospects on the ground. The rebels' apparent target for capture was not Richmond but a small county seat of 175 people, whose only significance lay in its biblically evocative name, Jerusalem. After seventy-two hours of violence that left fifty-five dead, the rebellion was quelled. Several weeks later Benjamin Phipps thrust his shotgun in Nat Turner's face and forced him from his hiding place, putting an emphatic end to the last mass rebellion against American slavery before the Civil War.

Richard Allen died in March 1831, five months before Nat Turner's terrible swift sword sliced through the tidewater Virginia countryside. During the last year of his life, he had called together the aspiring leaders of northern free black communities to meet and organize for the long resistance he knew lay before them. It was already clear that that resistance must now take a very different path than the violent overthrow of slavery attempted by Gabriel and soon by Nat Turner. The meeting in 1830 was the first of a series of "Negro Conventions" in which blacks would meet, debate, organize, and sometimes fight among themselves. Members of these gatherings were united, however, in their conviction that the truth claims that had justified the formation of the American nation should apply with even greater force to the conditions and aspirations of American slaves and their descendants. Like the rebels in Boston in 1775, or in Guadeloupe in 1793, they seized upon these contradictions of a slaveholding republic to argue the necessity of destroying slavery and accepting former slaves as "citizens and friends."

4

"A NEW BIRTH OF FREEDOM"

The Destruction of Slavery and Reconstruction of Black Life

"lo! The chattel becomes a man."
—Frederick Douglass to William Lloyd Garrison, January 1846

Frederick Douglass was anxious to get home when he boarded the *Cambria*, a British steamer bound for Boston in late April 1847. Just four months earlier his former master, Thomas Auld, had been prevailed upon by intermediaries to renounce all rights to him in exchange for £150, or rather its dollar equivalent (about $1,250). No longer a fugitive, the twenty-nine-year-old Douglass prepared to enter a new stage of his long struggle against slavery, for which this personal manumission would be merely the means and prelude. Likely his mind was so busy laying plans for a new, militant abolitionist newspaper that he would have scarcely bothered to take notice of the racial slight of being once again relegated to steerage, just as he had been on the trip over two years earlier. He had used that shabby treatment to open and focus his attacks on "the American Slave Power," which he held responsible for the insult, but now, so buoyed was he by the enthusiastic reception his speeches had received in Ireland, Scotland, and England, this latest affront merited only an acerbic aside. He returned home knowing firsthand of many Britons' deep hostility to slavery and recognizing how crucially important their sentiments would be to the continuing struggle against it. Neither he nor his fellow abolitionists could have known, of course, the momentous change that was eminent as the nation's sectional crisis wound to its conclusion less than two decades later.

The American sectional crisis over slavery was about to enter a new and dangerous phase. The cultural and institutional fissures between northerners and southerners had peaked even before Douglass left for Britain, as first Presbyterians, then Methodists, and finally Baptists formed regionally separate congregations. While Douglass was abroad, two new slave states, Texas and Florida, had been added to the Union, completing the political geography of the future Confederate States of America. The Mexican-American War, now entering its twelfth month, seemed destined to add more slave states, making it ever more unlikely that the sectional divide could be papered over with yet another political compromise, like those securing the Constitution itself in 1787 and then the admission of Missouri in 1820.

In fact, yet another compromise over slavery's expansion did come to pass in 1850, but it started to unravel scarcely before the ink was dry. Within a decade of Douglass's landing in Boston, American party allegiances would be fractured and reshuffled for the second time in a generation, supporters and opponents of slavery would draw blood in guerrilla-style clashes in Kansas, and the highest court in the land would declare not only that slavery's geographic expansion could not be legally restricted but that black Americans—free as well as slave—had no civil rights that white Americans were obliged to respect. The Supreme Court's decision proved more symbolic than practical, merely hardening a schism that many already deemed "irrepressible."

Ironically, then, as Douglass sailed home, slavery's final destruction was actually far closer than he would have dared imagine, the interval measurable by a child's coming-of-age. His then two-year-old son, Charles Remond, would be a month shy of celebrating his eighteenth birthday when Lincoln proclaimed his intent to abolish slavery in the rebel states. No doubt Douglass's hopes upon his return would have been encouraged if he could have foreseen how imminent the day of Jubilee actually was, but those hopes would have been dashed in equal measure had he known of the reversal of fortunes to follow shortly thereafter. He would live to witness new systems of social and labor controls being fastened onto black Americans during the waning decades of the century, the fruits of a lifetime's struggle seemingly lost.

By any measure Frederick Douglass was an exceptional man, but the main currents of his biography—embracing the roughly seventy years during which slavery was consolidated, destroyed, and reborn in new guises—was hardly unique. Rather, his life's course was, in the main, exemplary of an extraordinary generation of African American leaders. Like Douglass, many of the men and women born just before or shortly after America's second war with Great Britain not only lived to see slavery's immolation in the Civil War fifty years later but also the postwar social and political reconstruction of the nation and its reversal. Some—such as Henry Highland Garnet and William Wells Brown—had also escaped slavery and devoted their lives to the campaign to destroy it, mobilized black Americans to support the Union war effort, and lived to witness the war's bitter aftermath. Many of them had preceded Douglass or would follow in his wake to Britain, bearing as he did personal witness to slavery's systemic evil. Like Douglass, a few of them committed their experiences to writing, in the process finding a voice and together forging a uniquely American literature. Historians might choose to divide the experience of slavery from that of freedom, but these men's lives straddled that historic and experiential divide, as did the collective struggle they would wage to give full meaning to emancipation, to what Lincoln would later call "a new birth of freedom."

Of Bondage and Freedom

Douglass's life in bondage was very different from that of most other slaves, but in one key respect he shared the common lot: he knew well the pain and threat of separation from family and kin. Born and reared in slavery on a farm on Maryland's Eastern Shore, just across the Chesapeake Bay from Charles Ball, Douglass would experience that institution in its many diverse forms—in both urban and plantation settings, as a relatively "free" slave hireling and as utterly degraded chattel. Like Ball, he had lost his mother and siblings to the system's increasingly predatory appetite and had been left in the care of grandparents. He had never known his father, a white man—perhaps his mother's owner—and he had seen his mother only during her rare, furtive visits to his grandmother's cabin. She died when he was seven.

Born in 1772 of a family that traced its roots in Talbot County to early in the previous century, Frederick's maternal grandmother, Betsy Bailey, had enjoyed a relatively stable life compared with what awaited her children and grandchildren. Married to a free man, Isaac Bailey, Betsy had a household that straddled the boundary between slavery and freedom, a boundary that would soon harden. In contrast with her daughter, whose maternal ties to her son were fragile and tenuous, Grandma Betsy's simple log cabin was the spatial and emotional anchor for multiple generations of Bailey kin during Frederick's childhood. By the time she died in 1849, however, Betsy had seen nine children, grandchildren, and great-grandchildren sold away. The relative stability she had known was no more; the slave trader or his lurking presence would henceforth be a dominant fact of slave life.

Douglass's early childhood, therefore, provides another glimpse of the ongoing transformation of slavery in the Upper South during the century's second and third decades, the same changes that had so profoundly shaped Charles Ball's life. In the same year his mother died, Frederick was moved to his master's compound at Wye House, the property of a Tidewater aristocrat Edward Lloyd for whom Frederick's owner, Aaron Anthony, worked as general manager. Lloyd's fortune had been built originally on tobacco, but by Frederick's youth he had already made the switch to wheat. The material value and moral values of Wye House, however, were still thoroughly rooted in the eighteenth-century social order that had produced the great planters of the Chesapeake.

At Wye House, young Frederick had come under the care of Anthony's childless daughter, Lucretia, and her husband, Thomas Auld. When Anthony died in 1826, followed by Lucretia shortly thereafter, Frederick became the property of Auld. Typically, the death of an owner and the subsequent dispersal of his holdings was a catastrophe for slaves, but for the eight-year-old Frederick it was a stroke of good fortune. He was sent to Baltimore to reside with Auld's brother Hugh, a ship's caulker who owned no slaves. Except for a three-year stint back on the Eastern Shore during his mid-teens, Baltimore would be the main site of Douglass's formative experiences. There he learned a trade, was allowed to hire out his time at the docks, lived for a while outside his master's household, socialized and worshipped with free blacks at Baltimore's Zion Methodist Church, learned to read, and dreamed of freedom.

The bulk of Douglass's own narration of his youth, however, focuses on the events that transpired during his brief return as a teenager to the Eastern Shore. Hired out to Edward Covey—yet another former overseer trying to claw his way up the social ladder working hardscrabble land with hired slaves—fifteen-year-old Frederick tasted the bitter humiliation and brutalization common to slave labor that he had otherwise been spared. Covey's sadistic beatings and Douglass's ultimate retaliation provided the core material for the latter's autobiography and stump speeches for years to come. The overarching theme of his story was how resistance rekindles the manhood that slavery, by its very nature, must seek to destroy. In Douglass's telling, he became a man through that resistance and moved inexorably toward his total freedom as a consequence. Two years after he fought Covey to a standstill, Douglass joined five others in an aborted escape attempt. Back in Baltimore four years later, he tried again and succeeded, borrowing or buying a seaman's papers and making his way to freedom in Massachusetts.

As William McFeely, Douglass's most perceptive biographer to date, has noted, there is much more to this story of resistance and escape than Douglass's stripped-down stump narrative lets on. As in so many other narratives of slave flight, the central image is of the psychological transformation of an individual: the heroic slave, finally aroused, casting off his or her chains. Individual heroism there was certainly, but these accounts are incomplete renderings of the complex relations both among slaves and between them and the emerging free black communities. Douglass's confrontation with Covey, for example, was tacitly supported by the "civil disobedience" of slaves who refused to obey Covey's pleas for assistance, even if they stopped short of overtly aiding Douglass. Moreover, Douglass's escape attempt two years later was likely inspired less by his victory over Covey, as he suggests, than by the bonds of comradeship he later forged with other slave hirelings on William Freeland's farm: Handy Caldwell and two brothers, John and Henry Harris. These men were the real models for the heroic slave Douglass sought to become, especially the formidable Henry Harris, for whom Douglass appears to have named his firstborn son, Lewis Henry. Indeed, their fine character may well have saved him from hanging or worse after that first escape attempt went sour. None of them broke under interrogation and, echoing the resolution of Gabriel's conflict with Absalom Johnson a quarter century earlier, their owners' sensitivity to their inherent value clearly played a role in winning their eventual release from the sheriff's custody.

Equally crucial, but more complicated perhaps, were Douglass's relations with free blacks. As with Grandma Betsy and Isaac Bailey, Douglass moved in a world peopled by blacks born free or recently freed. A free black laborer, Sandy Jenkins, who aided him in his initial attempt to escape Covey, gave him a "magic" root that was to shield him from the slave breaker's wrath. For a while Jenkins had been a co-conspirator in Douglass's first, abortive escape attempt, even though he was already a freeman. Douglass's narrative never explains either Jenkins's earlier solidarity with his enslaved co-workers or Douglass's suspicions that it was Jenkins who later exposed the plot to authorities. In any event, this relationship remains emblematic of the complex, multifaceted ties and tensions between free and slave in antebellum America.

Nonetheless, free blacks were crucial enablers for slave fugitives like Douglass. Like the free black sailor from Philadelphia whom Charles Ball met in the Washington Navy Yard, freemen modeled liberty and often encouraged slaves to escape. Douglass's second, successful escape was probably inspired by similar encounters as he moved and socialized with Baltimore's free community, and it certainly would not have been possible without their aid. First among his helpmates—and indicative of the intimacy of his social relations with that free community—was Anna Murray, Douglass's future wife. An illiterate domestic servant and daughter of parents who migrated to Baltimore after their manumission, Anna probably met Frederick in a church that, much like Richard Allen's Bethel, embraced both slaves and free folk in its congregation. She encouraged Frederick to study the violin, which suggests her support of his compelling ambition to remake himself. Undoubtedly she contributed both financial and emotional support to his escape—some of the money to purchase forged free papers and for train and ferry fares perhaps; a place to hide his sailor's disguise and supplies for the trip probably; money for her own fare to New York certainly. His indebtedness to her is clear, even if his love is not. As soon as he reached New York, he sent for Anna and they were married. The emotional content of their relationship remains opaque, however; on such matters, Douglass's narrative is silent.

The historical record is silent, too, about the tensions that logic suggests must have followed the insertion of slave fugitives into these already fragile free black communities. Their succor was obviously crucial to the newcomers, most of whom could not make it as far as the relative safety of Massachusetts or the security of British Canada. At the same time, it could not have gone unnoticed that the fugitives in their midst brought greater scrutiny and danger, sometimes ensnaring the legally free in the slavers' net as well as the fugitives. New York, for example, was infamous for unscrupulous kidnappers on the lookout for unattached blacks to seize and sell south. Such work depended also on black interlocutors and spies who assisted the kidnappers in spotting their prey. During his own flight, warned of such predators, Douglass was wary of asking for directions from strangers, black or white.

Free blacks found themselves lumped with slaves also in the rhetorical counterattack by slavery's defenders. The more slaveholding came under attack, the more southern slaveholders defended it as the "natural" status for all blacks. Slavery was the southerner's way of life, and slaves were part of their extended patriarchal families, a child race for whom they gave nurture and support in exchange for their labor. By wrapping their admittedly "peculiar institution" in a reassuring domesticity, they made black character the rationale for slavery's peculiarities, ultimately grounding the institution's defense in the assertion that *all* blacks were unfit to live free. To support their case, they gathered and published statistics on the deplorable living conditions and the allegedly degraded social character of northern free black communities.

Consequently, northern free blacks were put in the position of fighting on two fronts: first, to condemn slavery, and second, to mobilize their communities behind associations and movements aimed at self-help and reform, including education, welfare assistance, temperance, and moral reform. The self-help agenda was greatly advanced by the flowering of newspapers, books, and national conventions of black leaders who met with increasing regularity through the two decades leading up to the Civil War. Unwittingly, by moralizing and politicizing the social ties linking free black and slave communities, southern counterattacks against abolitionism both stimulated the mobilization of northern black communities and underscored enduring tensions between freemen and slaves, which was sometimes evident even in African American protests against slavery. At a convention in Buffalo, New York, in August 1843, for example, Henry Highland Garnet made a speech calling on all slaves to resist their bondage. The speech was controversial at the time because of its open call for violent resistance at a moment when the abolition movement was still dominated by the principles of moral suasion and nonviolence promoted by William Lloyd Garrison. Douglass was present at that meeting and is reputed to have made a fierce response to Garnet's call to arms, leading to its narrow defeat by the convention. We have no record of the specific arguments Douglass made, but one can only wonder whether he pointed out how much Garnet's address impugned the courage and manhood of the slave. Echoing Rousseau, Garnet imperiously declared that slaves had nothing to lose but their chains, which in effect blamed the victim for his victimization. Douglass—having been in bondage much more recently than Garnet, and as a full-grown man rather than a child—should have known better. One hopes Douglass said so.

In many ways, however, Garnet's address merely echoed a dominant theme running through abolitionist propaganda generally. The abolitionists had to strip away the mythology southern defenders had woven around slavery, exposing it instead as the utter degradation of human beings. Far from the benign domesticity southerners touted, slavery was an abomination, the destroyer of normal domesticity, and incompatible with basic human values and relationships. It corrupted the moral character of the slave as much as it demeaned his body. It robbed slaves not simply of the fruits of their labor but, more damningly, of their manhood and woman-

The horribly scarred back of this Louisiana slave was discovered during his medical examination upon enlisting in the U.S. Colored Troop.

hood. These charges formed the abolitionist's most compelling lines of attack against slavery, perhaps because they resonated with the general anxieties of northern white people, themselves confronting an encroaching capitalist social order that disrupted traditional domestic relations.

Though highly effective, the abolitionists' fiery sword was also double-edged, leaving them with an intractable dilemma. Portraying slavery as an inhuman travesty left slaves themselves looking something less than human, which might ultimately prove counterproductive. Slaves might be objects of pity, surely, but not candidates for admission to the body politic. Unmanned men and deflowered women could command sympathy but not empathy, which implies imagining oneself in the other's place. For black abolitionists the dilemma was especially poignant. Such negative images of the so-called slavish personality constituted an enduring experiential barrier between slave and free communities that would be manifested for many years after emancipation.

Douglass's fabled confrontation with Covey modeled one solution to the dilemma: the moral transformation achieved through "manly" resistance could be redemptive. In truth, however, it was not the endangered male who most aroused revulsion against slavery, but the degradation of womanly virtue. A half-naked woman bleeding under the driver's lash; a woman, often with child, on the auction block; a woman raped—these were the most searing and enduring images of slavery's brutality. Indeed, these images lay at the core of the male's emasculation as well, for men unable to defend their women and children were not really men. The redemption of lost womanhood would be far more complicated than the resistance of males, and far more fraught with moral pitfalls.

That of Which "no words can speak"

On January 29, 1856, less than ten years after Douglass returned from Britain, the *Cincinnati Daily Gazette* ran a story about what it called "great excitement" in the city the previous day, "in consequences of the arrest of a party of slaves, and the murder of her child by a slave mother, while officers were in the act of making the arrest." In what must have been a complexly organized mass escape from three different properties, seventeen men, women, and children had crossed the frozen river from Kentucky.

Their owners and a deputy U.S. marshal tracked them to an abandoned house in Cincinnati and attempted to serve federal arrest warrants as authorized by the recently passed Fugitive Slave Act of 1850. When they broke into the house, however, the slaves put up a fierce resistance, even shooting off two of the marshal's fingers. In fact, all of the slaves except members of one multigenerational family managed to escape. Apparently, "old Simon and his wife, and young Simon and his wife and [their] four children . . . , the oldest near six years and the youngest a babe of about nine months" were either too elderly or too young to outrun the posse. Knowing this, they had resolved apparently to die rather than return to slavery, because when the slave catchers finally broke into the room, they found a horrific scene. One of the children lay bleeding on the floor, its head almost entirely cut off. The oldest had "a gash about four inches long," while another had suffered "a wound on the head."

Although the headline of the story read "Slave Mother Murders Her Child," it is clear that Margaret Garner had her husband's and perhaps the grandparents' assistance in the execution of this deed. This was not a spontaneous act but a deliberate family decision; all of them supported or took a hand in the bloody deed that day. Later, as Margaret stood on the deck of the riverboat that would carry what was left of her family back to slavery, she quietly released her grip on the baby who had survived, letting it slide into depths of the water below.

The abolitionist press quickly picked up this story and made it the centerpiece of its ongoing attack on slavery, particularly the operation of the Fugitive Slave Act, which implicated northerners in slavery's guilt. Here, finally, was the female counterpart of the heroic male slave resister. Abolitionist Lucy Stone, who interviewed Margaret Garner in her jail cell, provided one of the most dramatic contemporaneous renditions of how to think about what she had done.

> When I saw that poor fugitive, took her toil-hardened hand in mine, and read in her face deep suffering and an ardent longing for freedom, I could not help bid her be of good cheer. I told her that a thousand hearts were aching for her, and that they were glad one child of hers was safe with the angels. Her only reply was a look of deep despair, of anguish such as no words can speak. I thought the spirit she manifested was the same with that of our ancestors

to whom we had erected the monument at Bunker Hill—the spirit
that would rather let us all go back to God than back to slavery . . .
Rather than give her little daughter to that life, she killed it. If in
her deep maternal love she felt the impulse to send her child back
to God, to save it from coming woe, who shall say she had no right
to do so?

The gentle reader might recoil in horror from Margaret's act, Stone
lectures, but her impulse was thoroughly human, one that whites surely
must share. Certainly, she herself would "with my own teeth . . . tear open
my veins and let the earth drink my blood, rather than to wear the chains
of slavery." What Margaret Garner had done, therefore, was at once
heroic—like the American patriots memorialized at Bunker Hill—and
natural, as natural as a mother's love.

Framed this way, the radical abolitionists' imagery of the slave's moral
choice is chilling. Reduced to its essence, however, it reflects the continuing difficulty—of historians and laypeople alike—of comprehending
the slave experience. Hovering over all is Henry Highland Garnet's question: Why do they not resist? Even to the point of death, of oneself and
one's loved ones, resist! Historians have gone to great lengths to offer
answers to this question, but their analyses almost always come down
to an effort to explain, or explain away, the mysteries of the individual
relations between masters and slaves. Slaves either internalized somehow
the master's justifications for their bondage, or they stood ready to cut his
throat at the first opportunity. Neither explanation has proved entirely
satisfactory.

Part of the difficulty is that neither slaves nor masters faced each
other merely as individuals. Both were enmeshed in larger communities
that mediated their thoughts and actions. First, it was not some mysterious psychic power of the master that held the slave in check, but a larger
community of slaveholders and the mobilization of their collective power.
As Charles Ball knew very well, the slave patrols were a practical and
highly effective manifestation of that power. Behind them lay the state
militias and, ultimately, the military and institutional powers of the nation, which in essence the Fugitive Slave Law of 1850 sought to tap. But
there were yet more subtle ways in which a region organized to defend slavery posed formidable obstacles to effective slave resistance. As historian

Eugene Genovese has shown, southern law disciplined not only the slave but also the master. Covering every detail from whether and how manumissions might transpire to standards of diet, clothing, and punishment, by the 1840s, southern law mobilized and rationalized a social order so as to render any alternative to black bondage inconceivable—to whites as well as blacks. It is not an accident that the lively southern debates about and experiments with emancipation that transpired in the early postrevolutionary years had ceased by the antebellum era. Moreover, the lesson of the American Revolution for any who paid attention was that the southern defense of slavery might crack with the appearance of internal class fissures or when attacked militarily from without, or both. In due course that lesson would be driven home once more.

Historians have also been too slow to reckon the broader material interest in slavery among the larger white population, many of whom were financially dependent on slave property even if they did not own any. The hiring of enslaved labor—a growing and extensive practice throughout the antebellum period—helped rationalize and stabilize the system as a whole by offering a profitable outlet for surplus productive capacity. It satisfied the labor needs of non-slaveholders, offering them an efficient allocation of labor and capital resources. With little or no fixed capital investment they could increase production. Moreover, much as the twenty-first-century pensioners' interests are linked to capital markets, many nineteenth-century southerners' economic interests were linked to slave markets. Most whites could not stand aside, therefore, entirely disinterested in the defense of the institution. Even those who were disinterested financially might find the racial ordering that slavery anchored a comforting, taken-for-granted part of their everyday lives.

For the slaves, on the other hand, the negotiation of everyday life was more like moving through a chaotic maze in which the very integrity of one's psychic being was in constant danger of being smashed to pieces. One was ever vulnerable to dispossession—of goods, of children, even of oneself. Being chattel property subject to the normal laws of commerce, slaves could be sold for a profit or to cover a debt, used as collateral for loans, and put up as a wager in a game of cards or a horse race. With the intensification of slave production, its geographical expansion after the War of 1812, and the soaring slave prices that followed, the sense of menace and chaos deepened.

By our best estimates, more than 1 million slaves were moved from one southern region to another between 1820 and 1860, and well over half to two thirds of them were sold to slave traders. More than a quarter of these transactions, 285,000, occurred during the 1830s alone, which meant that a community of 100 slaves would lose 17 of its members within a ten-year period. Indeed, the most apt standard against which to measure the human losses suffered by some border-state slave communities may be the European communities denuded over a comparable thirty-year period by two world wars in the first half of the twentieth century. By 1860, Maryland had lost half its slave population to such interregional transfers; Kentucky and western Virginia, one third. Altogether an Appalachian region framed by the mountains and upcountry of seven southern states sent as many as 300,000 slaves to plantations in the Deep South, nearly two thirds of them children separated from their parents.

Parts of the upcountry fell on the demand side of the interregional equation as well. Once the Cherokee and Creeks had been completely removed from the upland areas of the Southeast, those lands were also opened to settlement by cotton planters and the forced migration of slaves to work them. As Charles Ball's experience illustrates, whether slaves were moved as individuals or with family members, the lives and social relations they had known theretofore were disrupted or put at risk. In short, they could be, and often were, deprived of all that other human beings held dear: family life, community life, life itself. All they valued was at risk in ways no other laborers had to endure or fear.

And yet it is quite clear that out of this disorder and threat arose reasonably coherent social organizations and relationships. In sharp rejoinder to Garnet's injunction, slaves did indeed have more to lose than their chains, did indeed feel that life was worth living. It could hardly have been otherwise. From the master's perspective, absolute chaos was surely not conducive to productive work getting done. From the slave's, the fashioning of some kind of social order of their own was but a rational response to the ever-present threat of disruption to their lives. Lawrence Levine's magnificent study of slave folklore suggests some of the motivations at work. In sharp contrast to the innocuous tales of animal tricksters their stories are often mistaken for, the slaves' folktales stared point-blank at the moral and social chaos at the core of their existence. These were not simple moralizing tales of how the weak might triumph over the strong, but reflections of and on the lived experience slaves knew: a dog-eat-dog world in which morality had little purchase. With these oral portraits—"magical realism" before there was a term for it—slaves taught their children what to expect and how to survive.

If the master confronted the slave from the safety of a mobilized white political community, therefore, the slaves stared back from slave quarters that were also mobilized, however brutalized and ravaged by the slave trade and arbitrary rule. The ideal slave, that ultimate tool, standing alone before his or her master stripped of relations to significant others, was largely a figment of slaveholders' (and a few historians') imaginations. Slaves cared about and for one another, valued relationships with other slaves above those with their owners, felt bound to and responsible for one another in ways that would become even more evident once the yoke of slavery was lifted. Even the unfortunates sold south managed to quickly integrate themselves into new communities, while those they left behind typically found support in the networks of intergenerational kin, even fictive kin, that remained. However difficult it has been to penetrate the human relations within the slave quarters, therefore, it is now clear that family and community shaped slaves' productive as well as their emotional lives. Many slaves—perhaps most—experienced these kin relations within nuclear families, and in some of these the parents enjoyed relatively stable marital ties that endured for decades.

On the other hand, there is also evidence that thousands of other slaves lived in nonnuclear households where child rearing fell largely on the mother, sometimes with the assistance of other kinspeople. For example, historian Wilma Dunaway suggests that two parents living with their children accurately described only one fifth of the households in the Appalachian states. Thus, four out of five households in the geographical heart of the South resembled the shattered, matriarchal families for which slavery has been long condemned. These disparate portraits—nuclear families and broken families—likely reflect the regional and temporal variations within American slavery rather than direct factual contradictions. First, there was a sharp schism in the South's political economy that put the Southeast and Southwest at opposite ends of an economic seesaw. In the economically booming Lower South, new planters arrived to establish large cotton and sugar plantations on fertile delta lands, while much of the Upper South endured relative decline as many planters shifted from tobacco, whose price was depressed for most of the period, to grain crops, which could be better worked with free wage labor or a mixture of hired slaves and free workers. And even those who stuck with tobacco found it prudent to take advantage of the high prices their excess slaves could fetch in the New Orleans slave markets. In some sense, the Upper South's primary crop became the slaves themselves.

In the Virginia Piedmont and the Appalachian upcountry, conversely, the units of production tended to be small, even where land and slave ownership were concentrated, and thus the slaves' opportunities to establish and sustain co-residential, nuclear families were severely limited. The reasons are fairly obvious: the smaller the co-resident population, the less likely that there would be a gender balance within the same age cohorts, notably the marriageable cohort, and the more devastating the impact of ordinary plantation operations, such as slave sales or hiring out. The fact that it was also men and women of marriageable age who were most likely to be sold or hired out exacerbated the imbalance. By contrast, on large plantations worked by scores of slaves, as one often found in the Carolina and Georgia lowlands, the Mississippi and Louisiana delta, and sometimes even in the Virginia Tidewater, not only were mothers and fathers able to forge enduring marriages, but even when such nuclear bonds were broken, new ones could be found. Most of the slaves who were unable to establish enduring marital relations were incorporated nonetheless into households with other blood relatives. This pattern held true on many small properties as well. Although discounting the importance of nuclear, two-parent families in Virginia, for example, historian Brenda Stevenson describes the typical slave child as living with its mother, siblings, and often an extended, intergenerational community of kinfolk.

Despite all this, slaves still valued familial relations even where they could not keep their households intact or conform to prevailing bourgeois ideals of normal domesticity. Some of their letters to or inquiries about one another have survived in the papers of their masters or been marooned among the documents swept up by the government's Civil War bureaucracy. "Send me a lock of the children's hair," pleaded a father separated from his family. "Oh! My Dear children how I do want to see you," pined another. Just as often, however, the messages embraced not simply spouses and children but a broader network of kin and community left behind. "Give my love to all at home," begged a man involuntarily removed with the owner's family to a refuge in the Deep South. Thus the relationships invoked here were not limited to what most of their contemporaries, and many of their descendants, might recognize as family. Perhaps a legacy of their African ancestors, perhaps a response to conditions in America, perhaps a bit of both, the valorization of kinship was the fundamental core of all these relationships. And whether that kinship was defined by blood or marriage, or was simply fictive, it constituted an enduring resource for meeting life's challenges. Much as Equiano and his shipmates responded to the ordeal of the slave ship, therefore, American slaves created a space from which to meet and resist their masters' demands.

Indeed, evidence of slaves' reliance on kin relations to lend order to their disordered world can be found even in the part of their lives most controlled by their masters: their work. In areas such as the South Carolina and Georgia low country, where the task system prevailed, most of the responsibility for organizing and allocating the work and its product fell to the slaves themselves, and it appears that kinship was a principal basis for assigning tasks and distributing rations, garden plots, and other perks. Out of slavery's chaos, then, an oppressed people forged tools with which to fashion liveable lives, tools that could be turned into not only weapons against slavery but resources with which to rebuild their lives in freedom. When sectional hostilities finally erupted into violent confrontation, southern slaves, to almost everyone's surprise, stood ready to make good Garnet's call for "manly" resistance.

The War: The Fires of Jubilee

It is only retrospectively that historians make sense of war, all too neatly arraying its chaotic movements into straight lines, and recasting with seeming ease its disparate motives and fractured sequences of time as clear causes and effects. Ordinary folk experience war as all twists and turns and utter confusion. War came to slave quarters as the distant rumble of cannon, as the sudden appearance of ravenous Union or Confederate foragers pillaging their meager supplies, as confused messages that the white folks' war was to set them free or that it had nothing to do with them. As is often the case on the battlefront, at any given moment one could not be certain who was friend or foe. Slaves such as Nancy Johnson and her husband in Liberty County, Georgia, risked their lives to hide and feed stranded Union soldiers, and later gave similar succor to Confederate deserters. Slaves frequently supplied Union troops with vital information; others hid the master's silver and protected the mistress from harm. One thing they all knew, however, as their grandparents had learned in the Revolutionary War era: such conflicts could open opportunities to better their situation or to escape their bondage. It was simply a matter of watching and waiting.

Slaves residing in the Virginia Tidewater did not have to wait too long. Within days of the firing on Fort Sumter, the Union reinforced its garrison at Fortress Monroe, situated at the mouth of the Chesapeake Bay less than thirty miles from colonial Jamestown. Relatively insignificant militarily, the site soon became a veritable thorn in the belly of the rebellion politically and a source of disquiet for the Union. On the twenty-fourth of May, just over a month after the war began, Sheppard Mallory, Frank Baker, and James Townsend ran away from their putative owner, Colonel Charles Mallory, and made their way to the fortress, where they asked for refuge. It was a scene that would be repeated at every Union beachhead thereafter, and indeed it might well have happened even earlier had Union policy toward slaves been clearer. Slaves could not entirely discount their owners' warnings that the Yankees were not liberators but would sell them to the West Indies at the first opportunity. Indeed, charges surfaced later that a few Union soldiers did in fact make tidy sums moonlighting as slave catchers for grateful Tidewater slave owners. Slaves could not have been reassured either to learn that the commanding officer at Fortress Monroe was none other than General Benjamin Butler, then infamous among abolitionists for having vowed, while marching his troops through Maryland a few weeks earlier, that he would put down any slave insurrection that the war's disruption might inspire—a vow soon repeated by at least two other generals. There is no reason to think that the slaves' legendary systems of communication were any less efficient at that time than they had been earlier. Thus they might also have learned that Butler, a Democrat, had supported Jefferson Davis for the party's presidential nomination in 1860 and had voted in the November elections for John Breckinridge, the South's favorite candidate. Nor would they have been reassured to know that Butler's convictions were entirely consistent with the policies then being loudly proclaimed by the Lincoln administration: to put down the Confederate insurrection, not to interfere with slavery.

War can alter the strongest ideological convictions and intentions, however. Once in the field, Butler soon recognized the absurdity of protecting slave property. His interview with the three fugitives Mallory, Baker, and Townsend revealed that they had fled Colonel Charles Mallory because he was preparing to join his regiment in North Carolina and intended to take them with him. Butler also knew that the Confederates were organizing slaves to build fortifications against a possible Union assault. Putting down the South's insurrection clearly required some interference with slavery. Rather than returning the three fugitives to Mallory, therefore, Butler decided to put them to work for the Union. By July, Butler had coined a discursive framework for depriving the enemy of slave labor while avoiding the appearance of emancipatory intent: he called the seized slaves "contraband," thus classifying them with mules, guns, and other captured war materiel. The name stuck, to fugitive and slave alike, throughout the war.

A contemporary photograph of fugitive slaves seeking refuge within Union Army lines.

Although Butler's contraband policy was motivated by military expediency, it could not long be confined to that politically safe terrain. The able-bodied males he seized were attached to families and dependents, and these women and children—though hardly qualifying as material instruments of the southern war machine—eventually came under the Union Army's protective umbrella as well. The wives and children that male fugitives left behind were often brutally mistreated by planters for whom they were now a liability—more mouths to feed with fewer male hands to raise the crops. Physically abused and driven from home, so many wives followed their menfolk to the Union encampments that one exasperated officer in Missouri demanded of his superiors, "What are we to do with the women and children?" Several more years would pass before Congress provided a coherent policy response to the officer's question, by summarily freeing the families of enlisted freedmen. Meanwhile their presence simply widened the breach that the "contraband" gambit had rent in the slave regime.

Six months after authoring the initial contraband policy, General Butler was in New Orleans organizing the military occupation following the Union naval victory there. Although he repeated his earlier mistake of trying to placate white southerners at first, by the end of the year he had reverted to the policy of deploying the South's human and material resources against it. By then it was the southerners' turn to revile the erstwhile southern sympathizer as "beast Butler."

Meanwhile, the Lincoln administration had seized on Butler's formula, writing it into law, in August 1861, as the First Confiscation Act, which declared forfeit any ostensible owner's claim to a slave "employed in hostile service against the Government of the United States," while maintaining a studied silence on the ex-slave's future status. The mutation of the government's policy on emancipation tracked the generals', though laggardly, as pressure built for more aggressive action against the slave labor system. As Frederick Douglass had long insisted, to fight the rebellion without freeing the slaves was tantamount to fighting with one hand tied behind your back. Eventually Lincoln would also adopt that view and urge passage of a Second Confiscation Act, in August 1862. In place of the original legal formula—focused on slaves used in aid of rebellion—the new law freed the slaves of disloyal owners, regardless of whether they had been deployed as military laborers. In the meantime, Congress had abolished slavery in the nation's capital and the territories and amended the articles of war to make it a court martial offense for Union soldiers to return fugitive slaves to their owners. A few weeks before the Second Confiscation Act was passed, Lincoln informed his cabinet of his decision to issue a preliminary proclamation of emancipation, which would apply to all slaves residing in areas still in rebellion on January 1, 1863.

The road to this policy shift was littered with political and strategic barriers that were for Lincoln far more compelling than the moral injustice of slavery. During the presidential campaign, the Republican Party had been careful to embrace opposition to the further expansion of slavery while keeping its distance from the slaves themselves. The outbreak of hostilities only exacerbated that disposition, at least initially. A war against slavery could not expect to garner broad support among a northern population that had just given 46 percent of their votes to Lincoln's opponents. Such a policy, moreover, was certain to send four slaveholding border states (Maryland, Delaware, Kentucky, and Missouri) and the antisecessionist counties of western Virginia into alliance with the Confederacy. The geographic region controlled by these loyal slaveholders was the linchpin of Lincoln's war strategy, constituting the veritable "breadbasket" of the South, and embracing the bulk of its metals, minerals, mules, and other war-related materiel. If the Union was to prevail in this fight, he reasoned, it must deprive the Confederacy of these resources.

The necessity of depriving the South of the kind of foreign support that had been so decisive in the nation's own bid for independence eighty years earlier pressured Union war policy from the opposite direction, a pressure likely to strengthen the longer the war dragged on. As long as Lincoln insisted that slavery was *not* an issue in the conflict, Britain and France could flirt with the idea of lending covert if not open support to the Confederacy. Cutting the upstart North American power down to size was not an unwelcome prospect in many European capitals. Having recently freed their own colonial slaves, however, and with significant sectors of their citizens strongly committed to its abolition in America, British policymakers in particular were not inclined to support a war to preserve American slavery.

It took fifteen months of war to frame Lincoln's policy choices so clearly, however. Meanwhile, the actions and initiatives of the slaves themselves, who embodied what Lincoln later famously summed up as the "mere friction and abrasion," "the mere incidents of war," steadily undermined the Union's preferred policy of neutrality on the slavery question. The three slaves who had presented themselves to Butler in the spring of 1861 swelled to nine hundred two months later and reached three thousand by the end of the following year. Every beachhead, every incursion into Confederate territory thereafter brought the same result, until the total numbers of "contraband" reached the tens of thousands. Altogether, it was in effect, as W.E.B. Du Bois perceptively labeled it, "a general strike." And as that designation suggests, its impact went beyond even the specific slaves who fled their plantations. The tremors arced throughout the entire social order that lived on the myth of the slave master's personal and absolute authority.

Before the end of the first full year of war, naval incursions along the South Carolina coast and a major victory at New Orleans brought tens of thousands more slaves, together with the plantations on which they had labored, under Union military control. Although the freed slaves were still called contraband, Butler's discursive sleight of hand soon outlived its usefulness, since neither military labor nor relief in refugee camps was an adequate solution any longer to the problems they posed. However unwelcome and untimely for the Lincoln administration, the urgency of those problems—the need to provide for their subsistence, to deploy their labor, and to order their living arrangements—reopened the issue of their immediate status and broached the question of their postwar fate.

Meanwhile, the freed slaves were witnesses to unprecedented fissures opening up in the systems of governance that had once dominated them. On November 7, 1861, U.S. naval forces sailed into Port Royal Sound, opening the Sea Islands off the South Carolina and Georgia coasts to Union occupation, forcing the planters there to flee to the mainland and leave behind most of their slaves, who had refused to accompany them. This left the Union government with the problem of fashioning an alternative labor and social regime for the former slaves of "Fugitive Rebels," as one Union officer impishly described them. By contrast, Louisiana planters did not abandon their slaves and plantations when the navy captured New Orleans two months later. Consequently, military authorities there were forced to mediate slave-master relations, which had the unintended effect of undermining those relations. In both places, therefore, traditional systems of slave production unraveled.

Since they had not been employed in support of the rebellion, neither the abandoned slaves at Port Royal nor those under occupation in Louisiana conformed technically to the criteria of Butler's contraband rule and the Confiscation Act that legalized it. Union boots on the ground, however, transformed the conditions of possibility for the management of slave labor. Given a federal policy rapidly morphing from neutrality to hostility toward the slave regime, officers in the field improvised solutions to problems they confronted daily. In August 1862, General Alfred H. Terry wrote his superiors from Fort Pulaski in Georgia, noting that by the terms of recent amendments to the articles of war, the army could not return fugitives to their masters. "Fugitive" in this case must also include, he surmised, slaves who remained on a given plantation but whom the master could not command to "render him obedience and service." As far as Terry was concerned, such a slave had effectively "escaped." Since Terry also forbade the use of violence against slaves within his jurisdiction, threatening to remove abused slaves from their "master's custody and control," the planters were deprived of their traditional means of sustaining their authority. Perhaps inadvertently, therefore, Terry exposed the true basis of the master's authority: not affection, as the master claimed, nor the internalized obedience that some historians posit, but a monopoly of violence. All the rest was mystification and rubbish.

The question of what might replace the sanctions of the whip pressed upon northern occupation forces, too. In the Sea Islands the reorganization of production on the abandoned plantations presented an early opportunity to test the former slaves' adaptability to the wage labor system many northerners expected to replace slavery. Within four months of the beginning of the occupation, plantation managers, missionaries, and teachers were sent to South Carolina as part of a collaborative effort by the federal government and private groups to restore cotton production and to tutor former slaves to live as free wage workers. Among this band of reformers intent on a root-and-branch reformation of the slave South was James Forten's granddaughter, Charlotte, whose personal diary records the tensions involved when northern bourgeois expectations and preconceptions encountered a people shaped by years of bondage. The northern reformers quickly discovered that their charges had minds of their own. Their self-consciously experimental mission to reshape the slave mentality was itself reshaped by men and women determined to make freedom meaningful in terms they

were familiar with; they thereby reframed the postwar labor problem in unexpected ways.

Slaves *were* indeed capable of adapting to wage labor, but they much
preferred to work for themselves on their own land. This was especially
true in the Carolina and Georgia lowlands, where labor had long been
organized by tasks, allowing slaves to work independently and to accumulate substantial property. For example, in Liberty County, Georgia, Samuel Elliott's father had acquired twenty head of cattle, seventy hogs, and
an extensive stock of poultry, which he left to his children upon his death.
Samuel went to war briefly as a servant to his master; he returned only to
see his inheritance confiscated, first by the Confederates and then by the
Yankee soldiers who arrived with General Sherman. Indeed, the reticence
of Sea Island slaves such as Elliott to flee as the fighting drew closer was
clearly influenced by their material investment in the plantations on which
they labored. When they did flee, they often took their possessions with
them, lining the riverbanks with their animals and household goods. More
was at stake than material goods, however. Slaves saw clearly that freedom had little meaning without property, which had given them a measure of independence even within slavery. The meaning, even the reality
of their liberation from slavery, therefore, depended on the economic and
moral independence that landownership seemed to assure them.

The tensions between the ex-slaves' aspirations for land and the North's
anxiety to sustain southern productivity evolved differently in the western
theater. Midway through the war, General Ulysses S. Grant captured Vicksburg, which cut the Confederacy in two and brought hundreds of plantations and thousands of slaves along the Mississippi River under Union
control. Many of the slave owners resident in these areas took refuge in
Texas, taking approximately 150,000 slaves with them. The federal government seized their plantations and leased them and their remaining laborers to private northern entrepreneurs. In some cases, however, they arrived
to find that the abandoned slaves had themselves taken charge of the
production process. The most famous instance of this were the properties
of Jefferson Davis and his brother Joseph, located some twenty-five miles
south of Vicksburg and known as Davis Bend. Joseph Davis had evacuated the property in the summer of 1862, leaving the blacks in control. In
the absence of their fugitive master, Davis's slaves organized a farming
collective and took care of themselves.

In Louisiana, where plantations remained under planter control, both Union policy and slave initiatives evolved very differently. For its part, the military sometimes acted to reinforce the slave masters' authority and sometimes to undermine it. Many slaves, on the other hand, seized upon the occupation as an opportunity to escape, challenging federal authorities and their masters, both of whom treated them as "outlaws." Aided by a swampy terrain that provided ample hiding places, such "outlawry" had long been among the slaves' repertoire of responses to Louisiana's plantation regime. Indeed, sometimes whole camps of runaways banded together, such as those who joined Octave Johnson near New Orleans. Burning cypress leaves to keep off the mosquitoes, and with the bloodhounds of a professional slave catcher baying in the distance, these men and women managed to stay at liberty for a year and a half. The war in southern Louisiana offered them a final escape route; Johnson made his way to Union forces at Camp Parapet, where he enlisted in the Corps d'Afrique. He and his companions were already experienced adversaries of the slave regime, therefore, even before the first shots were fired. The presence of federal troops, though sometimes hostile to their actions, encouraged defiance even among slaves who stayed put. Sometimes they seized control of the work process, ignoring the directions of their overseers and deciding what to plant—usually their vegetable gardens rather than sugar or cotton—as well as when and where. Sometimes they drove off the whites and seized control of the plantations altogether.

Oftentimes the threat to the slave system of production came from an even more unexpected source, the Confederacy itself. The Confederate military's need for slave labor forced it to impress able-bodied plantation hands. This unprecedented interposition of state authority confounded the notion of the master's ostensibly absolute power, as did the military camp experiences of the impressed slaves. Slave owners regularly complained that their allegedly docile laborers returned from military service prone to disobedience and presumptuousness.

All across the Confederacy and often well beyond the echo of Union cannon, therefore, masters were forced to adjust to the exigencies of war. Their authority undermined by Union advances on one side and Confederate requisitions on the other, many masters were forced to negotiate deals with their slaves to keep them at work. Reticent to concede too much, some planters offered harvest time "gifts," but their slaves generally refused to be satisfied by the mere perquisites of the old regime. Soon negotiations turned variously to a portion of the crop, the elimination of the overseer, a shorter workday, wages or payments in kind, and even manumission at some future date. Thus the essence of the master-slave relationship dissolved: labor was compensated rather than simply coerced, and its terms were negotiated rather than commanded. As in any wage-labor relationship, the matter came down to control of the means of production: land, tools, and seed. If the master remained on the plantation and still controlled access to those resources, he had a superior position from which to bargain, and the "slave" was forced to deal; if he didn't, the slave's dependence was over and he went to work for himself.

Mackley Woods from Hardaman County, Tennessee, worked for William Woods for twenty years. When Union forces seized nearby Bolivar, there was a general exodus of black laborers. Woods negotiated a deal with Mackley and several other of his slaves, promising them *"one fourth* of the crop that we would raise while we stayed with him," together with clothing and food and doctor's bills. Later Woods reneged on the deal, running off with the cotton and fourteen slaves, including three of Mackley's children. Meanwhile, some rebel planters in middle Tennessee turned their plantations over to the slaves to manage in their absence, with the understanding that they could claim the product of their labor. Other planters in occupied west Tennessee, having lost control of their slaves completely, sought to have them enlisted in the Union Army, even bribing recruiters to take them.

Slave owners looked on in amazement, moreover, as their government's efforts to prosecute the war undermined the very rationale for the conflict. A Confederate assistant secretary of war justified impressments of slave labor by comparing the ship of state to a distressed ship at sea. Much as a captain has a right to throw his cargo overboard to save his ship, he patiently explained to an officer, military necessity compels the forcible requisition of plantation supplies, including laborers, however devastating it might be for a particular property. For the planters, this was hardly a reassuring analogy. Certainly it was not unreasonable of slaveholders to assume that the whole raison d'être of the war was to save, not destroy, their way of life. Nonetheless, the government's actions early in the war presaged what was to come. In the spring of 1865, confronting the inexorable encroachment of Grant in northern Virginia, and with Sherman's rapid approach from the south, the Confederate Congress in Richmond

authorized the recruitment of slave soldiers. Although the legislation conditioned their recruitment on the master's approval and insisted that the
relation between master and slave would not be affected, the army's order
of implementation recognized that a slave soldier must be granted "the
rights of [a] freedman." It was a stunning reversal of the very justification
for the war. But it hardly mattered. Less than a month later, Lee surrendered at Appomattox.

A New Order: Reconstructing a Nation and a People

Just twelve months after Lincoln proclaimed the emancipation of slaves
in the rebel states and more than a year before General Lee's surrender,
Frederick Douglass—with optimism that his audience probably found
stunning—sought to shift attention from the ongoing war to the task of
reconstructing the nation. A group of women abolitionists had begun preparing the public for that next step by sponsoring a series of lectures at
New York City's Cooper Institute aimed at mobilizing support for a thirteenth amendment to the Constitution that they hoped would make slavery's abolition complete and irreversible. Douglass's gaze, however, was
focused on a yet-more-distant task: the social transformations necessary to
make black freedom real. First, the nation needed to recognize that the old
Union was dead, he declared, that they were no longer "fighting for the
dead past, but for the living present and the glorious future." The country
had to understand that that future would require "a new order of social and
political relations among the whole people." Slaves must not only be freed
but made citizens, armed to defend their new status through access to the
political process on an equal basis with whites. Black men must vote.

Like the abolition of slavery, the mandate to reconstruct the nation that
Douglass laid before his audience that winter evening would only emerge by
fits and starts over the next three years. Although the South was now clearly
on the defensive, the hammer blows of Sherman's capture of Atlanta and
decisive March to the Sea were still almost a year away. Only after that
victory—coupled with Lincoln's reelection a week earlier, which closed the
door on Democratic schemes for a compromised peace—did Congress begin in earnest to craft an abolition amendment. Union control of Louisiana
had forced the Lincoln administration to experiment some months earlier

with some preliminary protocols for readmitting the rebel states. At that time, eyeing his coming reelection campaign perhaps, Lincoln adopted an approach to the task that proved as ambivalent and cautious as his decision on abolition had been. The emphasis, he insisted, must be on reconciliation rather than reconstruction, on cultivating the leadership of southern white Unionists rather than incorporating black men into the body politic. Perhaps, he mused, black veterans of the war might be allowed to vote. Little did he realize that this small concession would eventually open a wide breach in the nation's racialized political boundaries.

Historians have fantasized about what kind of reconstruction process might have emerged had Lincoln survived John Wilkes Booth's fatal attack, but it is reasonable to assume that his reconciliation policy would have been no less vulnerable to "the mere incidents" and frictions of postwar conflicts over land, labor, and power than his earlier reluctance to emancipate the slaves had been to the pressures of war. In any event, although there was scant evidence by April 1865 of any movement toward Douglass's vision of a nation transformed, that prognosis would ultimately prove the more prescient. Within two years, the Republicans, who had come to power on a platform opposing only the expansion of slavery, would be committed to full citizenship and equal rights for African Americans. A nation whose highest court had declared black men incapable of citizenship just a decade earlier would soon welcome them to seats in the Congress and the Senate. For a brief moment, former slaves and freeborn African Americans could reasonably anticipate "a glorious future" in a more perfect union.

It is hardly surprising that most of Douglass's contemporaries could not anticipate such a radical change in the nation's political order. There was little historical precedent for it, certainly. Following the democratic revolutions of the late eighteenth century, the emancipation of slaves posed a substantial political problem for any putatively democratic polity. In theory, societies constituted of rights-bearing citizens rather than subjects should have extended to ex-slaves and their descendants the same civil rights as other citizens. And yet former slaves had not generally become voters and officeholders in the northern states following their emancipation. Although equal rights were declared to be the guiding principle for the post-emancipation social order in the British West Indies in the 1830s and '40s, only in Jamaica did former slaves become a formidable political force, an experiment aborted just as American Reconstruction began. None of the other New World societies that had abolished slavery by mid-century followed Britain's example. Partly because slavery's abolition emerged out of a bloody civil war, partly because of the depth of America's institutional commitment to republicanism perhaps, freed slaves posed a more fundamental challenge both to democratic theory and to its practice in the U.S. political order. The nation's ruptured political fabric had to be mended. With the founding constitutional compromise between slavery and freedom now mooted, the Constitution's original democratic-republican promise had somehow to be revitalized.

Still, as the guns fell silent at Appomattox, there was little reason to think that that revitalization would entail an attack on white supremacy. The Republican Party's stronghold lay in seven midwestern states—Ohio, Indiana, Illinois, Iowa, Michigan, Wisconsin, and Minnesota—each of which had recently demonstrated a firm commitment to white supremacy. All of them had passed some form of anti-black legislation ("Black Codes") during the decade preceding the Civil War, and several had reaffirmed their opposition to racial equality in various ways during the war. All barred blacks from voting or serving in the militia. Several had laws on the books hostile to black in-migration. Blacks could not testify against whites in Illinois and Indiana courtrooms and could not serve on juries in Iowa, Ohio, and Illinois. In some states, lax enforcement or the development of enclaves more receptive to black civic participation softened the practical impact of some of these laws. Ohio's Western Reserve, for example, attracted substantial numbers of black settlers with its racially integrated schools and the college at Oberlin, and black men voted and held municipal offices there. Indeed, it was there that a future Virginia congressman, John M. Langston, first held political office in the 1850s. Similarly, Quaker communities in Indiana, Michigan, and Ohio became islands of racial tolerance. These exceptions did not alter the fundamental political arithmetic, however, of a northern electorate opposed to slavery yet hostile to black equality with whites.

Racial attitudes need not remain static, however, and in the heat of battle, political calculations can mutate in complex, even contradictory ways. The war exacerbated northern whites' old fears of being deluged by black migrants escaping a hostile South, which reignited exclusionist sentiments in some places during the war. On the other hand, the war could also have an ameliorative effect on racial prejudices, as reflected in the repeal by 1865 of exclusionary laws in Ohio, Wisconsin, Illinois, and Minnesota and the acceptance of black suffrage in Minnesota and Iowa in 1868. During the spring and summer of 1864, congressional Republicans, fearful of a backlash in the upcoming presidential election, deleted suffrage rights for black men that earlier had been inserted into legislation organizing the territorial governments of Montana and Louisiana. That those provisions had won even their momentary consent, however, suggests that a significant political evolution was in progress.

These initial glimmers of greater receptiveness to black inclusion in the body politic, at least among some sectors of the northern public and some political leadership, surely reflect the exigencies of war and postwar adjustments. The decision in July 1862 to open militia service to blacks was practically simultaneous with Lincoln's decision to issue his preliminary emancipation decree. A year later, as manpower needs and resistance to the draft mounted, the initial racist opposition to broader recruitment and deployment of black troops flipped to enthusiastic advocacy that blacks bear more of the burden in what was now officially an antislavery war. The increased deployment of black troops, however, pressed upon Lincoln's government the difficult question of whether African Americans would be officially recognized as equals.

The Confederacy's response to the Union's deployment of black soldiers was immediate and fierce: they considered them no different than rebellious slaves, who if captured would be either sold or put to death. The southerners' challenge provoked northern condemnations of its inhumanity and threatened a key part of the Union government's scheme for addressing its growing military manpower needs. Lincoln's rejoinder, therefore, was equally fierce and uncompromising: for every black soldier enslaved, a captured rebel soldier would be put to hard labor; for every black prisoner shot, a Confederate prisoner would be executed. The immediate effect of General Order No. 100, issued on July 30, 1863, was that the South backed down. A more subtle, and perhaps enduring, effect was the order's backdoor affirmation of racial equality: that black life and liberty were equal to white life and liberty.

The second challenge that black recruitment posed developed around policy conflicts within the Union government itself, which prompted a more protracted struggle. The amended Militia Act of July 1862 stipulated unequal rates of pay for white and black recruits: thirteen dollars per month, plus a three-dollar clothing allowance, for the former; and ten dollars, with a three-dollar clothing deduction, for the latter. Initially the rationale for this discrimination was that black soldiers would be laborers not fighters, but it was no doubt also responsive to public distaste for the human equality implied by equal pay. In any event, the laborer-fighter distinction was soon rendered moot as blacks were repeatedly thrown into battle, enduring high casualties and garnering praise for their valor. Furthermore, as Attorney General Edward Bates pointed out repeatedly, the Militia Act did not in any case apply to units raised for regular army deployments as opposed to state militias. The War Department steadfastly refused to acknowledge Bates's ruling, however, and the unequal pay rates stood. Meanwhile, faltering efforts to fill manpower needs only with white troops underscored the necessity of attracting black recruits, for whom the pay dispute remained a powerful disincentive. For more than a year, civilian protests mounted, and several black units, some risking and enduring punishment for mutiny, refused to accept any pay at all rather than concede their putative unequal worth. After several false starts, Congress passed legislation on June 16, 1864, equalizing pay for all black recruits who could declare that they had been free (or, more craftily, "owed no one labor service") as of April 19, 1861, the day the war began. A year later, during the war's final days, equalization was extended retroactively to former slaves as well. At roughly the same time, the War Department authorized the commissioning of black officers. At last, a black man's service to the nation was putatively equal to a white man's.

Indeed, black men's military service had become increasingly difficult to ignore. By war's end, one of every four Union men who had served under arms was black. The thirty-eight thousand blacks who had died constituted a mortality rate 35 percent greater than their white comrades. Their valor attested by twenty-one Congressional Medals of Honor, black soldiers had taken part in 449 battles, 39 of which were classified as major, including all of the significant battles during the war's final months. When Richmond fell, a black regiment led the Union Army into the city.

The unique social circumstance of black soldiers would exaggerate their presence even more during the postwar demobilization. Blacks mustered out of the service much more slowly than whites, in part perhaps because they had fewer opportunities awaiting their return home, and in many cases no homes to which they could return. In July 1865, there were 123,156 black troops left in the army, 120 regiments of infantry, and 12 of cavalry. By December 1865, all but one of the 12 infantry regiments in Mississippi were black, as were almost 3 of every 4 soldiers stationed in the Louisiana-Texas military district. Many black veterans also knew that remaining in the military during the postwar period could prove useful for beleaguered southern black communities. Pervasive complaints by whites about black soldiers' alleged "demoralizing" effect on the freedpeople near their encampments signal their determination to protect and mobilize former slaves. Fully cognizant of their political potential, the War Department was determined to discharge black soldiers as soon as feasible; failing that, it sought to isolate them from other blacks by stationing them in far western posts. General Grant, who had so ostentatiously granted Lee's troops the right to keep their sidearms when they surrendered at Appomattox, issued orders that black soldiers of the U.S. Army not be allowed to purchase their weapons when they left the service.

Notwithstanding these anxious responses to black men under arms, their service did recast the political discourse regarding black enfranchisement. The moral-psychological impact of mobilizing black soldiers as the slave empire collapsed had been profound and unanticipated. One by one, the efforts to define black soldiers as something other than warriors for their own liberation—restricting them to labor battalions and off the battlefield, paying them "nigger" wages, denying them commissions as officer—had collapsed. The lowly chattel, as Douglass had once put it to Garrison, was now a man, and his fight to save the Union had a transformative effect not unlike Douglass's defiance of Covey. Black soldiers' brave service, a generation of leaders would constantly remind them thereafter, had saved the nation and cemented a people's title to full and equal citizenship.

The theme of entitlement emerged even before their actual wartime service and only grew more powerful thereafter. During what proved to be a premature effort to enlist black troops during the first year of the war, Douglass had formulated a powerful rationale for their prospective service: "He who fights the battles of America may claim America as his country and have that claim respected." Only the most intrepid abolitionists would have endorsed this proposition in 1861; by 1865, however, the idea that military service implied equality of civic rights had long since

These before and after pictures of the Georgia slave Hubbard Pryor graphically illuminate the transformation from chattel to man similar to that which Frederick Douglass celebrated in his victory over the slavebreaker Covey.

emerged as a core theme in discussions of postwar reconstruction. Even northern Democrats invoked the linkage between service and rights, albeit as part of their opposition to any black military recruitment. From newspapers to stump speeches, the notion of entitlement won through bearing arms to save the Union had emerged as a major theme of blacks' political claims on the postwar nation. "Above all," declared a New Orleans editor, "our devotion to our flag, and our manly conduct must be our last appeal and the ground of our hope." On December 13, 1865, a congressman from Indiana introduced a resolution urging citizenship rights for black veterans, a notion Lincoln had urged unsuccessfully for the Louisiana constitution the year before.

The notion of a veteran's "entitlement" to full citizenship may have predisposed the northern public to admit blacks to the body politic, but other developments turned that disposition into political necessity. The reconvened Congress underscored well-founded fears that southern congressional representatives might actually be more powerful upon their return than when they left. Slavery's abolition having rendered the "federal ratio" moot, the next national census would count former slaves as whole persons rather than three fifths as it had in the prewar political calculus determining the size of the South's congressional delegation. This 20 percent augmentation of the section's postwar voting power suggested to some that it might have been Lee rather than Grant who emerged victorious at Appomattox. The uneasiness was heightened no doubt when the Congress anticipated that Alexander Stephens, the former vice-president of the Confederacy and just recently a military prisoner, would soon present his senatorial credentials, having been elected by the Georgia legislature to represent the state. Notwithstanding its war-weary mood, the northern public could not readily concede so blatant a loss of the fruits of its victory. Meanwhile, congressmen read letters from soldiers and other constituents attesting to the mounting evidence of southern whites' intransigence: blatant efforts to reestablish slavery in all but name and violent attacks on white Unionists and freedpeople. Veritable carnivals of violence swept Memphis and New Orleans during the spring and summer of 1866, confirming the necessity for a more thoroughgoing reconstruction of the southern political order. The Republicans' landslide victory in the congressional elections the following fall gave them the power to seize control once more and restart the reconstruction process.

Between March 2, 1867, and March 11, 1868, Congress passed four statutes that provided a new basis and rationale for readmitting ten of the eleven former Confederate states to the Union. In sum, these laws created five districts in which military governors would supervise the process of preparing the former states for readmission, including writing new state constitutions stripped of the taint of slavery and racial distinctions and ratifying the Fourteenth Amendment, all proceeding under strictures wherein "male citizens . . . of whatever race, color, or previous condition" would be free to participate on the same basis as whites. In essence the Congress acted on the premise that a postwar settlement must secure the fruits of war and slavery's abolition and that it could achieve this only by admitting black men to the political process. Thus the Reconstruction Acts set the stage for a mass political mobilization across the South, of a scale and intensity not to be matched for another century. Indeed, black men registered and voted at rates unequaled to this day. Black women and children joined them at outdoor political rallies, crowded into the packed balconies at party conventions, and waited anxiously around the sites of constitutional conventions. In the process they together forged the notion of entitlement into a powerful communal ethos, a political will and strength that enabled them to resist the bribery and blandishments and the waves of violence and economic intimidation unleashed by defenders of the old order.

Securing the fruits of victory would depend, however, on transforming the social relations of labor and ensuring the relative autonomy of freedpeople's households and communities. The image of manliness that Douglass invokes in his autobiography, which proved so crucial to the transformation of black political consciousness during and after the war, was more complex than a mere assertion of masculine pride; it was a multivalent trope of self-making. Douglass invoked the image more than once and under very different circumstances. First was his description of his changed psychological and moral state after the fight with Covey. Then came the moment he took the podium to address his first abolitionist audience in Nantucket, becoming a speaking subject. And finally, when he wrote Garrison from Ireland, proud that he had commanded the attention of white audiences with his voice. Becoming a man, then, was the assertion of will, the defense of dignity, and the power to shape events rather than simply be victimized by them. This image fit well with the white South's own masculinist representation of political claims. As the historian Hannah Rosen has shown, their notions of manhood grounded southern white males' rejection of blacks as legitimate political actors and accounts for the peculiar forms their reign of terror took during the early postwar years. Rape and other forms of sexual violence against women emerged as overtly political weapons gauged to demean black women and emasculate black men.

As we have seen, however, Douglass's representation of his victory over Covey and of his assumption of a manly personhood was blind to the supporting role of his larger community, including its women. Efforts to build political community after slavery followed a similar script. Women such as James Forten's granddaughter Charlotte sensed as much when they went South to teach and minister to the needs of black communities. Women field hands enacted it when they withdrew their labor from plantation production and redirected their energies to sustain their households and families, creating a labor crisis in the process. Wives and mothers sustained it when they steeled their menfolk to assert the community's political agenda, while quietly building up the infrastructure of an independent black community that would survive long after that political edifice was destroyed by racial violence.

Contemporaries, astonished and surprised by the freedpeople's political sophistication and capacity, blamed their assertiveness on outside forces, missing entirely these indigenous resources and developments. To be sure, new, external agents of change were pouring into the postwar South: Union veterans, New England schoolmarms, and religious missionaries; the Freedmen's Bureau and the Union Leagues; northern and southern freeborn African Americans; and white political and economic opportunists. These outside forces could be effective, however, only because the mobilizations they sought to inspire were supported by former slaves.

Evidence of the former slaves' collective political capacities and sagacity had emerged well before the war's end. On January 12, 1865, almost a year to the day after Douglass addressed the abolitionists at Cooper Institute, General William T. Sherman and Secretary of War Edwin M. Stanton met with twenty black religious leaders in Savannah, Georgia. Sherman sought solutions for dealing with the tens of thousands of black refugees who had followed him out of Atlanta on his forced March to the Sea and now inundated his camps. All but one of the group of black men gathered that day were southern-born; all but four of the southerners were former slaves. A few had purchased their freedom or been freed by an owner's will before the war, but nine had been liberated by grace of the Union occupation. Almost all of them were ministers who had rendered an average of thirteen years of service to their respective flocks. They were part of the social architecture buttressing communal authority among a people excluded from the formal body politic and constrained by slavery's demands. The churches these men ministered had supplied spaces within the interstices of the Slave Power where an alternative worldview could be cultivated and modes for forging and enforcing the collective will could be perfected. Calling upon those resources and protocols, they elected a spokesman, Reverend Garrison Frazier, a sixty-seven-year-old former slave from Granville County who had managed just eight years earlier to save the $1,000 purchase price for himself and his wife. He had spent thirty-five years, half his lifetime, ministering to the surrounding community.

Did the men gathered here understand the difference between slavery and freedom? Stanton asked the group. Yes, replied Frazier, slavery meant taking "by *irresistible* power the work of another man and not by his consent," while freedom meant that the people would now "reap the fruit of our own labor and take care of ourselves." How could the government deal with the refugee problem? By giving them land isolated from white interference, Frazier replied, and the tools to work it so that they could feed themselves.

Four days later, Sherman issued his Special Field Order No. 15, adopting the principal suggestions he and Stanton had heard that evening in Savannah. A coastal reservation thirty miles wide, stretching from Charleston, South Carolina, to St. John's River, Florida, was set aside for exclusive settlement by freedmen. Forty-acre plots were to be assigned to black heads of households or the families of enlisted soldiers. Sherman also made available some of the army's broken-down mules so that the families could work the land, giving origin to the phrase "forty acres and a mule." "Provisional" titles were issued to the new landholders under Sherman's martial law authority that were to be confirmed by congressional action later. Unfortunately, that crucial provision soon fell victim to the growing dispute between Congress and President Andrew Johnson over control of the reconstruction process. Nine months after Sherman's order, just as the crops the refugees had planted were ready for harvest, Johnson ordered General Oliver O. Howard, head of the Freedmen's Bureau, to clear the black settlers off the land and return it to the previous owners.

General Howard's dutiful effort to carry out this order provoked an early and notable moment of political mobilization and resistance among the former slaves, including a petition embodying what is arguably the clearest articulation of the freedmen's shrewd understanding of the postwar political order and their place within it. The freedpeople on Edisto Island, South Carolina, elected a committee—Henry Bram, Ishmael Moultrie, Yates Sampson, and a few others—to draft the petition to the president and a response to General Howard. While their address to President Johnson was formal and proper, their appeal to Howard was personal and emotional. Perhaps they dared hope that he might be educated about the historical, political, and moral justice of their claims to the land. Indeed, their understanding of what the new postwar order required was strikingly astute. If they were to have any hope of avoiding being snared in a new slavery—helplessly dependent on their former masters—then they needed land, because that was the only way to ensure their self-determination and opportunity for self-realization in an agricultural economy. If evicted from the Sherman reservation, they would have to "remain on them working as In former time and subject to their [former masters'] will as then." "Landless, Homeless and Voteless," they would not be able to realize or protect the freedoms so recently won. Given this prognosis, it was inconceivable to the Edisto Islanders that the government would betray its most loyal supporters in order to reward "its late enemies." If Howard had sought to justify this breach of "common faith" with an appeal to abstract notions of the sanctity of property right, their ready answer was their own rights to the land, long since won with their sweat, tears, and blood: tied to a tree and given "39 lashes," a mother and sister "stripped and flogged."

Clearly, the Edisto Islanders' political consciousness was widely shared among the South's former slaves. Just a few months after the Edisto meeting, another freedman, Bayley Wyatt, rose to address a similar gathering in Yorktown, Virginia, where settlers had just been informed that they, too, had to surrender their land to its former owners. The news went down like "a dose of pizen," declared Wyatt. Freedpeople, who had "made bricks widout straw under old Pharo," now felt betrayed and dispossessed. Echoing the Edisto petition, he painstakingly laid out the argument that the purchase price for this land had already been extracted through their enslavement. "Our wives, our children, our husbands, has been sold over and over again to purchase the lands we now locate upon"; he insisted, and "for that reason, we have a divine right to the land." Elaborating a moral economy no doubt organic to slave communities everywhere, he declared, "And den didn't we clear the lands and raise de crops of corn, ob cotton, ob tobacco, ob rice, ob sugar, ob everything? And den didn't de large cities in de North grow up on de cotton and de sugars and de rice dat we made? . . . I say dey have grown rich and my people is poor."

Even before the Edisto Islanders drafted their petitions to the president and General Howard, southern planters had made clear what kind of postwar order they desired—one that looked a lot like the old order. Tobacco planters in central Virginia formed cartels to set uniform wages and terms of employment, including the stipulation that no worker be hired without the permission of his former owner, who would have first refusal of his services. Tennessee planters adopted a similar scheme, to which they added the threat of death to any violator. Shortly after the Edisto Islanders met, the South Carolina constitutional convention gathered to write a new code of laws for a society without slaves, a task soon undertaken throughout the former Confederacy. These "Black Codes," as they were called, generally recognized and sought to regulate the new civil status of former slaves—including marriage—while imposing extraordinary restrictions on their ability to earn a living outside plantations and farms. Black artisans were assessed large discriminatory taxes in South Carolina, aspiring black farmers could not own agricultural tracts in Mississippi, and throughout the region apprenticeship laws were dusted off to compel children to provide labor to their former owners, with or without the consent of their parents or kinspeople. Interdicted initially by Union military authorities or the Freedmen's Bureau and superseded by the Civil Rights Act passed in April 1866, most of these laws never came to fruition or were short-lived. Freedpeople did not wait on outside intervention, however. At the onset of the hiring season in freedom's first new year in the former Confederacy, they simply refused to sign contracts or continue working on the plantations.

Many white observers attributed this "strike" to the freedpeople's allegedly deluded expectation of a general land reform, their silly expectation of receiving "forty acres and a mule." They might have looked closer to home for explanations, however. Many planters did not pay well or regularly, and in some cases not at all. A free labor relationship hinged on the cash nexus was distasteful to people accustomed to securing labor through coercion, an attitude that could only exacerbate the structural dislocations shaping the postwar labor struggle. Deprived of the property in slaves that had served as one of their two principal sources of collateral, cash-strapped planters found themselves unable to pay wages regularly or reneged on their commitments. Meanwhile, their uncertain command of labor to produce crops diminished the value of their land, the second source of collateral, thus undercutting further their ability to borrow operating capital secured by a future crop. It soon became readily apparent that the impoverished planter's survival depended on solving the problem of labor supervision, without overseers or whips, and on postponing the final accounting of his labor bill until after the crop was harvested.

The ultimate solution to the planter's problem, it turned out, was to make the laborers his creditors, securing their wages with shares of the prospective crop. Black workers would receive their pay in the form of a share of the harvested crop, thus relieving the planter of meeting a payroll and ensuring labor throughout the year. Production would be organized around families, who would be assigned plots and work under the supervision of kinsmen rather than overseers. While waiting for their pay at the end of the crop season, these families would subsist on supplies provided by the planter, either directly or through a local merchant, and secured by a lien on their share of the crop. Thus the planter surrendered control over the labor process but gained the labor of the whole family once again, all while avoiding paying labor costs up front or the costs and aggravation of direct supervision. For their part, freedpeople may have seen in the arrangement—a tenure system that gave them a claim on the crop and immediate control of their family's labor and the work process—a path to eventual landownership. Black families could dream of climbing the ladder to agricultural success, gradually accumulating cash to buy tools and mules with which to strike a better deal as renters rather than share tenants and eventually buying the land denied them after emancipation and farming on their own account. Absent viable economic alternatives, it may have seemed like a good deal.

And so it was, initially. As long as staple prices remained high and the governing authorities that arbitrated their contracts were fair, sharecroppers had a reasonable chance of getting ahead. For roughly five years, those preconditions held throughout much of the South, and the new birth of freedom that emancipation had promised seemed to be realized. In 1868 there was an incredible political mobilization of black voters, shocking even their most fervent supporters, as illiterate farmers and workers organized, registered, and voted in overwhelming numbers. Rebuffing their former masters' efforts to entice or bully them, they voted their own interests. And despite some glaring exceptions, the white and black Republicans they elected to the constitutional conventions and legislatures responded to those interests. In most reconstructed states, they were able to establish public school systems—some for the first time—and outlaw various forms of racial discrimination. Where black political representation was strongest the Republicans legislated rules governing crop liens that favored tenants and appointed magistrates who would litigate them fairly.

The postwar economic boom crashed in 1873, however, beginning a prolonged secular depression that saw cotton prices tumble to historic lows and remain low for two decades. Less than seven years after the initiation of the radical phase of Reconstruction, the national political tides shifted, becoming more hostile to black aspirations. Democrats, now reconciled to the abolition of slavery but not black enfranchisement, regained control of the House of Representatives in 1874 and came close to winning the presidency two years later. Racked by vicious in-fighting and terrorized by white vigilantes, southern Republicans were chased from statehouses and rendered powerless to resist the systematic reversal of the legal protections that sharecroppers and tenants had briefly enjoyed. Over time, the new free labor regime that had seemed to promise a measure of autonomy and opportunity twisted into new forms of economic enslavement. Laws were passed or amended to ensure that the crop, and thus the lien on it, belonged to the planter, not the worker. The planter's control of the crop's disposition and settling up after the harvest provided means of cheating workers of the fruits of their labor. Falling staple prices ensured that there was little fruit to be shared. The gathering storms that destroyed the centuries-old institution of slavery had risen with incredible force and rapidity. The political transformations that swept away the economic foundation of a hard-won freedom came with even greater force and rapidity.

Making a Free Life

To meet the challenges of reconstructing their own lives and the life of the nation, freedpeople were forced to mobilize both the traditional resources nurtured during slavery and the new institutions born of the war and in its aftermath. Neither the freedpeople's immediate, and in some cases decisive, response to the former ruling class, nor their eventual political mobilization can be understood apart from the communities from which they came, communities forged in slavery, tested by a long war, and now reconstructed in a chaotic peace. Garrison Frazier and Bayley Wyatt were spokesmen for communities that were capable of identifying and nurturing their own indigenous leadership, crafting an analysis of their situation and needs that were organic to their lived experience, and drawing on that political consciousness to articulate the ends and means for achieving the "glorious future" Douglass had envisioned. They would draw on the world they knew—its work processes, its structures, and the dynamics of its social authority—and on the visions of divine and secular justice they had carefully extricated from the master's religion, a faith they had made their own. They were also fully conscious of the potential of the new world being remade around them, however, and sought to bend it toward their own ends.

The war experience had transformed many black Americans, slave and free, providing them with new incentives, a sense of self, and new tools to act collectively and individually in their own political interests. Reeducation for some of them had begun during military service, where they debated around army campfires the postwar transition, the right to vote, and other timely issues. It continued under the auspices of the Union Leagues, the Freedmen's Bureau, and their now fully independent churches. And yet the roots of black political life after slavery may also be found in the slave experience itself, which helps explain their otherwise amazingly rapid mobilization scarcely before the guns had cooled and the smoke cleared.

Recent historical studies suggest that the very ways in which slave labor had been mobilized and the laborer's property rights customarily defined may have inadvertently fostered social relations within the quarters that enabled the political solidarities and leadership that emerged in freedom. Churches and ties of kinship also proved essential to grass-roots mobilizations. And where work regimes and demographic patterns may not have favored such internal community structures, other developments may have compensated, fostering internal cohesion and the elaboration of social networks that proved politically efficacious after emancipation.

These traditional resources and predispositions were called upon immediately, since the defeated ruling class was in no mood either to maintain the social supports provided during slavery or to open to blacks the meager public support previously provided to impoverished whites. Blacks were excluded from public relief in Georgia, for example, and were assessed a special, separate tax to take care of black paupers in Mississippi. Newly independent black churches and mutual aid societies attempted to fill the breach in social services, but all struggled to provide an adequate social safety net.

The transition from a social order founded on slavery was complicated by the rapid and disconcerting transformation of the private sphere, where the fundamental social relations of both labor and welfare would be determined. With emancipation the planters' vaunted notion of paterfamilias collapsed, because there was no longer a rationale—even as pretense— for the notion that black workers' families were an extension of the white plantation family. Many planters quickly shed responsibilites they had previously assumed for their slave property, refusing to care for the elderly after their working lives had ceased or for the young before their work capacity had begun. The gender values associated with slavery were suddenly and radically reversed, which affected labor and family relations. In a system where slave babies were assets, women's reproductive capacity had been as highly valued as their productive capacity, if not more so—as evidenced by the fact that young women fetched high prices on the auction block. With slavery gone, vulnerable women—those pregnant or caring for young children—were much less valuable, and many were summarily evicted. On the other hand, men's value to the planters and to women was enhanced, as they became the most productive workers in the eyes of the former and potential protectors to the latter. The market price of labor reflected this reversal of value: freedmen were paid more than freedwomen. Moreover, it appears that the emerging gender differentials in pay may have encouraged many freedwomen to accept the otherwise alien notion that males were now the heads of their households.

On the other hand, many of the new ideas and sentiments induced by postwar structural changes resonated strongly with prewar mores and experience. By their actions throughout the years of bondage, slaves had left little doubt that they valued familial and kin relations. Once free, they showed a strong disposition to embrace legal sanctions for their marriages, the domestic relation that had been most vulnerable under slavery. Across the South, thousands flocked to army chaplains and Freedmen's Bureau officials seeking to solemnize their marital bonds. More than romantic sentiment was involved in these ceremonies. As Corporal Murray of the U.S. Colored Troop declared in Virginia in 1866, "The Marriage Covenant is at the foundation of all our rights. In slavery we could not have *legalised* marriage: *now* we have it . . . and we shall be established as a people." In form at least the corporal's words mirrored the arguments white southerners had made for the importance of marriage more generally, and which they would reiterate for newly freed slaves. Marriage anchored the community, made coherent the collectivity of individuals, and grounded the nation-state. On more practical grounds, both northern and southern state authorities encouraged ex-slaves to marry in order to instantiate the private obligations that might limit their claims on the public treasury. Not only federal authorities and southern planters but black and white missionaries had all strongly encouraged ex-slaves to marry. It was the one new civil right affirmed in all the southern Black Codes.

For their part, freedpeople embraced marriage, too. They readily recognized, it appears, that in American jurisprudence this long-denied civil right enabled one to claim *other* rights and legal protections, such as the privacy of one's household, protection from outside demands for one's children's labor, and the right to make civil contracts. A few, such as Corporal Murray, intuited that if marriage could ground the nation—as many legal experts contended—it might also form the foundation for rebuilding black communities. White contemporaries and latter-day historians have often misinterpreted this fundamentally political aspiration—to establish "a people"—as mere conformity with existing bourgeois values and households, and thus missed the crucial insight of a people emerging from a world where family and kinship held entirely different meanings. Within their living memory, after all, were Margaret Garner's bloodstained hands and stony visage.

Among the key transformative institutions shaping black life after emancipation were a vast array of churches—most of them now severed from controlling white entities—which succored freedmen's psychic health and political mobilization, and mutual aid associations, which provided everything from medical and death benefits to depositories for penny savings accounts. Union Leagues were organized, a vibrant political press proliferated, and political mass meetings enlivened normal routines of work and leisure, drawing in women and children as full participants. Now that black families were scattered across the individual tenant holdings that had replaced plantation villages—a physical isolation that eventually made them more vulnerable to political violence and economic intimidation—they used these new institutions as bases for collective action. A growing contingent of educational institutions, ranging from primary schools to colleges and universities, many supported by private rather than public funds, began the slow, decades-long process of educating future black leaders and professionals.

The 1876 election and federal military "withdrawal" from the South surely changed the balance of political and economic power, even if it did not immediately or completely eliminate black southerners as an important and sometimes decisive force in the region's and nation's political life. That was still at least two decades in the future. Nor did the end of the political phase of Reconstruction stall the institutional development that freedom from slavery had allowed to flourish. The growth of mutual aid societies, churches, and church-supported schools continued and would provide crucial institutional bases for renewed political mobilizations a century later.

When a congressional committee studying labor conditions toured the South early in 1883, therefore, they were met at every stop with optimistic assessments of a prosperous and progressive black future, if not quite the "glorious" one Douglass had envisioned two decades before. Later that very year, however, part of the legal infrastructure underpinning that optimism would be pulled away. In this twentieth-anniversary year of the Emancipation Proclamation, African Americans would confront once more the prospect of a revolution going backward; once more their standing as citizens would be put in doubt.

"[he] ceases to be the special favorite of the laws"

More than two thousand people pressed their way into Washington Hall in the nation's capital on the evening of October 22, 1883; they were bewildered, shocked, and angry. Hundreds more milled around outside the hall, unable to get seats. All had come to hear their leaders assess the latest blow to the freedom and dignity that their two-decade-old emancipation had seemed to promise. "Like a clap of thunder from a clear sky," as Douglass remembered the event some years later, the U.S. Supreme Court had struck down the Civil Rights Act passed eight years earlier. At the meeting that evening, Douglass sought to capture the crowd's mood. "We have been, as a race, grievously wounded," he began, "wounded in the house of our friends, and this wound is too deep and too painful for ordinary and measured speech." The possibility, even if fleeting, that the greatest orator of their era might be rendered speechless provided some measure of the gravity of the moment. The wound, conveyed by a nearly unanimous decision announced just one week earlier by Justice Joseph P. Bradley, speaking for a court dominated by Republicans and northerners, was that African Americans could no longer look to the national government to protect their newly acquired civil status as equal citizens, enjoying rights regardless of their race or former servile condition. The justices had been considering five cases, all involving some form of racial discrimination in public accommodations forbidden by the Civil Rights Act of 1875. Arising in different regions of the country from widely varying circumstances, the cases formally addressed the constitutionality of that particular act, but at heart they questioned whether the hard-won fruits of slavery's bloody destruction would endure.

The lead case among the five had reached the court in the fall of 1876. Bird Gee was refused service in the dining room of an inn operated by Murray Stanley in Kansas. Shortly thereafter, on October 14, 1876, Michael Ryan, doorkeeper at a San Francisco theater, prevented George M. Taylor from taking his seat. Less than four months later, on February 5, 1877, W.H.R. Agee was denied lodgings at Nichols House, an inn in Missouri. Because of the Court's decision to couple the Stanley and Nichols cases, and due to delays, these three cases were eventually joined with two others adjudicated in the early 1880s. On November 22, 1879, William R. Davis was refused a seat at the Grand Opera House in New York City. A ten-year-old slave in South Carolina at the time of emancipation, Davis was well educated and politically active. *The New York Times* described him as "a tall, good-looking man, intelligent and educated, converses and dresses well" and "of full African blood." This case appears to have been a deliberate test of the federal civil rights law. The business manager of a black weekly, *The Progressive American*, Davis had attempted a similar test of racial discrimination at Booth's Theatre two years earlier, but it had never come to trial because his witnesses failed to appear in court. In a ruse much like twentieth-century discrimination tests, the dark-skinned Davis had his female companion, "a bright octoroon, almost white," buy two tickets for Saturday's matinee performance. When they arrived at the theater, however, they were told that the tickets were somehow no longer valid. Davis immediately went outside and hired a white boy to buy tickets for them. Again, when they appeared to claim their seats, they were refused, and after a brief scuffle Davis was arrested.

The fifth and final case appears to have arisen under very different circumstances. Whereas Davis clearly anticipated the discrimination he encountered in New York, Sallie Robinson expected equal treatment in Tennessee. Boarding a train for Lynchburg, Virginia, at Grand Junction, just outside Memphis, on May 22, 1879, Robinson and her nephew made their way toward the first class, or "lady's," car for which they had purchased tickets. Suspicious that the "young and good-looking woman" traveling with a young white man was actually a prostitute, the conductor, "one Reagin," denied her entrance until he could investigate the matter further. Later, satisfied that she was not a prostitute—perhaps having learned that the young man was actually not white but a very light-skinned mulatto—he permitted them to take their assigned seats. The railroad's defense, therefore—which had been successful at trial—was that this was not a case of discrimination because of race. The plaintiff's response was essentially that Reagin's assumptions about Sallie Robinson's character were quite obviously grounded in racial prejudices notwithstanding the conductor's subsequent acquiescence. It was not simply that Ms. Robinson had been humiliated, but that it was inconceivable that a white woman would have been treated in the same manner.

The burden of defending the validity of the Civil Rights Act fell to Solicitor General Samuel Field Phillips, a southern-born opponent of secession who had joined the Republican Party after the war. Phillips's two-pronged argument insisted first that these acts of discrimination were not merely private initiatives but actions authorized by private enterprises licensed and regulated by the state and possessed thereby a quasi-public character, as attested by a substantial body of precedent. Second, he argued that the Thirteenth Amendment decreed "universal civil and political freedom throughout the United States" and thus protected black Americans from even private acts that sought to reimpose upon them "a badge of servitude," that is, a status "incident" to or derivative from their former civil subordination. Acts of racial discrimination must be nipped "in the bud," Phillips argued, or these early expressions of the white majority's *public* sentiment about the unequal treatment of former slaves would ultimately become institutionalized.

Ignoring Phillips's argument against the application of the Cruikshank precedent, which had limited the Fourteenth Amendment only to state actions in cases involving publicly regulated accommodations, Justice Bradley declared that solely "individual invasion[s] of individual rights" were involved in these cases, and thus federal protection was not constitutionally justified. Heatedly rejecting Phillips's second argument as to the applicability of the Thirteenth Amendment as "running the slavery argument into the ground," Bradley delivered a chilling assessment of what African Americans might expect from the courts in the future.

When a man has emerged from slavery, and by the aid of beneficent legislation has shaken off the inseparable concomitants of that state, there must be some stage in the progress of his elevation when he takes the rank of a mere citizen, and ceases to be the special favorite of the laws, and when his rights as a citizen, or a man, are to be protected in the ordinary modes by which other men's rights are protected . . .

Henceforth, less than a generation after emancipation, black Americans were on their own.

One of the many ironies of this case was that Bradley, a Yankee from New York, was the spokesman for the majority, while the lone dissenter was Justice John Marshall Harlan, scion of a Kentucky slaveholding family. Harlan's father was in many ways the archetypical patrician, paternalistic slaveholder, complete with the mulatto offspring whom his son inherited with the rest of his estate. The senior Harlan, allied politically with Henry Clay's moderate wing of the Whig Party, had remained faithful to the Union during the Civil War. Following in his father's footsteps, John attempted to tread a middle path politically, experimenting with a number of parties after the Whigs collapsed over the slavery question, and balancing loyalty to the Union with his continued defense of slave property rights to the bitter end. Although he raised a regiment to fight for the northern side in the Civil War, he resigned his commission after his father's death in 1863. He regarded Lincoln's Emancipation Proclamation as a betrayal of southern loyalists and went so far as to support Lincoln's opponent, General George B. McClellan, in the 1864 elections. As Kentucky's attorney general, he resisted federal efforts to free the families of freedmen who enlisted in Union armies. Indeed, it remains something of a mystery just how he made his way to the Republican Party within less than a decade after the war, although his law partnership with Republican presidential aspirant Benjamin H. Bristow may have had some influence on that decision. After two losing campaigns for governor during the 1870s, Harlan came to the attention of President Rutherford B. Hayes, who, looking for a southern Republican moderate consistent with his own conciliatory policies, chose Harlan for a seat on the Supreme Court. It probably didn't hurt that Harlan had supported Hayes's contested nomination and served on the electoral commission set up to resolve the disputed count of the 1876 election, a commission that Justice Bradley had chaired.

Judge Harlan's eloquent, impassioned dissent from Bradley's reasoning was not read that October Monday. Indeed, Harlan was still immobilized by an untimely writer's block, and only a subtle maneuver by his wife shook him from his paralysis. She placed on his desk an inkstand once used by Judge Roger Taney, author of the now-infamous Dred Scott decision that had declared black people bereft of any civil right that whites were bound to respect. With that inspiration the words flowed in virtual torrents that lifted the spirits if not the hopes of African Americans across the nation, making Harlan a nineteenth-century white hero for them second only to Lincoln. Building on Phillips's line of argument, Harlan declared that the Thirteenth Amendment did more than just prohibit slavery; "it decreed universal freedom throughout the United States." To have simply outlawed formal ownership while leaving the practices "incident to it" in place would have been the height of folly. He did not add, as Douglass would insist until his death, that such a limited gain was hardly worth the blood shed to destroy slavery. In a stinging rejoinder to Bradley's cavalier disclaimer that blacks should now be "mere citizens" with no special claims to the law's protection, Harlan declared that it was the continued white resistance to their being "mere citizens" that prompted the need for such laws in the first place and for the government's continued vigilance.

Not everyone, either then or later, accorded much weight to what was at stake in the Civil Rights Cases. In the decision's aftermath, practically every newspaper commentary described the decision as "widely expected" by knowledgeable lawyers. The Civil Rights Act, they insisted, was little more than a symbolic gesture to the memory of Charles Sumner, the Massachusetts senator and veteran abolitionist who had long fought for such legislation. It had been passed in a lame-duck session as the last hurrah of Republicans who had been defeated in the congressional elections of 1874, which brought into office the first postwar Democratic Congress. A dead letter from its inception, they insisted, the law's enforcement had been lax and more often an irritant and obstacle to good race relations than genuine insurance of equal treatment. A few black spokesmen publicly endorsed such obituaries, but most felt as Bishop Henry McNeal Turner did. A maverick former Georgia legislator and sometime immigrationist, Turner flatly declared that "Nothing has hurt us so much since the day we were emancipated . . ."

Turner's assessment was premature, to say the least, since many other injuries followed in rapid succession. Two weeks after the civil rights decision a bloody riot in Danville, Virginia, crushed a hopeful biracial political movement that had taken control of that state's government. The following year, Democrats won back the White House for the first time since 1860. In stark contrast with the chronologies most professional historians would later adopt, those who lived through the 1880s might well have dated Reconstruction's final interment with this grim constellation of events.

Two years later, in 1885, blacks commemorated the twenty-second anniversary of Lincoln's publication of his draft proclamation of emancipation. As he had on so many previous occasions, Douglass rose to speak to a Washington gathering marking that historic event. He began by noting the changed tone of these proceedings from earlier anniversaries: "conditions are changed, or appear to be changed. We do not stand where we stood one year ago." In the last election, the Republicans had been "defeated, humiliated, and driven from place and power," and blacks now found themselves "under the rule of a political party which steadily opposed their every step from bondage to freedom." Straining to decipher just what this change portended, Douglass spoke in a tone that was unusually ambivalent and uncertain. Though deeply suspicious of the Democratic Party, he had been reassured by President Grover Cleveland's declarations of continued solicitude for black civil rights. Although a self-confessed "party man," he did not put partisan allegiance above principle and held out the possibility that the Democrats could and should enjoy a long lease on national power—if they did the right thing. He clearly had little confidence, however, that a party so beholden to former slave drivers would in fact "do justice to the Negro." Although white Americans were too quick to forget what slavery and the war to destroy it were all about, Douglass firmly believed "the heart of the nation to be still safe and sound." Republicans should remember their own roots and appeal to that heart rather than to narrow material interests in tariffs and hard currency. Remembering the long transatlantic campaign for freedom and justice, perhaps, Douglass argued that ordinary politics did not serve in times of extraordinary challenge. "The life of the nation is secure only while the nation is honest, truthful, and virtuous; for upon these conditions depend the life of its life." At this historic moment, his nation must be true to itself.

Despite this remonstrance, Douglass, in the final decade of a lifetime of struggle, was clearly uncertain about how to read the currents and crosscurrents of the moment. Ranging over a discursive terrain at times idealistic and hopeful, at others analytical and calculating, his speech was a veritable pastiche of contradictions. At one point he declared confidently that "slavery has now become an anachronism, a superstition of the past, having no proper relation to the age and body of our times," while later he conceded that the Supreme Court's recent civil rights decision had gutted the Fourteenth Amendment, leaving the Constitution "under the feet of the mob," and blacks at their mercy. "Of what avail is citizenship and the elective franchise," he seethed, "where a whole people are deliberately abandoned to anarchy by the Government under which they live, and told they must protect themselves from violence as best they may." The substance of black Americans' hard-won emancipation was endangered, and the remedies were as yet uncertain. Alternately hinting at revolution and cosmic justice, the man who had once broken the slave breaker Covey now warned his audience that "the Negro is not what he was twenty years ago." They should not be surprised that he might "some day make common cause and learn some of the dangerous modes of protest against injustice adopted in other countries." This abrupt, menacing image of world revolution was softened almost as soon as uttered, however. Far more imaginable for Douglass was the divine vengeance that had cleansed the nation of the sin of slavery a quarter century earlier. "God is just," he reminded his audience, and "His justice cannot sleep forever." For just a moment, anyone present that day old enough to have attended abolitionist meetings a generation earlier might have heard in these words echoes of a young fugitive slave.

5

RAGTIME

Race and Nation at the Dawn of the Twentieth Century

On October 21, 1892, the World's Columbian Exposition—known collo-quially as the Chicago World's Fair—opened with a grand parade down Chicago's Michigan Avenue. Riding in one of the carriages carrying the diplomatic corps and foreign ministers, Frederick Douglass was greeted with spontaneously warm applause by the mostly white crowd lining that broad thoroughfare. The crowd had instantly recognized the distinctive white mane of "the famous colored statesman," explained a Chicago *Daily News* reporter, referring to Douglass's recent service as the American con-sul in Haiti. One imagines that this might have been a bittersweet moment for Douglass, for in many ways his own reception at that historic moment reflected the enduring ambivalences and contradictions of his people's pu-tative place in the nation's life and politics. Although he was warmly re-ceived by the crowd as a living American hero, his official standing at the fair was, ironically, by grace of his association with Haiti, rather than his native land. The Haitian government had asked him to manage their pa-vilion, in recognition of his prior diplomatic service in that black republic, where he had sought not only to represent American interests but some-times to protect Haitians from America's imperialistic designs. Like so many others before (and after), Douglass lived the "double-consciousness" to which a decade later W.E.B. Du Bois would give a name.

The festivities in Chicago heightened that sense of duality for black Americans generally, but none more so than the men of the Ninth U.S. Cavalry, a detachment of which rode just a few blocks ahead of Douglass's diplomatic entourage. The Ninth was one of the four "colored" regiments that had been formed largely of black veterans at the conclusion of the

Civil War. The 120 men of A and F Troops, detailed to Chicago that day, were the legacy of the arduous efforts Douglass and other black leaders had made to convince Lincoln of the efficacy of blacks fighting for their own freedom. The sharp contrast between the warm applause that greeted them now and the skepticism and hostility with which the idea of arming blacks in defense of the nation had been received just thirty years earlier must have brought a smile to Douglass's lips. Now these veteran soldiers were among the core units of America's small regular army, and they had been prominently featured in the crowd-pleasing musters and parades in the days preceding the fair's official dedication. Contemporary accounts took special note of their proud military bearing, with one reporter declaring that they "seemed to feel the importance of the occasion" more than the white troops, and that the precision of their movements won "many rounds of applause along the line of march." All of this, of course, stood in sharp contrast to the typical minstrel-like portrayals of blacks found in most of those very same newspapers.

Unlike Douglass, these men lived and died in relative anonymity, leaving little historical trace beyond the fragments buried in military service or pension files. Like him, however, they embodied the living contradictions of black life in America, their lives and destinies echoing the "doubleness" of Douglass's more famous life history, and that of African Americans in general. At least two of these men, Frank H. Stewart and Charles McD. Carter, had first enlisted in the army in 1883, the very year the Supreme Court rendered its verdict in the Civil Rights Cases. Their origins rooted in an earlier struggle for freedom, by the 1890s the black troops' principal assignments on the home front were keeping peace between small ranchers and large capitalist landowners, maintaining control over striking miners and railroad workers, and most important, suppressing the last flickers of resistance among Indians in the trans-Mississippi West. Practically all of them had been at Wounded Knee Creek, South Dakota, two years earlier, just after the Seventh Cavalry massacred 150 Sioux men, women, and children. Marching eighty-six miles in twenty-four hours, they arrived in time to rescue a detachment of the Seventh from an ambush and to help suppress the scattered resistance of surviving warriors.

A few months before they joined the festivities in Chicago, some of these troops had been stationed in the more hospitable climes of Fort Myers, Virginia, as a reward for their services at Wounded Knee, but their outraged white neighbors soon forced the War Department to send them back to Fort Robinson, Nebraska. From there they made their way to Chicago. In a week filled with musters, dress parades, and the official dedication parade itself, the black unit was repeatedly sandwiched between the famous Seventh and an all-Indian cavalry troop recently formed from among survivors of the Wounded Knee massacre. It was as if a particular theme of national becoming was being ostentatiously played out: ex-slave soldiers and conquered Indians riding in tandem with white troops who epitomized the taming of the western frontier. This juxtaposition seemed to mark a symbolic closure to the two conflicts, slavery and the Indian Wars, that had driven national policy since the country's founding, two brutal usurpations, of labor and of land, that formed the basis of its very being. Even as they confronted the contradictions of their own sense of national belonging—their simultaneous assimilation to and exclusion from a reunited America—black Americans remained crucial foils to the nation as it remade itself.

Several members of the black troop parading in Chicago that day would go on to other campaigns in America's evolving imperial adventure—charging with Teddy Roosevelt up Cuba's San Juan Hill and slogging through the jungles of the Philippines to suppress a rebellion against the American occupation that followed the Spanish-American War. Private Henry Venable, born into slavery on the eve of the Civil War, would die in Cuba, succumbing to yellow fever. Charles McD. Carter, Frank H. Stewart, Charles Lewis, and Albert Harris, all born during slavery's final years, survived Cuba only to move on to the Philippines. There Harris would be listed as a deserter; if true, perhaps he had been inspired by David Fagen, another Cuban war veteran, who renounced his American nationality to become a legendary leader among the Filipino insurrectos. The others returned to America after twenty or more years of service to their country's imperial ambitions, just as the nightmare of injustice Douglass had so feared fell like a cloak over African American aspirations. Their moment of glory in Chicago would not last, the brief symbolic acknowledgment of place, of national belonging, would not long survive the opening day's parade.

White City, White Nation

Turn-of-the-century debates about African Americans' national status and place played out across multiple story lines and on a global stage, all inter-

The storied Ninth Cavalry was one of four regiments organized initially from black Civil War
veterans. It would play a prominent role in the Indian Wars, the Cuban campaign, and the
suppression of the insurrection in the Philippines following the Spanish-American War.

leaved with larger questions about the broader national destiny. The black
experience during these years cannot be plotted in simple linear frames
or a single script. To a degree not witnessed before or since, the 1890s found
black Americans in motion—to the Caribbean, to Africa, to Europe, even
to the Asian Pacific. Some searched for national belonging elsewhere,
some went as missionaries of American civilization and promise. To capture this era as its subjects lived it is to recognize that the quarter century
between the Chicago World's Fair and America's entry into World War I
unfolded as a varied set of vignettes whose final outcomes were as yet indeterminate. The African American experience during these years, therefore, might best be imagined not as linear threads of a narrative but a series
of sepia-colored snapshots, like picture postcards of faraway moments and
places.

The official dedication of the fair in the autumn of 1892 unfolded during a momentous year in the life of the United States, dubbed years later
as the hemisphere's "first new nation." It was a year in which tensions about
the nation's character and access to citizenship played out across many
domains. It was the eighth year of a decade-long interlude between reces-

sions that would sorely test the country's economic and political systems. Although challenged by a multitude of populist forces, the country's eventual return to prosperity found capitalist control of both the economy and the polity more entrenched than ever. Early in the year, José Martí journeyed to Ybor City, Florida, a settlement of Cuban émigré tobacco workers adjacent to Tampa's native black community, to recruit supporters for the next stage of Cuba's suspended war of independence. He found there Afro-Cubans whose fervent support helped reshape the liberation movement. He could not have guessed that U.S. intervention just a few years later would strengthen reactionary forces in newly independent Cuba and ultimately blunt its hopeful first moves toward an antiracist future. During the following summer, the Populist Party, the closest America itself would come to a biracial, working-class movement for a very long time, held its national convention in Omaha, Nebraska, a meeting that proved to be both its high point and the beginning of its end. In June, Homer Plessy boarded a first-class coach on a train in New Orleans for a ride of roughly sixty miles to Covington, Louisiana; his journey would end four years later in the U.S. Supreme Court, where a decision on the legality of his acting like an ordinary human being would seal African American's second-class legal status for the next half century. By year's end, America had recorded the highest annual body count of lynching victims in its history; the depths of depravity and horror lynch mobs could achieve, however, still lay in the future.

Scenes at the Chicago World's Fair capture something of the syncopated, contrapuntal pulse of that moment, as the nation's anxious efforts to rewrite its own story clashed with similar efforts by its black citizens. Though dedicated in October 1892, the fair did not open to the general public until the following spring. Celebrating the four hundredth anniversary of Columbus's discovery of the Americas—an event North Americans now freely appropriated much as they did the name given to the hemisphere as a whole—the organizers sought to link the Genoese admiral's feat with their own notion of embarking on a providential mission, full of self-congratulation for having completed a century of constitutional governance, despite the near-fatal interruption of civil war. The restless spirit of adventure and invention that drove Columbus across the seas, they avowed, had also propelled Americans to the threshold of great material prosperity and made their nation the democratic culmination of Western civilization. All of these themes were fully in evidence at the World's Columbian Exposition, making it an extended narrative of national becoming.

The nation that the fair promoters sought to exhibit was decidedly modern and white, however, an image fiercely challenged by an emerging generation of African Americans. Their conflict notwithstanding, both blacks and whites were engaged in the task of weaving new narratives of the nation in anticipation of the coming century. Those narratives, like the fair itself, were often organized around spatial and temporal dualities: not only America versus Europe and the West versus the rest, but also the primitive and the past versus civilization and modernity. The fair's spatial dualism was rendered visually and literally by the neoclassical stylings of the "White City" at its center and the darkly raucous, vaguely chaotic Midway on its periphery. In the first site were the formal official exhibits of nation-states and civil societies; in the second, one found ethnographic spectacles of ostensibly primitive peoples and a carnivalesque atmosphere. As cultural historian Alan Trachtenberg points out, however, the dualities traced in space were complicated by the fact that the White City itself straddled a temporal divide, being at once "a consummation and a new beginning," a dialectic playing out visually and aurally at the fair. Lingering sectional tensions led fair promoters to anchor these new beginnings in ostentatious symbolic reconciliations of North and South, while blacks sought comparable manipulations of their slave past to recast their aspirations for the future. Indeed, blacks and whites shared a heightened sense that a historic transition was in progress, with each suggesting in different ways that the past must be colonized in order to project a desired future. For each, the celebration of civilization would play on the proximity and vitality of the primitive. For each, histories of origin had to be rewritten.

Befitting the fair's nationalist agenda, for example, the historian Frederick Jackson Turner read a seminal paper on the significance of the frontier in American history before the nine-year-old American Historical Association, one of the many professional organizations holding meetings in Chicago in conjunction with the exposition. Then a young professor at the University of Wisconsin, Turner offered an updated version of America's providential mission, locating its energy and drive in the struggle to tame the savage frontier. His narrative of America's national formation aspired to be a coherent and scientific rendering of "the really American part of our history," but it also elaborated a new national imaginary and invented a new tradition, one that literally wrote blacks out of the nation's history. America, in an appropriately Columbian gesture, was being rediscovered. Challenging previous scholars' preoccupation with America's European origins and the slavery controversy—dismissing the latter as a mere "incident" in the nation's history—Turner argued that it was the frontier, that "meeting point between savagery and civilization," that had profoundly shaped American character and destiny. A source of "perennial rebirth" and "fluidity," the frontier gave America its vitality, kept the nation in "continuous touch with the simplicity of primitive society," and thus, much like the Mediterranean Sea had been to Columbus's world, opened vistas for exploration and revised destinies. Indeed, it was the frontier that made America but "another name for opportunity."

Turner's thesis was one of the many ways the fair showcased both America's providential origins in the westward march of English-speaking peoples and the genesis of an "exceptional" social order on its western boundary. The fair's location in brash and booming Chicago underscored these themes. The image of a kind of natural succession in which a virile America inherited the mantle of leadership from the aging nations of the Old World seemed manifest in the very geography of Chicago. Standing at the crossroads of both the national rail system and the Great Lakes, the city was like "a new Mediterranean" city, declared *Chicago Tribune* columnist "Gath." As if to underscore this double-edged reference, Gath reminded his readers that while Columbus had brought slavery to the Americas, Chicago stood for the triumph of free labor and new beginnings. Gath's own parents had reared a son of fugitive slaves who now worked as a porter for Chicago's own Pullman Company. Meanwhile, ex-Confederates poured into the city ready for a new start.

Although sharing the broad theme of heralding western expansion as the leading edge of the progress of civilization, Turner and Gath peopled their narratives differently. Indian peoples had vanished in Turner's account, much like the receding frontier, while the geographical shift from east to west and the discursive decentering of slavery and the Civil War rendered black Americans practically invisible as well. By contrast, the *Tribune* columnist deliberately juxtaposed an ex-slave, former slaveholders, and his own abolitionist forebears, hinting perhaps that newfound sectional and racial reconciliations should fuel any national resurgence. For Gath, rewriting the nation was a multiracial undertaking.

Indeed, America's remaking was very much a phenomenon centered in eastern and midwestern urban industrial centers such as Chicago, rather than on Turner's frontier. Fast emerging as a major power in the Atlantic world at the very moment in which the movement of people, goods, and ideas were achieving truly global dimensions, the nation was in the midst of a fundamental transformation. Between 1870 and 1900, total world production of goods and services increased fourfold, and America joined Britain and Germany in the forefront of that industrial surge. With industrialization came the growth of cities, increasingly rapid transportation and communication, and phenomenal movements of populations across the globe, especially across the Atlantic—all of which portended major changes in everyday life and how people "placed" themselves in the world. Within a very short time, white Americans would come to worry about America's racial destiny, including the survival of "white" America as such in the midst of a mushrooming, southern European immigrant population, many of whom were not yet accepted as truly white by their American hosts.

For their part, African American leaders shared a contagious sense of being poised for radical departures in the life of the nation and the race, notwithstanding the persistence of intolerance. Their ubiquitous use of various adjectives and synonyms for "newness" suggests their sense of entering a new era, one in which the nation itself would be redefined in positive terms. Haunting the Chicago World's Fair, in historian William McFeely's memorable phrase, like "a ghost of old commitments," seventy-four-year-old Frederick Douglass constantly reminded everyone how far the nation had slipped from the bloodstained promise of emancipation. But even Douglass could not resist a measure of optimism as he surveyed the scene. The solution to the misnamed Negro problem, he was fond of saying, was simply that America should try justice and the problem would be solved. In 1892, he still believed the nation would make that choice.

Over the century's final decade and well into the next, America brushed aside Douglass's challenge; that the nation was destined to be a white man's country seemed clear and inexorable. *Inexorable* should not be read as *inevitable*, however. In hindsight one might dismiss black optimism at this historical moment as myopic, even self-deceiving, but the inhabitants of a given moment are not privileged, or damned, to experience their lives through history's rearview mirror. They live within the moment, perceiving both defeat and possibility hanging in the balance. And thus did the nation's destiny and black folks' place in that destiny still appear, as late as 1892, to be matters for contestation rather than resignation.

"New Negroes" in the "White City"

When one of the principal orators intoned on the fair's opening day that "We celebrate the emancipation of man," he obviously did not have recently emancipated African Americans in mind. Despite the prominence of black troops in the inaugural parade, African Americans found no official place in the fair organizers' vision of the nation. Their exclusion may well have been less an intentional insult to the race, however, than the consequence of an avid pursuit of one of the fair's principal themes: the sectional reconciliation of North and South. Since showing how much the wounds of the Civil War had healed was a major goal of the exposition from the outset, the white South received numerous concessions in the fair's planning and administration. As a consequence, the same politics of reunion and sectional reconciliation that Douglass found so galling in other arenas also stifled African Americans' quests for representation on the various national and local planning boards. With the exception of the Women's Building, exhibits were organized through state boards, meaning that most black applicants had to be screened by all-white southern state committees. The predictable result was that except for New York State and a few southern black colleges, there were no official exhibits to highlight black American progress or contributions to civilization in the White City, a fact prompting the wry joke among blacks that this was truly a "white" city.

Black people figured prominently in exhibits intended to contrast modern civilization with humankind's primitive origins, however. Although the sovereign nations of Haiti and Liberia, the world's only black republics, were found in dignified pavilions, the fair chose to represent what was taken to be the *normative* state of African-descended peoples by an ostensible replica of a Dahomean village located on the Midway on the periphery of the fairground's center. In doing so, fair officials continued a tradition begun at the World's Fair in Paris in 1889, when the so-called ethnographic village was enshrined as a standard feature of these "carni-

This cartoonist's imagery of African Americans attending the Chicago Fair was typical of the verbal and physical portraits circulating at the time.

vals of the industrial age," as the historian Curtis Hinsley has dubbed them. Thus the Chicago fair, like most other world's fairs during the late nineteenth century, continued an unseemly blend of museum pedagogy and carnival showmanship. With the Midway strip and the White City as visual emblems of humankind's dual nature, its layout was a virtual mapping of relations of power, of control and subordination, of inclusion and exclusion, and, of course, of the relative weights of the different races and cultures in the scale of civilization. On the Midway, the Dahomeans (who came from present-day Benin), along with other exotic cultures, were displayed in their putatively native habitats like "an illustrated encyclopedia of humanity."

Already chafing from their losing battle for greater representation within the White City, many blacks threw their hands up in disgust at this final insult and urged a boycott of the fair. Others continued to plead for a separate Negro annex, where the progress and dignity of the race could be displayed. The latter idea, however, was vigorously attacked as surrender to segregation, as was the alternative plan of hosting a special Colored American Day for the celebration of black culture. As one black group from Chicago declared "there is to be no '*white* American citizen's day,' why should there be a 'colored American citizen's day'?" Surely this was but an unseemly concession to the idea that black Americans were not an integral part of the whole of American civilization. Others, including black fairgoer Thomas J. Bell, an alumnus of Atlanta University, thought such inflexible opposition to a separate African American exhibit was self-defeating. Given that blacks had emerged from slavery only thirty years ago, he lamented, "and for the good of those who would deny that they belong to the Nation, and declare that 'a Niger [sic] can't learn nothing,' it would have been well if they had made a special effort to get up an exhibit."

Frederick Douglass and Ida B. Wells came up with an alternative idea that had the virtue of sustaining a black presence at the fair but couching it in protest. Blacks would compose and distribute a pamphlet criticizing their exclusion, entitled, "The Reason Why the Colored American Is Not in the World's Columbian Exhibition." It would include an essay on black progress since emancipation and a fact-laden statistical demonstration of African American capacity—altogether a collective epic of a people's rise "up from slavery." Being seasoned international activists and thus conscious of the importance of world public opinion to white Americans' self-regard, Douglass and Wells proposed to translate their pamphlet into French, German, and Spanish and place it in the hands of as many foreign visitors as possible. Columbus's seed, they would show the world, had produced not a flower of human progress but a canker of moral regression. In the end, however, not enough money could be raised to distribute a multilingual pamphlet, so it was published in English, with only the preface translated into the three major European languages.

Douglass endorsed the separate "Colored American Day," convinced by performing artists such as violinist and composer Will Marion Cook that it would be an opportunity to showcase African American progress in the arts, specifically in classical music. Ida Wells and other activists broke sharply with Douglass over this decision, fearing that the day could be transformed into just one more occasion to ridicule black pretensions to cultivation and dignity. Ominously, while special trains were arranged to bring carloads of blacks to Chicago for the day, white opportunists made plans to distribute free watermelons.

In the end, the celebration hovered perilously between a disastrous minstrel-like carnival and a dignified African American showcase. Doug-

lass arrived early but then went home in disgust at disturbing signs that
the event was rapidly degenerating into just the embarrassing spectacle
skeptics had predicted. When he returned to give the opening address of
the program that afternoon, he was visibly shaken by catcalls from white
hecklers. He soon righted himself, however, and assuming the imposing,
authoritative posture of the fierce warrior of the abolitionist struggles of
old, he delivered an inspired condemnation of the rising tide of racial discrimination and of America's failure to live up to its own ideals. Drawing
a palpable counterpoint to the fair's official message, he trumpeted black
progress and protested blacks' exclusion. Douglass's august presence transformed the event into yet another occasion for protest. His address was
followed by performances of classical music and other orations, all giving
tangible evidence of African Americans' mastery of Western culture.
Firebrand Ida B. Wells rushed to the fairgrounds later to apologize and
acknowledge the elder statesman's sagacity.

Douglass's speech at the Colored American Day rehearsed many of
the points and much of the language he would invoke in another address
delivered the following year, variously entitled, "The Lesson of the Hour"
and "Why Is the Negro Lynched," one of the final speeches of his life. His
anger having abated with the passage of time perhaps, Douglass heaped
ostentatious praise on the fair as a whole in the later printed version of his
speech. The exposition was "glorious," a "grand ethnological object lesson,"
"one of the most grandest demonstrations of civilization that the world
had ever seen." The treatment blacks received at the hands of the Chicago
fair promoters still rankled months later, however, and the Dahomean
spectacle remained an open sore. Having preferred the Negro as minstrel
(as represented by the Dahomeans) to the educated Negro of culture, he
seethed, the fair promoters had squandered their credibility. In some of
the bitterest rhetoric of the speech, Douglass linked the acts of discrimination against African American culture and talent with the physical
violence of lynching that formed the core theme of his speech. The actions
of the fair managers announced to the world "that the colored people of
America are not deemed by Americans as within the compass of American
law, progress and civilization. It says to the lynchers and mobocrats of the
South, go on in your hellish work of Negro persecution. You kill their bodies, we kill their souls."

Soul killing was a strong metaphor for the injuries black Americans
endured, and its use suggests not only the depth of bitterness Douglass

and many other African Americans felt but also the measure of their expectations. With slavery's destruction they expected full and equal citizenship, not simply in law but in that larger sense captured in the debate over
the Civil Rights Cases ten years earlier—that the "badge of servitude"
must be destroyed as well. Those expectations had survived the dashed
hopes of Reconstruction and all the subsequent violent affronts. To be met
with ridicule at this moment, to be associated with the primitive and backward in the ubiquitous cartoons poking fun at the benighted Africans and
their dull-witted American cousins was soul-destroying indeed.

There is a profound historical irony, however, in Douglass's discursive
link of American minstrelsy and lynch mobs with the Dahomean exhibit.
If African Americans were not as they were depicted in the popular press,
neither were the Africans. If the ongoing narrative reconstruction of the
American nation—one that excluded blacks—was complicated and mul-
tivocal, so was that of the Fon villagers huddled against the cool Chicago
spring. Their putative performance of African village life enacted the fair
promoters' fantasies of timeless primitivity, but at that very moment their

"The Johnson Family Visit the Dahoman [sic] Village. MRS. JOHNSON:
'Ezwell Johnson, stop shakin' Han's wid dat Heathen! You want de hul Fair ter t'ink
you's found a Poo' Relation?'"

own lives and culture were undergoing a radical, historic transformation. Although we know little about the individual members of this group, it is clear that the village on the Midway was a constructed rather than an actual community. Some, if not most, of the "villagers" came from West African cities rather than the African bush. At least three of the "villagers" were reported to have been fluent in French, reinforcing suspicion of a cosmopolitan experience if not an urban provenance.

The world the Fon came from had already undergone profound economic and political changes since the height of the slave trade decades earlier. Upon his succession to the throne in 1818, Gezo, king of Dahomey, had embarked upon a kind of modernization campaign, demilitarizing the kingdom and shifting the economy from its reliance on slave trading to palm oil, which encouraged the development in turn of a wealthy and cosmopolitan African merchant class in the principal cities, Cotonou and Porto Novo. King Gezo's policies were reversed during the 1860s and '70s by his successors, Glele and Behanzin, who revived both militarism and slave raiding, but their policies had alienated the urban elite, opening a source of social tension and political weakness. When the French, who had been granted commercial privileges earlier, pressed for recognition of territorial claims as well, they found ready allies among that elite. Consequently, while the Dahomeans entertained the crowds in Chicago that spring and summer, their native country was being overrun by the French along with their Senegalese mercenary allies, the *tirailleurs*. Before fairgoers returned home, Behanzin had been deposed and exiled to one of France's American colonies, Martinique. Under these circumstances, the fierce anger with which Douglass and other black Americans greeted the African presence in Chicago would seem deeply misplaced. The Fon people's tragic situation certainly deserved more empathy than scorn, and their brutal loss of nationhood resonated with similar threats at that moment to African Americans' sense of national belonging.

A broader perspective on African and African American relations suggests an even more complex situation, however. For all his scornful rejection of what the Fon presence in Chicago symbolized, Douglass paid them a visit one evening and was received with the dignity and warmth befitting a chief. The more complex reality was that African Americans' attitudes toward Africa were neither simple rejection nor wholehearted identification but a profound ambivalence built on both engagement and

This photograph of a group of Fon people at the Chicago Fair belies the cartoon stereotypes typically published about the Dahomean Village.

distance. There was both pride in their African heritage and condescension toward the putative backwardness of contemporary Africans. Undoubtedly ignorance played some part in shaping African Americans' responses to Africa, but given the various immigrants, missionaries, and ordinary workers and travelers to Africa, black American contact with the continent was probably greater during the 1890s than it would be for another half century. Many black Americans watched closely as Europeans fundamentally recast Africa's place in the international order, carving out their respective spheres of influence in Africa preparatory to formal colonization.

Since Paul Cuffee's expeditions in the early nineteenth century, Africa's fate in the global order had weighed heavily on black American's sense of national identity. Throughout the nineteenth century, emigration movements waxed and waned in inverse relation to blacks' prospects in America, growing during the 1850s as slavery seemed more entrenched, and receding in the 1870s with slavery's destruction and the promise of emancipation. By 1892, scarcely a thousand emigrants had ventured to West Africa since emancipation and fewer still had been able to endure the privations long enough to establish permanent settlements there. Some expeditions had ended disastrously with erstwhile migrants returning home destitute. Others never made it to Africa at all, such as the estimated 410 black Arkansans who, during the same year the Chicago fair opened, collectively paid $3,000 for a chartered train to Brunswick, Georgia, where they were to board a ship to Liberia. The ship never came. Although such well-publicized failures probably discouraged many actual emigrants, the *debate* over emigration—fueled by post-Reconstruction economic and political violence—kept Africa before the black American public as a live option nonetheless. Indeed, back-to-Africa emigration movements continued to roil the internal politics of black communities well into the third decade of the next century.

More important than actual emigration and perhaps equally responsible for its continued resonance were the African missionary projects sponsored by black churches. The churches channeled black Americans' identification with Africa by giving it a religious framing. Thus it was not enslavement that connected black Americans to Africa but Christian duty, which transformed the alleged African heathenism that so profoundly embarrassed them into a challenging target for reform. Black Americans could be morally linked to Africans through their slave past but culturally distanced from them as the agents of their redemption. Thus did missionary work effectively sublimate the tensions African Americans felt between their African origins and their desired connection with an American future. As historian James Campbell has so perceptively observed, "African missions provided proof that history was progressive, that the ordeal of slavery had indeed meant something, that black Americans were yet a chosen people, destined to play a special role in the unfolding design of Providence." Here, African Americans found their own version of America's providential mission.

Foremost in the black missionary effort was the AME Church, whose episcopal structure better enabled it to concentrate funds and activities and whose traditionally militant, politically engaged ministry gave it the capacity to lead such ventures. Foremost among these political ministers was Henry McNeal Turner, who had become a major advocate of African emigration after the betrayal of Reconstruction in Georgia in the 1870s. Turner visited Africa four times during the 1890s; indeed, he was just returning from the continent when he arrived at the Chicago fair's Congress on Africa in August 1893. At that time Turner's African dream was still anathema to many of his colleagues, but AME women's groups gradually made African missionary work acceptable, aided by a new generation of ministerial leadership. These new leaders effectively changed the subject of the earlier debate: from renunciation of America for Africa, which emigrationists such as Turner insisted upon, to Africa as a moral challenge in which black America could prove itself and vindicate the race. Like Moses raised in the Pharaoh's household, they would go forth to lead their Israel out of Egyptian darkness.

Meanwhile a new generation of indigenous religious leaders was emerging in South Africa. Driven by conditions much like those confronted by Richard Allen and Absalom Jones a century earlier, several lay ministers withdrew from the white Wesleyan Methodist missionary society in 1892. Inspired by the prophecy in Psalm 68 ("Princes shall come out of Egypt; Ethiopia shall soon stretch out her hands unto God."), they called themselves the Ethiopian Church. Having come to see African Americans as models of progress and modernity, they eventually made contact (through Turner) with the AME and, by 1896, affiliated themselves with it.

Africans studying at African American colleges, especially Wilberforce, facilitated these first ministerial contacts, but the South Africans' exposure to aspects of black American popular culture laid the ground-work. Port cities such as Durban and Cape Town had always been impor-tant points of contact between Africans and African Americans, many of them black seamen who made up a significant share of the American mer-chant marine in the nineteenth century. The discovery of diamonds and gold in the 1880s and '90s brought an even greater African American pres-ence in southern Africa. And with them came cultural interactions, espe-cially the spiritual music introduced by traveling theater companies modeled loosely on the Jubilee singing groups first organized by black American colleges. These performances departed sharply from the American origi-nals, however. When Orpheus McAdoo's Jubilee Singers toured South Africa in the 1890s, for example, their performances were a bizarre mé-lange of spirituals and minstrelsy, which proved popular with whites as well as blacks. At almost precisely the moment Douglass was upbraiding the Dahomean's exhibit for reinforcing the American minstrel image, there-fore, black Americans were performing the real thing in southern Africa. The deeper irony, however, was that in neither case were things entirely as they seemed. What Africans seized upon from McAdoo's performers was not the idea of their catering to an archaic racial past, but their self-confident negotiation of the modern world, their savoir faire, their cul-tural modernity—or, in a word, their American-ness, the very identity de-nied them at home.

African American historian Rayford Logan famously dubbed the first de-cades of the twentieth century "the nadir" of black American history, and in some sense that gloomy narrative of exclusion has dominated histori-ans' accounts of this era ever since. But as Logan pointed out, the nadir was reached ironically "not because of lack of attention [to blacks' degraded status] . . . but because of the efforts to improve it." The 1890s had opened, he observed, with unsuccessful, but nonetheless viable, attempts to pass voting rights protections and national education funding through the Lodge election and Blair education bills, respectively. The success of either might have produced a more democratic polity and civil society in the twentieth-century South. The dynamism of the moment, therefore, gave racial exclu-sion a dual aspect and suggests a more complicated story than one simply of denigration and loss.

This dynamism was fully on display at the Chicago fair, where blacks constituted a far more significant presence than implied by their "official" absence. Sprawling over multiple sites and events beyond the White City, from which blacks *were* by and large excluded, the larger fair supplied a broad, synergistic terrain. As historian Christopher Reed has shown, ordinary black folk and their leading lights gathered to ponder and debate their past, present, and future claims on the American nation in the numerous meetings and conferences at other locations in the city, which often used the fair as an occasion to pursue parallel, unrelated, or even contrary agendas. Somewhere, at some time over this six-month period, the full range of issues and questions facing black Americans were addressed: sharecropping and convict lease, lynching and peonage, migration and emigration. Not one event, one place, one set of people, nor even one conversation, these multiple, intergenerational assemblies encompassed many of the major figures from the past and most of those who would claim leadership roles in black communities over the next decade. Of the two figures who would dominate black politics in the next decade, W.E.B. Du Bois was still in Berlin studying for his doctorate, but his future nemesis, Booker T. Washington, addressed a session of the Congress on Labor that met in Chicago that summer. Ida B. Wells met her future husband, Ferdinand Barnett, while working on the pamphlet protesting black exclusion from the fair, and stayed to make Chicago her home. Robert S. Abbott came to the fair as a member of the Hampton University Quartet; he returned later to found and edit the Chicago *Defender*, which would profoundly influence black public opinion over the first half of the twentieth century.

Fair events also offered national visibility to current Chicago residents: Charles Edwin Bentley; Fannie Barrier Williams and her husband, S. Laing Williams, one of the first black graduates of the University of Michigan Law School; all three were prominent among speakers or hosts during the festivities. Reflecting the shift in professional location of black leadership since Reconstruction, politicians were superseded as the dominant black spokesmen by young professionals such as Bentley and Williams, or educators such as Anna Julia Cooper, Fannie Jackson Coppin, and Booker T. Washington. All were figures with growing national reputations. There were also established black literary figures such as Francis Ellen Watkins, up-and-coming ones such as Paul Laurence Dunbar, and future greats such as James Weldon Johnson. The latter, a future leader of the

NAACP, was then an Atlanta University student working as a "chairboy," which involved pushing foot-weary visitors about the grounds in a rickshaw-like vehicle for forty dollars per month.

Foremost among the blacks attending the fair, of course, was Frederick Douglass, the grand old man and undisputed elder statesman, who was in demand everywhere. Yet the most striking aspect of this assembly was the manifest emergence of a new generation of leadership and their self-conscious assumption of that role. Talented and purposeful, optimistic and self-confident, most of these men and women were by the early 1890s in the prime years of their personal and professional lives and quite conscious of themselves as a special generational cohort, a "New Negro." Born in the years immediately preceding or following the American Civil War, few of them had reached their fortieth birthday and most were still in their early thirties. Although sexagenarian Henry McNeal Turner groused that there was no such thing as a "New Negro," it was clearly the one idea or trope most blacks of this era could agree on, even if they gave that idea different inflections and twists. The "New Negroes" were very conscious of the fact that they were the first generation born and/or reared after slavery, which for them was the collective childhood of the race, when blacks were dependent and not free to exercise their judgment or to prove themselves. The Civil War, so traumatic for their parents' generation, was for them, as David Blight beautifully puts it, a "history beyond memory," an event occupying a kind of netherworld between the living present and the irretrievable past. Now, witnessing the twilight of the old century and anticipating the dawn of the new, they were determined to make the most of their freedom, determined to seize upon their destined role as the vanguard that would lead their people to a glorious destiny.

Less anchored in the struggles of the past, they often projected an acute impression of self-fashioning, of being themselves living works of self-creation. Not only were they, like many of their elders, self-tutored, but they conveyed a sense of being the self-conscious authors of their own lives in secular narratives markedly different from those of their more biblically inspired parents. Washington's story of self-making, of rising from humble beginnings, was one many of them shared. Whereas young Booker swept floors at Hampton University to pay his tuition, the others of that generation also secured higher degrees and professional careers not by the grace of God but by sheer force of character and will. As a boy in Fayetteville,

Olaudah Equiano's autobiography would become the seminal saga of the rise from slavery to freedom, replicated in numerous American slave narratives in the early nineteenth century.

Having accumulated a fortune from sailmaking and real estate, James Forten was both a pillar of Philadelphia's African American elite, a militant leader of the early antislavery campaigns, and patriarch of generations of antislavery activists.

Founder of the African Methodist Episcopal Church, Rev. Richard Allen anchored Philadelphia's black community and mobilized the national Negro Convention Movement to fight for equal rights and the abolition of slavery.

This daguerreotype by an unidentified artist captures the brooding image of young Frederick Douglass shortly after he emerged as a fiery spokesman for the abolitionist movement.

Having just returned from a tour promoting her anti-lynching campaign in England, Ida B. Wells had just moved to Chicago in 1893 to lead protests against the exclusion of African Americans from the World's Fair when this photo was taken.

A rare portrait of Ned Cobb and his family taken in 1907 by an itinerant photographer and later passed on as a gift to Cobb's biographer, Theodore Rosengarten.

A photograph taken in Paris in 1900, where W.E.B. Du Bois presented a major photographic exhibit and other materials on African Americans to the Paris Exposition Universelle.

This oil portrait of Jean Toomer was one of the many by the German-born portraitist Winold Reiss that graced Harlem Renaissance publications in the 1920s.

This photograph of a mature Simon Owens was taken by the African American documentary filmmaker Allen Willis for the cover of the German edition of *Indignant Heart: A Black Worker's Journal*.

Birmingham's Sixteenth Street Baptist Church had been the major site for mass meetings and a staging area for civil rights demonstrations. Here, Rev. Fred Shuttlesworth preaches at the funeral for four black girls killed when the church was bombed on September 12, 1963.

Johnnie Tillmon (left) and Beulah Sanders led National Welfare Rights Organization demonstrators in a takeover of the offices of the Secretary of Health, Education, and Welfare on May 13, 1970.

Malcolm X was a prominent organizer for the Nation of Islam in Detroit and Chicago before moving on the New York City. This photo was taken in 1961, shortly before his rise to national prominence as the angry voice of a budding black urban rebellion.

North Carolina, for example, Charles W. Chesnutt was almost literally the figure Washington so often ridiculed in his speeches and writings—the poor black boy in a sharecropper's shack poring over a French grammar. Born of a free Negro family in North Carolina in 1858, Chesnutt taught himself German and French, keeping a journal in which he recorded various reading and writing exercises. To further his education in these languages he hired a white tutor—a German-Jewish immigrant not cowed by the strictures against teaching blacks above their station—and he continued with him until he exhausted what he had to teach. Perhaps the fact that both were self-made is what sustained the warm friendship between Washington and Chesnutt in later years, despite their growing political differences over the former's increasingly accommodationist policies.

Born in 1858, Anna J. Cooper also came up from slavery. She managed to go to Oberlin, where she secured a classical education, one sufficient to enable her later to earn an advanced degree from the Sorbonne, where in 1925, at sixty-seven years of age, she wrote a thesis on French attitudes toward the abolition of slavery. Neither Chesnutt nor Cooper saw any reason why black folk should not aspire to master the best that Western civilization had to offer, since they had done so themselves against great odds. They would have readily endorsed the sentiments Du Bois published later that decade in his essay, "Of the Training of Black Men": "I sit with Shakespeare and he winces not . . . I summon Aristole and Aurelius and . . . they come all graciously with no scorn nor condescension . . . I dwell above the Veil."

The notion of "dwelling above the veil" conjured a vision foreign to Douglass's generation. Perhaps that image could have been embraced only by a generation born and reared during years of war and reconstruction—an era of hope and progress—and yet coming of age in a period of retrenchment and retrogression. Perhaps the poignant contrast of their present with the recent past fired their defiance of efforts to stereotype them. Calls for self-help and self-criticism were common among them, reflecting, on the one hand, their self-confidence and, on the other, their self-regard as molders of their own and their people's destiny. It was, then, out of self-confidence rather than resignation or accommodation, that many of them, like Washington and the young Du Bois, at one time or another endorsed the idea of accepting literacy restrictions on suffrage rights as a spur to blacks to make greater efforts to acquire education—much to Douglass's chagrin. Later generations would seize upon such "elitist" positions and some of their rhetoric as indicators of class pretensions and bourgeois morality, but their positions were consistent with those of the "respectable" black working class who raised their children to be proud advocates for their people, steeled with the conviction that they could draw strength from racist denigration and "uplift the race." Indeed, as the black sociologist E. Franklin Frazier has suggested, this early black elite in the making often adopted as its own the code of honor affected by (if not lived by) the former southern aristocracy.

The Chicago fair itself seemed to offer ample evidence of African American accomplishment since slavery and the promise of excellence in their own generation. The celebrated forty-eight-year-old African American sculptor Edmonia Lewis exhibited her *Hiawatha* as part of the New York State women's exhibit. Thirty-four-year-old Philadelphian Henry O. Tanner arrived from Paris, where he had been studying since 1890, to collect an award for his painting *The Bagpipe Lesson*. In July 1893, just a few blocks north of the World's Fair, thirty-five-year-old Dr. Daniel Hale Williams performed the first successful suturing of the pericardium of the human heart at Provident Hospital, a racially integrated medical facility founded two years earlier to promote modern black medical practice. Meanwhile, a thirty-two-year-old student from Iowa, George Washington Carver, who would emerge as a major agricultural chemist in the coming decade, came to the fair to present his painting *Yucca Gloriosa*, which won honorable mention. Meanwhile, twenty-one-year-old Paul Laurence Dunbar, whom Douglass had met and hired as his assistant at the Haitian pavilion, read to fairgoers from his first poetry collection, *Oak and Ivy*.

It's little wonder, then, that a speaker was shouted down when she urged a boycott of the fair at the opening session of the Congress on the Negro in June. These men and women were determined to be seen and heard. At that same meeting, the proposed Colored American Day, which Douglass supported, was also roundly condemned. *How* they were seen and heard also mattered.

More often than not the New Negro whom one did meet at the fair was a woman. Since many of the women's events were organized and managed outside the regular committees—which were less likely to be controlled by white southern delegates—they offered more opportunities for black participation, despite the ambient condescension and racism. One such venue was the World's Congress of Representative Women, which met during the first month of the fair and included such luminaries as Jane Addams, Susan B. Anthony, and Lucy Stone. Six African American women also made presentations at the Women's Congress, among them the novelist Frances W. Harper and the essayist Anna Julia Cooper, both of whom had published important books the previous year, *Iola Leroy* and *A Voice from the South*, respectively. Fannie Barrier Williams delivered one of the featured addresses, a lecture on the intellectual progress of colored women since emancipation. These women spoke not just for black women but for the race, announcing the arrival of a new generation and the fashioning of a new agenda. They demanded justice, but they would not sink into either bitterness or hopelessness, Williams declared defiantly; they would proudly disdain both faultfinding and supplication. "The Negro people of America have reached a distinctly new era in their career so quickly," she went on, "that the American mind has scarcely had time to recognize the fact, and adjust itself to the new requirements of the people in all things that pertain to citizenship." In a brief address following Williams, Anna J. Cooper added, "We take our stand on the solidarity of humanity, the oneness of life, and the unnaturalness and injustice of all special favoritisms, whether of sex, race, country, or condition." Invited to the lectern to deliver impromptu remarks after these women spoke, Douglass fairly gushed with delight and optimism. "A new heaven is dawning upon us, and a new earth is ours, in which the discrimination against men and women on account of color and sex is passing away." Frances W. Harper echoed Douglass's sentiments when she spoke to that gathering two days later. Although a woman of Douglass's generation, she had articulated the overarching theme of the youngsters when describing in *Iola Leroy* the marital union of her schoolteacher protagonist with a young doctor: "grand and noble poses were lighting up their lives; and they esteemed it a blessed privilege to stand on the threshold of a new era and labor for those who had passed from the old oligarchy of slavery into the new commonwealth of freedom." When she spoke at the fair, the dawning era had become much more specific; she heralded "the threshold of a new women's era."

Whether male or female, these new Negroes were not oblivious to or naïve about the present conditions and future threats confronting the black majority who were still confined to lives as sharecroppers and tenants on southern plantations. At the Congress on Labor that met in August, Ida B. Wells warned of the perils of peonage, and young Booker T. Washington, arriving fresh from his inaugural Tuskegee conference of farm laborers—where he had learned firsthand the vagaries and injustices of crop liens, perpetual debt, and economic servitude—gave an analysis of these developments surprisingly close in tone and content to what Du Bois would write a decade later. Fully three fourths of all black farmers in the Deep South, Washington estimated, were at that moment in debt for the previous year's crop, and eight out of ten for the current crop. As he would do increasingly over the coming years, however, Washington drew back from a radical critique of southern labor exploitation, suggesting instead that the solution was hard work, thrift, and Tuskegee-style industrial training.

There were significant numbers of ordinary black Americans at the fair, and in various ways they made clear that they, too, were New Negroes. Participation of the black masses reflected the development of African American organizational life after emancipation and the black public sphere in general. Blacks arrived in Chicago not only as individuals but as part of national and local organizations such as the Masonic lodges and the Knights of Pythias. The Masons, for example, organized a system of referrals to help their members avoid the subtle housing discrimination they might encounter in Chicago. Members of these groups probably swelled the large "respectable" black working-class audiences that applauded the New Negro speakers, especially at the numerous meetings held in the various black churches close to the fairgrounds.

On the physical and temporal margins of the fair, too, one could witness a phenomenal transformation in the modes of black cultural expression. Building upon decades of experimentation in southern juke joints and red-light districts, ragtime was introduced to the nation in the demimonde environs of the fair and, according to jazz composer W. C. Handy, twenty-five-year-old Scott Joplin was its prime mover. The new music even won plaudits from Will Marion Cook, one of the new professional composers seeking to showcase black classical musical talent at the fair. Ragtime's complex time signatures and syncopation required that one hand carry the melody on which the other "signified" with rifts and counterpoints— all of which made for a music both technically complex yet seemingly effortless and irreverent. Sassy and self-confident, ragtime had, Cook wrote, "the zest of unexpectedness"—a characterization as apt for the times as for the music. Although anchored to the slave past through the "cakewalk," whose strong influences it bore, ragtime was an urban music, at once building on and breaking sharply with the black past as it poignantly invoked the multifaceted mood and tempo of that historical moment.

And yet ragtime, the most strikingly modernist musical form produced in this era, was generally sold through sheet music bearing minstrel images from the slave past; black "unexpectedness" had to be contained in a more predictable guise. As such, it mirrors the multiple ironic counterpoints to the image-building of the New Negroes found elsewhere in the fair's environs. Whether among the Fon villagers, with McAdoo's singers, or in the rhythms of ragtime, black people of this era appear often to have provided cultural spaces wherein the allegedly primitive and the ostensibly modern could meet.

As would happen with increasing frequency thereafter, modernity often arrived in a salesman's satchel, appropriating black imagery for commercial ends. At the fair, a comely black Chicago matron, Nancy Green, distributed a new product bearing her likeness, one of the earliest of the commercially prepared foodstuffs that would transform American domestic life: Aunt Jemima pancakes. Indeed, the 1890s was generally a decade of intensification of the lifeworlds and rhythms we associate with modern domesticity, and not only was that transformation common to the Western world but so was the use of black faces to peddle such commodities. Frequently, the message these black images conveyed were similar to that of Aunt Jemima: the comfort and nurture associated with the putatively defunct southern plantation being instrumental to advancing its opposite, a modernist ethos. In this as in so many ways, the era was not simply transitional but existed in a kind of time warp, or, as Trachtenberg suggests of the era as a whole, was Janus-faced, simultaneously gazing into the past and the future. Essentially, the past was co-opted and domesticated by linking it to the future, and thus, perhaps, enabling that future. Undoubtedly, Nancy Green sought her own future social mobility through this chance masquerade as a figure from a mythical black past. She could hardly have guessed that her smiling image would still contain, a century later, the idea of servitude, the image of the slave past, frozen in time.

Concurrent with the rise of Jim Crow, turn-of-the-century sheet music was illustrated with stereotypical images of black Americans. The title for this illustration is a pun on the word "rags," conflating ragtime music with literally picking up discarded rags.

Homer Plessy's Unfinished Journey

Roughly a week after the grand dedication ceremonies in Chicago celebrated America's providential origins and destiny, Homer A. Plessy was
arraigned before Judge John H. Ferguson in a New Orleans criminal court
on charges of having violated Louisiana's separate car law. This twenty-
nine-year-old shoemaker's challenge to the evolving Jim Crow order was
consistent with the New Negro generation's self-confident assumption
of their rightful "place" in the nation and with the significance of transportation by rail in the substantive and symbolic economy of America's
nascent modernity. Judge Ferguson's rejection of Plessy's claims two weeks
later set the stage for a decision by the nation's highest tribunal that confirmed black Americans' place, separate and—despite protestations to the
contrary—unequal.

In historical hindsight the Plessy decision seems predetermined, given
ample evidence of black folk's declining status in the nation's political,
social, and economic life. During the mid-1880s, however, T. McCants
Stewart of Brooklyn, New York, had traveled by rail through the South
Atlantic seaboard states without experiencing any discrimination. A militant attorney, Stewart would not have contended that his journey was evidence of a racially integrated South, but it did confirm that notwithstanding
the setback of the Supreme Court's recent decision in the Civil Rights
Cases, there was no unified system of racial separation: discriminatory
rules, lacking the force of law, were neither consistently nor strictly enforced. In several southern states, especially where blacks had enjoyed
significant political power during Reconstruction, civil rights laws had
been passed during the 1870s banning discrimination in public accommodation. These laws had to be dismantled before legal segregation could
be put into practice, a process that proved to be problematic in some of
the states where blacks still retained at least marginal political representation. Steamboats along the inland and coastal waterways had always been
and continued to be the most rigidly segregated mode of transportation, but
intracity streetcars were only slowly being segregated again after a period of
relative openness. Railroads, an increasingly essential component of the
national transport system and the very emblems of modernity, were still
the least segregated mode of transport.

The resegregation process came in two waves that bracketed the early
1890s: first, over the five-year period that preceded the opening of the

Chicago World's Fair, nine states, seven of them in the Lower South, adopted new regulations; thereafter, between 1898 and 1907, five others (two of them, border states) followed suit. Significantly, three of the latter states—Virginia and North and South Carolina—acted almost immediately after the Spanish-American War. Indeed, blunting the aspirations that conflict had raised among blacks may well have been a significant part of the legislators' intent.

The content of these laws varied tremendously, reflecting both the tentativeness with which this new challenge to the fruits of the Civil War was initiated and, in some cases, the fact that blacks were still a political presence that had to be negotiated or neutralized in some way. The case of Tennessee, which was the first state to legislate on the subject, in 1881, illustrates the ambiguity of this new departure. The "redeemed" Tennessee legislature of 1875, reacting to the federal Civil Rights Law passed that year, had enacted its own measure guaranteeing proprietors of public accommodations the right to refuse service to any patron as they saw fit. In 1881, when a split in Democratic ranks delivered control of the governorship and the lower house of the legislature to the Republicans, four black representatives sought to repeal this law. After their initiatives failed on two close votes, Republicans compromised on a so-called Separate Car Law, which did not require racial discrimination but simply obliged railways to make separate first-class accommodations available, a compromise designed to placate black complaints about being charged first-class prices for second-class accommodation. Ten years later, operating in a much different political environment, Tennessee amended this legislation so as to make segregation mandatory. Many of the other states that passed laws during that first wave simply followed Tennessee's earlier example, however, either requiring or authorizing separate first-class accommodation for blacks without explicitly mandating segregation.

One historian's survey argues that with the exception of Louisiana and perhaps Arkansas, "blacks commonly found themselves segregated into inferior coaches, regardless of the fares they paid." And, indeed, in 1883, Ida B. Wells was ejected from a first-class coach in Tennessee despite the 1881 law requiring that first-class ticket holders be given first-class service. Though holding a first-class ticket, Wells was assigned to a smoking car rather than the "ladies' car." The testimony of black witnesses throughout this period also makes clear that it was not the literal inability to ride first class that most rankled them but their constant exposure to insults and indignities. In the early 1880s, even so phlegmatic a voice as Booker T. Washington scarcely concealed his contempt and anger when he complained that "[when] a poorly dressed, slovenly white man boards the train he is shown into the colored half coach. When a white man gets drunk or wants to lounge around in an indecent position he finds his way into the colored department."

When a Separate Car Bill was introduced into the Louisiana legislature in the spring of 1890, it seemed likely to share a fate similar to that of the initial legislation in Tennessee. There were still eighteen black members in the legislature, and vigilant members of the recently formed Citizens' Committee immediately rallied and denounced the legislation in a memorial. "Citizenship is national and has no color," they declared, which went to the heart of the matter, because unlike measures in some other states, Louisiana's proposal explicitly mandated racial separation and threatened railway officials and passengers with fines and jail sentences for noncompliance. Black nurses attending white children were exempted, underscoring the fact that blacks' literal presence was not the issue but instead their presence on terms of equality. It was no longer—if it ever had been—merely the convenience and comfort of black travelers that was at stake, but the whole race's claim to equal citizenship.

Despite protests and deft legislative maneuvers by opponents, the measure eventually became law. Highly organized and enjoying a long and largely successful tradition of both legal and popular protests against racial discrimination stretching back to Reconstruction, the African American community of New Orleans immediately began planning a legal challenge. Louisiana's unusually large and well-educated antebellum free black population (18,647 in 1860, which was more than twenty-fold larger than neighboring states in the Lower South) had owned substantial property and vigilantly guarded its relatively elite status during the antebellum years. Unlike similar groups in both the Northern and Southern hemispheres, their privileged class and legal status had not necessarily encouraged political conservatism. A significant and vocal part of that community, with its ancestral roots in the French Antilles, maintained close connections with the French radical traditions of the Jacobin revolutions of 1789 and, more recently, 1848. Carrying these ideals into the post-emancipation politics of the U.S. South, many of them had campaigned ably, if ultimately unsuccessfully, for a more egalitarian national Reconstruction policy.

Members of the Roudanez family vividly illustrate the black Francophone community's trajectory. Dr. Louis Charles Roudanez, who had studied medicine in France in the 1850s and participated directly in the revolution of 1848, and his brother, Jean Baptiste Roudanez, a mechanical engineer, were profoundly marked by the radical currents of those years. During the American Civil War, Louis Charles founded the *New Orleans Tribune*, the state's first official Republican newspaper and the first African American daily published in the United States. Meanwhile, his brother, Jean Baptiste, was part of the Louisiana delegation that petitioned President Lincoln for voting rights early in 1864 and was an organizer of the National Equal Rights League formed that year. These were the people Lincoln had intended to placate with his proposal for limited suffrage for black veterans.

A member of the "New Negro" generation, Rodolphe L. Desdunes had not even been born in 1848, but his political vision was nurtured by the Creole activists from that era. Having earned a law degree from Straight University and founded a bilingual daily, *The Crusader*, Desdunes was a seasoned radical spokesman for New Orleans' Creole community by the early 1890s. Along with the *Crusader*'s editor, Louis A. Martinet, he organized the Washington-based American Citizens' Equal Rights Association and its local New Orleans branch, the Comité des Citoyens, which presented the first memorial protesting the proposed Separate Car Law in 1891 and organized the constitutional test that followed. The Comité des Citoyens contacted Albion W. Tourgée, a white Republican and former member of North Carolina's Reconstruction legislature, who already had written about the Louisiana law in the *Chicago Inter Ocean*. Taking the case without fee, Tourgée acted as the lead counsel, but relied on a New Orleans attorney, James C. Walker, to develop and prosecute the case through the local and state appellate process, which was initiated on January 2, 1892.

Although the trend in Louisiana had been, as elsewhere, toward increasing segregation, contemporary observers' impressions that racial separation was still not rigidly or consistently enforced in New Orleans is borne out by the difficulty the Citizens' Committee experienced initially in setting up a test case. The attorneys' strategy was to try to focus the case narrowly on the issue of color by having as a plaintiff a mulatto, perhaps a woman who was nearly white, thus exposing the arbitrariness of racial classification. But the peculiarities of New Orleans's racial climate made such a strategy difficult to execute. Louisiana's railroad companies resented the Separate Car Law because of the extra expense it entailed, and given New Orleans's large mulatto population, a nearly white person might not be refused admission to a white car anyway. The strategy worked, it appears, only because the committee was able to secure the silent cooperation of the Louisville and Nashville Railroad company to stage a test.

Daniel F. Desdunes, a twenty-one-year-old octoroon and the son of Rodolphe Desdunes, undertook the first test. On February 24, 1892, he was arrested for taking a seat in the "white" car on an L&N train traveling from New Orleans to Mobile, Alabama. After some delay, Desdunes's case was rendered moot by a decision of the Louisiana Supreme Court in another case that reaffirmed the principle that states could not impose regulations on interstate commerce. Since the central issue of the constitutionality of racial separation was not addressed in this case, attorneys set to work constructing a wholly intrastate case. For that test they chose a local shoemaker and friend of Rodolphe Desdunes, Homer Plessy, who also had roots in New Orleans's politically active Creole community.

Purchasing a ticket on June 7, 1892, for a trip from New Orleans to Covington, Louisiana, on the East Louisiana Railway, which operated wholly intrastate, Plessy boarded the coach reserved for whites. Apparently by prearrangement with railroad officials, since Plessy's race was not obvious to the uninitiated, he was arrested for violation of the state's Separate Car Law. On November 18, Judge Ferguson issued his written opinion that denied all of Plessy's claims and laid the basis for an appeal to the Louisiana Supreme Court, of which Francis T. Nicholls, the governor who had signed the Separate Car measure into law, was now chief justice. After receiving an unfavorable opinion from the state supreme court, Plessy's attorneys immediately filed an appeal to the U.S. Supreme Court. With the case having taken scarcely six months to get that far, however, its final disposition would not unfold for three more years.

That decision, handed down on Monday, May 18, 1896, not only upheld Judge Ferguson's denial of Plessy's claims that his equal rights as a citizen had been violated, but did so on grounds and in language that brutally undercut the optimistic hopes of the New Negro generation.

Seven justices endorsed Justice Henry Billings Brown's opinion upholding the Louisiana law, seeing no violation of Plessy's constitutional rights in what they judged to be a "reasonable" exercise of the state's police powers. The standard of what was reasonable turned clearly on the Court's view that racial differences were natural and obvious and "must always exist so long as white men are distinguished from the other race by color." This fact, they believed, underpinned the distinction between civil and political equality, which fell within the reach of the law, and social equality, which did not. Louisiana's law was not inconsistent, moreover, with those in northern jurisdictions requiring segregated schools or barring interracial marriages, and thus the Court must grant Louisiana "a large discretion" and defer to what local courts considered "established usages, customs and traditions." Not content merely to ground its decision in judicial restraint, however, the Court insisted not only that Plessy's complaint was not amendable to legal remedies but was also without substantive merit. By Brown's reckoning, Plessy had no legitimate grievance because the racial separation that Louisiana mandated was benign and neutral. The law weighed equally on whites and blacks, and any imputation of its being "a badge of inferiority" was "solely because the colored race chooses to put that construction upon it." Analyzing this passage some years later, Charles W. Chesnutt quipped, "I presume that hanging might be pleasant if a man could only convince himself that it would not be painful, nor disgraceful, nor terminate his earthly career."

Only Justice John Marshall Harlan saw the case as Plessy's attorneys did: that forcible separation denied civic belonging and amounted to "a badge of slavery." He grounded his dissent in the evolving legal doctrine that a railway was a public highway whose ownership entailed "the exercise of public functions." The majority's distinction between social and civil equality was irrelevant in this context. Harlan accepted the reality of racial difference and racial pride as readily as Brown, but insisted that one was free to act on those differences only to the point where another rights-bearing citizen was injured. And contrary to Brown's reasoning, racial separation did involve injury, for it marked blacks with "a badge of servitude." It was facetious for the majority to insist that the Louisiana law in question applied equally to whites as well as blacks, since everyone understood its clear intent: "under the guise" of equal accommodation, blacks would be compelled "to keep to themselves." "No one would be so wanting in candor as to assert the contrary." Although he did not say so, the fact that Louisiana was prepared to allow blacks into white coaches only when obviously in service to whites sustained his point.

Such egregious discrimination between citizens was reachable by the law, Harlan insisted, because it flew in the face of the intent of postwar constitutional amendments that guaranteed equal citizenship, "universal civil freedom," and an end not only to slavery but to "the imposition of any burdens or disabilities that constitute badges of slavery or servitude." These amendments "removed the race line from our governmental systems" and empowered the courts to "protect all the civil rights that pertain to freedom and citizenship." While it is true that the language of the amendments was simply prohibitory, Harlan conceded, given the political context of their passage, in response to "unfriendly legislation" (the Black Codes), they clearly implied "positive immunity" from laws that would have relegated blacks to an inferior status. Like the Black Codes, this Louisiana measure constituted an effort to defeat the "legitimate results" of the recent Civil War, Harlan lamented, and this could only plant "seeds of race hate" that future generations would reap.

Although many historians, and many of its contemporaries, read the Plessy decision as an inevitable and natural outgrowth of the racial trends of that era, Harlan clearly saw developments through a different lens, one much like that of the black plaintiffs. He rejected the various precedents in state law that Judge Brown had offered to establish the reasonableness of Jim Crow laws as exercises of police powers, because they were passed at times or under circumstances inconsistent with "the era [inaugurated] by the recent amendments of the supreme law, which established universal civil freedom, gave citizenship to all born or naturalized in the United States and residing here, obliterated the race line from our systems of governments, National and State, and placed our free institutions upon the broad and sure foundation of the equality of all men before the law." Though he did not say so explicitly, Harlan clearly implied the notion that both Lincoln and Frederick Douglass had articulated so clearly: the previous generations' terrible expenditure of blood and treasure had opened the prospect for achieving at last the constitutional guarantee of "a republican form of government." With this decision the final closure of that opening would be fully evident, the fruits of that bloody conflict would be squandered, and "a large body of American citizens, now constituting a

part of the political community called the People of the United States"
would be placed "in a condition of legal inferiority" and denied "the full
enjoyment of the blessings of freedom." This would make a mockery of
America's claims to a providential status among nations. "We boast of the
freedom enjoyed by our people. But it is difficult to reconcile that boast
with a state of the law which, practically, puts the brand of servitude and
degradation upon a large class of our fellow-citizens, our equals before the
law. The thin disguise of 'equal' accommodations for passengers in railroad coaches will not mislead any one nor atone for the wrong this day
done."

However thin the disguise, that it was required at all spoke powerfully
to the expectations many held for that era. The plaintiff's brief had attempted a kind of *reductio ad absurdum* by appending a long list of un-
thinkable practices that might follow acceptance of the principle of "equal
but separate." Where does it end, asked Harlan, echoing the plaintiff's
brief? Why not require that blacks and whites be separated in courtrooms,
swear on separate Bibles, ride in different sections on streetcars, or walk
on different sides of the public streets? Surely anyone would recognize the
absurdity of such social arrangements, he and the plaintiff's attorneys
thought, and abandon this first step into the abyss. The irony, of course,
is that many of the measures they held up to ridicule to discredit the
Separate Car Law would soon be enacted in many parts of an increasingly
Jim Crow South.

The Gathering Storm

On January 11, 1897, after his challenge to the constitutionality of the
Louisiana Separate Car Law had been denied and the case remanded
back to the state courts, Homer Plessy pleaded guilty to the charges, paid
a twenty-five-dollar fine, and settled quietly back into the Creole working-
class community of the Faubourg Tremé, just northwest of the French
Quarter. The seemingly quiet denouement of Plessy's four-year journey
was echoed in contemporary reactions to the Court's decision on his case,
which ranged from utter silence to muted resignation. The southern press
and national law reviews, and many northern Democratic papers, gave
brief approving notices of the decision. Some major papers ignored it alto-

gether. Although the black press gave the decision more coverage, there was nothing like the vigor of the outrage that had greeted the civil rights decision twelve years earlier. In a short response published in a Boston journal a month after the decision was announced, Booker T. Washington reiterated that black Americans' principal objection was to inequality of accommodations rather than a principled objection to their separation. He demurred on the constitutional principles involved, contenting himself with observations that while only inconveniencing blacks, "such an unjust law injures the white man in morals and ideas of justice." "The negro can endure the temporary inconvenience, but the injury to the white man is permanent. It is the one who inflicts the wrong that is hurt, rather than the one on whom the wrong is inflicted." There appear to have been no contemporaneous published reactions from Du Bois, Wells-Barnett, or others among the emerging spokespersons for the New Negro.

Given the decision's prominent place in racial jurisprudence in the half century that followed, not to mention Harlan's dire warnings, the relative disinterest or seeming apathy is surprising. On the other hand, one can imagine that many observers viewed this decision as merely a further confirmation of the reasoning and arguments of the earlier Civil Rights Cases, which marked a much sharper and obvious break with the mood and expectations of the emancipation era. Certainly Brown's majority opinion was narrowly framed and broke no new legal ground. Only Harlan's fiery dissent would be remembered and cited in the years to come. For many blacks, no doubt, the Supreme Court's edict may have been of far less concern than equally pernicious but more immediate ongoing developments. In retrospect, then, the response to Plessy may appear as the eerie calm that comes before a storm.

The "badge of slavery" that Plessy's lawyers had invoked was clearly etched on the back of Alabama sharecropper Hayes Cobb. "My daddy was a free man," recalled his eldest son, Ned Cobb, "but in his acts he was a slave." Although his son's harsh condemnation was intended figuratively, Hayes Cobb had in fact spent the first fifteen years of his life in slavery. According to his son's embittered recollection, Hayes "[d]idn't look ahead to profit hisself in nothing that he done," and then in frustration turned violently against his wives and children. A more objective reading of Ned's memoir, however, suggests that Hayes Cobb, who was in his mid-forties when the Plessy decision was handed down, had already been beaten down by the social relations of labor that evolved in the post-Reconstruction era.

Being at least six to eight years older than Booker T. Washington and some of the other more famous members of the New Negro generation, Hayes Cobb had experienced slavery firsthand, as a young man old enough for fieldwork. He had lived through the terrors of the Civil War and the heady first years of emancipation. Described as dark-skinned, slender, and "kind of rawboned," he had responded to freedom as had many other young men: by traveling through the South testing his new civil status. Although he made lots of money during his travels—which he brought home to his mother, turning "first one pocket to her and then another and just rak[ing] the money in her lap"—he regretted not taking advantage of the temporarily deflated postwar land prices to buy some of Alabama's abundant piney woodlands. There is evidence, nonetheless, that Hayes did prosper in his early years of farming after settling down and marrying. His son recalls that in the mid-1890s his father owned five or six head of cattle, three or four "fattening hogs," mules, harnesses, and farm tools; altogether enough to have raised Hayes up the agricultural ladder to renter rather than cropper. These possessions were impressed upon young Ned's memory, however, just as they were being forcibly taken away by landlords to whom his father was indebted. "I seed my daddy cleaned up twice," Ned recalled; "everything he had they took away from him . . . [H]e never did prosper none after that."

For Hayes Cobb, as for millions of other black sharecroppers and tenants, the social humiliation and economic victimization he endured mocked Justice Brown's neat distinction between the civil-political and social domains. Getting ahead in an economic system built on debt relations was already perilous, given the sharp cyclical movements of the world cotton market. A hostile racial environment increased the odds even more. In 1899, Hayes Cobb claimed to have received oral permission to sell one of his cows from Lloyd Albee, who held the mortgage on them; but after the sale, Albee denied giving his consent. When Hayes refused to settle the matter by becoming Albee's cropper, Albee had him thrown in jail. Jasper Clay, another landowner, bailed him out on condition that he work *his* property. Out of fear, Hayes accepted essentially the same proposition from Clay that he had turned down from Albee. The fear was justified.

Jasper Clay had recently killed in cold blood one of his black tenants, Henry Kirkland, who had had the gall to dispute his figures at settling-up time. It was probably not lost on Hayes that while his illiteracy might lead to his being cheated and jailed, literacy could get him killed. Hayes was put into the field working on halves but never saw any profits from his labor. He and his family, who by Ned's report had never known hunger before, were fed nothing but sorghum syrup and cornmeal. Fourteen years old at the time, Ned Cobb recalled years later some aspects of a deal his father made with Clay to win release from this seemingly permanent indenture. He would make the straw baskets with which to harvest the cotton in return for his and his family's freedom. Why the ruthless Clay accepted such an arrangement remains unclear. Given the fear he instilled, he surely could have had both baskets and labor; but apparently some arrangement was made that returned the Cobb family to the milder indentureship of ordinary sharecropping in a depressed cotton market. Forever thereafter, according to his disappointed son, Hayes Cobb "wasn't a slave but he lived like one."

From his impressionable adolescent years, Ned Cobb remembered his father as a beaten man who callously put his wife and children to work in the fields while he went off hunting and fishing. An alternative interpretation is equally plausible, however. Workers have known at least since before the Black Laws of sixteenth-century England that the game of fields and streams can provide a surer and more independent subsistence than domesticated animals and crops that were ever vulnerable to legal and extra-legal confiscation. Armed with an old double-barreled muzzle loader, Hayes "killed game goin and a comin . . . catch fish, great God almighty, Catch em in baskets, two or three baskets; sometimes he'd catch more fish than the settlement could eat. And he'd get him some steel traps and go down to the creek—trap eels. Fish, eels, wild turkeys, wild ducks, possums, coons, beavers, squirrels, all such as that." "I seed the day come and pass that he'd feed us just on his game." Through his bitterness, Ned appears to have never connected his father's prowess as a hunter-gather with his recollection that, except when working for Jasper Clay, the family never went hungry. Nor does he recognize that his father's response to the southern regime of labor and law anticipated that of Ned's own younger brother Peter, who "made up his mind that he weren't goin to have anything and after that, why, nothing could hurt him." It is likely that Hayes

Cobb had come early on to the same conclusion as his son Peter. Indeed, in a more reflective, perhaps forgiving, moment the hard-driving Ned acknowledged the rationality of the kind of passive resistance his father had embraced: "whenever the colored man prospered too fast in this country under the old rulins, they worked every figure to cut you down, cut your britches off you. So, it might have been his way of thinking that it weren't no use in climbin too fast; weren't no use in climbin slow, neither, if they was goin to take everything you worked for when you got too high."

As Homer Plessy settled back into his shoemaking trade following his brush with history, across the city thirty-year-old Robert Charles, who had migrated to New Orleans from Mississippi just two years earlier, continued his struggle to earn a living from a series of itinerant day labor jobs. It is unlikely that the Plessy decision made much impression on Charles, other than to deepen his already bleak assessment of black prospects in America. Already keenly interested in African emigration, he had joined the International Migration Society, an organization offering its subscribers transportation to Liberia, just days before the Court's decision was announced. Although Charles was no more representative of the larger population of southern blacks than was Plessy, his life course and plight surely reflected an important segment of the whole. Like many black residents of this city and elsewhere, Charles lived a life seemingly detached from the concerns of the likes of Desdunes, Martinet, or the other self-proclaimed New Negroes. It is highly unlikely that he would have had any contact with the Creole community's mobilization to challenge the Separate Car Law, for example. And yet Plessy's challenge to the "badge of servitude" implied by that law was just as relevant to Charles's life and work, just as much a part of his existence and consciousness as that of the African American elite.

Born in the early 1850s and mid-1860s, respectively, Hayes Cobb and Robert Charles were members of roughly the same generational cohort that had descended on Chicago three years earlier to celebrate a hopeful new era of black progress. Cobb and Charles found little in their lives to celebrate, and for them the term *New Negro* would take on a more sinister meaning. The commentaries of white southerners were filled with invidious comparisons between the generation coming of age in the late nineteenth century and their slave-born elders, comparisons that decidedly favored the latter. These "new negroes," white elites complained, lacked the deference and discipline of the older generation reared in slavery, their labor was unreliable, their demeanor surly, their manners brutish. The young men in particular were prone to vagabondage and disorder, especially rape; underworked and oversexed, they posed a clear and present danger to the white community. Those like Cobb, the lazy, ne'er-do-wells who stayed on the plantation but allegedly retarded southern development through their ignorant and slovenly ways, embodied a venerable regional stereotype now achieving national consensus. Those like Charles, the itinerant urban laborers who had escaped from the tight controls of the plantation regime, epitomized the racial panic of the turn-of-the-century South.

Robert Charles grew up scarcely two hundred miles as the crow flies northeast of New Orleans, farming on shares with his parents, Jasper and Mariah, on cotton plantations along Bayou Pierre in the northwestern corner of Copiah County near Pine Bluff, Mississippi. He was nine or ten years old when Mississippi was violently "redeemed" by marauding Democrats. As in many localities in the South, Copiah, with twenty-five hundred black voters still on the registration rolls, remained a contested area politically well into the early 1880s. Homegrown white Republicans joined with blacks to form a populist political coalition that occasionally managed to avoid being "counted out" in elections for critical local posts such as county treasurer, sheriff, or magistrate. There is no evidence that Charles's family was politically active, but seventeen-year-old Robert was surely marked by the explosion of political violence in Copiah in 1883. The white leader of the Fusion Party and several politically active blacks were gunned down, breaking the biracial coalition and ending black political activity until well into the next century. This story—biracial political and/ or labor coalitions violently disrupted—became an oft-told tale in the South, repeated six months later in Danville, Virginia; four years later in the bayous of Louisiana; and yet again in Wilmington, North Carolina, in 1898.

In 1888, shortly after the riot in Copiah, Robert and his brother Henry migrated thirty miles north to Vicksburg, where they eventually landed work as section hands with the Louisville, New Orleans, and Texas Railroad (LNO&T). They worked for the railroad until the spring of 1892, when their violent confrontation with a white fireman over a stolen pistol forced them to seek refuge again in Copiah County. It is not clear just how they supported themselves upon returning home, but having tasted city life, they appear not to have returned to farming on shares. Robert adopted an alias, Curtis Robertson, and may have engaged in bootlegging; he was arraigned on that charge in 1894. Although eventually acquitted, Charles moved to New Orleans shortly after his arraignment.

In New Orleans, Charles lived in a dozen shabby residences in the teeming, racially integrated working-class sections of the city, while working on the docks, in sawmills, and at various odd jobs. He obviously cut an imposing figure. At 6 feet tall and 180 pounds, he was described variously as "burly" by those who obviously feared him and as having an air of elegance by some of his women friends. Despite the limited educational facilities in Copiah County, several people in his lodging house described him as scholarly, and he struck many other people as well educated. Such impressions undoubtedly reflect Charles's self-education, evidenced by the worn textbooks and well-marked composition books found in his quarters after his death. Unlike the similar self-tutoring regime Charles Chesnutt embarked on a decade earlier, however, Robert Charles's efforts were fueled with political kindling.

The year Charles joined the International Migration Society (IMS), 1896, was the year not only of the Plessy decision but of political upheaval in Louisiana. In an echo of Copiah County of 1883, a Louisiana fusion party was counted out in a violence-drenched election campaign that April, and there were twenty-one lynchings in the state—a record. Two years later a state constitutional convention disenfranchised black voters by imposing racially disencriminatory property and literacy requirements for voting. By 1900, the black share of registered voters, which had been 44 percent of the total a decade earlier, fell to 4 percent. Scarcely more than 5,000 black voters made their way to the polls that year, compared with 130,000 before the new constitution went into effect. Witnesses reported later that Charles was deeply angered by these political developments and further enraged the very next year by news reports of the brutal lynching in Georgia of an itinerant farmworker, Sam Hose. Newspapers were filled with the gruesome details of how special trains had been chartered to bring spectators to see Hose's slow and agonizing death. In a ritualized scene of torture, Hose was hanged; his body was then burned and, finally, cut open so that souvenirs could be collected and sold.

As with many other African Americans, such blatant and unpunished racial injustice made Charles a fervent supporter of schemes for African emigration. He may well have become interested in emigration earlier, while living in Vicksburg, since well-known black missionaries to Africa lectured there during his residency. A member of the International Migration Society since May 22, 1896, he later volunteered to be one of its unpaid agents, canvassing for it in Mississippi at his own expense. On its face the IMS, formed by four Birmingham white men, had all the marks of an unscrupulous scam. Requiring one dollar in monthly dues for forty months, at which point the member had presumably accumulated enough to pay for the trip to Africa, the society could declare the entire sum forfeited if any payments were missed. The organization did charter two ships, however, and actually carried about five hundred blacks to Liberia in 1895 and 1896. After the IMS folded in 1899, Charles contacted Bishop Henry McNeal Turner and offered to be a subscription agent for his *Voice of Missions*, a monthly magazine the AME minister had published since 1893 to spread his religious and emigrationist messages.

In the sweltering first summer of the new century, Charles was still peddling Turner's paper and dreaming of his "return" to Africa. On July 27, however, he exploded in a violent rage against the society that still marked him with "the badge of servitude." On that evening a routine stop by two policemen erupted in gunfire, leaving Charles and one of the policemen seriously wounded. Cornered at his lodgings hours later, Charles coolly killed two of his pursuers and wounded twenty-four others before falling himself in a hail of gunfire. His death did little to stem the orgy of mob violence visited on the New Orleans black community over the next several days, or to stanch the legend that grew up around his person in the years to come.

Foolish or heroic, senseless or tragic, Robert Charles's revolt had no precedent in the historical memories of whites or blacks. From one angle of vision, perhaps, it anticipated black urban rebellions a half century later; from another, it prefigured the future of Hayes Cobb's son Ned, who would himself stand in a cabin doorway thirty-two years later with his ".32 Smith and Wesson" raining fire on police officers bent on enforcing a racist regime.

The New Negro Confronts the New South

Less than a year after Robert Charles met his violent end, thirty-three-year-old W.E.B. Du Bois described a tour of southern Georgia for northern white readers of *The World's Work*, an effort to acquaint them with "the Negro as he really is." Upon boarding the train in Atlanta, Du Bois warned his imagined companions that "If you wish to ride with me you must come in the 'Jim Crow Car.'" The trip took them to Dougherty County, at the conceptual and geographical "centre of the Negro problem." They moved through time as well as space, over a "historic" terrain where great Indian nations had been fought and crushed, where a slave empire had been forged and destroyed, and more recently, "where Sam Hose was crucified." Rolling south from Atlanta over the crimson soil of the Georgia Piedmont, they saw "brand-new cotton mills rise on every side," but below Macon the world grew darker, a "strange land of shadows" and "half-intelligible murmurs of the world beyond." Near Albany, where there were five black persons for every white and one could travel ten miles without seeing a white face, the ruins of a civilization built on slave labor were fully evident. Here half-ruined mansions stood "brown and dingy," their fallen fences and decrepit gateposts a synecdoche for a society's lost elegance and decay. Meanwhile, the scattered progeny of their former ruling families had retreated to nearby cities, to collect their rents from impoverished black tenants and feed "hungrily off the remnants of an earldom." The immediate cause of the distress and desolation were not difficult to discern, according to Du Bois: "a pall of debt hangs over the beautiful land," ensnaring planter, merchant, and tenant alike but coming finally to rest on the bent back of the worker, robbing him of all incentive to labor. "What rent do you pay here?" he called out to one. "All that we make," came the reply. "Let a white man touch me, and he dies," muttered another. "[T]hese were the extremes of the Negro problem which we met that day," sighed Du Bois, "and we scarce know which we preferred."

The diametrically opposed responses of Du Bois's unnamed personae echoed those of Hayes Cobb and Robert Charles. As with Cobb and Charles, their lives were being profoundly reshaped by the ongoing transformation of their region. Behind that transformation were the southern white capitalists and their publicists who noisily promoted the remodeling of the South's political economy. They were responsible for its "brand-new cotton mills." They counseled its political and economic elites to emulate the well-trod paths of industrial takeoff elsewhere: to build railroads to haul the coal and iron ores excavated from southern soil, to build steel mills to process it, to build cotton and tobacco factories to absorb the produce of southern plantations. With these steps the South could link the interests and welfare of countryside and city in a mutual commitment to a more modern future. Only in this way, they implied, would the South be rescued from the dark foreboding destiny lurking in Dougherty County.

The New South ideal called for a rejection of the archaic forms of labor and race relations of the antebellum era in exchange for more modern fashions appropriate to the new, progressive era. But as Du Bois guided his imaginary party over "a raised road, built by chained Negro convicts," he gave glimpses of the other face of the New South. The county prison, he informed his charges, "is ever full of black criminals,—black folk say that only colored boys are sent to jail, and they not because they are guilty, but because the state needs criminals to eke out its income by their forced labor."

The sharp distinctions that New South boosters drew between the past and future of the region obscured the melding of social relations characteristic of both, a mixture that, in fact, rendered labor and racial oppression more efficient. On the face of it, for example, Jasper Clay's brutal oppression of Hayes Cobb aped the behavior of Old South slave drivers, but in fact Clay was thoroughly enmeshed in the New South's modernized labor regime. Clay was not simply an individual planter but a cog in a corporate enterprise, a firm called Davis and Podell, which had bailed him out of jail after he killed Henry Kirkland and probably owned him as thoroughly as he did Hayes Cobb. For his part, Hayes was formally a cropper working for half the crop, but he went to the fields as part of a squad of laborers who "floated through and through the field and kept up one big crop." No doubt, Davis and Podell thought blacks were inferior beings, but they knew that men such as Cobb and Charles were also, as a Vicksburg paper put it, "the animate machinery which has largely produced our wealth." For them labor relations and race relations were but two sides of the same coin. Their objective was neither segregation nor exclusion per se, but supremacy.

The conjuncture of old and new regimes is perhaps even more striking with another of the key players in the drive to modernize the southern economy, the railway conglomerates. When, like many other farm laborers, Robert and Henry Charles abandoned the cotton fields to seek work in the industrial sector, they found jobs at the Louisville, New Orleans, and Texas Railroad. Unlike cotton mills, which long maintained a whites-only employment policy, railroad companies offered black workers an escape route from perpetual indentureship on the plantation. Rail companies such as the LNO&T—which was involved in one of the cases cited in Plessy's brief—also often found themselves at the center of the legal conflict over Jim Crow seating, and sometimes even ended up on the side of the plaintiffs who were challenging this "badge of servitude" so evocative of the Old South. As we have seen, this was almost certainly the role of the Louisville and Nashville Company, whose cooperation proved crucial to the Comité des Citoyens' test of the Louisiana Separate Car Law.

Even as such enterprises helped, however reluctantly, to modernize southern race relations, they were at that same moment instrumental in imposing a labor regime very much like the involuntary servitude of the antebellum era. Indeed, like most other southern railway companies, and the industrial clients they served, the L&N owed its very existence to the forced labor of black convicts. If railroads were emblems of the South's modernity, the convict laborers who built them provided an alter image of retardation.

"Involuntary servitude, except as punishment for a crime," the lone exception to the Thirteenth Amendment's prohibition of slavery, was seized upon to supply the labor needs of various New South industries. For much of the late nineteenth and well into the early twentieth century, leased convicts provided southern employers cheap labor under conditions rivaling the former slave plantations. Northern and western states also put convicted criminals to work, of course, but usually within prison walls making goods for other state institutions or for private contractors. Only thirteen states leased convicts to private employers' supervision outside prison walls; almost all of those were located in the South, and almost all of their convict laborers were African American.

Southern convict lease was not an initiative that originated with former slaveholders, however, nor were they the primary employers of such labor. Southern convicts built railroads, mined everything from phosphate to coal, made brick, felled trees, and paved roads far more often than they picked cotton. Indeed, in some cases, modernizing Republican governors had led the way during Reconstruction in their search for quick and cheap ways to spur the railroad construction they hoped would modernize the South. Their innovation was readily adopted and expanded by their successors, the "redeeming" Democrats who engineered a fivefold increase in the southern convict labor force during the last twenty years of the century. By 1880, Georgia convicts had added a thousand miles of rail track to the state's antebellum network, and Alabama had expanded its leased prison force threefold during the first five years after Democrats seized power. By 1888, the state of Alabama was leasing every able-bodied prisoner to just two companies, Tennessee Coal, Iron and Railroad, a subsidiary of the L&N, and Sloss Furnace, all entities that eventually merged to make up the Birmingham Steel complex, which was in turn bought out by US Steel twenty years later.

Indeed, steel, the icon of the modern industrial age, stood at the apex of a southern industrial conglomeration, for which the huge coal deposits in Georgia, Alabama, and Tennessee formed the base. Those coal mines soon became the region's chief employers of convicts. Complaining about the unreliability of free laborers, some coal barons boasted that convict labor saved them up to sixty-five cents per ton. Although others would dispute these figures, one advantage accorded by convict labor was beyond dispute: they provided what the owners called "reliability," by which they meant labor control. As the labor historian Alex Lichtenstein has astutely observed, for industrial employers, convict lease served much the same role as crop liens, vagrancy statutes, and the anti-enticement laws that criminalized outside labor recruitment did for planters. Indeed, Georgia discovered that it could dispense with issuing expensive railroad bonds—their favorite target in attacks against so-called Republican corruption—because their control of the labor supply was sufficient to reassure capitalists that their investments would earn profits. By the 1890s, as the depression and labor unrest intensified, mining companies laid off free workers and replaced them with prisoners. In an era of intense labor conflict, any free laborer was a potential striker, every convict laborer a strikebreaker.

Convict leasing posed a formidable constraint for organized labor in the South, but its weight fell far more heavily on people such as Robert Charles and Hayes Cobb than the white working class. Prisons that held just a few hundred inmates before the war, practically all of them white, processed thousands during the postwar era, practically all of them black.

With wicked humor, John Trowbridge, a northern traveler during the early postwar years, feigned awe at the sterling virtue of southern white men, since none had ever been sentenced to the chain gang. By 1898, nine out of ten convicts leased in Georgia and Louisiana were black, and many Black Belt counties in Alabama had never leased a white prisoner.

The overwhelming majority of the crimes the black convicts were charged with were property crimes, many of them newly minted for the post-emancipation economy. A frequent charge brought in Alabama, for example, was "larceny after trust," meaning violation of a labor contract. This law transformed disputes that in another context might simply have been matters for negotiation or settlement in civil courts—such as who should own or transport a crop to market—into felonies. A conviction for selling farm produce or cottonseed at night brought twelve months hard labor; actually stealing any part of a corn or cotton crop was defined as grand larceny, punishable by two to five years in prison. Many of these laws were intended to lay dragnets to ensnare not only croppers but black renters and owners, thereby denying them the small measure of independence gained in escaping the tenant crop lien system. Meanwhile, county court systems not noted for fairness even in the best of circumstances could not resist the temptation to further corrupt legal processes; the so-called court costs entailed in the arrest, imprisonment, and trial of misdemeanor cases, which often amounted to forty dollars or even a hundred dollars, became a pretext for leasing convicted prisoners. Forty dollars in court costs could result in one hundred days at hard labor—assuming that the system was administered fairly. In most cases it wasn't. Many black convicts served sentences far exceeding the time necessary to pay their fines and costs.

Coming under severe attack throughout the 1890s, convict lease systems were gradually abandoned in most southern states by the end of the first decade of the new century. Mississippi and Tennessee had abolished the system by 1898, and Georgia followed suit in 1908. Alabama held out until 1928. It has been argued that, much as with slavery, the inflexibility of a leased, bound labor force proved less efficient and less productive than free laborers in the long run. It is also clear, however, that attacks on this underside of New South progressivism were effective in eliminating it.

As the late historian C. Vann Woodward and a number of other analysts have shown, the New South image and programs were fraught with contradictions and ironies, and they sparked inter- and intra-class conflicts among white southerners. Across the South, significant enclaves of interracial political mobilization emerged, surviving the overthrow of Reconstruction and the political fraud and violence used to intimidate black voters throughout the 1880s and '90s. In political form the movements were much like that in the Copiah County of Robert Charles's youth, fusions of disgruntled populist Democrats and black and white Republicans. Much more threatening was the Populist Party, formed by white farmers and tenants to challenge the debt system that had ensnared Hayes Cobb and his son, and the railroads and banks that impoverished owners and tenants alike through discriminatory rates and credit arrangements. Similar organizations emerged among workers in the mining and timber industries. Rhetorically, and sometimes in practice, these movements sought to forge black-white alliances, thus partially challenging the Jim Crow social orthodoxy established by the so-called Redeemers who overthrew Reconstruction and the New Southers. More often than not, however, even the most promising of these movements faltered and shattered, easy targets for the race-baiting conservative opposition.

By the end of the decade, white conservative Democrats had honed a potent formula to destroy all of these coalitions—create a moral panic, cry rape. The race riot in Wilmington, North Carolina, in 1898 provides one of the more explicit demonstrations of this technique. There a coalition of white Populists and black Republicans had won control of many state and local offices in the mid-1890s. A white opposition formed, led by men born and/or reared largely in the postwar era—the counterpart ironically of the New Negroes. This particular group of "new men" was determined to win by violence and fraud what they had lost in fair elections. Seizing upon then-novel techniques of political mobilization and propaganda, they launched a campaign to demonize black men and drive them from public life, much like the metaphorical figure central to the disenfranchisement campaign two years later—the incubus, a winged demon alleged to have sexually violated white women while they slept. Thrust beyond the boundaries of human sympathy, blacks were effectively served up for the remorseless slaughter that followed a few days after election day: three hundred dead by one estimate, many more wounded, and fourteen hundred forced into exile.

A few months after the Wilmington riots, the newly Democratic state legislature began crafting a disenfranchisement law, including all of the by

This cartoon, published during the 1900 campaign for a new constitution aimed at disenfranchising North Carolina's black voters, graphically portrays the sexual panic that white conservatives had exploited before the Wilmington Riot.

then well-tested techniques that slipped under the broad, ambiguous language of the Fifteenth Amendment: poll taxes and literacy requirements, with the caveat of a "grandfather clause" for those whites who might be presumed to be sons of pre-1867 voters. The new law was approved in an August 1900 referendum and took effect on July 1, 1902. The U.S. Supreme Court had already upheld poll taxes in *Williams v. Mississippi* in 1898; the grandfather clause would escape constitutional scrutiny until 1915, by which time the one-party system that would define southern politics for half a century was well entrenched, and southern whites, occupying "safe" seats from small electorates, accrued immense institutional power in Congress.

White southern radicals' receptivity to race-baiting almost certainly confirmed many black leaders' skepticism of the efficacy of biracial insurgencies. Some of these leaders preferred to ally themselves with the conservative opponents of the Populists, men they hoped might restrain their violent underlings. No doubt many of them arrived at their skepticism independently, even before these betrayals. Although many black leaders of the new generation—such as Kelly Miller, Mary Church Terrell, and Booker T. Washington—had been among the most eloquent critics of convict lease, Du Bois alone embedded his critique within a broader dissection of the perils as well as the promise of a modernizing South. For many others, the impulse to make common cause with the northern and southern capitalists in forging a "New South" proved irresistible. The New South promoters' enthusiastic embrace of modernity paralleled the timing and echoed many of the themes of the New Negroes themselves. The whirl of industrial progress and economic development invoked by the white boosters resonated with their sense of progress and national destiny. For them, as for social analysts of many stripes thereafter, modernization promised the destruction of archaic and outmoded social oppressions such as racism and segregation.

The most prominent of the latter group, no doubt, was Booker T. Washington, the principal of Tuskegee Institute, who gained national celebrity in the fall of 1895 after a celebrated speech at the Atlanta Cotton States Exposition. Emulating the Chicago World's Fair of two years earlier—including, even, the reappearance of the Dahomean village—the events in Atlanta were intended to promote the New South advocates' particular vision of the future. Unlike the Chicago fair, there was no debate in Atlanta over the size and nature of a black presence; on the fairgrounds in Atlanta, blacks would be both prominent and separate. Indeed, a major motive in recruiting Washington to speak was that his and other southern black leaders' influence had been needed to persuade Congress to subsidize the event in the first place. Washington played a significant role in that lobbying effort, deviating from a fund-raising trip to testify in the nation's capital on behalf of its organizers, and he was rewarded with both considerable influence on the selection of the director of the Negro exhibit and the opportunity to deliver his historic address. In that address Washington sketched a New South where blacks would forego a presence in the public sphere—both the exercise of political power and voice—in exchange for participation in the new free labor economy. Well aware that he was addressing an audience fragmented by class and region as well as race, Washington shrewdly reasoned that the two regional capitalist elites were crucial to his success. Fostering the material progress of the South seemed the one theme these regional elites might unite around, and the central metaphor of his speech captured that goal beautifully: one as the hand in mutual material progress; separate as the fingers in all things social. Whether he was aware of it or not, it was also a platform many aspiring black leaders of his generation could endorse. Coming just seven months after the death of Frederick Douglass, Washington's speech appeared to secure his claim to the mantle of African American leadership.

Indeed, Washington's address was initially received warmly by many prominent black leaders. W.E.B. Du Bois, Francis Grimké, and Charles W. Chesnutt—the first two later counted among his fiercest critics—sent Washington congratulatory telegrams and letters. For several years following the Atlanta address, these men continued to express genuine admiration and respect for Washington's work at Tuskegee, and their goodwill seems to have been reciprocated. Indeed, for a while the opposition to Washington remained sporadic and confined to a relatively small faction, led notably by William Monroe Trotter in Boston and Ida B. Wells in Chicago. Charles W. Chesnutt, for example, arguably Washington's polar opposite on most issues, could hardly contain his enthusiasm about the Tuskegee Negro Conference he attended early in 1901. "Tuskegee was a revelation," he exclaimed, "as it must be to anyone upon the first visit . . . One who comes and sees, is conquered." After witnessing proud farmers and tenants testify about their struggles and accomplishments, he admitted to being "swept off his feet." "They had done well, these men, and knew it, and wished to have proper credit for it. But the finest thing about it all was the spirit of charity which filled these knotted and gnarled old men, whose lives had been spent with the sun and the soil." He knew very well that they were "picked men," because "if every Negro farmer in Alabama were as prosperous as some of them, there would be small need of Tuskegee." Chesnutt appreciated very well what Tuskegee meant to these men, however. "It has furnished them a center of thought, of interest, of communication, of light: a place where they can come once a year, meet in friendly intercourse, and exchange views and experiences, a place to which they will naturally think of sending their children for instruction." It is notable, perhaps, that Du Bois, for whom Washington had not yet given up his efforts to recruit to the Tuskegee faculty, was also in attendance.

Thus the bitterly personal, even vitriolic character of the conflict between the Washingtonian and Du Boisian factions that developed later can obscure the common ground from which they departed. Though often cast, at the time and by historians later, as a contest between elitist and popular values, between classical and industrial education, between economics and politics, the differences between the groups were, on many issues, much narrower in practice than their rhetoric would suggest. There was no necessary incompatibility between classical and industrial education, economic and political strategies, or even elitist and populist emphases. One can find individuals throughout the South who easily reconciled elements of both ideologies in their everyday political practice. Only after Washington's political and economic alliances with white elites gave him overweening power within the black community did the opposition to him become broader, deeper, and fiercer. The publication of Du Bois's *The Souls of Black Folk* in 1903 exposed that "Tuskegee Machine" to broader public view, and gradually a broad-based political and intellectual critique emerged. Thereafter, the New Negro leadership split into two hostile camps. That development, however, is in fact much more part of the emerging urban milieu of the early twentieth century than the receding world of Hayes Cobb and Robert Charles.

Early in February 1906, final discharge papers were issued to Frank H. Stewart, one of the many black men anonymous to history who had been so instrumental in the formation of the new American empire that now stretched from the Caribbean Basin to Asia's Pacific Rim. Six months later, black American soldiers suffered one of the more egregious insults and injustices in their long history of national service. In the small town of Brownsville, Texas, a dozen or so black troopers from the Twenty-fifth Infantry Regiment stationed at Fort Brown were falsely accused of murdering a local bartender and wounding a police officer. The incident followed a period of heightened racial tensions between the troops and local white townspeople that, ironically, bore striking similarities to the racial harassment black troops had encountered eight years earlier in Tampa, Florida, where they rendezvoused before attacking Cuba. The soldiers staunchly maintained their innocence, and there is reason to believe that the "evidence" townspeople offered to prove their guilt had been fabricated. Accepting the white townspeople's version of events, President Theodore Roosevelt ordered the dishonorable discharge of 167 men, some of them twenty-year veterans, who as a result would be ineligible for further civil service employment or pensions. Although many members of Roosevelt's own Republican Party condemned his action in what came to be called the Brownsville Affair, it was not enough to assuage the outrage of many black Americans. No doubt the unjust treatment of these soldiers resonated too perfectly with their sense of declining status in the nation more generally.

We have no record of how Stewart responded to this development, but we can well imagine its pain for the twenty-three-year veteran. More than a decade earlier he had ridden proudly down Chicago's Michigan Avenue to open the World's Fair. Then the question of what kind of nation America would become remained, for many at least, an open one. Now, just over a decade later, the two overarching issues that had roiled the nation's tranquility since its inception—the rightful status of Indians and the citizenship of people of African descent—seemed finally resolved: the one defeated militarily and stored in the recesses of national mythology, the other politically nullified and rendered the object of humor and pity. Now resolutely a white man's country, America was ready to take its place on the world stage.

Indeed, the insult to black servicemen at Brownsville prefigured Stewart's own humiliation in his final years. A veteran of the Indian Wars and campaigns in Cuba and the Philippines, Stewart passed his final years in a vain effort to secure an increase in his pension, claiming that wounds and ailments contracted during that service now racked his body with pain. Between 1908 and the summer of 1915, one plaintive petition to the Pension Bureau followed another, until the issue became moot. Stewart died on October 31, 1915, just as America was on the verge of entering the Great War and, with it, a new chapter in its national transformation. So, too, was black America.

6

"A SECOND EMANCIPATION"
The Great Migrations of the Twentieth Century

On a sweltering late September evening in 1906, Atlanta, Georgia, erupted in three days of unrestrained racial violence. Inflamed by largely false or exaggerated newspaper reports and rumors of black men attacking white women, mobs hunted down and beat or killed any vulnerable African American man, woman, or child they could reach. Black businesses in the city's downtown were wantonly destroyed. For two nights black neighborhoods were menaced with invasion and destruction as armed white men gathered at their perimeters, declaring their intention "to kill every damned nigger in the town." In the riot's aftermath, official reports counted 25 blacks dead and 150 wounded, but the numbers were surely much greater. The city that epitomized the South's "new departure," its veritable rebirth from the ashes of the Civil War, lay economically paralyzed and disoriented.

Though sharing many similarities with previous outbreaks of racial rioting, the violence in Atlanta unfolded in three distinct stages, moving from what black newspaperman J. Max Barber described as "primal savagery" in the downtown section on Saturday to more systematic efforts to terrorize black neighborhoods in the days that followed, first by the mobs and then by police and militia. Shortly after six o'clock on Saturday evening, a mob made up mostly of young toughs—though egged on at times by "respectable" businessmen—began to form at Peachtree and Decatur streets, near the city's principal red-light district, which had long been known for its indiscriminate mélange of whites and blacks seeking or selling alcohol, sex, and entertainment. This September evening would be different, however. Following a racially charged gubernatorial campaign that populist Democrat Hoke Smith won largely on his promise to disenfranchise the state's black men, the city's newspapers had been filled with daily stories and editorials about black men's sexual attacks on white women—almost all of which later proved false. As night fell, the mob began random attacks around the area known as Five Points, the main pedestrian intersection and transportation hub of downtown, chasing down and beating the black workers and shoppers they found there. By ten o'clock, augmented by the patrons pouring out of bars as they closed, the mob which had swelled to an estimated ten thousand strong, was sweeping through the downtown area, turning it into a killing field. Unsuspecting black people making their way to or through the area were pulled from streetcars. Men, women, children, cripples—the mob spared no one. Black businesses and their proprietors were prime targets. Mrs. Mattie Adams had operated a restaurant at the intersection of Fair and Peters streets for twenty years. A portion of the mob led by George W. Blackstock, who had come from Decatur for the express purpose of "hurting niggers," broke down the barred door of her business, beat her and her daughter with wagon wheel spokes, and shot bullets at her grandson's feet "to make him dance." He and his followers then proceeded to completely destroy her restaurant. The men working in one of the shops on Peachtree Street belonging to the wealthy black businessman Alonzo Herndon were less fortunate: four barbers were shot and the bootblack beaten to death. Two dead bodies were dumped at the foot of the Henry Grady Monument, as if to make a cruel commentary on Grady's "New South" vision.

By three o'clock on Sunday morning there was a pause in the violence as heavy rains forced the rioters to seek cover. It was a false calm. Their fury was unabated. With the dawn light revealing black corpses littering the downtown's blood-drenched streets, the mob's attention switched to two black neighborhoods on the city's periphery, and the riot became, declared Oswald Garrison Villard, a future founder of the NAACP, "a pogrom." On Sunday and Monday evenings, respectively, newly formed mobs marched on Darktown, a black working-class community, and then on Brownville, home to the city's amazing complex of black colleges and its growing professional and middle-class elite. Marching into communities of at least partially armed black folk was decidedly different from attacking the unsuspecting and unarmed, however. The mob paused on the edge of Darktown, where all the streetlights had been shot out by residents anticipating the invasion. Gunshots were exchanged, some whites were hit, and the

Le Petit Journal

Le Petit Journal   5 ....   SUPPLÉMENT ILLUSTRÉ   5 ....   ABONNEMENTS

DIMANCHE 7 OCTOBRE 1906

LES « LYNCHAGES » AUX ÉTATS-UNIS
Massacre de nègres à Atlanta (Georgie)

Accounts of the carnage in Atlanta reached Europe, as shown in this Parisian
illustrated newspaper.

mob retreated, redirecting its assaults onto stray blacks encountered in its path. The attack on Brownville, Monday evening, led by policemen and hastily deputized citizens, was also repulsed, and one of its leaders, police officer James Heard, was killed. These momentary victories would grow into a legend of black resistance enduring deep into the twentieth century, eventually underwriting an alternative narrative of black liberation.

Victory was short-lived. The obvious solution to a confrontation with armed blacks was to use the forces of law and order to disarm them. At dawn on Tuesday, an indiscriminate mix of police officers, sheriff's deputies, militia, and white citizens systematically began terrorizing blacks in the Brownville section. Using an alleged search for arms stashes as an excuse, they arrested hundreds of black men and boys, abused the president of the Gammon Theological Seminary, and disarmed the professors and students who had organized to guard terrified residents taking refuge in the college's buildings. Calculating correctly that further resistance to the police and militia would degenerate into an unimaginable massacre, the now-disarmed blacks were forced to stand by while "the law" extended the reign of terror. Fulton County police found one badly wounded man in his bed and shot him in cold blood. Blacks retaliated with attacks on stragglers separated from the posse, killing one and wounding four. Later that evening the militia returned, now armed with a Gatling gun. The body count of blacks mounted until the riot abruptly ended late Tuesday afternoon.

W.E.B. Du Bois, one of Atlanta's prominent black citizens and a professor of sociology at one of the nation's leading black universities, was in Lowdnes County, Alabama, the weekend the rioting broke out, conducting field studies of black rural communities for the U.S. Department of the Census. Finding himself two hundred miles from his wife and daughter as the frightening news flashed across the country, Du Bois was profoundly shaken. Indeed, he later described his mental state during the long train ride home from rural Calhoun as "hysterical." One can well imagine that harrowing voyage: a bumpy buggy ride to the station at Calhoun to catch the Nashville and Louisville train, the agonizingly slow progress to Montgomery, where he would have had to transfer to the Western Alabama line that passed through Atlanta on its way to Savannah. During that long, anxious trip Du Bois wrote a poem, "A Litany of Atlanta." Composed on the train in the white heat of fear and anger, his words were by turns fiery and plaintive, flirting at times with blasphemy. "O Silent God," he lamented, "Is this Thy justice, . . . ? Sit no longer blind, . . . deaf to our prayer and dumb to our dumb suffering. Surely Thou too art not white, . . . a pale, bloodless, heartless thing?" Spitting contempt at the mob's apologists, who justified the violence as retaliation for attacks on white women, he reminded them that black women had been systematically "debauched" by white men since slavery times. Falling back on a then-familiar argument among the aspiring black respectable class, however, he condemned rapists and criminals of any color, especially those who violated women and the sanctity of the home, pleading only that all black folk not be classed with "our devils." And yet any fair accounting would recognize, he added, that those black "devils" were not born but made, fashioned out of the detritus thrown off by the South's brutal racial oppression, their deviltry nursed in crime and fed on injustice. Drawn by temperament to intermix social analysis with plaintive lament, Du Bois could not resist a jab at the "uplift" prescription for black progress advocated by his nemesis Booker T. Washington. "They told him: *Work and Rise*"—but still he lay slaughtered in the streets.

It is a measure of the depth of frustration and anger among black intellectuals that Du Bois's poem soon became something of a classic. Perhaps it reflected so powerfully their own inner conflicts, the doubled burden of representing the race and uplifting it, the felt contradiction of standing apart from the embarrassing black underclass while speaking for it. The tensions were present but muted in many of the black elites' protests against lynching, in which, as Ida Wells so perceptively noted, white charges of sexual depravity could mute black expressions of outrage. The racial pogroms sweeping through American cities in the first decades of the twentieth century, however, simply left a sense of deflation and betrayal. As so often in the past, the principal target of mob violence was not black vice but black virtue.

The "virtuous" among Atlanta's black community were scarcely prepared for the terror of that late September weekend, whatever their class location, ideological predisposition, or background. That a growing, self-confident, and progressive black community should be targeted by the racial hatred unleashed in Atlanta that autumn appears to have struck a deep chord, and its damage—psychological as well as material—would be long-lasting. In the riot's aftermath, some of the city's most promising professionals left town for good, joining the ongoing "migration of the talented tenth," as black historian Carter G. Woodson would later call it. No doubt they were followed by an indeterminate number of working-class folk, all in search of more racially hospitable climates in other cities, southern as well as northern. Those who remained were forced to rethink what was then called "the Negro Problem" and the strategies for its resolution. It was not yet fully evident even to the most perceptive observers, however, that what they were witnessing was but the beginning of something not amenable to familiar analytical categories, or as the black intellectual Alain Locke described it some years later, "something beyond the watch and guard" of their previous experience.

Their failures to recognize the change are understandable, of course. The Atlanta riot bore many of the marks of previous racial outbursts. "Nigger-baiting" politicians had exploited white fears that black voting power might thwart their aspirations, a ploy that worked best when coupled with a more visceral metaphor of usurpation—white men's sexual panic at black men taking liberties with their wives and daughters. Echoes of lynching and riot scenarios of the past two decades were plain to see. More difficult to see, however, were the ways in which Atlanta's riot replicated the one in New York City just six years earlier and anticipated another in Springfield, Illinois, just two years later. Impossible to see, perhaps, was how all these events prefigured the future convergence of southern and northern black experiences and a fundamental transformation in black life.

The Atlanta riot fell toward the end of a ten-year period straddling the turn of the century that witnessed violent racial outbreaks in Wilmington, North Carolina, in 1898; New Orleans and New York City in 1900; and Springfield, Illinois, in 1908. Most of these outbreaks were sparked by very similar street encounters, which became more common with the heightened visibility of blacks in urban spaces. The mobs often targeted upwardly mobile blacks, who were perceived to be threats to white working-class voting power, economic well-being, or sexual honor. The New York riot, for instance, occurred just two weeks after Robert Charles's altercation with two New Orleans policemen triggered violence in that city, and it unfolded in a strikingly similar fashion. On August 12, Robert Thorpe, a plainclothes policeman in Manhattan's Tenderloin District, accosted May

Enoch, a black woman he suspected of being a prostitute but who was actually waiting for her boyfriend, Arthur Harris. The argument with Thorpe intensified with the arrival of Harris, who did not realize Thorpe was a policeman. Hot words followed by physical violence left Thorpe wounded and near death. Manhattan's Irish immigrant community, already restive about its competition for space and jobs with a growing black population, exploded in two days of rioting. As much as it echoed the violence in New Orleans that year, however, the riot in Manhattan also prefigured downtown Atlanta six years later: blacks were pulled from streetcars and attacked at their jobs in restaurants, hotels, and barbershops; white policemen dispatched ostensibly to restore order disarmed the blacks instead and joined in the violence against them.

This striking convergence of southern and northern racial violence during the first decade of the twentieth century signaled an ongoing and permanent transformation in black life in America. No doubt the almost fourfold increase in New York's black population over the preceding decade, fed mostly by southern migrants, contributed significantly to the escalating violence. Notably, Atlanta's black population, starting from a comparable base (28,177), had also increased substantially over that same period. Although Atlanta's increase (84.2 percent) was much smaller than New York's, it was politically fraught because it boosted an already sizable black plurality that had emerged three decades earlier during Reconstruction. In the decade following the Atlanta riot, the social and political import of the steady, then suddenly dramatic, expansion of the black population in many northern and southern cities would become fully evident.

In 1906, these harbingers of a coming transformation of black life in America would have been obscure for most contemporaries. Du Bois journeyed to Lowndes County, Alabama, that year to study the so-called Negro Problem because he assumed, reasonably enough, that solutions must be found where the overwhelming majority of black Americans still lived and worked: in the rural South. When Du Bois was born, three years after the Civil War, more than nine out of ten black Americans lived in the South, a distribution that had scarcely changed forty years later when the census of 1910 found 89 percent of the black population still there, despite a steady four-decades-old movement to northern and border cities. Du Bois could not have known that in another four decades *most* black Americans would be living in cities and that the problems of the rural economy he was laboring to decipher would already have faded into near irrelevancy. Indeed, a closer look at that 1910 census would have revealed that even then well over a quarter of the nation's black population resided in cities and towns.

With industrial activity exploding and railroad mileage nearly doubling in the 1880s, the southern economy, though still overwhelmingly agricultural, was being reoriented in significant ways. There was a decided shift away from the port cities that had served as entrepôts to the plantation economy toward new or reviving interior cities. Railroads replaced seaports, integrating those southern cities into regional networks and promoting economic exchange within the region and with the outside. The result was a tremendous intraregional migration that would ultimately transform southern life: whereas southern cities were home to one of every ten of the region's inhabitants in 1880, they sheltered one of five by 1910 and one of three by the eve of the Second World War. Although the South remained the most rural region in the nation, therefore, its urban growth rate would actually exceed all others.

The changes in the black population distribution closely tracked that of the region as a whole. There were many fewer city folk among southern blacks than nationally (18.8 percent versus 27.3 percent), but the rate of increase was far greater. Indeed, using twenty-four cities as a standard of measurement, the Census Bureau found that during that first decade of the twentieth century, blacks poured into urban areas at a rate two and a half times faster than the general population; that pace quickened to six and a half times faster in the decade that followed. In contrast with rural whites, however, black southern migrants during the earlier decades tended to favor older seaports such as Charleston and Savannah over inland cities such as Atlanta or Montgomery, reflecting perhaps the more hospitable welcome of already well-established black communities in those historic cities. Nonetheless, by 1910, a total of 329,166 blacks lived and worked in the South's six largest cities—Atlanta, Birmingham, Memphis, Nashville, New Orleans, and Richmond—all of which would be among the principal feeders of the great northern migration in the century's second decade.

Clearly, then, the great wartime migrations of African Americans during the first half of the twentieth century cannot be understood apart from the emergence of the New South as the region grew commercially and industrially during the late nineteenth century. In hindsight, we can see that contemporaneous developments in New York and Atlanta signaled the imminent displacement, in time and space, of the so-called Negro Problem. In the future, it would be renamed "the urban problem" and would require different analytical perspectives and perhaps different strategies for social change. For the second time since blacks' arrival on the North American continent, then, the material and logistical basis of their life chances were being fundamentally altered. Their social and cultural lives, their political prospects and possibilities, their means of shaping the present and future—all were new. Ten years after the Atlanta riot, a black newspaper editor, who had himself only recently migrated to Chicago, would hail this constellation of changes "a second emancipation."

"Of the Wings of Atalanta": New South, Old South

Du Bois opened the fifth essay of *The Souls of Black Folk* with a trenchant description of Atlanta: "South of the North, yet north of the South, . . . peering out from the shadows of the past into the promise of the future." Like most of the other essays in the volume, "Of the Wings of Atalanta" is by turns historical and prescient, argumentative and lyrical. Taken together, the essays of the collection straddled the centuries as much as they did genres of literary expression: one foot in past debates over slavery and black adjustments to emancipation, the second in an era not yet discernable. Henry Grady's so-called New South Creed and Booker T. Washington's complicity with it are clear targets. Thanks to Grady's relentless propaganda and the two world's fairs—in 1881 and 1895—that touted its rise from the ashes of civil war, Atlanta was already the very emblem of New South aspirations. The question, of course, was which "new south"? The one celebrated in John Greenleaf Whittier's poem that Du Bois used as the epigraph for his essay, where master and slave, both liberated by emancipation, join hands in the region's moral redemption? Or the one celebrated by Grady and endorsed by Booker T. Washington, where capital liberated from the dead hand of the slave oligarchy would make the South an industrial workshop? Like a number of other black intellectuals, Du Bois was himself beguiled by images of an Old South aristocracy, of the "Southern gentleman [who was the] new-world heir of the grace and courtliness of patrician, knight, [and] noble," who, though wrong about

slavery, was decent and honorable, nonetheless. Now these men were being submerged and subordinated to new men mired in a crass, materialist
ethos of moneygrubbing. Like Atalanta of Greek myth, whom Du Bois chose
to allegorize its likely fate, the city of a hundred hills seemed destined to
profane its true mission, "the Gospel of Work befouled by the Gospel of
Pay." The city's salvation lay with its black people, or rather with that part
of the black populace, "unthought of, half-forgotten," who resided and
worked in the black universities that three years later would be menaced
by riot. Along with his own Atlanta University, founded in 1865, to serve
the children of slaves, these institutions were representative of others elsewhere, such as Fisk and Howard, all dedicated to teaching the higher
meaning of life, how to reconcile "real life and the growing knowledge of
life"—in sum, "the secret of civilization." The South, he declared, needs
"knowledge and culture," and the "Wings of Atalanta are the coming universities of the South." His hope and plea was that such centers of learning would produce black and white men "of broad culture, catholic tolerance,
and trained ability, joining their hands to other hands, and giving to this
squabble of the Races a decent and dignified peace."

Much of this would soon come to seem pathetically naïve after the
violence of 1906—even to Du Bois. Developments in the immediate aftermath of the riot prefigured the template of race relations that would evolve
in the most economically progressive areas of the South during the first
half of the twentieth century. Embarrassed by the carnage produced by
irresponsible racial populists such as gubernatorial candidate Hoke Smith,
Atlanta's white leaders of business and civic life acted quickly to reassert
control and restore the city's reputation. A riot victims' fund was established, and rewards were offered for the apprehension of rioters. Even
before the riot ashes cooled, the leaders met to form two committees, the
most powerful of which was the Committee of Ten, a coalition of business, religious, and political leaders that assumed overarching authority
over the rebuilding process. The other was a biracial committee designed
to promote interracial peace, whose nonconfrontational style provided a
model for the Commission on Interracial Cooperation formed in Atlanta
in 1919 and similar groups that sprouted in "progressive" southern cities
over the next half century.

The spirit and agenda that Booker T. Washington had advocated a
decade earlier seemed to animate these developments, but the class com-

promises in this case took a form that he and many other black leaders badly misread. Seeking to reconcile a new commercial-industrial ethos with a reinterpretation of the old order, New South boosters enlisted allies among the emerging black elites, repudiated the Civil War as "a mistake," and touted the abolition of slavery as freeing whites from the chains of social and economic backwardness even as it liberated their slaves. It became clear, however, that the price of racial peace was stricter policing of racial separation, by which the elite sought to placate white populists, who were otherwise skeptical about their economic schemes. Rhetorically, the new white elite embraced the putatively paternalistic master-slave relationship as a model for all black-white relations. What they really wanted, Ray Stannard Baker so perceptively observed in 1908, was "the New South and the Old Negro."

Many African American leaders embraced these post-riot initiatives, nonetheless, hoping to find openings for class unity across racial lines. They would be disappointed by and large. Blacks were excluded from any meaningful role in rebuilding Atlanta, for example, and there and elsewhere black businesses formerly located in the downtown sections were displaced to segregated neighborhoods. Like Atlanta, other New South cities tended to be far more racially segregated than their Old South predecessors, and in all of them, black neighborhoods were likely to endure official neglect, their demands for paved streets, sanitation, streetlights, parks, schools, health care, equal education, and police protection going unanswered.

Whatever their posture toward the New South regimes, however, black leaders were fairly unanimous in their determination to turn the new segregation to their advantage. Black colleges and universities would prepare the next generation of leaders, they argued. Black businesses and professional classes, some of which had formerly served an exclusively white clientele, would now be supported by these black neighborhoods. Indeed, black businessmen regularly invoked the virtues of segregation to anchor their marketing campaigns. "[A]n Afro-American policy," blared an advertisement by Charlotte, North Carolina's Afro-American Mutual Insurance Company, sold "by an Afro-American agent, made by Afro-American clerks, on an Afro-American husband[,] an Afro-American wife, or an Afro-American child, makes an Afro-American home independent in the hours of sickness or death." The black elites of New South cities, then, were the first to advance the notion of a black renaissance in segregated urban enclaves.

The development of the black community in Charlotte is exemplary
of the ecological, temporal, and ideological patterns found in Atlanta and
other New South cities. Beginning in the late 1890s, as elsewhere, pressure from white politicians forced into new areas the black businessmen
and black residents who had previously occupied downtown districts
and wards, thus shifting the city's racial map by 1910 from a mixed,
salt-and-pepper pattern to a patchwork of all-black and all-white blocks.
Suburban expansion brought new developments, ranging from cheap
shotgun-style rental units for working-class folk to substantial houses like
those occupied by the business and professional residential enclave around
Biddle Memorial Institute (later renamed Johnson C. Smith University).
There was also a diversified business and commercial district, anchored
since 1894 by the AME Zion Publishing House, later joined by the Afro-
American Mutual Insurance Company. There was even a plausible, though
unsuccessful, effort to establish a black-owned cotton mill. It is not surprising, therefore, that one of the principal streets in one of Charlotte's
black neighborhoods was named for Booker T. Washington.

Indeed, the materialist, self-help philosophy that Washington had
made famous by the turn of the century had been trumpeted decades
earlier in Charlotte. "Get knowledge. Get money. Get land," William C.
Smith declared in the 1880s. "Use these things properly taking Christ as
our guide, and all will be well." Of course, black Charlotte's endorsement
of racial solidarity should not be confused with segregation. As the historian Earl Lewis reminds us in his study of Norfolk during this period, the
desire for "congregation" as a means of empowerment is not the same as
enduring "segregation" and the insult of racial exclusion. The brief boycott
movement protesting the onset of segregated seating on streetcars and
trolleys in 1907 indicates that Charlotte blacks still resented the denial of
public services and accommodations, or access to them on insulting terms.
As elsewhere, however, with the emergence of Jim Crow, most of Charlotte's black leaders appeared to have acquiesced to the admonitions of
the former consul to Sierra Leone, Dr. J. L. Williams, who advised a close
friend in 1905 that "money will accomplish what legislation will not." Sensitive to and critical of poor blacks whose behavior reinforced racial stereotypes, the "best men" and "best women" of black Charlotte formed a
social web of book clubs, churches, and other institutions to foster and
display moral rectitude. Though wary of Fusionist politics, some of them

were drawn into alliances with white Prohibitionist parties, in the name of biracial and bipartisan uplift. In the aftermath of Prohibition's defeat at the polls, whites blamed blacks, however, which may have discredited biracial political engagement for several decades. Nonetheless, the basic notion of racial accommodation built on a rapprochement between the "better classes" of the two races remained operative for several decades more, ebbing briefly with the rise of a new urban economy and black leadership in the New Deal era and reemerging during the Civil Rights Movement that followed.

Developments after the Atlanta riot underscore how much the rise of the Jim Crow South was linked to its urbanization and suggest why resistance to that system would also appear first in southern cities. Obviously, hostility to blacks and rejection of anything suggesting racial equality was a long-standing sentiment in the South as in the nation as a whole. But in the South these attitudes had existed side by side with a racial intimacy that startled most northern visitors. The consistent, institutionalized prohibition of practically all interracial contact was new, therefore. Indeed, the Jim Crow that arose in the early twentieth century was modern, rigid, systematic, legalized, and distinctly urban. Only while in or moving between cities did whites begin to worry about close proximity and physical contact with black folk. Such worries made no sense in the rural South, where social proximity was as unavoidable as southern whites' dependence on black labor. And, in fact, that very labor dependency lent physical contact a different meaning in rural areas: blacks were clearly not equal or capable of presuming equality, and thus physical racial intimacy resonated differently. The riots in Atlanta and other southern cities, therefore, heralded the evolution of a different racial order than the nation had known before.

This evolution to a new racial ordering of southern everyday life was slow, however, because most blacks continued to live and work in the rural South until the mid-twentieth century. There was, historian Mark Schultz has written, "a rural face to white supremacy" in the early twentieth-century South. Or, more precisely, this was true mainly in areas where plantation management had not succumbed to large corporate conglomerates. As Schultz so poetically phrased it, race relations in the rural South looked more like "a sprawling thicket" than the "tightly manicured lawns" of southern cities and suburbs. Many of the counties in the Georgia Black

Belt just south of Atlanta were exemplary of the complexities of rural Jim Crow. A region Du Bois had described so graphically and poetically in *The Souls of Black Folk* was, by the eve of the First World War, a mere shadow of its better days, with only a faint scent of wisteria and magnolia hanging over its now-decrepit mansions. The Jim Crow social regime then evolving in southern cities such as Atlanta was still largely irrelevant there. To be sure, the white folks' commitment to racial supremacy was as strong as ever, but the idea of strictly segregating the races would have been dysfunctional in an economy and social order wholly dependent on black folks' close proximity. The physical residential separation that did exist was of entire subregions rather than neighborhoods. It arose because, since slavery days, black labor had been massed on the large plantations that monopolized the rich soils of the Atlantic seacoast and southern Lowlands. Consequently, many of these counties would continue to have three-to-one black population majorities deep into the twentieth century. The lesser soils of the Piedmont and hilly regions were left to white yeomen farmers, who wrested from them an oftentimes marginal existence. In the decades following emancipation, significant numbers of black farmers settled in these regions as well, often taking up the less productive lands white folks didn't want. A few black landowners did gain a foothold in the plantation districts, however, securing titles to plots exhausted by almost a century of abuse from cotton monoculture.

Roughly one hundred miles southeast of Atlanta, Hancock County lies astride the historic path Sherman took in his March to the Sea. It exemplified all the economic and demographic patterns, and the associated social etiquette structuring relations between the races, that were peculiar to the rural South in the decades before and during the Great Migration. In 1910, notwithstanding the significant pockets of sandy soils claimed by black and white smallholders, large landowners monopolized the richest soils. That year, in one of Hancock's most fertile militia districts, for example, 43 percent of the land was owned by just ten men; following the boll weevil infestation and agriculture's economic depression in the 1920s, that concentration would grow to 54 percent. Meanwhile, the numbers working on shares as opposed to renting comprised a third of all tenants in 1910 and fully half by 1920.

Almost by definition, paternalism develops in contexts where social relations are unequal, and it is sustained by a monopoly on violence. In the

Black Belt, white elites controlled the law and the land, thus leaving blacks little alternative but to seek their goodwill and protection. In return they might have expected their children to be pulled from school whenever their labor was needed, their wives and daughters to provide domestic services to the big house when called, their husbands and fathers to render personal services on demand. Thus James Wilson's father regularly missed Sunday services at his own church in order to wait on the planter's family, standing at the ready to hitch their buggy when they went to the white church and to unhitch it when they came home. Meanwhile, powerful planters such as Sam Innis readily interposed their authority between their workers and the law, refusing to allow the state to prosecute them. As some survivors of that era recalled later, the ultimate safety for blacks, whether workers or landowners, was that some powerful white man would be willing to declare, "That's my nigger."

Within the political logic of white supremacy, this peculiar patron-clientage, or "paternalism," provided the overall structure for rural black-white relations, but it did not account for or contain the unruly thicket of interactions across the color line. Unlike the anonymity of the city, rural economy and geography required face-to-face, often intimate contacts and exchanges. Its conventions, taboos, and etiquette governing racial interactions could vary with location, age of the participants, and even posture, such as, incredibly enough, whether one was sitting or standing. Blacks and whites might intermingle and eat together out of doors but not indoors, while standing but not while seated, as preadolescents but not thereafter (when one was presumed to have become a sexual being). Given their control of the livelihoods of lesser whites as well as blacks, however, powerful white planters freely flouted even these racial conventions and taboos. Hancock's Lynn Rives, a substantial white landowner, brought his black grandsons into white restaurants to eat with him. Percy Moore drove around openly with his black mistress. Others maintained interracial households. And no one whose loan or livelihood was vulnerable to their say-so was likely to challenge them.

At the other end of the class spectrum, interracial boundary crossing was also rife. Much as in pre-riot Atlanta, blacks and whites joined together in illicit spaces and activities, such as gambling, drinking, and prostitution. In the recreationally impoverished countryside, they watched one another's baseball games and sometimes even played against one another. Until the 1930s, or shortly thereafter, they paid occasional visits to each other's churches, although some observers noted that whites were more likely to have been the visitors and blacks the gracious hosts.

Hancock's black landowners—who by 1920 owned 34,700 acres of the county's land—secured thereby a ticket to greater independence from white control over the minutest details of their daily lives, but their security often depended on having a white patron. Someone had to be willing to sell land to them in a culture hostile to "uppity" blacks moving beyond their place. And, at some point, someone might be needed to intervene with authorities to help a black family sustain its claim to the land. The largest black-owned properties were usually legacies from white kinspeople secured during the previous century, while the smaller, but more numerous tracts were secured during the first two decades of the twentieth century, many of them by virtue of favorable prices and abundant crops during the First World War. Kinship across the color line played a role in many of these purchases or legacies, especially for some of the more substantial landed black families. In some instances, a landlord risked the opprobrium of his white neighbors to reward a tenant's years of faithful service.

Nonetheless, while it was prudent for even substantial black landowners to show the proper racial deference to whites, it is also clear that owning, and even renting, the land one worked lent a measure of independence and room for maneuver that was unavailable to most rural blacks. The children of landowners attended school more regularly and for more years than did those of sharecroppers. Where black schools were nonexistent or inaccessible, landed families often sent their children to live with urban relatives or to boarding schools. Although many farm girls sought work during the dead season as domestics and laundresses, the wives and daughters of landed families were much less likely to risk the dangers of working in white homes. Their fathers and sons traveled to nearby cities or out of the region altogether to find seasonal or permanent jobs to supplement the family income. It is very likely, then, that young men and women from such families were among the first responders to the great urban migration that began during World War I and continued well after the Second World War.

Restive and underemployed young men and women like these had swelled the growing ranks of black southerners who made their way north during the first decade of the twentieth century, as opportunities for a decent life and personal security in the South rapidly diminished. By 1916, however, the then-two-year-old war in Europe had choked off the European immigrant sources of labor for northern industries at precisely the moment workers were most needed to supply the Allied war machine, and labor recruiters looked to black as well as white southerners to fill the void. Given the lack of precise census data, determining the origins of these migrant workers remains conjectural, but there are strong indications that at least this first wave emerged either from southern cities and towns or from among the sons and daughters of owners and renters like those in Hancock who had already experienced seasonal work off the farm. Migrants' diaries and letters describe work in logging and turpentine camps, on railroad construction crews, and other non-farm labor.

By the time the guns went silent on the Western Front in the fall of 1918, the migration north had become a veritable social movement, one that would mark a fundamental rupture in black life, culture, and consciousness, one that would transform the black South as well as the North even as it forged profound bonds between them. By war's end, entire families and communities had pulled up stakes for what they called "the promised land." The migrants' seeming rhetorical hyperbole should be taken seriously, for their "exodus" cannot be reduced to impersonal economic forces, rendered in demographic statistics, or visualized simply in spatial terms. Rather than an image of anonymous human vectors flung aimlessly northward by forces beyond their control, one might imagine an unfolding web braiding two spaces, north and south, intertwining them through the lives of people moving along its connecting strands, with people and places left behind remaining intimately part of the new habitations. Even as they built new lives, migrants drew on and transported their experiences and cultural resources—and their limitations—from their communities of origin into those new lives. They also transmitted a bit of that new life back again to their old homes, to places and people that forever remained "down home." Migration, then, involved multiple acts of transformation—of self and others, of sending and receiving communities. In neither the North nor the South would black life be the same again.

On the Southern

For young Jean Toomer, northern-born and bred, the South was a place of mystery and foreboding danger. He had accepted an invitation to teach at a rural school in Hancock County, Georgia, in the fall of 1921, substituting for the regular teacher who was traveling in the North raising funds for the school. Like the young Du Bois more than three decades earlier, Toomer encountered for the first time a black southern culture as foreign as it was mesmerizing. Unlike Du Bois, Toomer had familial roots in the South. His estranged father had been born there and would die there. His mother's father, P.B.S. Pinchback, briefly governor of Louisiana during Reconstruction, had been born in nearby Macon, and the teacher for whom Toomer substituted was his grandfather's old friend.

Toomer undertook this assignment for the money and to gain a brief respite from caring for his aging grandparents, but the experience was personally and professionally transformative. The almost literal embodiment of Du Bois's "seventh son," Toomer truly lived in "a world which yield[ed] him no true self-consciousness." Raised largely by a grandfather and grandmother who looked white, Toomer was a stranger to black American culture, his contact limited mostly to his final years in a black Washington, D.C., high school. Seeing for the first time these simple people "strong with the tang of fields and soil," hearing their "folk-songs rolling up the valley at twilight," empowered his writing and opened doors to new creative possibilities. He described the visit to Hancock County as a kind of rebirth; its people "gave birth to a whole new life." It is no small irony, then, that he was also keenly conscious of witnessing a dying way of life. "'Cane,'" he wrote later, "was a swan song . . . a song of an end." On the train home to Washington, Toomer began to compose passages for *Cane*, the book that arguably inaugurated the black literary and cultural explosion known as the Harlem Renaissance, or if not that, surely emblematized its highest creative aspirations. The final section of that book recounts the experience of a character much like himself among a people like those he had encountered in Hancock. By December 20, he had completed a full draft of the book. The next day his grandfather, one of the last survivors of the heady days following emancipation, passed away.

As Toomer settled down to work in a coach, very likely on the Southern Railway, that took him back to Washington, he almost certainly found himself seated among scores of black folk much like those he was writing about, perhaps even people he had met, taught, and studied during his brief sojourn in Hancock County. Ironically, their very means of transport was a legacy of the Reconstruction-era triumphs and defeats of his grandfather's generation. The subsidies for start-up rail lines, the leasing of convict labor to build them, the ideological conviction that the South must be economically integrated with the North established the basis for the eventual emergence and consolidation of the principal southern rail networks that would now facilitate the rapid movement of black folks out of the region. Rolling up the Atlantic coast from Florida through Georgia, the Carolinas, and Virginia was a vast, interconnected East Coast rail system, of which the Southern was a key link. From the Union Station terminus in the nation's capital, Toomer's fellow passengers could make their way to lines connecting with cities farther north or west. Farther west, those coming out of the Gulf states would board the same Louisville and Nashville train to Montgomery that Du Bois had taken on the first leg of his harrowing journey from Calhoun, making connections in Cincinnati for Detroit, Cleveland, and other midwestern cities. And, finally, the Illinois Central ran up from New Orleans through Memphis to Chicago, fed by trunk lines that stretched like fingers into the isolated hinterlands of the Mississippi Delta. These three rail networks provided the main thoroughfares of the great northern migration that would ebb and flow over the next three decades. Though beckoning to the future, then, they were also silent metaphors of the umbilical links between a present and a past reconstruction of black life and folkways, links to the emancipation of the previous century.

Upon reaching Washington's Union Station, Jean Toomer parted company with a substantial number of his fellow passengers from southern Georgia, as they fanned out for connections to destinations farther north and west. No doubt many of them would have been headed for New York City, which by the second decade of the century had become the emblem of a putative black emancipation and rebirth, perhaps not unlike Toomer's own. Their arrival in New York would be heralded and celebrated by an earlier generation of southern migrants who had already fashioned impressive—indeed, unprecedented—communal and institutional infrastructures that would accommodate them. Seizing the advantages that a rapidly, aggressively modernizing city had to offer, this "talented tenth"— though as much heirs to Booker T. Washington as Du Bois—had set out to build a "black metropolis" within the larger metropolis, a black cultural capital within the nation's cultural capital, and through these a black identity to counter the traditional rural southern stereotypes. As a result,

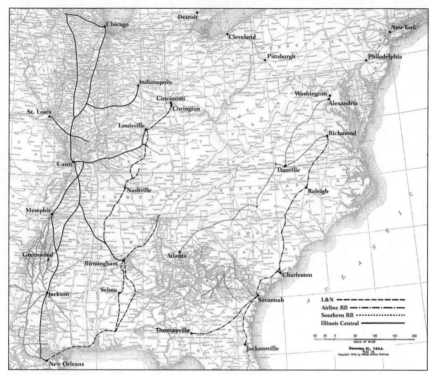

This 1920s railway map highlights the three principal routes for migrants leaving the South during the Great Migration.

New York's Manhattan borough, especially the Harlem precincts, claimed what many later groused was an undeserved central place in the transformation of black life and culture during the first half of the twentieth century.

Four years after the Atlanta riot, Du Bois had abandoned the deteriorating situation in that city for New York, where he assumed directorship of the newly formed NAACP's house organ, *The Crisis*. Ironically, the NAACP was itself formed in response to the kind of racial terror Du Bois had fled, one that now seemed to threaten northern cities as well as southern. In a scenario not dissimilar to Atlanta's, rioting broke out in Springfield, Illinois, in 1908. Such an event in the city claiming Abraham Lincoln as its favorite son, and just seven years before the nation would celebrate the half-century anniversary of emancipation from slavery was a troubling indicator of deteriorating race relations and of the threat to black citizenship nationally. A biracial meeting was convened in New York City the following year, and the NAACP formed to combat racial violence and discrimination. Many saw this as a direct challenge to the leadership of Booker T. Washington—including Washington himself. And, indeed, despite the best efforts of its principal white founders to placate Washington, the NAACP's commitment to aggressive and public legal protests of the evolving Jim Crow order did in fact challenge all that Washington stood for. The fact that his most prominent and influential critic had assumed a leading role in the new organization didn't help matters.

In reality, the Du Bois–Washington controversy that had so roiled black leadership over the previous decade faded rather rapidly after 1910. Indeed, a protégé of Washington's, James Weldon Johnson, joined the NAACP's staff in 1916, following a diplomatic career that had taken him to Venezuela and Nicaragua. Far more important for the emerging generation of black leaders were the problems and opportunities unfolding in this new era. Although legal challenges to peonage and disenfranchisement were among its first major initiatives, and anti-lynching legislation remained a central objective for several decades more, the new organization quickly became embroiled in matters that older controversies and paradigms had not anticipated, such as racial zoning and residential covenants in New South cities and the representation of blacks in new cultural media such as movies. Having its headquarters in Manhattan, the rising cultural and economic capital of twentieth-century America, was immensely helpful to the NAACP in pursuing this agenda. Magnet to diverse media, a mélange of foreign peoples and cultures, and political ferment—in short, America's emerging cultural capital—New York City was fast becoming the black cultural capital as well. The unprecedented migration of southern blacks at precisely the moment of the city's rapid ascent was the "favorable conjunction," argued Arna Bontemps, that enabled Manhattan's Harlem community to assume a primary role in the black cultural renaissance of the interwar years. Indeed, most movements for revitalizing the national black community during the interwar period eventually found their home in New York, even if they did not start there. Moreover, whatever the validity of New York's claims to cultural priority, it is indisputable that, as with many other political exiles, the city provided black migrants and immigrants an institutional space for sustained challenges to southern Jim Crow regimes and to the politics of accommodation, then and for long thereafter.

One of the seven principal destinations of the wartime migration— the others were Philadelphia, Chicago, Detroit, Pittsburgh, Indianapolis, and Cleveland, which together embraced 40 percent of the North's black population in 1920—New York City had a black population two-thirds larger in 1920 than when Du Bois arrived in 1910. Almost all of the increase was credited to the massive inflow that had begun just four years earlier, and most of those newcomers squeezed into the space framed on the west and east by Seventh and Lenox avenues and by 110th and 135th streets on the south and north. This was Harlem, formerly a white suburb of the city in the nineteenth century, that had been overbuilt by real estate speculators in the early twentieth century in anticipation of a proposed subway extension. Desperate landlords stuck with vacant apartments agreed to lease some of them to Philip A. Payton, a black, underemployed, college-educated janitor in a white real estate office, who subletted the units to black tenants. A veritable "race war" ensued thereafter: white investors bought the buildings and evicted the black tenants; Payton and other black speculators leased or purchased other buildings for rent to blacks. Ultimately white flight from the neighborhood left blacks in possession of large sections of Harlem's real estate, encouraging further in-migration from the Tenderloin District and scattered parts of the city.

A product of a small black college in North Carolina but Massachusetts-born, Payton was representative of the Tuskegee machine's northern phalanx. He and his associates were all members of the National Negro Business League, which was founded in Boston but heavily influenced by Booker T. Washington, and many of them attended its 1905 meeting in New York, where they proudly reported their Harlem triumph. Though later described as pioneer black nationalists by some historians, Payton and his allies began with distinctly integrationist goals. Their Afro-American Realty Company was a response to what they called "the forced colonization" of Negroes in New York's undesirable Midtown neighborhoods, where respectable blacks were forced to live side by side with "the low-down, loud-mouthed, razor-carrying, shiftless Negro." They set out to deliberately limit black occupancy to only one or two flats in any one building, so as to avoid white flight. That strategy failed miserably, however, as did the company itself, during the severe recession of 1907–08. Nonetheless, they had opened a breach that other black Realtors—such as James Weldon Johnson's father-in-law, John Nail—quickly filled. Soon large institutional investors such as St. Mark's Methodist Episcopal Church entered the fray, buying up entire blocks of Harlem at a stroke. Payton's guerrilla incursion became a multi-front crusade.

The war metaphors were appropriate because this was truly a struggle for control of territory, involving mass maneuver, strategy, and a collective sense of moral victory at its end. A quarter century later a typically judicious James Weldon Johnson could not contain his racial pride at the uniqueness of the Harlem community that had been won: a black urban space. First of all, he noted, it was "situated in the heart of Manhattan [in] one of the most beautiful and healthful sites in the whole city. It is not a fringe, it is not a slum, nor is it a 'quarter' consisting of dilapidated tenements." Instead one found there "handsome" apartments built to code; paved, well-lighted streets; and two main highways connecting it to the rest of the city. "Harlem," he declared, "is not a section that one goes out to," but that one goes through. The aesthetic and psychological value of a community that *one goes through* rather than *out to* must be measured against all those black communities relegated to marginal areas, often across an actual physical barrier or divide—a railroad track, a river, a red-light district. By creating a concentrated enclave for black folk in a socially and economically diverse community, the migration to Harlem provided a market for the development of black businesses and professions and a population sufficient to support black institutional life more generally. In other words, it replicated in the North the urban black enclaves established in a few southern cities some two decades earlier. The northern enclaves would soon outpace their southern predecessors. Between 1910 and 1920, Harlem was the magnet drawing the majority of black migrants to the city, as evidenced by the fact that eight out of every ten of the black newcomers to New York City settled there. Their presence, in turn, enabled an explosion of media outlets, professional services, entertainment, and, eventually, political empowerment.

A new generation of men and women—many of them southern-born and most barely in or approaching their twenties—could sense in Harlem's teeming streets that it could be "the laboratory of a great race-welding," even before Howard University professor Alain Locke hailed it as such in the 1925 publication, *The New Negro*. Among them was the remarkable Ella Josephine Baker, a native of rural North Carolina, who arrived after completing her studies at Shaw University in Raleigh in 1927. Like many others, Baker found a cultural vitality and political dynamism in Harlem that changed her consciousness and redirected her life's ambitions. Shaw's education had prepared her to be either a prim schoolteacher or a selfless missionary, but her reeducation on Harlem's streets gave her a taste for political insurgency. She acquired organizational skills that she would lend successively to the NAACP and other civil rights organizations over the next forty years.

Southern migrants were not the only ones peopling Harlem's streets, however. An unprecedented influx came from the larger black Atlantic world. Suddenly African Americans had to negotiate physical and psychological space with West Indians, some of whom were even more cosmopolitan and politically radical than they. New York may have been a West Indian's second or third stop after travels in Europe, Panama, and Costa Rica. Their black identity might be but a part of a complex, often contradictory, self-conception that embraced British nationality, anticolonialism, socialism, and the color prejudices peculiar to Latin tripartite racial regimes. The differences in national background produced misunderstandings and tensions, but they also introduced new thinking and stimulated debate, all of which helped make New York one of the principal cities of the black Atlantic world.

A heightened awareness of an enlarged black world was unavoidable for those settling in postwar Harlem. More than any previous generation, these African Americans scrutinized and reacted to American policies abroad—to America's occupation of Haiti in 1915, to U.S. relations with Liberia in the 1920s, to Italy's invasion of Ethiopia in 1935, to how the peace treaty signed at Versailles would affect Europe's current and former colonies after World War I. Soon after his arrival in the city in 1916, the Jamaican Marcus Garvey discovered that British colonial black folks' concerns about national belonging and identity resonated deeply with those of politically disinherited and economically dispossessed African Americans. Although his world headquarters remained in New York, where the message of racial rebirth was palpable and ubiquitous, Garvey soon moved far beyond his fractious West Indian base in Harlem to the southern heartland. Like young Arna Bontemps, however, most admirers of Garvey probably discounted his "back-to-Africa" scheme, the notion of a mass migration to Africa, as yet another imagined community, much like the promised land after the exodus from Egyptland described in the familiar lyrics of spirituals. What mattered most was Garvey's message of racial revitalization; it resonated with the diverse experiences of black Americans, despite long-standing regional, class, and color differences and tensions among them.

Black newcomers to the urban North discovered prospects for rebirth in many venues and forms, however. Unconsciously echoing the more modest touting of the benefits of racial solidarity in New South cities such as Atlanta and Charlotte two decades earlier, Howard University philosophy professor Alain Locke declared in 1925 that the creative potential unleashed in Harlem provided an opportunity "to repair a damaged group psychology and reshape a warped social perspective," "to convert a defensive into an offensive position, a handicap into an incentive." In striking contrast to earlier spokesmen, however, Locke was thinking less of African American achievements in business and the professions than of blacks' cultural achievements. James Weldon Johnson's mentor had long lived by the aphorism that no race that has material wealth is for long excluded and oppressed. His protégé subtly substituted new terms into the Tuskegee Wizard's equation, however: "No people that has produced great literature and art," Johnson wrote, "has ever been looked upon by the world as distinctly inferior." By those terms black gains should rightly have been considerable. In a mere ten years, between the mid-twenties and the mid-thirties, African Americans published twenty-six novels, ten volumes of poetry, five Broadway plays, and countless short stories and essays.

Perhaps the very scale and intensity of its cultural output left the Harlem Renaissance vulnerable to criticism when the pace of production subsided. By the 1930s it all seemed to have been a brief "vogue." More seriously, later critics declared, the black cultural industry had been built on foundations of white patronage and approval that were both inauthentic and unreliable. There was no black theater and no consensus on the aesthetic standards and community values that should govern an authentically black cultural expression, they complained.

Such criticisms might be faulted in turn, however, for taking a much narrower perspective on the value and depth of cultural change than is warranted—either temporally, geographically, or with respect to just how *culture* is defined. Black creativity certainly did not cease with the crash on Wall Street in October 1929, as the works of southern migrants such as Richard Wright and Jacob Lawrence and northern natives such as Ann Petry and James Baldwin will attest. Gritty hard times inspired a second renaissance of black cultural creativity. But the most important limit on the utility of such critiques for assessing the far-reaching transformation during these years is the narrow definition of culture on which they are premised. The criticisms are almost totally irrelevant to the actual lives of most black people in this period. Their cultural world was much less dependent on white "patrons," for example, than the more literary arts.

The material and symbolic anchors of the culture black Americans had known were also in the midst of transformation—much as Toomer had sensed in Hancock County—but moving with even greater intensity in the northern cities. As Charles Spurgeon Johnson, James Weldon Johnson's counterpart at the Urban League, who actually surpassed him as a culture broker, put it in a 1925 essay, "In ten years Negroes have been transported from one culture to another." All the guideposts that enabled them to negotiate their everyday lives were different. Where and how they worked, worshipped, and played required adjustments and adaptations of received traditions. They, like the urban subjects in the middle section of Toomer's *Cane*, were "a new people." They synthesize the "freedom" and "boldness" of the black tradition with the "jazzed, strident," and ultimately "crude" modernity of black urban life. Yet that culture was intensely "American," because "the shows that please Seventh Street [in Washington's black community] make their fortunes on Broadway."

Cultural historian Lawrence Levine describes the main chords of this transformation as moving from the basically oral forms of cultural expression to the written, and from a communal ethos to an individualist one. In 1865, ninety-three of every one hundred blacks could not read or write, but by 1930, only ten of every one hundred suffered that disability. For them as for any other human community, the architecture of consciousness, the structures of communication, changed with this increased access to the written word. Words are part of a visual world, while the spoken word is animate and dynamic. Words on a page are static, impersonal, and separable from the writer, while speech is personal and tied to a speaker. And most important, spoken words are necessarily social phenomena; they depend upon an actual rather than a virtual audience.

The negotiation of this divide—what was in essence the tension between tradition and modernity—had emerged first in the late nineteenth century, finding expression in African American minstrel performances and vaudeville, in ragtime, and in classic blues. The complex interpolation of these cultural forms, however, suggests that Levine's distinction between traditional and modern should not be drawn too starkly; much like the demographic shift from South to North, the cultural shift was neither complete nor irreversible. "Tradition" need not remain merely static under the pressure of "the modern"; rather the tension between them could be a source of creative energy, as old forms were urbanized and accommodated new technologies. Itinerant musicians, marching bands, and entertainers in red-light districts pushed the boundaries of creativity and innovation in their respective crafts. The freedom and infrastructure of postwar northern cities provided the means and spaces for a renaissance in popular culture that was arguably more profound and enduring than anything in the literary domain. Wax recordings provided musicians wider distribution and influence; an estimated five to six million blues records were sold each year during the 1920s.

Although white companies initially resisted recording black performers of black music, Mamie Smith broke through that barrier in February 1920. Her success led to a recording of "Crazy Blues" with a black band and singer. Bessie Smith followed three years later, recording "Down Hearted Blues," which sold 750,000 copies. She would go on to sell more than 6 million records before her recording career ended in the early 1930s. Stories abound of long lines on the Chicago South Side to snap up Smith's latest releases and of Pullman porters carrying copies to rural districts for sale at inflated prices. To be identified as a maker of "race records" was pejorative, but the work was profitable. Between 1920 and 1942, a total of 5,500 different blues recordings would be issued by a thousand black musicians.

Thus did the "great race-welding" of which Locke spoke operate on levels he was probably unaware of. Mechanical reproduction of music recast the creative context of local producers. But as Levine points out, oral traditions sustained a dialectical relation with the more modern forms, because commercial recordings remained dependent on folk sources. The cultural world of black folk not only expanded, but became integrated and enriched. Thus call-and-response was not replaced but took a different form, as the live audience's reception figured into and shaped the performance. As they stomped and moaned and talked back, their repartee fed the mood and blurred the distinction between performer and audience. Blues spoke directly to the immediate experiences of people ripped from familiar surroundings and enduring new or heightened social and economic repression. It established a common baseline of experience despite a growing difference of life worlds between North and South, urban and rural. As Levine so eloquently describes it, "the blues allowed individuals greater voice for their individuality than any previous form of Afro-American song but kept them still members of the group, still on familiar ground, still in touch with their peers and their roots."

Popular music, therefore, provided a ubiquitous medium for sustaining a long-term cultural communication within the black American world—between North and South, city and country, and, to some degree perhaps, the class strata within that world. It achieves, perhaps, the syncretization that Toomer seemed vaguely to sense when researching and writing *Cane*. The phonograph and the radio played central roles in this process, argues Lawrence Levine, as "the music and dance of the country and city, of white and black, of the folk and the commercial music hall, of the church and the street corner, met and amalgamated." By the 1940s, the effects were clear. A sociological survey of the Mississippi Delta reported that black folk were not as isolated as they had once been. From a small town in Florida, Zora Neale Hurston complained to her anthropologist mentor, Franz Boas, that her sources for black folklore were all listening to recorded music on phonographs and the radio and spending their leisure time at the movies. In some sense, then, black southerners moved North, yet brought back, "down home," something of the world they had created there.

The Louisville and Nashville

Like thousands of other southern youth during the postwar years, Simon P. Owens caught the first train north as soon as he came of age in the mid-1920s. Recalling that journey in his lively memoir published thirty years later under the pseudonym Charles Denby, Owens describes the emotionally charged moment when his train paused at daybreak in Covington, Kentucky, which lay just across the Ohio River from Cincinnati, a historic entryway into the free states during slavery days. Someone yelled excitedly that they were about to cross the Mason-Dixon Line, and Owens searched for what he imagined to be its physical embodiment, "a row of trees with some kind of white mark like the mark in the middle of the highway." He saw nothing of the sort, of course, and in time he would learn that the North, where he no longer had "to worry about sitting in the back," had its own version of racial proscriptions. Upon reaching Detroit, he would discover entirely different worlds of work, community, and interracial dynamics, but in each of those worlds black people continued to struggle for equal life chances with white Americans. There were opportunities unlike any they had known south of Mason and Dixon's imaginary line, but there were also Jim Crow rules and violence—northern style.

Owens was born in Lowndes County, Alabama, in 1907, within hailing distance of Calhoun. He describes a somewhat less promising state of affairs there than Du Bois pictured excitedly in his letters to Mary White Ovington. There was no sign in his corner of Lowndes County of the farm cooperatives that Du Bois had studied so hopefully; indeed, there was little hope of any kind for progress in these rural environs. In this historic Black Belt that the intense demand for slave labor had wrought, Owens's worlds of work, school, church, and sport were densely peopled by near and distant relatives. Some, like his maternal grandfather, owned small farms, while the vast majority labored on shares for the few large planters who monopolized the land. Owens's father had been able to buy a small plot of land during the First World War, which enabled his family to enjoy a measure of independence that most of their neighbors did not, but Simon had still spent his early childhood with his parents and three siblings in a one-room frame house with dirt flooring, their food prepared in a nearby shed that served as a kitchen. And much as with fellow Alabamian Ned Cobb, his father's modest advantages could not protect the family from brutal southern racial mores. Owens's grandmother's vivid memories of being ripped from her mother's arms when she was twelve years old and sold away from her family in Georgia hung over their present and formed the prologue of a continuing struggle.

Certainly to Owens's mind, the world he inhabited seemed barely changed from the one his grandmother encountered half a century earlier. As then, the relations between black labor and white property were Janus-faced: a seemingly benign paternalism on one side, a brutally violent repression on the other. In this world, labor and sexual exploitation of blacks by whites was embraced within the single fist of economic and social dependence. Notwithstanding Alabama's law ostensibly outlawing convict labor and a Supreme Court decision in 1911 that peonage was unconstitutional, Lowdnes County planters were kept well supplied by their relatives and friends on the judicial bench. It was, then, a closed, rural province in which a few large landowners alternately controlled and feuded over land and law and privileges. One of them, Berger, for whom Owens's father once worked, built a village on his vast property holdings and installed his daughter as head of the local bank. He employed an armed "riding boss" to oversee his several plantations. Like the overseers of slaves in earlier days, their job tenures were uncertain and often brief, and most conflicts between workers and overseers were resolved in favor of the former, since they were more essential to plantation operations. Berger bound his tenants to the property further by offering them easy credit—and thus perpetual debt—at his plantation store. Much like some slave-owning planters of another era, he required the young workers on his plantation to intermarry with other tenants, thus avoiding "abroad' marriages and divided loyalties. He built churches and schools for tenants on the property. Not surprisingly, school sessions were closely correlated with the labor needs of the plantation. The five-month school year that Ned Cobb described was typical, and most black boys were done with schooling of any kind by their twelfth birthday.

The Great War that drew other blacks North, leaving labor short and cotton prices high, enabled Owens's father to save enough to make the down payment on his forty acres in 1917. Small of stature but tough-minded, Owens's father worked at the sawmill for extra cash and hoped that cotton prices would stay high enough long enough to enable him to finish paying for the land before the inevitable postwar swoon. Owens tells us little about how he managed to escape Lowndes, but like his counterparts in Hancock County and many other similar communities, it is likely that his father's relative success provided the material and perhaps the moral wherewithal for the trip. As with them, too, the journey to Detroit was not his first venture outside the county, since before migrating north, he claims to have worked in the foundries in Anniston, Alabama.

Owens's prior industrial employment suggests the complex history preceding the exodus of nearly two hundred thousand blacks from Alabama and Mississippi between 1910 and 1920. Though direct and indirect evidence points to an urban origin for many of them, Owens's story suggests that even those still resident in the rural South were not as isolated from a more modern life as is often assumed. This may have been especially true of migrants from Alabama, where the exploitation of coal and iron deposits had attracted northern and foreign capital and forged a major industrial complex around Birmingham by 1910. After US Steel absorbed the TCI and Sloss plants in 1907, the new management relied on the black labor reserves of the Black Belt much as had its predecessors. By one estimate as many as 75 percent of the unskilled labor in the steel mills was black in 1910. And although practically all of the skilled positions were reserved for whites, blacks occupied a substantial number of the semi-skilled jobs during the prewar period. Access to these niches in the grow-ing industrial economy can be attributed to white disdain for the dirty, often dangerous unskilled work, and the impact of technological innova-tions that actually rendered some jobs less desirable. For example, blacks held 48 percent of the positions for molders (the makers of forms for the molten metal) in 1918, but these jobs no longer held the status in the pro-duction process that they had earlier. The pattern of black employment reversed during the interwar period, however: large numbers of jobs were deskilled as the pace of technological change quickened, and whites took most of them. By 1930, total black employment had been cut by 40 percent. There is no way to determine how many of these displaced southern work-ers made their way north, but black Alabamians' affinity for Detroit is striking. Indeed, "AlabamaNorth," a term one historian uses to describe Cleveland, Ohio, during the Great Migration, could as readily be applied to Detroit. By 1920, Alabama already accounted for the second-largest concentration of black migrants in Detroit, a trend that would continue into the 1930s.

Already ninth in total population and the sixth-largest American man-ufacturing city in 1910, with its foundries, stove manufacturers, and lum-ber yards, Detroit would soon become as emblematic of the nation's industrial muscle as New York City was for its cultural infrastructure. The increase in the number of people employed by and capital invested in Detroit's in-dustrial production between 1909 and 1914 was, respectively, three and two times the national average. In 1910, Henry Ford had inaugurated pro-duction processes and a management regime that revolutionized Ameri-can industry, thus beginning a new economic age that many analysts have since dubbed "Fordism."

Blacks had not been a part of the initial surge in industrial growth spurred by the automobile industry. In 1916, only about fifty blacks were employed in the entire Ford complex in Detroit. That same year witnessed a transformation in Detroit's black population more far-reaching than in any other American city, economically and demographically. A population that had never exceeded six thousand increased more than sixfold by 1920, a four-year period that also saw dramatic gains in black male industrial em-ployment. Two years after the Armistice, an astonishing 70 percent of De-troit's black males were employed in some form of factory work, a sizable proportion in automobile plants. In fact, roughly one of every five black men worked in an auto plant in 1920, a number that grew to one of every three by 1930.

Pittsburgh, the other industrial anchor of what came to be called the Fordist economy, was Detroit's nearest competitor for industrial employment on this scale. There black men also found a significant niche in the evolving modern economy. By 1920, blacks made up almost 8 percent of Pittsburgh's male labor force and held almost 9 percent of its factory jobs, accounting for over half of all employed black males. As in other urban centers, the situation for black women was much less favorable, their jobs differing little from those they had held in the South. In 1920, more than 80 and 90 percent in Detroit and Pittsburgh, respectively, were relegated to some form of domestic labor or personal service, compared with roughly 20 percent of white women. The few who gained jobs outside that sector—in retail stores and light industry—lost them to returning soldiers, or to white women who had themselves been displaced by white veterans. The postwar recession exacerbated the problem, and the 1930s Depression compounded it further. As late as 1940, half of black women workers were still domestics.

Disproportionate numbers of the black autoworkers in Detroit were employed in Ford plants, especially its massive complex at River Rouge. Although Packard had led the way by introducing blacks into its labor force, by 1919 African Americans made up more than a tenth of Ford's fifteen thousand workers in Detroit. The total number would grow to five thousand by 1923 and ten thousand by 1926. By the late 1920s, these Ford employees, together with their families, constituted roughly a quarter of the city's black population.

Given Henry Ford's racist and anti-Semitic views, his company's leadership role in hiring blacks is a bit puzzling. Blacks may have benefited from the ostensible contrast between well-worn stereotypes of them versus those of the Jews Ford loathed even more: quiet and docile, blacks made good workers and potentially useful citizens, whereas the radical, foreign Jews did not. In Ford's mind, apparently, their alleged inferiority did not mean that blacks should be excluded from the opportunities of a better job and a decent life, no more than his willingness to pay his workers a higher wage (five dollars a day in 1914) meant that he would hesitate to use black strikebreakers to undercut his workers' bargaining power or white goon squads to beat them up. The race question would disappear, he argued, "when every man shall have opportunity to go forth in the morning to perform the work he is best fitted to do, and to receive a wage which means a secure family life."

It is also noteworthy, however, that racial opportunity at Ford was limited to its Detroit plants, especially to River Rouge. The peculiar conjuncture of Ford's wartime labor needs with the character of Detroit's black community may explain why it was the beneficiary of this unique bounty. Ford established close relations first with Rev. Robert L. Bradley, pastor of Detroit's oldest and largest black church, Second Baptist, and later with Father Everard W. Daniel, who headed the third-largest black congregation, St. Matthew's Protestant Episcopal. Both men were themselves relative newcomers to the city, Bradley from Canada and Daniel from the Virgin Islands by way of New York, where he had attended New York University and the Union Theological Seminary. Bradley's congregation was made up largely of southern black migrants, whereas Daniel's was an upper-class, old settler congregation. The relations these men established with Henry Ford manifested yet another form of paternalism, one differing from the patterns found in the South but equally pernicious. The ministers supplied Ford with laborers in exchange for his financial support. It became virtually impossible to get or keep a job at Ford without going through them or their associates, which gave them considerable power in the black community. What Ford received in return was a labor force that had been vetted to ensure him responsible and probably anti-union workers.

The ministers' services to Ford were replicated by the Detroit Urban League, which provided similar referral services for the other automakers and other employers. The Detroit branch had opened in 1916 under the direction of Forrester B. Washington, a product of Tufts University who had received graduate training at Harvard and Columbia universities, and later by John Dancy, a North Carolinian educated at Livingstone College and the University of Pennsylvania. Forging close relations with Detroit's fiercely anti-union Employers Association, Washington and Dancy enjoyed extraordinary success in placing southern migrants in jobs.

Washington and Dancy were representative of a new generation of black social and political leadership, yet another New Negro group. Like their counterparts in literary and cultural fields, they had been born just before or after the turn of the century, mostly educated in southern colleges that had been influenced by Booker T. Washington, but often receiving graduate training at elite northern white universities. The re-segregation of the nation's capital after Woodrow Wilson's election now denied them access to the government jobs and political appointments that their predecessors, such as James Weldon Johnson, had held, so many of them turned to careers in what might be broadly described as social work. Eventually, Washington would leave the Urban League for the Labor Department's Division of Negro Economics, but Dancy came to Detroit from the Norfolk YMCA. By and large, they gave a distinctly conservative cast to black political and social strategies, or rather reinforced those tendencies that many ministers and other community leaders already embraced. Given the almost universal hostility of white-controlled unions to black labor, on the one hand, and the largesse of white capitalists such as Andrew Carnegie and John D. Rockefeller, on the other, conditions were ripe for the ascendancy of these conservative New Negro leaders. Urban League chapters in Chicago and Detroit were heavily subsidized by the principal employers of blacks in those cities, meatpackers in the former and automakers in the latter. Indeed, the real surprise is that as many black workers bucked the trend and identified their interests with organized labor as did. Not until the depression crisis of the 1930s, under pressure from young intellectuals on the East Coast— economist Abram Harris, lawyer Charles Houston, and political scientist Ralph Bunche, all at Howard University, along with A. Philip Randolph, who had recently organized the railroad porters—did the national Urban League office shift to policies more friendly to organized labor.

Black workers' distrust of unions was well earned, however. Since its inception, the white union movement had been almost uniformly hostile to black membership. Other than the United Mine Workers, most of the exceptions—the Knights of Labor, dockworkers' unions in Baltimore and New Orleans, the Brotherhood of Timber Workers, and the Industrial Workers of the World—were unfortunately also the most short-lived, ineffectual, or internally segregated. The powerful and relatively racially progressive United Mine Workers often relegated blacks to segregated locals, while most American Federation of Labor affiliates and the formidable Railway Brotherhoods excluded them altogether. Organized workers at the forefront of the emerging modern economy, such as the Amalgamated Association of Iron, Steel, and Tin Workers, which was formed in 1876, excluded blacks entirely until 1881, and continued to have uneasy race relations throughout the early twentieth century.

Notwithstanding this unsavory history, black workers did ally with unions that accepted them. The labor movement did garner a favorable image among some regional pockets of southern blacks, whose work experiences may have included mining or railway jobs. Simon Owens, for example, would become a stalwart union man despite being a severe critic of the leadership of the UAW in later years; he recalled fondly the leadership of John L. Lewis and the sit-in strikes.

The obstacles to forging an interracial workers' movement were considerable, however, and began with the very nature of the workplace itself. Blacks and whites might be employed by the same companies but not necessarily in the same jobs, under the same conditions, or with the same pay and benefits. Consequently, there was neither a social basis upon which to forge the kind of labor solidarity born of a common work experience and grievances, nor a physical context in which such social interactions might transpire. Even lunch breaks found Detroit's black autoworkers confined to the few overcrowded restaurants that would serve them, according to Owens. Like the segregated neighborhoods they lived in, black and white workers inhabited different job spaces, with different tools, and even performing tasks with different rhythms. "Nigger work" was dirty, dangerous, and degrading. At Detroit's River Rouge, black workers breathed toxic chemical and industrial dust while grinding, spray-painting, and working in the foundry. In Pittsburgh's steel mills, they sweltered in skin-searing heat, carrying hot metal "craps" and cleaning slag from the hearths. At Swift's packinghouses in Chicago, they worked the killing floor amid the squeals of dying animals. These job assignments were not necessitated by the problem of integrating inexperienced farm boys into an industrial regimen. Skilled, experienced black migrants fresh from US Steel plants in Birmingham were consistently demoted once they reached Pittsburgh. Contemporary industrial surveys document systematic underemployment of black workers.

Racially differentiated labor experiences were exacerbated by the intense seasonality of the work. Labor turnover was unusually high, especially among younger workers confined to the dirtiest, most disagreeable, and dangerous work. But cyclical employment rhythms were built into the very fabric of the industrial economy. Jobs fluctuated with consumer demand, alternating between a hectic pace to meet orders followed by idleness during temporary shutdowns, for example, when retooling for model changes in the automobile factories. Black migration from the South was roughly attuned to these cycles. Thus after the recession in 1921, the numbers arriving in Detroit fell to just 3,500 the following year but rose again to 14,000 with revived production at Ford in 1923. Although these cycles affected all workers, the impact on black employment prospects was greater. There was a 33 percent decline in iron and steel employment in Pittsburgh between 1920 and 1930, for example, but among black workers it was 43 percent. Not surprisingly, then, many younger workers came north for short, intense spells of employment, returned south for extended periods when laid off, and came north again when industrial activity picked up. Simon Owens's movements illustrate this pattern. He had easily secured work at the foundry of the Graham-Paige Detroit Motor Car Company upon his arrival in Detroit in 1924, when the automobile factories were humming. He was laid off four months later, however, getting his first taste of the seasonality peculiar to an industrial as opposed to an agricultural regime. Like many black migrants, Owens returned south to wait out the extended downturn after the crash in 1929.

Finally, lack of contact at work was reinforced by residential segregation far exceeding the typical southern experience, and with far fewer opportunities to fashion bonds of class that transcended racial boundaries. In Detroit, blacks lived on St. Antoine Street, next to the red-light district, where their death rate was twice the norm for whites and overcrowding was so severe that, as one observer put it, often "the most convenient way to dress was to stand in the middle of the bed." As in most northern cities, residents took in boarders to make ends meet, rendering many private homes more like hotels.

It is hardly surprising, then, that during the intense labor struggles that erupted in the postwar decade—especially the steel strike in 1919 and coal in 1925–28—black and white workers often found themselves on different sides of the picket lines, hardening images of blacks as scab labor and whites as vicious race mobs. The reality was far more mixed, however. Some black workers supported these strikes, and some whites, most notably the skilled steelworkers, deserted them. It was the stereotyped images that would endure, however, deepening the racial fault line in the struggling labor movement. As the black urban population grew, these tensions flared up in conflicts over access to housing and urban leisure spaces as well as employment.

Owens returned to Detroit in the second wave of the Great Migration during World War II to find the racial situation only slightly changed. He found more black and white social interactions on the shop floor, but continued resistance to racial equality within union management, which often seemed to collude with the company in discriminatory job assignments. On his very first day back, he reports losing a coveted riveter's job to a less qualified white southerner. Meanwhile, racial tensions in the city over housing and access to recreational facilities were building, exacerbated by a national wartime environment that had already led to race riots in Harlem and Los Angeles. On June 20, 1943, just three months after Owens's return, Detroit was gripped by a week of violence. According to Owens the trouble began when recently drafted young black males determined that if they had to fight and possibly die for their country, they would have access to its beaches and amusement parks before they left. Hundreds of white sailors were just as determined to deny them that access. On a particularly hot Sunday, full-scale violence erupted when many of the city's residents sought relief at the Belle Isle beaches. By the time it was over, thirty-one people were dead and two hundred injured.

The wartime riots in Harlem and Detroit in 1943 had eerie echoes of the early twentieth-century outbreaks in Atlanta, New York, and Springfield. There were some striking differences, however. The most notable was that blacks were as likely to be initiators of the violence as its victims. The destruction of businesses and property in black communities was perpetrated largely by blacks, who singled out mostly white-owned establishments against which they had grievances. Anticipating racial conflicts later in the century, these were not pogroms intended to wipe out black communities but rebellions against intolerable material conditions, policing, or racial subordination more generally. The migration from the South to the North was now more than a quarter-century old, and black communities in both regions had been radically transformed.

The Illinois Central

Running practically due north from New Orleans through Memphis to its terminus at Twelfth Street in downtown Chicago, the Illinois Central Railroad was like a mirror image of the Mississippi River during the third decade of the twentieth century, draining the Delta floodplains of southern blacks headed north much as the storied river washed rich soils south from the Upper Midwest. Spilling onto both sides of the river, these soils formed an alluvial empire one hundred miles wide that drew southeastern Arkansas and west central Mississippi into one social-economic domain—the Delta, once poetically described as beginning "in the lobby of the Peabody Hotel in Memphis and ending on Catfish Row in Vicksburg." A much darker poetic imagery infused NAACP staffer William Pickens's description of that region in 1921, however. Striving to capture the otherwise unimaginable terror uncovered by his investigation of the gruesome fate of Henry Lowry, an Arkansas sharecropper who was burned to death while six hundred spectators looked on, Pickens dubbed the region the "American Congo," his metaphor provocatively equating the heart of the American South with the infamous heart of darkness that constituted Belgian king Leopold II's bloody fiefdom in central Africa. Lowry's troubles began when he had the impudence to demand a fair settlement of his wages before moving off O. T. Craig's plantation on the Arkansas side of the Delta. Their heated dispute turned violent, and Lowry killed Craig. Apprehended in Texas, to which he had briefly escaped, Lowry was abducted by a mob and hanged as he was being brought home for trial. His death was slow. His abductors took advantage of the delay to enjoy dinner at the Peabody Hotel.

Perhaps the best measure of the complex interplay of natural beauty and human ugliness, of the past and the present of this "most southern place on earth," is to be found in novelist William Faulkner's historical fiction. Sutpen's Hundred eschews gauzy images of mint and magnolia, evoking instead a plantation empire that was, as one of Faulkner's narrators declares, "ripped violently from a wilderness." Contrary to the account in *Absalom, Absalom*, however, most of the men of Sutpen's ilk arrived long after the Civil War, during which the region had remained mostly an untamed frontier, and most of them were black, by a margin of ten to one. The Delta was tamed in the New, not the Old South. Federally funded levee construction in the 1880s and railroad expansion beginning at the dawn of the twentieth century spurred a cotton and timber boom that brought in thousands of black migrants bent on mastering this new frontier. Indeed, as late as 1900, blacks made up a majority of the landowners in seven of the nine Mississippi Delta counties and constituted 66 percent of their farm owners overall. Their tenures would be short-lived, however, and in time it was they who would be "mastered."

By the eve of World War I, railroad companies such as the Missouri Pacific and the Illinois Central had cleared the land of its hardwood, leaving scarred landscapes that have sometimes been compared to central Georgia after Sherman's March to the Sea. On the Arkansas side of the river, after the Missouri Pacific's extension there in 1903–07, Phillips County emerged as America's second-largest hardwood producer, while nearby Memphis became the world's premier hardwood market. In that city, Delta lumbermen met to form the Southern Alluvial Land Association in 1916, to promote and sell the cut-over land for plantation cultivation.

These were not the plantations familiar to the Old South, however, but entirely novel, often vertically integrated, huge corporate enterprises. By 1913, few were less than 360 acres and some encompassed 5,000 to 10,000 acres. Lambrook, a moderately scaled example, was a 4,000-acre property near Elaine worked by six hundred black laborers and owned by Gerard B. Lambert, proprietor of St. Louis's Lambert Pharmacal, which made Listerine. At the other end of the scale was the Mississippi Delta Planting Company (later Delta and Pine Land Company), which had amassed 45,000 acres of cotton land in Bolivar County by 1917. Its migrant entrepreneur, L. K. Salsbury, hailed from England, where in 1911 he had convinced a combine of textile manufacturers to invest in property depressed by the collapse of cotton prices after the boll weevil infestation from the 1908–10 seasons. Though formed by a very different racial and class regime, this new and largely foreign (to the South) planter class built a totalitarian society that grounded a fierce labor regimentation of renters, croppers, and wage hands into an all-encompassing industrial welfare system that might have made even the fiercest of the Old South patriarchs blush. They built schools and churches for their workers, but for the same reasons as they opened their workers' mail and controlled their movements: absolute hegemony. Workers were required to buy at the plantation store, which supplied salt pork, sugar, beans, flour, and shoes. They had to rent the company's mules and plows at interest rates of 25 to 35 percent. Many plantations, such as Sunnyside in Chicot County, which was owned by New York banker Austin Corbin, also employed convict labor.

The First World War shook the alluvial empire to its core. First, it created a critical shortage of labor as young people streamed into southern and northern cities. By 1917, the reported losses of black population had already reached 23,628 in Arkansas, 35,291 in Mississippi, and 22,632 in Tennessee. The formation of the Mississippi Welfare League—designed to discourage further migration by offering better pay, living conditions, and schools—is indicative of the migration's impact. Once America joined the actual fighting, military recruitment exacerbated the labor problem. Despite persistent efforts by planters to secure deferments, more blacks than whites were drafted from the five states at the core of the southern Black Belt. The pay received by the family dependents of soldiers loosened plantation bonds further, enabling more to escape to the city. Even the sharp, war-induced spike in the price of cotton, which climbed from eleven cents per hundred pounds in 1915 to forty-three cents by 1919, had its downside for the planters. Given increased demand and a labor shortage, their workers were able to bargain for better wages. As a consequence, picking wages more than tripled, rising from sixty cents per hundred pounds in 1915 to two dollars by 1917.

As these figures show, the rate of increase in wages still lagged behind the increase in cotton prices, and while some Delta workers' improved bargaining positions enabled them to extract weekly rather than annual settlements and other concessions, many others did not see much improvement. By 1919, when the South was on the verge of harvesting its first $2 billion cotton crop, tensions heightened as landowners could no longer conceal the outright cheating that diverted a disproportionate share of profits into their own pockets. The return of soldiers, black and white, only made things worse. Many black soldiers returned from the war expecting a new deal in a world now saved for democracy. Many whites feared that such demands were an inevitable consequence of the black soldiers' life-changing experiences of travel and combat. For example, Fred Sullens, a Mississippian and captain in military intelligence, warned fellow Mississippians "that the negro soldier returning from France will not be the same sort of negro he was before donning the uniform." Other whites, especially soldiers and sailors, were convinced that the very presence of uniformed blacks threatened the racial order. During a period later dubbed the "Red Summer" of 1919, there were more than forty outbreaks of racial violence across the country, many of them beginning with attacks on black soldiers or veterans. The massacre in Phillips County, Arkansas, near the small town of Elaine, completed this deadly cycle of violence.

Frank Moore was one of the roughly one thousand African American men from Phillips County who had served in the military during the Great War and returned expecting better. He and his wife had worked their fourteen acres of cotton and five acres of corn on shares, but had just $678 worth of household goods to show for it. Moore joined with other Delta workers to demand fairer treatment, especially the right to sell their crops directly rather than through the landowner. In the spring of 1919, they organized the Progressive Farmers and Household Union of America (PFHUA) to press their case. Although taking the familiar organizational forms and rituals of religious and fraternal orders, the PFHUA was well aware of both the race and class dimensions of its struggle. Their slogan declared, "We Battle for the Rights of Our Race; In Union Is Strength."

As harvest season approached in September 1919, sixty-eight members of the PFHUA working on the northern-owned Theodore Fauthauer plantation hired Ulysses S. Bratton, a Republican lawyer who had served as assistant U.S. attorney during Teddy Roosevelt's administration, to bring suit against the owners to halt their fraudulent practices and to secure a fair share of the crop. A meeting scheduled with Bratton's son to take depositions was broken up by six to eight armed men, as was another union meeting at the Hoop Spur Church, just three miles outside Elaine. Armed guards posted outside the church returned fire when attacked by a white posse, killing W. A. Adkins, a white special agent for the Missouri Pacific Railroad. News of the shooting led to the mobilization of an even larger, three-hundred-man "posse," including many white combat veterans. Seeking revenge, they burned the church and proceeded to "hunt negroes . . . shooting and killing them as they came to them."

With permission from the secretary of the army, Arkansas's governor sent in 583 federal troops, including a machine-gun battalion just returned from France, to put down the "insurrection." Authorized to shoot any black person who did not surrender, the troops and vigilantes slaughtered scores of people in cold blood and confined hundreds of others—women and children as well as men—in the Elaine schoolhouse, releasing only those ready to return to work on the cotton harvest. Witnesses, including Gerard B. Lambert, the Listerine magnate, described a barbarism that echoed the atrocities in the Belgian Congo referenced in Pickens's protest later: the "cutting off the ears or toes of dead negroes for souvenirs and the dragging of their bodies through the streets of Elaine," the burning to death of a recalcitrant witness. The most recent scholarship estimates a final death toll of two hundred but makes clear that official cover-ups render any accurate count impossible.

Frank Moore managed to escape the first assault on the Hoop Spur Church, but was forced to seek refuge with his family in the woods when the vigilantes arrived near his home the next day "shooting and killing men, women and children." The Moore family made it only to the relative safety of the troops, however, who carted them off to the schoolhouse jail in Elaine. Frank's wife was separated from the family during their flight and hid in the woods for four weeks. She emerged to discover all their household goods confiscated by their landlord and threats of death and burning if she remained. Frank and eleven other union men were subsequently indicted and convicted of murder. Four years later in *Moore v. Dempsey*, the U.S. Supreme Court overturned the convictions of Moore and five of his fellow defendants on the grounds, as Justice Oliver Wendell Holmes argued, that they had been deprived of due process of law by the torture used to extract their confessions and that a mob spirit had enveloped their trial. The Moores disappear from the available public record after Frank's victory in court, but it is highly likely that they were among the thousands of blacks who made their way to Memphis or Chicago during the 1920s. John E. Miller, the prosecuting attorney for Moore's trial, fared better. He went to Congress in 1931 and on to the U.S. Senate six years later. In 1941, President Franklin Roosevelt made him a federal judge in the western district of Arkansas, where he served until 1967. Among his duties was overseeing the implementation of school desegregation cases— to which he was, predictably, unalterably opposed.

If Frank Moore did, in fact, make his way to Memphis or Chicago, he may well have crossed paths with another black refugee from the American Congo. Although born in 1908 just south of the Delta to a sharecropping family on a plantation twenty-two miles east of Natchez, Richard Nathaniel Wright also migrated to Chicago in response to violence in the Delta. His family gave up farming and moved to Memphis in 1913, where shortly afterward his father abandoned his mother with their two preschool-age boys. His mother, a former schoolteacher, struggled to raise the boys alone from her earnings as a cook, but finally put them in an orphanage. Some time in 1916, her younger sister, Maggie Hoskins, brought them all to live with her in Elaine, Arkansas. Richard became a favorite of Maggie's husband, Silas, who ran a successful saloon, catering to workers in the local sawmills. In 1917, local whites enraged by Silas's refusal to sell the highly profitable saloon, shot him down in cold blood. Threatened with further violence, the family fled. After enduring a migratory adolescence through various cities—Jackson and Greenwood, Mississippi; West Helena, Arkansas; and finally Memphis—Richard moved to Chicago with Aunt Maggie in 1927, bringing his mother and younger brother up to join them a bit later. This was in many ways a migration story typical of that place and time, except for the literary fame that awaited Wright in the decades to come. In his autobiographical and fictional works *Black Boy* (1945) and *Native Son* (1940), Wright would chronicle in vivid terms the lived experience of a generation of Mississippians—the social and physical violence that set them in motion, the triumphs and disappointments that awaited their arrival in the North.

The Chicago that Wright found already ranked second in absolute numbers and third in proportionate increase of its black population among the northern cities during the First World War. By 1920, more than eight of every ten black Chicagoans had been born in some other state, almost half of them in either Tennessee or Mississippi. A decade later both the overall black population of the city and the Mississippi natives among them had doubled again (to 233,903 and 38,356, respectively). Wright's fellow Mississippi natives now made up one of every five black migrants to the city.

Black workers had achieved impressive economic progress in the Chicago labor market by the time Richard Wright settled there, holding almost a third of the jobs in the meatpacking industry, for example. The war had stimulated demand for meat exports at the same time as it reduced the supply of immigrant labor, creating an opening for the recruitment of ten thousand to twelve thousand black workers by 1917, a fourth of the packers' labor force. By 1920, meatpackers were African Americans' largest employer in Chicago, and by 1928 they made up almost 30 percent of the industry's work force as a whole and a third of some of its biggest firms. For African Americans in Chicago, the industry was comparable to automaking in Detroit. And, indeed, meatpackers such as Armour had actually pioneered assembly line production processes later credited to Henry Ford. Thus blacks, who in many cases may well have been recruited as strikebreakers initially, benefited from employers' conscious efforts, following the labor unrest of the 1920s, to replace native whites with black and Mexican workers, as well as from the general deskilling of a labor force in which common manual labor made up two thirds of the whole. Their supposedly good fortune, however, was to work in one of the filthiest, noisiest, most unhealthy jobs in America. Stimulated by urban growth and the appearance of refrigerated rail cars, these vertically integrated corporations found profit in every aspect of an animal's carcass—glue, fertilizer, soap and oil, as well as meat. The rhythms of meatpacking work were in many ways not unlike those of farm labor: intense on Mondays and Tuesdays, when the cattle arrived, dropping to a half day on Fridays. Moreover, seasonal fluctuations in demand brought frequent layoffs.

Differing in many respects from those in Pittsburgh or Detroit, however, Chicago's southern black migrants were not as likely to have emulated Simon Owens's back-and-forth movements between Detroit and Alabama, in rhythm with the fluctuations of the automobile labor market, since at least a fifth of them came from the nation's most rural and least industrialized state, Mississippi, which had little to offer returning migrants. Moreover, escape from the American Congo had required careful collective mobilization and quiet plotting to evade planters, who literally pulled their workers off northbound trains. The Mississippi migrants were marked in other ways. Theirs was not a migration of individuals set in motion by abstract social forces, as the classic narrative may have had it, but one built on networks of family and kinfolk, some of whom were already in the North, and on the dense communal infrastructures of southern cities and towns. Migration clubs were organized, with memberships ranging from forty to eighty, to pool resources and secure group discounts from the railroads. These clubs were typically led by small businessmen and a strikingly large number of women, both of whom were relatively independent of the white power structure and economically mobile. Robert Horton, proprietor of the Hattiesburg's barbershop and deacon of the First Baptist Church, exemplifies the leadership that made the Mississippi migration what historian James Grossman has called "a grass-roots social movement." Between the fall of 1916 and January 1917, Deacon Horton recruited forty men and women to form a migration club and to secure a group discount on the Illinois Central. Like many other preachers, whose interests were best served by stable communities in which their positions were well established, Horton's pastor, Rev. Perkins, opposed the migration at first. But he was soon compelled to follow his departing flock to Chicago. Teachers, the other principal professional group, also opposed the movement, because of their vulnerability to reprisals by the white political authorities. Eventually, many of them also found the northbound tide irresistible.

Mississippi migrants differed, too, in their striking efforts to replicate much of their former institutional lives in their new surroundings. The South Side of Chicago was indelibly marked with their "Old Country" origins and the sense of collectivity that informed their presence. When Horton reestablished his business on the South Side, he called it the Hattiesburg Barber Shop, and it quickly became a gathering place for the home folks. Meanwhile, his reluctant fellow migrant, Rev. Perkins, opened the doors of his transplanted church for his displaced congregation.

For all that was familiar in their new surroundings, however, the migrants confronted, and reveled in, a profoundly different world, one transformed in its social relations not only of labor but also of leisure. The churches and mutual aid organizations that had structured much of the social life of the black South, urban and rural, now merged into a complex infrastructure of communications media, musical and sports entertainment, political and business activity—all of which were peopled and in some measure controlled, if not always owned, by blacks. All made for a world, as one migrant testifying before the Chicago Commission on Race Relations put it, "full of life." Like Harlem's 125th Street, Memphis's Beale Street, and Eighteenth and Vine in Kansas City, "the Stroll," stretching along Chicago's South State Street from Twenty-sixth to Thirty-ninth (later down to Forty-seventh) rendered the fullness of this new life visible and audible, a virtual theater for self-realization and self-display. Black institutional life merged with everyday life to fashion a sense of community in what to an outsider's gaze was merely a ghetto. These were spaces, once again to use historian Earl Lewis's distinction, of congregation not segregation, and thus the fiercest of "race men" could embrace them. Despite occasional tensions arising from the conflicting agendas and styles of newcomers and old settlers, the respectable folk and those linked to the underworld, aspiring middle class and struggling working class, all could embrace the vibrant vision of a new life emerging in what they called "the black metropolis."

The emergence of this new black public life had preceded the Great Migration by several decades, but it was greatly enhanced and consolidated by the dramatic population influx later. Robert Abbott's *The Chicago Defender*, which overlapped with or influenced almost all aspects of this new public life, had been founded in 1905. A relatively recent migrant himself, the Georgia-born Abbott had settled in Chicago in 1897, returning after graduation to the city he had visited with the Hampton University Quartet during the 1893 World's Fair. Modeling the Horatio Alger rags-to-riches story favored by Booker T. Washington and his admirers, he reputedly started his newspaper with twenty-five cents in capital, but built a national circulation network by currying favor with black porters, waiters, and other railroad workers. By 1916 he had achieved a phenomenal distribution of thirty-three thousand, which he more than quadrupled just three years later. Since readers typically passed the paper around, read it aloud, and discussed it in barbershops and at other gathering places, it had a virtual circulation many times larger. Like his hero Booker T. Washington, Abbott had actually opposed southerners moving north earlier, but reversed himself once the Chicago labor market opened to blacks in the summer of 1916. Of course, as with many other northern black enterprises, it didn't hurt that Abbott's business would benefit economically from the expansion of local readers.

Theaters and clubs, institutions that would also become critical to the refashioning of black culture and consciousness during the first half of the twentieth century, also had origins predating the Great Migration by at least two decades, but flourished with it. An important venue for vaudeville, Chicago emerged as a center for African American cinema—its production and its spectatorship—in the years before and after the First World War. Chicago was home, too, to a vibrant and innovative music scene, with an infrastructure of recording studios and radio programming that would soon nurture an impressive diversity of styles and genres, including blues, jazz, and gospel. In Chicago's churches and studios, Thomas Dorsey and Mahalia Jackson crafted and popularized a new gospel music. Meanwhile, Delta migrants Sonny Boy Williamson, Charley Patton, Son House, Robert Johnson, and later Muddy Waters pioneered new secular sounds that spoke of "down home," but for an urban audience.

The migration north, then, provided space and time for the *re*-creation of the black world—a world in which the past was not forgotten but ever present, where old memories infused new forms and technologies of expression, where the collective consciousness emerged more politically inflected, and where, as with other dual nationals, the sense of home was doubled and complex. No less a witness than young Richard Nathaniel Wright reveals how determinedly the memories of life and death in the Delta resonated even in the construction of this new world. During his first decade in the North, while sharing a small apartment on the South Side with his family—including the brutally widowed Maggie Hoskins—Wright worked at odd jobs and perfected the craft skills that would make him one of America's finest writers. Finally, years later, after rendering his masterpiece dissection of the black metropolis, *Native Son*, he was ready to commit his memories of coming of age in the Mississippi Delta to print. The result was a memoir rife with images of deprivation, hunger, and violence. Remembering the family's flight after his uncle Silas was gunned down on the streets of Elaine, he wrote, "Somewhere in the unknown the white threat was hovering near again." To understand him, to understand a people whose present was haunted by "a thousand lynchings," one must begin with that past.

7

"A SECOND RECONSTRUCTION"

The Freedom Movement

Mamie Bradley had warned her son. She had told him to enjoy the charming, languid pace of life in the Mississippi Delta, but to know that the rules were different for black people down there than on Chicago's South Side. "I told him to be very careful how he spoke" to white people, she said. Perhaps it was all too much for a spunky fourteen-year-old raised in the relative freedom of the black metropolis to absorb. Perhaps his mother's voice lacked the authority of direct experience, since, though she was born in Tallahatchie County, she had migrated to Chicago in 1924, when she was just two years old, with her parents, John and Alma Carthan. She knew the American Congo mostly through the stories her parents and relatives had told, and the lurid atrocities regularly reported in the *Defender*. Like most northern blacks with southern roots, she had made summer pilgrimages "down home," but these were likely to underscore its distance from her life in Chicago while rendering its more familiar touches faintly nostalgic. She knew it well enough to expect that a boy who spoke "sass" to a white woman might be whipped; she never expected that such a childish prank would get him killed. Now, though devastated by inconsolable grief, she waited at Chicago's Twelfth Street Station for the Illinois Central's *City of New Orleans* to bring his body home. She had already determined that she would show "everyone . . . what they did to my boy."

What had been done to young Emmett Till was gruesome even by American Congo standards. The story of exactly what transpired between him and Carolyn Bryant at the general store in Money, Mississippi, may never be known for certain: a crude attempt to kiss her, a sassy "Good-bye, baby" tossed over his shoulder as he walked out, a wolf whistle when she

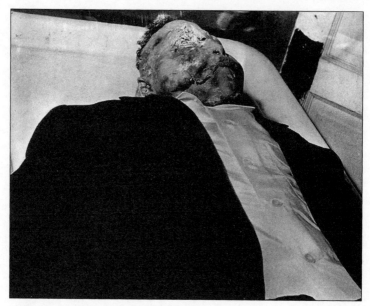

This image of Emmett Till's mutilated face was witnessed by the hundreds
of Chicagoans attending his funeral and thousands of readers of the *Chicago
Defender*. An even more gruesome photograph appeared in *Jet* magazine days
earlier, but Johnson Publications has not allowed historians to reprint it.

followed him out? What *is* known is that Carolyn's husband, Roy Bryant,
and his half-brother, J. W. Milam, came to the shotgun cabin of Emmett's
uncle Moses Wright at about 2:30 a.m. on August 28, 1955. We know that
they took Emmett to their car and demanded of someone inside whether
he was the one, to which a soft voice replied, "Yes." We know that three
days later his body, tethered by barbed wire to a seventy-five-pound cotton
gin fan, was pulled out of the Tallahatchie River near the boundary separating Leflore and Tallahatchie counties. We know that his skull was so
badly crushed that a piece of it fell out into the boat that fished him out of
the water. We know there were conflicting reports as to whether the mysterious hole above his right ear, which the sheriff declared was made by a
bullet, was actually made by a drill bit. We know that tens of thousands
of people viewed this young boy's mangled body while it lay, as if in state,
at A. A. Rayner Funeral Home on Cottage Grove Avenue, as did hundreds
of thousands more who read John Johnson's *Jet* magazine. We know that
what they saw there inflamed black America. We know that after that,
black-white relations would never be the same.

Much had changed in America since the Carthan family left Mississippi for Chicago. Mamie Bradley and her companions signaled as much with "the sensation" they created when they walked briskly into the Sumner County courthouse to witness the trial of her son's murderers. Her bearing as much as her eventual testimony suggested a person in remarkable command of herself despite an unimaginable grief, a poised young woman, demure yet determined, calculatedly deferential yet fiercely proud. All evoked a vast distance between the world she inhabited in the North and the one so familiar to startled blacks and whites in that sweltering Mississippi courthouse.

Despite her self-description to reporters as "lower middle class," Mamie Bradley was a civilian employee of the U.S. Air Force, residing in a comfortable two-family house in Chicago's Bronzeville. She arrived at the trial accompanied by her father, John Wiley Nash Carthan, then a resident of Detroit, and a cousin, Rayfield Mooty, president of a Congress of Indus-

Mamie Bradley at the murder trial of her son. Left to right: John Wiley Nash Carthan, Willie Reed, Mamie Till Bradley, Dr. T.R.M. Howard, Congressman Charles Diggs, Jr., and an unidentified woman.

trial Organizations steelworkers' local in Gary, Indiana. Also present were
two African American congressmen, William Levi Dawson from Illinois's
first district, and Charles Diggs, Jr., from Michigan's thirteenth. Each of
these lives evidenced the profound changes in the social, economic, and
political situation of black Americans over the three decades since the
Carthans had left the South.

Like many other World War I–era migrants, John Wiley Nash Carthan had benefited from the relative advantages offered by growing up in
a landowning family. His father had run a plantation store and employed
sharecroppers to work his land. When he came of age, however, Nash sought
work in Chicago, finding it making cornstarch, oil, and syrup at the Argo
Corn Products Refining Company, located in a community bearing the
same name a few miles southwest of the city. Soon his wife, Alma, their
children, and other members of the extended family joined him in a rapidly growing enclave that came to be known as Little Mississippi. Nash
abandoned the family during the Depression years, eventually finding his
way to Detroit. In the Motor City he worked in a drugstore but apparently
learned something about auto repair as well, given descriptions of his
occupation later. The dissolution of the Carthans' nuclear family under
the economic and social strains of the urban environment prefigured patterns that would grow to crisis proportions in the latter half of the century,
and the difficulties their daughter would confront much sooner.

Taking full advantage of the better public education available in the
North, Mamie graduated high school with honors in 1940 and went on to
secure various clerical jobs, benefiting from the relaxation of racial discrimination in the federal civil service during and immediately after the
war and the threefold increase in nonwhite employment in white-collar jobs
more generally between 1940 and 1950. Prior to taking her job with the air
force in 1953, Mamie worked with the induction center at Fort Wayne, near
Detroit, during the war and with the Social Security Administration in
Chicago during the early 1950s.

Perhaps it was the contrast between her own achievements and ambitions and what she regarded as rather unimpressive male suitors in provincial Argo that clouded her judgment of the brash young Louis Till, a migrant
from Missouri working at the corn refinery. A gambler and amateur boxer,
Louis Till was physically imposing, restless, self-assured, but fatally prone
to getting into trouble. The positive valences of these traits no doubt made
him attractive to the impressionable young Mamie, who joined him to

stage a spontaneous, if inadvertent, sit-in that led to the integration of Argo's only drugstore. The less favorable inflections of his character traits, however, rendered him abusive and uncaring, and eventually embroiled him in legal troubles, from which he escaped only by enlisting in the army. In 1945, Mamie received an oblique notice from the War Department informing her of Till's death while serving with the liberating troops in Italy. Years later, a search of military records revealed that a troubled Louis Till had not died in action in Italy, but was court-martialed and executed for the brutal rape of two women and the murder of a third. In the end, all that remained to Mamie from this brief, unhappy marriage was a four-year-old son and a silver ring returned in the packet of Louis Till's personal effects. Just as he embarked on his fateful trip south, Mamie gave the ring, a memento of a father he had never known, to young Emmett. Two weeks later, Louis's ring would help her identify her son's mutilated body.

High school diplomas and white-collar jobs were still out of reach for most black southern migrants then. As with Mamie's cousin Rayfield Mooty, the work experience of the luckiest among them was far more likely to be in the industrial sector of the economy, which had seen a phenomenal expansion during the war. Born in 1907, Mooty had migrated from the rural South to find work in the industrial North, beginning in a Dayton, Ohio, foundry in 1923 and ending up as a shop steward at Reynolds Aluminum Company in Gary, Indiana, by the mid-1950s. His brief employment in a Pennsylvania coal mine in 1928 suggests that he may well have been among the black workers recruited to break the massive strikes there that year, but just a decade later found him firmly embedded in the Amalgamated Association of Iron, Steel, and Tin Workers, and by 1942, a charter member of a Chicago local of the steelworkers' union. Like Simon Owens, Mooty endured a love-hate relationship with his union, acting as both its fierce advocate and among its most militant critics, and eventually co-founding a black workers' caucus to demand fairer treatment within the union as well as on the job. Mooty's life course maps the overall promise and disappointments of the economic transformation that African Americans confronted by the mid-1950s. He would have been one among an estimated eighty-five thousand to ninety-five thousand newly unionized black steelworkers in 1945. There were at least an equal number of blacks in the United Automobile Workers, and perhaps as many as forty thousand blacks in the Marine and Shipbuilding Workers' union. Altogether, there were somewhere between a half million to seven hundred thousand black unionized industrial and craft workers by the end of the Second World War, roughly evenly divided between the AFL and the CIO. They were a long way from the hate strikes of the previous decades, but as Mooty well knew, stubborn interracial tensions remained to be overcome.

Perhaps the most striking evidence of change in black Americans' prospects was the presence of the two congressmen accompanying Mamie Bradley's party to the courthouse. Like many of the political and business leaders who rose to prominence in the migration years, her congressman William Dawson had been born and educated in the South but soon seized upon educational, economic, and political opportunities in a rapidly changing North. Born in 1886 in the Georgia regions immortalized by Du Bois and Jean Toomer, Dawson moved to Chicago to work on a law degree at Northwestern University after graduating from Fisk University in 1909. Following combat service as a lieutenant in the 365th Infantry during the First World War, he practiced law in Chicago and was elected alderman for the second ward from 1933 to 1939. In 1943, he succeeded Arthur Mitchell as the second black Democrat to occupy the congressional seat formerly held by black Republican Oscar de Priest, the first African American elected to Congress in the twentieth century.

By contrast, Nash Carthan's congressman Charles Diggs, Jr., had been elected only recently to represent the rapidly expanded black population of Detroit. The thirty-three-year-old Diggs had formerly served three years in the Michigan state senate, occupying a seat his father had won in 1937 during a moment of labor and political insurgency in Detroit. Although he had also been educated at Fisk, his earlier matriculation at the University of Michigan in Ann Arbor suggests a significant generational change from his father's social and political formation. Like Congressman Dawson, Charles Diggs, Sr., was a southerner who had migrated to the North before the Great Migration, having come to Detroit from Tallula, Mississippi, in 1913. Diggs's political career built on the eclectic political brew of interwar Detroit: he was by turns an officer in Marcus Garvey's Universal Negro Improvement Association and a Republican activist in the 1920s, a union stalwart and Democratic organizer by 1932. Diggs's shift in political allegiance anticipated a more general political transformation in black urban communities across the nation four years later. In 1932, 60 percent of his black contemporaries had voted against Franklin Roosevelt's New

Deal, but in 1936, 76 percent of northern blacks supported Roosevelt's re-election, confirming a historic partisan realignment begun in the congressional elections of 1934. In that same election, Diggs, Sr., became the first African American elected to the Michigan state senate, a position his son would occupy briefly before his election to Congress in 1952. Although the presence of Dawson and Diggs in Congress, along with Adam Clayton Powell, Jr., of Harlem, was scarcely more than symbolic of African Americans' political resurgence, the postwar growth in northern black voting strength could now reputedly determine the presidential election in as many as seventeen key northern states.

The very idea of black congressmen astounded white and black Mississippians alike. There was confusion in the days leading up to the Emmett Till murder trial in Sumner about how they would be accommodated in the racially segregated courtroom. Diggs was eventually seated with the out-of-town reporters, whose deference to him was a further cause for consternation. But even those hailing from ostensibly more enlightened parts of the country were probably unaware that a quiet political revolution already in progress in many southern and northern cities would soon bear fruit. Although blacks were still almost completely excluded from the ballot box in Mississippi and much of the rural deep South, there had been a surge in black voter registration in southern cities. By 1954, the South had more than two and a half times the number of registered black voters as it had on the eve of World War II. Indeed the change in the political climate of some states was even more dramatic, ranging from Virginia, where there were roughly four newly registered black voters for every one on the rolls a decade and half earlier, to Mississippi, with eighty-six new voters for every one who had dared venture to the courthouse before the war. It is surely no accident, for example, that the prominent place among Movement flashpoints eventually occupied by Alabama cities—Montgomery, Birmingham, and Selma—owes something to the fact that twenty-three new black voters had been registered in that state by 1954 for every one inscribed on its rolls before the war.

In heavily rural states such as Mississippi, however, the absolute numbers remained pitifully small and the political impact negligible, notwithstanding a dramatic rise proportionally. Even there, however, the winds of change were evident. Three of the principal leaders of voter registration drives in that state during the first two postwar decades—Medgar Evers,

Amzie Moore, and Aaron Henry—were all active during the 1950s in the Regional Council of Negro Leadership, an organization headquartered in Mound Bayou, an all-black town founded in the last century, and directed by Dr. Theodore Roosevelt Mason Howard, a black surgeon and entrepreneur there. Howard provided accommodation and armed protection at his residence for Mamie Bradley and her party while they attended the trial in nearby Sumner. Weeks earlier Medgar Evers and Amzie Moore had joined in the search for Emmett Till's body and then for witnesses to the killing, finding in the process disturbing rumors of many other blacks who had disappeared into Mississippi rivers and swamps after perceived breaches of the southern racial order—unnoticed and unavenged. Like many others, Evers, Moore, and Henry formed their political consciousness during these years, and they would emerge at the center of far greater challenges to the Mississippi order less than a decade later.

In 1955, however, any serious political challenge was confined mostly to urban population centers, and it was there that the earliest tremors of the Civil Rights Movement emerged. These areas proved to be the most vulnerable spots in Jim Crow's armor, as a rapidly growing and increasingly assertive black electorate posed difficulties for urban southern white politicians trying to reconcile their progressive agendas for economic development with an internally fractured defense of suddenly anachronistic social practices. In more ways than one, then, the spectacles witnessed in the Sumner courthouse in the early fall of 1955 were but harbingers of the momentous changes at work.

Coming scarcely more than three months after the U.S. Supreme Court's cautious injunction to implement its landmark school desegregation decision *Brown v. Board of Education*, "with all deliberate speed," atrocities such as the Till lynching seemed relics of a distant past, "another country," as James Baldwin would write later. Indeed, nothing reflected the sense of a new day coming more than the sight of the diminutive, sixty-four-year-old Moses Wright throwing off a lifetime of deference to white folks and identifying his grand-nephew's abductor's in that Sumner courtroom. His testimony signaled the "dying present" of that racial regime, wrote correspondent Murray Kempton in a dispatch filed with the *New York Post*. Once again, America would endure the pangs from what Lincoln had once called "a new birth of freedom," or what contemporaries would come to refer to as "a second Reconstruction." Mamie Bradley would indeed show the world "what they did to my boy"—and the world would never be the same.

Tremors in Montgomery

Just sixty-eight days after the Leflore County jury declared Roy Bryant and J. W. Milam not guilty of Emmett Till's murder, Rosa Louise McCauley Parks took her seat in the first row of the "colored" section on the Cleveland Avenue bus in Montgomery, Alabama, headed home to the public housing apartment she shared with her husband and aging mother. With the sudden influx of white riders at her bus's third stop in front of the Empire Theater, the driver, James Fred Blake, moved the sign marking its racial divide and ordered the four black passengers in front of it to surrender their seats to the new, white arrivals. After some hesitation, three blacks moved to the rear. Rosa Parks did not. Recounting the moment years later, she recalled her act as at once spontaneous and overdetermined by her people's accumulated grievances. "[M]istreated and humiliated," she simply decided that she "had been pushed as far as I could stand to be pushed." It was time "to know once and for all what rights I had as a human being and a citizen."

Parks scarcely suspected that her actions that day would reframe a decades-old struggle for citizenship rights and human dignity. Anger at the Mississippi verdict still rippled through black communities across the nation. Indeed, just four days earlier, at a mass meeting in Montgomery, Parks herself had listened to Dr. Howard, Mamie Bradley's host at Mound Bayou, condemn the virtual reign of terror in his state. She might well have recognized elements of her own life story in that of Till's grieving mother. Though a life-long resident of the South and eight years older than Mamie Bradley, Parks also had familial roots in the rural Black Belt. Like the Carthans, Rosa's carpenter father and schoolteacher mother had moved a step above their own farmworking parents, making a home for their infant daughter in the black community gathered around Tuskegee Institute. Rosa was also raised by a single mother, her parents having divorced when she was two. She spent the next nine years of her childhood on the tenant farm of her maternal grandparents, just outside Montgomery, but after her eleventh birthday she was sent to live with cousins in that city so that she could attend a private school. Like Alma Carthan, Leona McCauley insisted that her daughter get the best education a single mother could afford, entrusting her first to the New England schoolmarms at the Miss White's Industrial School for Negro Girls and then to the laboratory school attached to Alabama State College, one of the scores of schools founded for freedpeople during the first Reconstruction. At Miss White's she studied stenography, typing, and the seamstress skills that now earned her a living at the city's largest department store, Montgomery Fair. Unlike Mamie Bradley, she would find no opportunity to employ her secretarial skills to earn a livelihood, not even during her wartime employment at Maxwell Air Force Base. Superficially, she seemed a far better fit for Mamie Bradley's self-description as "lower middle class," and yet, as with Mamie, Rosa's demur exterior concealed sturdy ambition, a shrewd intelligence, and steely determination.

African American residents of southern cities had been testing the limits of their rights as human beings and citizens in various ways since the turn of the century, but with increasing aggressiveness and political

This mugshot, taken shortly after her arrest during the Montgomery bus boycotts in 1956, reveals the dignity and steely resolve of Rosa Parks.

savvy during and shortly after the Second World War. The dramatic explosion of the South's urban black population was a necessary but not sufficient explanation for this increased militancy. The increase in black population was more than matched by the influx of whites to cities such as Montgomery, which had been growing at the torrid pace of 30 percent each decade of the twentieth century. Consequently, the rough racial parity of Montgomery's interwar years gave way to a 63 percent white majority by 1955. The influx of white migrants destabilized an elite-controlled political machine, however, which, following civil service reforms in 1949, lacked either the patronage or other institutional and social ties to sustain its hold over a residentially segregated white working class. Such splits among whites enhanced the political leverage of the small but growing number of black voters. Edgar D. Nixon had organized the Alabama Voters League in September 1943, and black registration had doubled by 1955. By the mid-1950s, black leaders in Montgomery had chalked up some impressive successes: the city was one of sixty-two southern municipalities that had hired black police officers, and it had built two high schools for blacks, raising the proportion of African Americans holding high school diplomas from 6 to 10 percent. Indeed, in 1953, an envious black newspaper editor in Birmingham had declared Montgomery the state's "most enlightened city."

Blacks' new political power was on full display in the 1953 municipal election, when they supplied the margin of victory for Dave Birmingham, an anti-machine candidate supported by blacks and working-class whites. Birmingham's victory prompted some among the city's white political elite to shift their strategy from racial paternalism to aggressive race-baiting in an effort to disrupt blacks' tacit alliance with white workers. The new political realignment would greatly complicate later efforts by more moderate whites to respond to blacks' political grievances, and the increased racial polarization produced political paralysis. On the other hand, the stalemate solidified black support for more militant action against the city's racial regime.

The slow but steady emergence of a more militant black leadership in Montgomery followed a pattern evident in other southern cities in the late 1940s and early 1950s, a number of which—notably Atlanta, Birmingham, Durham, and Memphis—experienced sharp labor conflicts as the black rural migrants pouring into industrial and service jobs chafed at demeaning treatment and discriminatory wages. Even more common, however, were complaints about police brutality, especially sexual violence against black women, and physical and verbal abuse on the buses. Thus intense community mobilizations to protest the rape of Gertrude Perkins by two Montgomery policemen in 1949 mirrored a very similar incident in Memphis in 1945. As in the Memphis case, these protests often exposed the political and class fissures within black communities. Often a younger, more militant working-class cohort of newcomers challenged an older, more conservative and petit bourgeois establishment to push farther and faster than they were willing to go. Similar, though less overt, fractures along class and gender lines could be observed among black leaders in Montgomery, notably labor leader Edgar D. Nixon, businessman Rufus Lewis, and Alabama State English professor Jo Ann Robinson, each of whom led constituencies that competed almost as often as they cooperated. And yet, the deep humiliation to which Rosa Parks referred in explaining her act of defiance was a common thread running through the grievances articulated by *all* blacks in Montgomery—and elsewhere. It was that shared experience—a daily confrontation with raw subordination that challenged their very humanity—that enabled a fractious black community divided by class, religious affiliation, gender, and political philosophy to unite in protest.

The first ten seats on Montgomery's buses were reserved for whites, and the last ten designated for blacks. The middle sixteen fluctuated with the relative proportion of white and black riders at any given time, which meant that blacks must surrender their seats to whites as the front sections of the bus filled up. This vague, ever-shifting racial boundary exacerbated racial tensions, serving as an everyday reminder of white supremacy and black inferiority. Drivers shouted preemptory orders laced with racist insults; white passengers felt empowered to heap verbal and sometimes physical abuse on black riders perceived as resisting or insufficiently obeisant to their assigned place in the social order. In theory and practice, black riders were untouchables. After paying their fare to the driver up front, they were required to reenter through the center door so as to avoid the possibility of brushing against white passengers. All too often impatient drivers sped off before they could reenter. Indeed, Rosa Parks recalled that Fred Blake left her standing in the rain one evening several years earlier, when she had not managed to reenter through the back door quickly enough. Whatever their class status, therefore, blacks shared a common visceral anger, one focused less on racial segregation per se than on the everyday abuse it authorized. The Montgomery story illustrates how the struggle against the latter evolved into a broad-scale attack against the former, and indeed against the whole racial order.

Black grievances against their demeaning treatment on southern buses were long-standing, occasioning both spontaneous and organized protests. Acts of resistance were especially common during the wartime migration and after. In the archives of Birmingham's bus company, for example, historian Robin Kelley uncovered 176 cases of racial conflict in a single year, including at least 88 instances of defiance of segregation ordinances. Most of this resistance came from working-class women, which appears to have been the pattern in Montgomery as well. As an active member and officer in the NAACP, Rosa Parks was very familiar with these cases. She had only joined that civil rights organization in 1943, but had long been familiar with it through her husband, Raymond, a member for a decade longer, early enough to have been active in protests against the Scottsboro Boys trial. At first Rosa simply lent her secretarial skills to aid the local branch, headed by Edgar D. Nixon, but over time she grew more intensely involved, attending conventions and a leadership training retreat in Jacksonville, Florida, in 1946 (where she met Ella Baker), running one of the local offices, and serving as a youth adviser in the early 1950s. Nixon had introduced her to the white Montgomery activists Clifford and Virginia Durr, who, the summer before her bus protest, arranged for her to attend a two-week conference on school desegregation at the famous Highlander Folk School. Earlier that same summer, Parks herself arranged for Claudette Colvin to share with NAACP members an account of her defiance of the segregation ordinance. In a confrontation similar to the one Rosa Parks would endure eight and a half months later, the fifteen-year-old Colvin was arrested for refusing to surrender her bus seat to white passengers. In fact, black leaders had planned to use her case to challenge the segregation ordinance in a federal lawsuit, but discovered that the unmarried girl had become pregnant and feared that this would discredit their case.

Rosa Parks suffered no such disabilities, and quickly emerged as a unifying symbol of blacks' collective grievances with the bus company—and helped prompt the resulting boycott. Whether a reflection of the limitations of their political consciousness or of their sense of political efficacy, the black leaders' initial goals were very modest: to stop the insults rather than end segregation as such. They were willing to abide by the current arrangement, with seats reserved for whites at the front of the bus and in the rear for blacks, but with the caveat that blacks no longer be required to surrender their seats when the number of white passengers exceeded their allotment. To minimize confrontations with racist and abusive drivers, they demanded black drivers for predominantly black routes and company instructions to all drivers requiring greater courtesy. What they appeared to want, sneered NAACP executive Roy Wilkins, was simply a "more polite segregation." Wilkins's acerbic characterization aside, it is certainly arguable that white acquiescence to these demands might well have deferred the imminent frontal attack on segregation.

There is undoubtedly some truth to historian J. Mills Thornton's argument, however, that these first modest demands of boycott leaders were a somewhat perverse product of their sense of electoral empowerment, and thus faith in the possibility of achieving negotiated solutions to their community's grievances. By the mid-1950s, however, in Montgomery as in many similar southern cities, local politics were echoing regional leaders' hysterical declarations of "massive resistance" to the recent Supreme Court decision mandating the integration of public schools. In that context even modest movements toward reform became major threats to the entire racial order, arousing violent and implacable white resistance and crushing any hint of dissent by more moderate whites. Within roughly four months of Parks's arrest, membership in the White Citizens' Council (judged by some to be simply Klansmen in business suits) had surged from six hundred to twelve thousand in Montgomery, an increase that put pressure on white politicians there to conform to the massive resistance strategy. In response, a hitherto fractious, cautious black leadership united behind a more militant and frontal legal attack on segregation.

In tandem with the boycott, Montgomery's black leaders sued to end segregation on the buses and won a smashing victory before the U.S. Supreme Court. The Court's decision in *Browder v. Gayle* affirmed a lower court's ruling that the rationale for integrated education articulated earlier in the *Brown* decision applied to transportation as well. The Montgomery newspapers were technically correct, therefore, when they insisted that blacks owed their victory to a court decision rather than to the 381-day boycott, implying thereby that the direct-action campaign was unnecessary. For blacks across the nation and in Montgomery, this logic was beside the point. With the boycott, blacks had proven their capacity for disciplined collective action in the face of economic intimidation and extreme violence. The explosive growth of protest activity, soon known simply as "the Movement," underscored that interpretation.

Black Montgomery's actions resonated powerfully with black youth, especially in the greatly expanded network of southern colleges and universities. Even before the boycott reached its midway point, students at Florida A&M began their own boycott of buses in Tallahassee, with a former Montgomery minister providing leadership. Meanwhile, with the federal government forced repeatedly to reaffirm court rulings mandating equality of treatment in interstate transportation and terminal facilities, bus terminal restaurants, toilets, and water fountains became choice targets for assaulting the southern racial order, attracting sit-ins by local residents and travelers and opening a new front in a veritable war on Jim Crow.

A little more than four years after the Montgomery bus boycott's successful conclusion, four freshmen from a local black college demanded service at a Woolworth lunch counter in Greensboro, North Carolina. Their action drew support from students at surrounding colleges, and within weeks had spread like wildfire through more than eighty southern cities. Fourteen months later, in the spring of 1961, the Congress of Racial Equality (CORE) revived a tactic it had used in 1947 to test earlier court and administrative rulings. In December 1960, the Supreme Court had ruled in *Boynton v. Virginia* that discrimination in bus terminals violated the National Motor Carrier Act of 1935, reviving institutional memories of a similar decision in June 1946 (*Morgan v. Virginia*). Most black leaders understood, however, that the recent decision was destined to have no more practical effect in ending discrimination than the first. Thus, on May 2, 1961, under CORE's auspices, two small groups of racially mixed "Freedom Riders" boarded Greyhound and Trailways buses bound for New Orleans. The Freedom Riders encountered some minor resistance in the Carolinas, but when they reached Alabama they were attacked with firebombs outside Anniston and by a vicious mob in Birmingham, forcing them to abort the rest of the trip to New Orleans. A group of Nashville college students, veterans of sit-in demonstrations in that city, resumed the test, only to meet a Klan-organized riot in Montgomery that forced federal intervention to protect them. The determined students pushed on to Jackson, Mississippi, where they were promptly arrested and confined in that state's notorious Parchman Penitentiary. The segregationists' victory proved to be pyrrhic; from Parchman and other southern jails emerged a battle-hardened leadership for future attacks on the Jim Crow regime.

Clearly, the Montgomery bus boycott marked a fundamental shift in the long struggle against Jim Crow. Understanding that shift and accounting for its timing require that we place the city and that moment in a context at once local and national, personal and broadly sociological. Nothing in the arsenal of tactics deployed in Montgomery, or in similar struggles later, was new. Drawing on a tradition at least as old as the abolitionists' refusal to buy slave-grown staples in the early nineteenth century, African Americans had already deployed the boycott weapon at the turn of the twentieth century in their effort to strangle Jim Crow in its cradle and again in the 1930s, when "Don't Buy Where You Can't Work" campaigns erupted in at least a dozen northern cities. In addition to freedom rides, the pacifist militants of CORE deployed picketing and sit-ins—tactics perfected during the 1930s by striking autoworkers in Flint, Michigan—to protest restaurant discrimination in several northern cities, including Chicago. Mass marches and street demonstrations, with roots too numerous to count, had been deployed to draw

A sit-in at F. W. Woolworth's in Greensboro, North Carolina, in 1960. Left to right: Ronald Martin, Robert Patterson, and Mark Martin.

national attention to racial violence during World War I. None of these efforts had led to a sustained social-political movement, however. None had succeeded in destroying Jim Crow.

The movement launched in Montgomery—or, perhaps more accurately, by Emmett Till's murder—would ultimately succeed not because its tactics were new, but because of newfound conditions of possibility, a new context for their implementation. First, this was clearly a youth movement, the indispensable core of its full-time activists being drawn from Emmett Till's generation, those born during or shortly after the war. At the same time, it was an intergenerational movement, one in which young people drew sustenance and inspiration from some members of the interwar generation, the contemporaries of Mamie Bradley, and people like Ella Baker, whose lives had been transformed by migration and war. Most important, following the massive migration to northern and southern cities and towns, neither generational cohort was constrained, as their parents or grandparents had been, by the southern plantation regime. Finally, this assault

Organized by the NAACP, this march down New York City's Fifth Avenue in 1917 was one of the earliest mass protest demonstrations demanding equal rights for African Americans.

on the racial order would unfold within a political-economic system that was radically transformed, especially with respect to federal-state relations, from the prewar political order. Not only was the federal state now a more powerful force in the everyday life of its citizens—a phenomenon begun by the New Deal but greatly accelerated by the mobilization for war—but the balance of forces shaping the policy needs of the national state were shifting inexorably from a local to a geopolitical axis. In this environment old tools acquired a sharper edge and, as black leaders soon realized, local protests could no longer be contained on local terrains.

Thus the southern segregationists' familiar characterization of the confrontations in literally scores of cities and communities following Montgomery was at least partly correct: they were often aided if not stimulated by "outside agitators" intent on provoking overreaction by the keepers of a system that suddenly appeared vulnerable in ways hardly imaginable to local folk a decade earlier. A more militant generation of leaders emerged to challenge the now-cautious and relatively conservative legal strategies of the NAACP. CORE, formed by northern white and black pacifists during the war, and the Student Nonviolent Coordinating Committee (SNCC), formed by southern student veterans of the sit-in movement in 1960, committed themselves to undertaking more direct assaults on the Jim Crow regime. These young "agitators" soon recognized that their struggle against the American racial order required a broad movement rather than merely local skirmishes, the engagement of national political authority and law rather than negotiations limited to discrete southern communities and city ordinances. To achieve this, they determined that the recently elected Kennedy administration must be forced to abandon its policy of accommodating its southern Democratic allies and become more proactive in the fight to dismantle segregation. In turn, the confrontations with Jim Crow had to be dramatic and morally unambiguous, which meant that a cadre of seasoned veterans—"freedom fighters"—must be prepared to carry that struggle across the South.

Explosions in Birmingham

Some ninety miles to the north and roughly six years after its first tremors in Montgomery, the nascent Movement emerged with explosive force in

Birmingham. Much had changed in America and among African American leadership in that brief interval. Martin Luther King, Jr., had left Montgomery in 1960 to become his father's co-pastor at Atlanta's Ebenezer Baptist Church. The Southern Christian Leadership Conference (SCLC) that King, Jr., had organized in 1957 to coordinate local challenges to Jim Crow was now headquartered in Atlanta. Although King had emerged as the preeminent civil rights leader on the national stage by the early 1960s, CORE and SNCC were now staffed by battle-hardened veterans. During the resurgence of militant attacks on northern Jim Crow practices during the Second World War, the strongly pacifist activists in CORE had led sit-ins and pickets demanding integration of restaurants and recreation sites, most notably in Chicago and New Jersey. SNCC, meanwhile, had long ceased to be a mere "coordinator" of local sit-in activities, as envisioned when it was founded in the winter of 1960. Now its seasoned organizers were dispatched from its Atlanta headquarters to help mobilize civil disobedience campaigns in scores of southern cities and towns where local black leaders had shown sparks of resistance. Scarcely more than a year after SNCC was founded, for example, Freedom Rider veterans Charles Sherrod and Charles Jones moved to Albany, Georgia, and began mobilizing a broad-scale attack on that city's Jim Crow regime. Initially targeting high school and local college students, they pioneered community-organizing techniques that SNCC later replicated in both the rural and the urban South. Through the town's youth, they reached the older generation, forging the first of the urban mass movements that characterized civil rights activity during the first half of the 1960s.

Meanwhile, the conservative and overly cautious Republican administration of Dwight D. Eisenhower had been replaced by the liberal but almost equally cautious Democratic administration of John F. Kennedy, whose first full year in office would be dominated by intense cold war crises. Blacks had expected a great deal from Kennedy, but he proved to be more of a hardheaded realist than the idealist his campaign rhetoric had suggested. It is clear, moreover, that Kennedy faced a domestic political situation not unlike Roosevelt's some thirty years earlier. The Democrats' New Deal coalition joined African Americans from the major northern cities increasingly impatient with racial discrimination with southern whites just as firmly committed to the racial status quo and a northern white working class increasingly (and sometimes violently) resistant to black competition for jobs and housing. Moreover, given their seniority in and command of the legislative process, disproportionate power over legislation and its implementation still rested with a small southern congressional delegation whose electorates were kept small and easily manipulated by the systematic exclusion of black voters.

In contrast with Roosevelt's era, however, new countervailing developments in the 1960s challenged these inertial forces. More and more, the cold war pitted America and its European allies in a deadly contest with the Soviet Union for the allegiances of unaligned nations, most of them "colored" by America's racial reckoning. The impact of this confrontation on national policy calculations had become evident a year after President Harry Truman openly acknowledged East-West hostilities in 1947. Between the fall of 1947 and the summer of 1948, he warmly embraced a government commission's report advocating expanded civil rights legislation, issued an executive order ending segregation of the armed services, urged an end to racially discriminatory housing covenants in an amicus curiae brief to the Supreme Court, and fought to keep a civil rights plank in the Democratic Party's platform. The last action sparked a southern walkout and formation of the Dixiecrat Party, arguably the first stage of the so-called massive resistance campaign that would emerge seven years later. The fissure—papered over in subsequent years by pairing northern Democratic presidential candidates with southerners in the VP spot—would rupture completely seven years after Kennedy's inauguration, with the reemergence of a lily-white southern Republican Party.

In the short term, however, it was the geopolitical dimensions of the situation that commanded policymakers' attention. The cold war conflicts that dominated Kennedy's abbreviated tenure—the Bay of Pigs and the Berlin Crisis in the spring and fall of 1961, followed by the Cuban Missile Crisis in the fall of 1962—threatened to turn cold war face-offs into hot war nuclear conflagrations. Given these circumstances, world public opinion assumed unprecedented importance, and the South's racial conflict effectively became a national security issue. America's image in newly independent African and Asian nations—twenty-five new nations by the end of Kennedy's first year in office—was not improved, for example, by the discrimination their ambassadors and staff frequently encountered during road trips from the UN in New York through southern New Jersey, Delaware, and Maryland to the capital in Washington. The quaint south-

ern custom of denying colored travelers access to meals and toilets suddenly became an issue of state.

Consequently, Montgomery was arguably the last largely local struggle and local victory of the Civil Rights Movement. The victory in Montgomery resonated nationally, of course, and it clearly provided a model for
mobilizations in other communities, but such mobilizations and victories
had followed the frustrating pattern already evident in school desegregation cases. Implementation of the Supreme Court's decision practically
required the replication of the original struggle in scores of communities,
entailing not only costly legal fees and court costs but often broken limbs
and lives—with little assurance of lasting success. Indeed, it is noteworthy that when Birmingham tried to emulate Montgomery's bus boycott in
November 1958, it failed. Four years later a campaign to boycott Birmingham's downtown stores also failed. As the insurgency around civil rights
issues in Birmingham evolved, however, a crucial turn was made in the
strategy and tactics of the Movement as a whole, shifting the focus from
piecemeal legal victories to an effort to achieve a national mandate for
broad structural changes through a massive, direct assault on the community power structures supporting segregation. It was a bold but dangerous strategy, ultimately threatening the loss not only of recently acquired
federal institutional support but sometimes promoting dangerous splits
within the African American community itself.

In many ways the initial stage of the civil rights insurgency in Birmingham evolved much as it had in other southern cities, despite the
undeniably unique features of the city's political and economic character:
a southern city shaped by heavy industry. As in Montgomery, there had
been dramatic population growth in Birmingham during the war and
postwar periods—20 percent between 1940 and 1950—and the white
community was politically divided roughly along class lines between a
development-oriented ruling elite and a socially anxious working class,
the now-familiar template for political coalition building and dissension in
the postwar South.

With Birmingham aspiring to supplant Atlanta as the South's leading
metropolis, its "business progressives" were even more anxious than Montgomery's to sustain the aura of social progress and order they deemed essential to attracting capital investment. There was a significant fissure
within their ranks, however, since the more progressive elements among

them tended to be dependent on an expanded community of local consumers fueled by economic growth, while the interests of many old-line
industrialists, catering to more distant markets, were better served by keeping wages and production costs low, leading them to look less favorably on
programs to attract new industrial competitors to the area.

Differing class interests were evident in Birmingham's black community as well. Counting at least one millionaire and many well-to-do businessmen and lawyers within its ranks, the city's growing black elite depended
less on teachers and other vulnerable professionals than other southern
cities. Its rising upper middle class included owners of a major bank (Citizens Federal Savings and Loan), and substantial real estate and insurance
enterprises. Despite racially discriminatory allocations, FHA and veterans' housing benefits spurred the city's black homeownership in the postwar period. Indeed, struggles over housing for this expanding black middle
class precipitated the first wave of racial violence in 1947, including a
dozen bombings that became characteristic of racial terrorism in a city
soon to be derisively labeled "Bombingham."

In contrast with most southern cities, Birmingham's working class
was heavily industrialized and unionized. When factories had operated at
full capacity, black steelworkers made up 30 percent of the work force and
actively participated in the coal and metalworkers' unions. Nonetheless,
the unions' ability to bridge the racial divide was even less successful in
the South than in the North. Unions typically colluded with employers to
preserve white control of a dwindling supply of skilled jobs, especially in
the context of the drastic de-skilling of metalwork during the postwar period. These tensions are evident in the experience of Hosea Hudson, who
migrated to the city from Atlanta in 1924 to take a job in the steel mills.
Like Rayfield Mooty, Hudson was elected president of his union local,
serving from 1942 to 1947. Countering this evidence of integration into the
workers' movement, however, were numerous instances of racial exclusion.
In one such instance, Hudson recalls that he and several other blacks were
elected to the Birmingham Industrial Council, a steelworkers' committee
assigned the task of interviewing local political candidates. The white members connived to hold the interviews in a segregated hotel, however, which
effectively excluded the committee's black members from participation.
This was but one of many instances where pressure from the national
union leadership encouraged nominal recognition of blacks as fellow union
members but could not ensure equality in practice.

As in other southern urban communities, African Americans of all classes could unite around grievances all too common in the postwar urban South: public humiliation on buses, policemen's sexual abuse of black women, and police brutality more generally. The Klan-led bombing campaign targeting middle-income black homeowners in the new housing developments left all blacks feeling vulnerable to racial violence. For a brief time, black residents were able to suppress white terrorism in these communities through officially authorized neighborhood patrols. Their success may well have encouraged them to make the hiring of black policemen a principal demand of their postwar negotiations. Much as Edgar D. Nixon's postwar voter registration efforts in Montgomery sought to join middle- and working-class folk in a common effort, Hosea Hudson's Right to Vote club had attempted a similar mobilization of workers and schoolteachers in Birmingham during the spring of 1938.

As in Montgomery, the success of voter registration efforts paved the way for negotiations with factions of the white elite aimed at alleviating some common black grievances, interactions eventually formalized with the formation of the Interracial Committee in April 1951. This was, of course, a model of biracial interaction pioneered in Atlanta following that city's devastating riot in 1906. And as in Atlanta, the group was hobbled by mutual misperceptions that, while they would prove fatal in the long run, may well have been crucial to the group's formation in the first place. The black participants of such interracial committees were likely to see whatever modest reforms they achieved as mere harbingers of more thoroughgoing changes, while white "moderates"—glancing fearfully over their shoulders to monitor the reactions of violence-prone whites—were likely to see them as completely forestalling the need for any further change.

Police brutality, an issue in every southern city, was even more egregious in Birmingham, where the department overseen by T. Eugene "Bull" Connor was known to be "a sink of corruption and racial prejudice." Elected in 1937, Connor had hitherto done the bidding of the city's business elite while burnishing his populist appeal to the white working class. Given their desire to promote a more progressive image for the city, however, business progressives grew increasingly restive with Connor's corrupt and brutal regime. He also posed a formidable obstacle to their ongoing efforts to assuage black grievances regarding police misconduct. Their protracted battle to rid themselves of the embarrassing commissioner of public safety eventually succeeded when the scandal-plagued Connor declined to run for reelection in 1953. The elevation of more moderate men to authority over public safety, however, produced little progress toward meeting the black leaders' principal demand—the hiring of black police officers—despite the precedent set by numerous other southern cities, including Montgomery, Mobile, and Memphis.

Meanwhile, events elsewhere shrank the window for action that Birmingham's more progressive elements had briefly enjoyed. The Supreme Court's implementation order for the *Brown* decision, Emmett Till's murder, the bus boycott in Montgomery, and riots following Autherine Lucy's attempt to enroll in the state university in nearby Tuscaloosa—this rapid succession of events between the spring of 1955 and the fall of 1956 effectively closed the door to further biracial negotiations. The Interracial Committee was dissolved in 1956, and Bull Connor returned to power in the spring of 1957.

Political and racial polarization also undercut the leadership position of the black elite, whose community influence rested on their ability to extract concessions through negotiations with their white counterparts. As in Montgomery and other cities, white intransigence would eventually force them to embrace more militant tactics and ally themselves, at least temporarily, with more militant groups. Thus, following the collapse of biracial negotiations in the spring of 1956, Birmingham's black militants formed the Alabama Christian Movement for Human Rights (ACMHR), augmented by former members of the NAACP, who were stranded after an onslaught of lawsuits in several Deep South states crippled their organization's local operations. As a result the ACMHR was able to forge a relatively diverse constituency of middle-, lower-middle-, and working-class members into a more aggressive attack on segregation.

The mixed-class location and militancy of the ACMHR reflected that of its leader, Fred Shuttlesworth. Born in 1922, the son of an unmarried couple—a farm woman and a carpenter who was also an itinerant Baptist minister—Shuttlesworth took the surname of the retired coal miner and bootlegger his mother married when he was four years old. Before he turned thirty, Shuttlesworth had sold bootleg whiskey, been ordained as a Baptist minister, worked for the U.S. Army Air Corps in Mobile, and received a degree in education from Alabama State College. He returned to Birmingham to pastor Bethel Baptist Church in 1953, the year Bull Connor was driven out of office by scandal. Arguably, Shuttlesworth was well prepared to work at the class interstices of the emerging Civil Rights Movement. Certainly under his leadership blacks in Birmingham launched the largest, most militant, direct action campaign in African American history, making 1963 a watershed year in the centuries-long freedom struggle.

The Birmingham Movement made direct action, involving the mobilization of broad and diverse segments of a given community behind its demands, the central paradigm for movement activity thereafter. Although mass participation had certainly characterized the boycott movements, too, their action was relatively passive compared with the direct confrontations involved in street demonstrations. The subsequent shift of emphasis in direct action campaigns was subtle but significant. With the exception of an unsuccessful effort in Albany, Georgia, in 1962, previous civil rights campaigns had typically deployed small groups of dedicated activists to challenge Jim Crow laws, usually with the goal of testing federal rulings or changing local ordinances. Such actions were often designed to produce "facts on the ground" that would frame a subsequent legal test case. The issue would ultimately be resolved in the courts. For tactical and strategic reasons the Birmingham Movement launched in 1962 had, by the spring of 1963, evolved into a test of a new form of direct action. Thousands of people would challenge not simply Jim Crow laws but police ordinances and court injunctions designed to blunt their right to protest those laws, filling the jails beyond capacity and forcing a national as well as local crisis.

The strategy of attacking the racial regime at its weakest point through direct-action tactics and dramatic mass mobilizations made access to public accommodations seem like the Movement's central demand. Indeed, for many, the simple act of ordering a Coke at a lunch counter, seemingly a mere consumer demand, emerged as the emblem of the early Civil Rights Movement. In reality, however, in Birmingham and elsewhere, the direct-action innovation always built on existing and/or simultaneous campaigns for voter registration, municipal employment, and reforms in urban policing. The clashes over access to public accommodations drew attention because, in these public arenas, ordinary blacks and whites confronted each other more directly and those confrontations aroused visceral responses from each group—blacks experiencing gratuitous insult, and whites threats to a status long dependent on black subordination. Second, in campaigns designed to attract national attention, Jim Crow laws proved to be the racial regime's most vulnerable pressure points. They were directly vulnerable to economic pressure because, as on the buses, blacks were often an important if not majority bloc of consumers; and even where they were a minority, their boycotts often represented a company's crucial profit margin and their demonstrations could scare away substantial numbers of white customers. Most important, perhaps, in a thoroughly urbanized and increasingly globalized political economy, the white South's adamant and violent defense of this form of racial distinction was incomprehensible to most people outside the region, reinforcing the South's image of backwardness and irrationality. As would become readily apparent within that same decade, racial discrimination was a *national* problem, and northern whites were as prone to defend racial privileges in employment and housing as were their fellow citizens in the South, but to them, white southerners' violent defense of separate water fountains and toilets just seemed bizarre. Thus southern white reactionaries' self-characterization as defenders of a unique "way of life" had the perverse effect of reinforcing their isolation from potential northern white allies. As the human toll in black lives mounted, national sentiment, and thus federal power, was turned decisively against those defenses.

Shuttlesworth's invitation to King to join his movement was a deliberate effort to shine a national spotlight on the Birmingham struggle. Their subsequent, controversial decision to enlist high school students in that struggle worked to achieve the numbers necessary to foster a crisis, to frame the moral bankruptcy of the old order, and to recruit a hitherto passive older generation of blacks to the campaign. Given these strategic and tactical commitments, the complaints by "moderate" whites and some among the black elite that there should be a pause in the direct-action campaign to allow the old-style negotiations to resume and bear fruit were largely irrelevant. What was needed, after all, was not simply a changed racial and political regime in Birmingham per se, but the broad transformation of the southern, and then the national, racial order.

Several weeks of mass demonstration did build national support, which authorized more active federal intervention to broker negotiations and, eventually, a deal between the Birmingham Movement and the more moderate elements of Birmingham's white power structure. Although civil rights leaders' claims of victory have been questioned, given problems with the settlement's actual implementation later, clearly their nationally focused strategy had borne fruit. A day after articulating a new cold war strategy at Ameri-

This photograph of a seventeen-year-old boy attacked by a police dog during a Birmingham street demonstration in 1963 became an iconic image of the Civil Rights Movement.

can University, President Kennedy addressed the nation about its racial crisis, promising new legislation and a determination finally to redeem the promise of the Emancipation Proclamation in this its centennial year. Pressure for passage of the proposed legislation built that summer as scores of southern cities emulated the Birmingham model—mass street demonstrations, filling municipal jails beyond capacity, clogging local judicial systems, and disrupting ordinary commerce. These local campaigns culminated, on August 28, 1963, with a massive demonstration in the nation's capital, where more than two hundred thousand white and black demonstrators gathered before the Lincoln Memorial under banners demanding "Jobs and Freedom." During the ceremonies, news arrived from West Africa that William Edward Burghardt Du Bois had died earlier that day in Ghana. The symbolism of the coincidence was obvious even to those with only a casual familiarity with African Americans' long freedom struggle. It is not clear whether anyone realized that that very day also marked the eighth anniversary of the death of Emmett Till.

• • •

Eleven months after demonstrators gathered on the Washington Mall, civil rights legislation even more comprehensive than that Kennedy had proposed or that the demonstrators had dared hope for was passed by Congress and signed into law by President Lyndon Johnson. No doubt the Civil Rights Act's authors, most casual observers, and probably some activists considered its passage a successful culmination of almost a decade of intense civil rights agitation. It outlawed racial discrimination in publicly funded facilities such as parks and recreation sites and in privately owned public accommodations such as restaurants, hotels, and movie theaters. It addressed in some measure the continuing problem of segregated schools and job discrimination.

For the veteran activists most intensely engaged in the southern revolution, however, events during that fateful summer of 1964 mooted any inclination they might have had to celebrate. The law's passage came just days after the foreboding disappearance of three civil rights workers, Michael Schwerner, Andrew Goodman, and James Chaney, which underscored the continued urgency of issues that had troubled the Movement from its inception—voting rights and police misconduct, matters largely tangential to the major provisions of the new legislation. Even less evident, perhaps, was the fact that this crowning legislative success actually marked the beginning of a crucial shift in the Movement's relation to the national state, and ultimately to the northern white public, the addressees of its insistent appeals to dismantle the southern racial order. Within days of the bill's signing, the nation's attention shifted to northern manifestations of racial inequality. On July 17, 1964, blacks in Harlem rioted following a police shooting of an unarmed young black man, their anger and grievances posing a somewhat different political scenario than attacks on Jim Crow in the distant South. Scarcely a month later, events at the Democratic National Convention in Atlantic City offered further evidence that the political or economic self-interests or prejudices of the Movement's northern white audiences would henceforth set limits on the effectiveness of moral appeals based on southern "outrages." For those familiar with African Americans' centuries of struggle, the parallels with the demise of the first Reconstruction were disquieting—and painful.

The Revolution Comes to Greenwood

In the early evening of the day preceding the historic March on Washington, a small group from Mississippi picketed the offices of the U.S. Justice Department. Some passing motorists yelled insults expressing their disapproval of this seemingly premature beginning of the scheduled protest march. For the group's leader, Robert Parrish Moses, this protest was designed to address a blind spot in the demands that would be showcased in the larger demonstration the next day. For the Mississippians the issue was not just the slogan officially prescribed for march placards, "Jobs and Freedom," but the failure of their national government to protect their most fundamental means of securing full and equal citizenship—the right to vote. Perhaps, better than most of their fellow demonstrators gathered in the capital city that day, they recognized that black disenfranchisement—one of the two main pillars of the southern Jim Crow regime erected at the turn of the century—undergirded power relations not only in the South but nationally. "Jobs and Freedom" would not become realities anywhere until that issue was fully and decisively resolved.

Although the Birmingham Movement had compelled Kennedy to propose the new civil rights legislation, his announcement on June 11, 1963, gained renewed urgency and moral force because it came just hours before Medgar Evers was felled by an assassin's bullet in Jackson, Mississippi. Born in 1925, Evers led a life that epitomized the origins of a generation that played a preeminent role in forging the long civil rights struggle in Mississippi. He came of age just in time to go to war, serving in France with the famed truck unit "the Red Ball Express." When he returned in 1946, he found his native state on the verge of a fundamental economic transformation, albeit at a slower pace than elsewhere in the postwar South. With plantation labor demands shrinking, abetted both by government-subsidized cuts in acreage and the gradual but inexorable mechanization of non-harvest work, thousands of Mississippi's young men either migrated or continued working on military bases and in the war industries that had sprouted along the state's Gulf Coast during the war. Ambitious young black men who chose, like Evers, to stay in the South had to seek work off the plantations, and, where successful, they gained a measure of independence that their fathers never dreamed of. Drawing benefits from the GI Bill, Evers completed a degree at Alcorn College, despite being a high school dropout. His first job after college was as an agent for Dr. T.R.M. Howard's Magnolia Mutual Life Insurance Company in Mound Bayou, which brought him into direct contact with the extreme poverty and human devastation of the Mississippi Delta. The experience would spur his social consciousness and no doubt offer valuable lessons relevant to his later work as an organizer, first with Howard's Regional Council of Negro Leadership and then with the NAACP.

As a field secretary for the NAACP, Evers was on the front lines of the one-sided racial warfare raging in Mississippi during the postwar years. He named his first child after the African revolutionary leader Jomo Kenyatta and dreamed of emulating Kenya's Mau Mau warriors by seeking armed vengeance for the carnage he had witnessed in the Delta. By 1963, he was the NAACP's principal representative and spokesperson in the state—and thus a target for assassination. In a symbolic gesture to his service at home and abroad, President Kennedy authorized his burial at Arlington National Cemetery. This was but the first of many such ceremonies to come for the fallen warriors of the freedom struggle.

That war veterans loom large among the older Mississippi activists may simply reflect the timing of their maturity, their sense of entitlement, or the fact that their exemption from the poll tax by state law encouraged their registration efforts. There can be little doubt, in any case, that for black veterans, the war broke the mold within which their racially circumscribed lives would normally have been confined. Amzie Moore's reaction to the blatant contradiction between the professed ideals of a war for democracy and the army's systematic humiliation of black soldiers was fairly typical: What, he asked, did citizenship and the loyalty it presumed mean for a black man in Mississippi? Serving in Europe and the Pacific, respectively, both Evers and Aaron Henry were transported a world away from Mississippi, but this simply reinforced their determination to make the state a genuine home for themselves and other blacks. Each of them seized upon the GI Bill to seek more education after the war, Evers at Alcorn and Henry at Xavier University in New Orleans. All three men would throw themselves into postwar voter registration campaigns.

They were no doubt encouraged when these campaigns soon bore fruit. Although the obstacles in Mississippi were more formidable than those in most southern states, registration increased tenfold during the first postwar decade, peaking at nearly twenty-five thousand black voters in 1955. The growth of the NAACP was even more impressive: more than ten times as many branches and a fiftyfold increase in membership since 1949. One year after the Till lynching, however, racial terror, economic reprisals, and legal suppression had driven the number of black voters back down to just over eight thousand. The NAACP had lost 246 of its branches and forty-eight thousand members. It is no surprise, then, that when young Bob Moses arrived in Greenwood in 1961 seeking counsel on how to mobilize a civil rights campaign in the Mississippi Delta, Amzie Moore urged him to target the right to vote.

Moore would have been surprised, however, if he had known that his plea to Moses was soon to be effectively seconded by federal authorities and to gain material support from some of the nation's foremost philanthropic foundations. By a twist of fate, the Delta's nearly two-decades-old indigenously led voter registration campaign happened to coincide with the Kennedy administration's anxious desire to turn the Movement away from Birmingham-style confrontations. Early in 1961, Stephen R. Currier, president of the Taconic Foundation and founder and president of the Potomac Institute, had initiated discussions with Martin Luther King, Jr., regarding the possibility of funding a large-scale voter registration campaign in the South. Shortly after, once the crisis over the Freedom Rides subsided the following spring, Attorney General Robert Kennedy urged a similar refocusing of strategy to a group of student activists, no doubt seeing it as a way to deflect their energies into less violent confrontations. Through the summer and fall, Robert Kennedy pressed the issue through his lieutenant Burke Marshall and presidential adviser Harris Wofford, who met with various civil rights groups, the Southern Regional Council, and representatives of philanthropic groups to fashion a plan of action and a conduit for the plan's funding. Planning was completed at a meeting in January 1962: the various civil rights field staffs would, over a two-and-a-half-year period, receive $870,000 from three philanthropic foundations that had long funded social reform initiatives (the Stern Family Fund, the Field, and the Taconic foundations), to be funneled through a newly formed Voter Education Project directed by Little Rock lawyer Wiley Branton. Although mere observers at these meetings, the Justice Department representatives had offered "full government cooperation" in this endeavor, which was understood to mean the crucial commitment to ensure legal protection for the field workers. The Civil Rights Act of 1957, which then-senator Lyndon Johnson had shepherded through Congress and President Eisenhower had signed, made voter intimidation a federal crime, and thus federal intervention to protect registration efforts was clearly authorized. And, indeed, in March 1962, Robert Kennedy did instruct his Civil Rights Division to make greater use of the FBI to investigate cases of voter suppression.

Over time, however, the promised federal protection proved much more politically problematic. As had often been the case during the long struggle to ensure African American citizenship, legal authority and political will were two very different things. Any notion that the Kennedy administration might have had that registering voters would be less contentious or would arouse a less violent resistance than street demonstrations was as fleeting as its commitments for protection. In Delta counties, where blacks made up as much as 60 percent of the population, voting could quite literally be a matter of life and death. Ultimately, the "outside agitators" who ventured into Mississippi discovered that they were on their own.

It was fitting, perhaps, that the first of these "outside agitators" to arrive in the Delta was SNCC worker Sam Block, a Mississippi native and air force veteran who had once attended classes at the Highlander School. Block was not dispatched, however, before satisfying the objections from some SNCC veterans of the earlier sit-in campaigns, who feared, correctly, that the Kennedys' proffer of assistance was intended to deflect the Movement into less radical channels. Ironically, if perhaps unwittingly, they shared the Kennedys' central premise that voter registration work was indeed a less direct, less radical challenge to the southern racial regime. Neither group fully appreciated, perhaps, that the roots of the southern crisis were actually in black southerners' long-standing struggle for citizenship rights—or as Rosa Parks had put it, "what rights [they] had as a human being and a citizen." Perhaps Bob Moses, the newcomer from New York, intuited that the Movement must ultimately become political in order that its fundamental challenge to the established order have a lasting effect.

Certainly, the veteran organizer Ella Baker understood that the hit-and-run strategy then being pursued by Martin Luther King, Jr., and the SCLC could never achieve fundamental and enduring change. Baker's long activist apprenticeship—organizing local chapters of the NAACP in the 1940s and as chief of staff for SCLC in the 1950s—had taught her that lasting change must come from a people and communities fundamentally transformed. Those people and their communities must learn to trust their own capacities and to grow their own indigenous leadership. Organizers could not begin that learning process, therefore, by ignoring the community's own articulation of what was needed. Thus Amzie Moore's analysis of need must be honored and his request responded to. However suspect its motives, therefore, the establishment-sponsored Voter Education Project provided material means for shaping that response. In the end, the two sides of the debate decided to live and let live: SNCC would have two branches, one devoted to organizing direct-action campaigns and a second focused on voter registration under Moses's general direction in six Mississippi Delta counties (Bolivar, Coahoma, Leflore, Marshall, Sunflower, and Washington).

Thus Block began his work in Greenwood, a principal spawning ground of the White Citizens' Council and hometown of Medgar Evers's assassin, Byron De La Beckwith. With a population of barely twenty-two thousand, Greenwood was still the largest town between Memphis and Jackson. Greenwood's most relevant distinction for Block, however, may have been that it lay in Leflore County, where Emmett Till was murdered and his killers set free. Following what had become a standard SNCC organizing strategy, Block focused his efforts on enlisting young people and lower-middle-class adults—yardmen, maids, cab drivers, beauticians, barbers, custodians, and field hands. It was the kind of patient, painstaking organizational labor that Ella Baker, SNCC's unofficial mentor, had long emphasized. Designed to tap into the dense, interlocking, intergenerational networks of kinship and organizational experience, it sought to mobilize the indigenous leadership and support structures necessary to wage what was sure to be a dangerous and difficult struggle.

Registering voters in the largely rural, black majority counties of the Mississippi Delta would prove even more difficult than anticipated, however. In sharp contrast with its long history of racial violence, Mississippi's initial response to the Movement challenge was surprisingly bureaucratic and legalistic. In 1956, it established the Sovereignty Commission to monitor and coordinate its responses to civil rights agitation. Like Alabama, it introduced new procedures and requirements for voter registration, including a questionnaire ostensibly to test literacy and a requirement that appli-

Organizing at the grass roots. In a scene replicated in numerous communities across the
South, SNCC field Secretary Charles Sherrod (standing) and activist Randy Battle (seated)
visit a prospective voter in Albany, Georgia, in 1963.

cants register at county courthouses, making the process more cumbersome
and surveillance easier. An even more formidable obstacle, however, was
the state's wrenching poverty. Living conditions in the Delta were poor
even by Mississippi standards, already among the lowest in the nation.
Delta whites earned half the per capita income of whites in the rest of the
state, and only 10 percent of the region's homes had indoor plumbing. The
situation for the Delta's blacks was much worse, of course; the median
income for them was less than half that of their white neighbors, and their
infant mortality twice as high. Economic retaliation offered ready weapons
with which to squash registration activities, therefore. Planters evicted
their tenants, and local authorities cut off federally funded surplus food
supplies. Consequently, substantial Movement resources were channeled
into organizing food and clothing drives among northern supporters, and
these also proved to be powerful organizational tools, because they involved those supporters more deeply in the southern struggle. By the early
1960s, as registration efforts intensified, the state reached for its traditional arsenal of weapons—jailing, high bail fees, and raw violence—to

deplete the Movement's resources, terrorize its local supporters, and blunt its efforts. By the winter of 1963, even Bob Moses had grown frustrated and doubtful about the project's prospects.

As was so often the case during these crisis years, however, such extreme measures filed a double edge of resistance onto repression's sword. Although southern reactionaries often did succeed in temporarily blunting Movement objectives, they could also inadvertently turn victims into leaders. Fannie Lou Hamer's story demonstrates both the obstacles the Movement confronted and the courage aroused to fight through them. Born Fannie Lee Townsend in 1917 to a sharecropping couple in Montgomery County, Hamer would emerge as an icon of Mississippi's indigenous movement. Her powerful oratorical skills were sometimes attributed to her father, another Baptist preacher who turned to bootlegging to make ends meet. While others went north during the Great Migration, Fannie's parents made it only as far as E. W. Brandon's Ruleville plantation in Sunflower County. Ten years later, they had earned and saved enough to buy a wagon, tools, three mules, two cows, and a car. Like Ned Cobb, however, they quickly discovered that too much success brought retaliation. Unnamed whites poisoned their animals and destroyed their prospects. The family never recovered. Ten years after being "cleaned out," Fannie's father died of a stroke on the eve of the Second World War. Shortly thereafter an accident rendered her mother an invalid. During the war, Fannie Lou married Perry (Pap) Hamer and moved with her mother onto W. D. Marlow's plantation in Ruleville, where Pap worked as a tractor driver and Fannie became a timekeeper.

In the late summer of 1962, Bob Moses, James Forman, and several other representatives from the Council of Federated Organizations (COFO) spoke at a mass meeting at a Baptist church in Ruleville in an effort to recruit prospective registration applicants in Sunflower County, where blacks made up 61 percent of the voting-age population but barely more than 1 percent of the voting rolls. The speakers succeeded in persuading eighteen people to accompany them to register in Indianola, the county seat and birthplace of the White Citizens' Council. Fannie Lou Hamer was among those recruits. She did not succeed in registering, of course, having failed to answer to the registrar's satisfaction the mandated twenty-one questions about the Mississippi constitution, including one demanding an explanation of an obscure clause called "the de facto law." During the registration process, however, she was required to provide a full accounting of her personal background, including place of employment. News of her registration attempt reached the Marlow plantation that evening before she did. Marlow confronted her and demanded that she withdraw her application or face eviction. She refused, and was forced to move off the plantation. Over the coming months she would endure threatening phone calls, repeated drive-by shooting attempts, and a brutal beating in the Winona jail that left her with kidney damage and blind in one eye. Unfortunately for her, to secure legal protection from such harassment, she would have needed to appeal to Sunflower's sheriff, S. L. Milam, brother of J. W. Milam, one of Emmett Till's murderers.

Hamer's transformation demonstrates both the power and limitations of Ella Baker's grass-roots mobilization strategy. Meaningful change—not simply to register voters but to empower them politically—could have been achieved only through the kind of transformed worldview that the Movement made possible. At the same time, it soon became abundantly clear that those structures of oppression would yield to nothing less than the superior force of national law and the external imposition of a new social order. Neither the existing civil rights laws, nor the one Kennedy would soon propose, was likely to initiate such a radical federal intervention. Moreover, the FBI, the principal agency charged with their protection, maintained suspiciously close relations with local police forces.

Little more than a year after its inception, therefore, COFO undertook the complex maneuver of redeploying the local mobilization around voter registration with the goal of achieving the national pressure necessary for a more thorough political reform. First, they organized a mock election, demonstrating to the nation evidence of voter suppression and laying the basis for a subsequent challenge to the national Democratic Party's continued embrace of the state's political establishment. The following summer they recruited hundreds of white college students to join their voter registration campaign, a deliberate effort to bring the glare of national publicity that might force greater federal protection for their organizing activities generally. At summer's end, they challenged the seating of Mississippi's all-white delegation at the Democratic Party National Convention in Atlantic City.

With Aaron Henry heading the ticket as a candidate for governor and garnering eighty-three thousand votes, the parallel "freedom ballot" in the

November 1963 elections did indeed demonstrate that Mississippi blacks would have exercised their citizenship rights if permitted. Unfortunately, that message was probably lost on a nation—and a Movement—preoccupied with the murder of four black girls in the bombed Sixteenth Street Baptist Church in Birmingham seven weeks before, and then John F. Kennedy's assassination three weeks after the election. Similarly, when the Mississippi Freedom Democratic Party (MFDP) organized the following April, attention was focused on southern senators' filibuster of the Civil Rights Bill, which as noted contained little that addressed the most pressing voting rights issues that Mississippi blacks were then confronting. On June 10, after fifty-seven days, the filibuster was broken, just as COFO activists were completing preparations to train the northern volunteers for the summer's activities. They probably devoted even less attention to the bill's final passage and President Lyndon Johnson's elaborate signing ceremony on July 2, for they were now fully riveted on the search for three of their own— Schwerner, Chaney, and Goodman—who had disappeared on June 21 while investigating the burning of a black church in Meridian, Mississippi. The three young men's bodies were found on August 4, just seventeen days before the MFDP delegation arrived in Atlantic City to challenge Mississippi senator James Eastland's party.

Those relatively insulated from the ongoing struggle in the Mississippi Delta failed to appreciate the context of the black Mississippi delegation's historic journey to reach this convention. On the face of it, the issue before the convention was whether black voter suppression in Mississippi justified the denial of seats to the regular state Democratic Party and the seating of the MFDP delegation in its place, not whether deep historic wrongs would finally be righted a hundred years after emancipation. Thus the legal and moral debates played out against the backdrop of President Johnson's fear that seating the MFDP would chase the party's southern wing into the arms of his presidential opponent, Barry Goldwater, a conservative Republican who had just voted against the Civil Rights Act. Johnson was also well aware that Alabama governor George Wallace had exceeded all expectations the previous spring in garnering Democratic votes in several northern-state presidential primaries. Thus, he reasoned, embracing a radical civil rights agenda risked two key pillars of the already fraying Democratic coalition. He determined to use the full weight of his office to defeat such an outcome. Black and white supporters found judgeships

dangled or withdrawn. Walter Reuther's UAW, heretofore a labor ally of
the Movement threatened to withdraw donations from SCLC and to fire
the lead attorney for the challengers, the labor lawyer Joseph Rauh. The
Movement itself was in danger of splitting as King, James Farmer of
CORE, and Roy Wilkins of the NAACP spoke in favor of the MFDP, but
Bayard Rustin, the main organizer of the 1963 March on Washington, ridiculed their refusal to compromise as naïve and ignorant of the necessity
of embracing realpolitik. An Oregon congresswoman proposed a compromise allocating the MFDP two nonvoting delegates, which was rejected
by the group "as a back-of-the-bus offer." In the end, realpolitik prevailed,
but only after the white southern regulars had walked out and their challengers had been rebuffed, leaving both sides alienated from the Democratic Party.

Events in Atlantic City embittered a generation of activists. Many in the
Movement's core groups—SNCC, CORE, and the MFDP—grew more
radical after Atlantic City. Shaken by unavenged martyrdom, angered by
unacknowledged betrayal, many were drawn irresistibly to the rage articulated so forcefully by Malcolm X, the separatism embraced by the Nation of
Islam, and the siren call to revolutionary violence. SNCC's faith in a biracial, nonviolent movement—what some called "the beloved community"—
began to unravel in the months immediately following the showdown in
Atlantic City. Traveling through West Africa later that fall, some of SNCC's
principal leaders were drawn to alternative visions of racial redemption,
after seeing African peoples in apparent control of their national destinies. Less than two years later, following a flurry of tense staff meetings
and a blizzard of position papers, the organization became fully committed to a black separatist agenda and expelled its white staff.

    By that time tensions between MFDP and SNCC had already led
Fannie Lou Hamer to leave the latter in the spring of 1965. Along with
Unita Blackwell and other MFDP stalwarts, she turned her attention to
issues of welfare and poverty, focused on the creation of the Mississippi
Freedom Labor Union (MFLU), an organization of truck drivers, day laborers, and domestics. The MFLU emerged out of discussions promoted
in some of the "freedom schools" that SNCC had organized earlier. Attracting forty-five people at its first meeting in Bolivar County in April

1965, it soon grew to five hundred members spread over six Delta counties. Although the union supported strikes by aggrieved farmworkers in 1965, most of its organizational efforts were directed at promoting land owner- ship and building homes and businesses. Organizing farm laborers was beating against the winds of change, however. The already substantial losses of rural population and agricultural labor had accelerated by the late 1960s, and many of the planter barons now relied as much or more on gov- ernment subsidies as on growing cotton. As early as 1961–62, Mississippi senator James Eastland, for example, was receiving $500,000 in subsidies. Given declines in labor and production over the following decade, he surely was even more wedded to the government dole by 1965.

Not for another decade, however, would structural changes in the nation's political economy that were reshaping the possibility for achieving funda- mental social change become fully evident. In the meantime, black citi- zenship, particularly the issue of ensuring black voting rights, remained on the front page of the nation's political agenda and conscience, notwith- standing the MFDP's defeat at Atlantic City. Wielding their now-well- honed strategy of massive mobilization, Movement leaders were able to rouse the nation one last time to confront and destroy the remaining pillar of southern white supremacy—black disenfranchisement. Even as they did so, however, three of the leading civil rights organizations—SNCC, SCLC, and CORE—stood just months away from virtual if not actual dissolution as significant national forces. By the end of 1965, the nation was already poised to move onto a far more complex racial terrain, for which the strategies and tactics honed over the past decade would prove much less useful. Less than a year after rebuffing the MFDP challenge— and still losing all but two southern states in his landslide victory over Barry Goldwater—President Lyndon Johnson championed strong voting rights legislation, which would eventually transform the nation's political order. Even at that moment, however, he was making fateful foreign policy decisions that would profoundly shape not only his own political fate but the future of the Civil Rights Movement he had so briefly embraced. More than ever before, African Americans' claims to equal citizenship would be framed by tensions generated within a political arena shaped by national and international forces.

The Roads from Selma

There is an almost poetic historical symmetry in the fact that Dallas County, Alabama, the birthplace of Bull Connor, should have been the site of the dramatic climax of the Civil Rights Movement and of the most intense decade of civil rights agitation in American history. The county's principal town, Selma, was home to twenty-eight thousand residents in 1960, evenly divided between whites and blacks. It lay just fifty-four miles southwest of Montgomery and just an hour or two away from the bloody ground of Ned Cobb's shootout at Camp Hill, from Simon Owens's family home in Lowndes County, and from the Calhoun school where Du Bois undertook his final empirical research into "the Negro Problem" of the rural South in 1906. Indeed, by 1965, Selma and its rural Dallas County environs epitomized the phenomenal half-century evolution of the southern Black Belt.

From the decade preceding the Civil War until the first decade of the twentieth century, Dallas County produced more cotton than any other in the state, but after 1910 it would endure a thorough remaking of its social and economic order. The Great Migration, the New Deal agricultural reforms, and the Second World War undermined the cotton monoculture and the social relations of labor it had produced. By the end of the Second World War, the shift to cattle ranching signaled the rapid end of the old plantation regime and with it the panoply of social controls built upon the white landlord–black tenant relationship. The number of black tenant farmers declined from seven thousand in 1910 to just one thousand by 1964. The furnishing system whereby grocers financed farm production through their credits to workers either shifted into ordinary banking or disappeared altogether. Those blacks who did not move north crowded into Selma, where their relatively greater access to education and a denser institutional life provided the basis for what one historian has called "a new social order."

Consequently, a political system formerly dominated by the planter class and its urban allies and dependents was transformed, and political patterns observed elsewhere in the urban South emerged. Long an important rail junction with a substantial non-farm employment, Selma saw a rapid, steep decline in this sector during the postwar period, triggering the systematic, contractual exclusion of blacks by white union laborers. At the other end of the political spectrum was a small group of relatively progressive white businessmen, anxious to attract outside capital for expanded industrial development. In Selma in the fall of 1962, they had formed the "Committee of 100 Plus," which, like similar groups in Montgomery and Birmingham, sought to modernize the local economy.

As elsewhere in the postwar South, Selma benefited from the war-induced growth of federal infrastructure. Nearby Craig Air Force Base, established to train fighter pilots, provided jobs for many of the city's residents and subsidized the local schools. Although Selma's black community never achieved a measure of political leverage comparable to Montgomery's or Birmingham's, the federal installation and local businessmen's development aspirations did moderate an otherwise thoroughly reactionary racial regime—at least somewhat. Black voters supplied the margin of victory for the election of Joe T. Smitherman, a young appliance store owner with a social and political profile similar to Montgomery's Dave Birmingham. Smitherman's ally, police chief Wilson Baker, also adopted a "moderate" approach to enforcing white supremacy. *Moderation* is a relative term, of course; Wilson Baker was a charter member of the White Citizens' Council. At the council's urging perhaps, Selma followed Mississippi's example of deploying economic intimidation as its weapon of choice to discourage voter registration. For example, in 1955, the Selma school board had fired black teachers who signed a petition asking that it obey the recent Supreme Court decision and desegregate its schools. Blacks boycotted the Cloverleaf Creamery in response, but met with violent reprisals against an activist black employee there. In a similar incident seven years later, Dallas County dismissed thirty-six teachers who had testified in a suit brought by the Department of Justice against voter suppression.

The combination of "moderate" and violent repression stymied local efforts to mobilize the black vote. Despite the fact that SNCC began organizing there at roughly the same time it went into Mississippi, by 1964 there were still only 250 blacks registered out of an eligible population of 5,744. Veteran organizer Bernard Lafayette had moved into Selma in October 1962, followed by Worth Long several months later. Registration had been boosted for a while by nightly mass meetings during the spring and summer of 1963, but declined precipitously shortly thereafter. Discouraged by the setback, veteran local leader Amelia Boynton made a presentation to the SCLC in Atlanta, ending with a request for Martin Luther

King's personal assistance. King made his first visit in October 1964, just two months before receiving the Nobel Peace Prize. He returned during the early months of 1965, when the Selma movement had regained its traction through mass street parades and arrests, peaking at two thousand arrests in early February 1965.

The increased activism culminated on Sunday, March 7, 1965, when a sheriff's posse viciously attacked voting rights demonstrators led by the SNCC chairman John Lewis as they crossed the Edmund Pettus Bridge for an intended march on the state capital in Montgomery. Beamed live to a national television audience, the scenes of Sheriff Clark's mounted posse charging into the crowd wielding batons and beating back the marchers shocked and outraged the nation. Blanket media coverage over the following weeks, including the brutal beatings and deaths of other civil rights supporters, built intense pressure for federal action on the unfinished agenda of the Movement. On March 15, 1965, President Johnson spoke to the nation on the moral necessity for new legislation, a moment reprising Kennedy's address two years earlier. Echoing Rosa Parks's justification of her refusal to surrender her bus seat ten years earlier, Johnson

In Martin Luther King, Jr.'s absence, the SNCC chairman John Lewis (center) led the initial march to Montgomery, which was attacked by a sheriff's posse with clubs and tear gas.

declared that the movement in Selma was simply "the effort of American Negroes to secure for themselves the full blessings of American life." After a century of ambivalence and betrayal, the national government once more had to stand firmly behind the cause of full citizenship. Quoting the long-standing anthem of the nonviolent movement, Johnson declared, "We *will* overcome." Another line in Johnson's speech attracted less notice, but it turned out to be prophetic. Even with this most fundamental right of citizenship secured, he warned, "the battle will not be over."

The Selma campaign, however, was the last of the classic battles that had come to define the Civil Rights Movement. Immediately after Johnson signed the Voting Rights Act on August 6, 1965, the Justice Department dispatched federal registrars to congressional districts in the seven southern states that had shown a demonstrable historical pattern of voter exclusion. The new registrars were authorized to suspend literacy tests and poll taxes, devices that southern registrars had deployed to disfranchise black voters since the turn of the century, and to register voters for federal elections directly. Within a month of the signing ceremony, a quarter million black southerners were registered, a figure that would double again within four years. A struggle for African American citizenship stretching back to the closing decades of the previous century seemed to have reached closure and success. The 6 percent of eligible black Mississippians who were registered in 1964 mushroomed to 60 percent by 1971. The 75 black elected officials counted in southern states in 1965 grew to 3,685 by 1987. Black mayors and city councilmen became a common sight in southern cities, including many that had been sites of violent struggle in the 1950s and '60s. Atlanta, scene of the 1906 riot, elected its first black mayor in 1974. Birmingham followed suit in 1979, as did Memphis and New Orleans several years later. Black congressmen were elected from southern districts for the first time since Reconstruction, including prominent Movement leaders such as Julian Bond and John Lewis from Atlanta.

The Movement's sudden and dramatic success brought a strangely bittersweet denouement, however. Although Movement activists continued to mobilize around electoral politics and an array of social and economic issues, rarely were they able again to frame those issues for a national audience as clear moral choices requiring federal legislative remedies. In that narrow but significant sense, the Civil Rights Movement was over, leaving in its wake an odd sense of incompleteness, of goals yet unfulfilled. The triumphant euphoria of the Voting Rights Act signing ceremony was quickly overtaken five days later by the frightening violence that for six days ravaged the Watts community in Los Angeles. It was the first of several urban rebellions that would shake northern and western cities over the next three years, each sparked by confrontations between the black community and white police officers—ominous echoes of the grievances that had fueled protests in southern cities a decade earlier. With amazing swiftness the century-long struggle for voting rights was made to seem irrelevant, as the escalating violence shifted attention to racial conditions and tensions elsewhere. The major civil rights organizations pivoted to address this new front in the struggle for social justice, only to be overwhelmed by the complexities of the problems and the northern political environments they confronted. For a brief moment Martin Luther King, Jr., seemed on the verge of readapting the tactics of the southern movement and rearticulating civil rights as a struggle for economic justice with a "Poor People's Campaign" that would march on and set up an encampment in the nation's capital during the summer of 1968. On April 4, 1968, he was felled by an assassin's bullet in Memphis, Tennessee, and the Poor People's March disintegrated the following summer much as had the 1920s Bonus March by World War I veterans on which it was modeled. Fittingly, King's fateful stop in Memphis was to lend support to a strike by black garbage workers seeking improved wages and working conditions. However, "I Am a Man!", the slogan emblazoned on their picket signs, suggests that higher wages and better working conditions were mere stand-ins for human dignity and respect, echoes of a theme that had run through the southern civil rights campaign since Rosa Parks took her seat on the Cleveland Avenue bus in Montgomery.

Rosa Parks observed all these changes from her new home in Detroit, to which she had moved with her husband and mother in 1956, after losing her job at Montgomery Fair. Eventually she found work as a secretary-receptionist on the staff of Congressman John Conyers, himself a legatee of the earlier black political revolution in the North. She returned to her native state to participate in the Selma-to-Montgomery march in 1965, but found herself repeatedly excluded from the line of march by the young marshals who "didn't know who I was and couldn't care less about me because they didn't know me." More disturbing still were the vast changes she witnessed in black Americans' life chances and status, dictated for her memoirs in the last decade of the twentieth century. Referring to voting rights laws, black officeholders, and access to ordinary public spaces, she expressed pleasure at the racial progress she had lived to see. "I look back now and realize that since that evening on the bus in Montgomery, Alabama, we have made a lot of progress in some ways." Recent Supreme Court decisions and national indifference or hostility to sustaining those civil rights gains suggested "a resurgence of reactionary attitudes" that was disturbing, however. "Sometimes I do feel pretty sad about some of the events that have taken place recently," she said. She had witnessed the deteriorating social fabric of Detroit's black community that followed the explosive violence of 1967. For the generation born from those ashes, the struggles and heroism of the Civil Rights Movement were but a distant, perhaps even irrelevant, memory. On August 30, 1994, twenty-eight-year-old Joseph Skipper, drug-addicted and looking for money to support his habit, broke into Parks's modest home on Detroit's east side. Although he recognized Parks, that did not stay his senseless assault: after extorting fifty-three dollars, he punched the eighty-one-year-old "mother of the Civil Rights Movement" and fled, leaving in his wake the anguish, shame, and rage of a generation. It was as if, but for a moment, a nation and a people had come face-to-face with its amnesia and unfulfilled promises.

More than a decade after Selma, Mamie Till Bradley reconnected with the movement her son's murder had launched and found new forms of solace for her brutal loss. In the aftermath of her public mourning, she had quietly devoted herself to securing her graduate degree in education and teaching in the Chicago public schools. There she used her son's martyrdom to challenge her students to diligence and self-improvement. Finally, in 1976, a statue of Emmett was raised in a public park in Denver, alongside one of Martin Luther King, Jr. A decade later, at a Movement commemoration in Atlanta, Bradley met Coretta Scott, King's widow, and Rosa Parks, with both of whom she became close friends. With these events, Emmett's death ceased to be solely a personal tragedy "for me to hug to myself and weep, but a worldwide awakening that would change the course of history." Like the grieving young mother of that other moment, two decades earlier, she refused to allow a struggle's history to be washed away.

8

CITIZENS OF THE NATION, CITIZENS OF THE WORLD

African America in the Twenty-first Century

In far too many ways American Negroes have been another nation.
—President Lyndon B. Johnson, Howard University, June 4, 1965

I speak to you not as a candidate for President, but as a citizen—a proud citizen of the United States, and a fellow citizen of the world.
—Democratic presidential candidate Barack Obama,
Berlin, Germany, July 24, 2008

Roughly three months after the bloody confrontations in Selma and two months before he signed the Voting Rights Act, President Lyndon Johnson spoke to that year's graduating class at Howard University. It is not clear whether Johnson was aware that the title of his speech, "To Fulfill These Rights," echoed the report, "To Secure These Rights," issued by President Truman's Committee on Civil Rights in 1947, but clearly much had changed during the intervening eighteen years. The president proudly ticked off the civil rights gains black Americans had made, most of them legislated during his brief eighteen-month tenure: the Supreme Court's decision outlawing segregated schools now strengthened with new enforcement tools, laws against job discrimination, laws requiring equal access to public accommodations and facilities, and the Voting Rights Act he expected to reach his desk within a few weeks. Notwithstanding this rapid and undeniable progress in fulfilling the century-old promise of emancipation, he warned, no one should expect black men and women simply to walk through the gates of opportunity these new laws had thrown open. One might as easily expect that after striking chains from the ankles of a runner you could then bid him or her to compete equally in a race with other runners who had not been shackled. "Freedom is not enough," he declared. Black Americans were finally recognized as full citizens of the nation, yet in "far too many ways American Negroes have been another nation." Caught in "a seamless web" of poverty and disability, too many blacks inhabited an "inherited, gateless poverty." Their full integration into the life of the nation would require another, "more profound stage of the battle for civil rights," one whose goal was "equality as a fact and as a result."

Except for a few demonstrators among the graduating seniors who were angered by recent signs of escalating military activities in Vietnam and by their disappointment with the president's initial response to the violence in Selma, the largely black audience was both surprised and encouraged by Johnson's address. Their warm reception had been anticipated by the NAACP's Roy Wilkins, the Urban League's Whitney Young, and SCLC's Martin Luther King, Jr., all of whom had read and endorsed an advance copy of the speech. The necessity of moving on to a "second stage" in the struggle to ensure racial justice, which Johnson now endorsed, had been part of debates and discussions among civil rights leaders since their preparations for the March on Washington. It was no accident that *Jobs* had been coupled with (and preceded) *Freedom* on the banners of the marchers two summers earlier. The idea for the march, originating with the venerable labor leader A. Philip Randolph and elaborated by younger lieutenants and associates, had from the first been focused on advancing social-democratic state policies to address racial issues within the context of what they recognized as broader structural barriers to social and economic justice. Other black leaders shared their concerns, if not their socialist commitments. Indeed, Whitney Young, the new executive director of the relatively conservative National Urban League (NUL), had arrived at quite similar conclusions. In September 1962, just his second year on the job, he had warned that blacks might end up with "a mouthful of rights and an empty stomach," unless the historical roots of deprivation were addressed through job retraining, education, and increased social welfare expenditures. The following year, Young won the League's endorsement of his "Marshall Plan" for black America, which seized upon cold war logic and rhetoric to justify a massive infusion of public funding to address poverty at home much as the nation had rebuilt Europe in its effort to contain communism.

Meanwhile, King's complex ideological formation, a blend of Christian ideas of social responsibility and secular notions of social justice, made him receptive as well to a social-democratic inflection of Movement goals. Among King's key strategic interlocutors were A. Philip Randolph's protégé Bayard Rustin and the author Michael Harrington. In the February 1965 issue of *Commentary*, Rustin reiterated the arguments he had made for compromise during the MFDP challenge in Atlantic City, urging social justice advocates to move "From Protest to Politics," but now coupled that plea with insistence that the political focus be on the deeper systemic problems that underlay racial injustice. In 1962, Harrington had published *The Other Americans*, which documented the broader crisis of white as well as black poverty and made a case for mobilizing government programs to address it. Already, in his testimony before the Democratic National Convention the previous summer, King had endorsed federal spending on public works and a guaranteed minimum income for every American family. Finally, that July, a Louis Harris–*Newsweek* opinion poll revealed that blacks "wanted jobs more than they wanted hotel rooms or hamburgers."

The warm applause washing over President Johnson on Howard's campus that sunny morning, therefore, reflected a rare moment of rough consensus about the next steps in the movement for racial equality. The historic transformations set in motion by the Great Migration were now irreversible. An even larger proportion of the black population now lived in cities than whites, and the general shift out of agriculture, along with expanding educational opportunities in the South as well as the North, had boosted a sizable middle class now poised to seize upon the benefits of the rights revolution. Most blacks, however, had not benefited from these changes. More were unemployed in 1964 than in 1954, and the jobless rate—roughly equal in the early postwar years—was now twice as high for blacks as whites. The gap between the median income for white and black families had grown wider. The number of white families in poverty had decreased by 27 percent since 1947, a pace of amelioration nine times higher than that experienced by nonwhite families. Infant mortality, once 70 percent higher among nonwhites, now stood 90 percent higher. Although the grim statistical portrait of black America etched in Johnson's speech was drawn from an unpublished, but soon-to-be-controversial government report, he would have found quite similar assessments in recent studies of black urban life by contemporary black social scientists: Robert Weaver's *The Urban Complex* (1964) and Kenneth Clark's *Dark Ghetto* (1965). Alarmed at the growing social pressures on black families and communities, these students of the contemporary urban crisis were no doubt comfortable with Johnson deploying the devastation of urban black families as justification for new government initiatives aimed at ensuring "equality as a fact and as a result."

Writing in a period of relative economic expansion, however, even the most sophisticated analysts of the late 1960s failed to appreciate the ongoing structural transformations in the global economy that would complicate any effort to address what had come to be known as "the urban problem." The brief political rapprochement between the Johnson administration and the civil rights leadership evaporated before summer's end, taking with it the possibility for a concerted campaign to make the nation whole. Just two years after Johnson's speech, a presidential commission graphically underscored the unfinished business he had recognized: a nation "moving toward two societies, one black, one white—separate and unequal."

Two Nations, Two Cultures

Johnson's speech was inspired and co-authored by Daniel Patrick Moynihan, an assistant secretary in the Labor Department who had just completed a report on the subject. Born in Oklahoma but reared mostly in and around New York City, Moynihan had finished high school in East Harlem. Exposure to Manhattan's ethnic mélange, together with a history of emotional disruptions within his own family, may well have colored his subsequent academic and professional commitments and views. He reports feeling devastated by the loss of his alcoholic and philandering father, and he sometimes suffered straitened material circumstances growing up in a household headed by his twice-divorced mother. Moynihan had joined the Labor Department during the Kennedy administration, after stints at the London School of Economics on a Fulbright fellowship, in the New York governor's office, and at the Fletcher School of Law and Diplomacy, where he received his doctorate. He had already made his mark in government with an analysis of data on draft rejectees that supplied the conceptual basis for President Kennedy's manpower programs in the early 1960s. After President Johnson made the Great Society and civil rights the signature policy initiatives of his administration, Moynihan and his staff undertook a study of what had once been called "the Negro Problem." Their report, "The Negro Family: The Case for National Action," was at once a treatise on historical sociology and a white paper documenting the case for new policy initiatives, all held together by a moral discourse on the failings of the nation and a people. Citing Bayard Rustin's recent *Commentary* article and prefiguring the theme of Johnson's later speech, the report opened with a declaration that the nation had arrived at a new stage in the struggle for racial equality. Looking backward, the report drew on a soon-to-be controversial study by historian Stanley Elkins that argued that American slavery—"'the most awful in the world'"—destroyed the black family and fundamentally crippled blacks' capacity for normal human relations. Using the work of the preeminent African American sociologist E. Franklin Frazier to document developments after slavery, the authors argued that the deterioration in the status and capacities of black males could be traced to the dysfunctional matriarchies inherited from slavery that still distorted gender relations in contemporary black communities and exacerbated urban unemployment. Given this self-perpetuating "tangle of pathology," a crisis was building in northern ghettos where alienated "Negro youth appear to be withdrawing from American society."

Completed in March, the report was distributed as an internal document and never subject to the cross-departmental reviews and vetting normal for such a major policy initiative. It reached Johnson's desk in May and became the basis for his commencement address, which, also contrary to usual procedures, was not vetted by the bureaucracies it would implicate. Indeed, the report's cool reception by many social scientists in and out of government suggests that it might well not have survived such a review. At that very moment, most of the relevant agencies were deeply engaged sorting through the programmatic and administrative challenges posed by Johnson's declaration of a "war on poverty," which Congress had written into law a few weeks after passing the Civil Rights Act in 1964. The new law set up the Office of Economic Opportunity (OEO) to oversee a broad range of rural and urban programs to retrain adults and youth for the changing job market, teach literacy to poor people and immigrant workers, and provide housing assistance to rural residents and legal services for the poor. The black urban crisis was just a part of this larger effort initially, but would soon overwhelm it. While certainly recognizing the broad social and emotional impact of historical conditions and ongoing structural disloca-tions, the evolving logic of the poverty warriors was to mobilize communi-ties to ensure delivery of existing services to the poor and to provide that "target" population with the resources to address its own problems.

The consensus that had briefly formed around Johnson's speech be-gan to dissolve once Moynihan's report was made public a month later. The grim statistics that Johnson had cited—and that black social scien-tists had long warned of—had been marshaled in the report to support an argument that seemed to suggest that black people's cultural deficiencies were the root causes of their economic and social deprivation. With one quarter of all black marriages dissolved, one quarter of all black families headed by a woman, and one quarter of all black children born out of wedlock, the conclusion seemed clear to Moynihan and his co-authors: "At the heart of the deterioration of the fabric of Negro society is the de-terioration of the Negro family." The irony, of course, was that Moynihan's report not only tapped into the anxious conclusions of at least two gen-erations of black sociologists but echoed a concern, now at least a century old, that the integrity of the black family was at risk. Thus, for example, Moynihan's major premise—"The family is the basic social unit of Ameri-can life; it is the basic socializing unit"—is one that Corporal Murray would have readily affirmed. Murray's declaration to a meeting of freed-people in 1866 that the "Marriage Covenant is at the foundation of all our rights" was intended, however, to draw attention to the economic dispos-session and legal inequities that put black families at risk. In Moynihan's formulation, that relationship seemed reversed, shading toward an accu-sation that broken black families were the *cause* of a cultural dysfunction that contributed to their unemployment and poverty. Whatever Moyni-han's intentions, this inflection attracted the attention of both his sup-porters and critics. Ultimately his report could be, and was, read less as "a case for national action" than a rebuke of black America's deficiencies and an injunction for self-help. Given this public reception, even black leaders such as King and Young, who had welcomed Johnson's speech initially, soon turned critical of the government's stance.

By late August, Johnson had retreated from the policy initiative he had embraced so passionately and boldly at Howard in June, especially after the Watts rebellion in Los Angeles required the National Guard to restore order after thirty-four were left dead, nine hundred injured, and thirty-five hundred arrested. Some in the press seized on the outbreak to underscore the emerging theme of black dysfunction and irresponsibility. Those charges would soon overtake the administration's war on poverty as well, especially as the program came to be associated with the black urban poor rather than the many white and rural recipients of OEO services as originally conceived. Johnson's proposed federal poverty expenditures were now suspect, being portrayed as undeserved rewards for lawlessness and laziness. The White House conference Johnson had announced for the fall as a bold first step "to fulfill these rights" was put off until the following spring, for which the autumn meeting would be merely a planning session. Meanwhile, the White House worked to dampen the controversy: packing the council overseeing arrangements for the spring conference with more businessmen than civil rights leaders, deleting discussions of the black family as such from the agenda, and managing plenary discussions so as to produce the least dissent. Although present at these meetings, Moynihan was reduced to watching in virtual silence as his presence was mostly ignored and his report systematically repudiated.

By then, Johnson had more serious distractions from the now-murky domestic politics of poverty. The debate over civil rights and social policy transpired as his administration slipped into a fateful decision about the conflict in Vietnam. Having decided on a gradual escalation of America's military engagement early in the previous year, Johnson reluctantly approved a bombing campaign against North Vietnam during the first three months of 1965, followed by the quiet introduction of American combat troops. By August, the nation was deeply and fatally engaged, having dispatched 125,000 men to Vietnam in July, with many thousands more destined to fight and die there over the next decade. The new war policy necessarily shifted the administration's budget priorities, despite denials to the contrary. That month, Johnson asked Congress for a supplemental appropriation of $1.7 billion to prosecute the war through the next fiscal year, bringing the total for that year to $5 billion. The cost would double the following year and reach $33 billion in 1968. Meanwhile, OEO's budget never exceeded $1.8 billion, roughly 1.5 percent of the total federal budget. By early 1968, the war in Vietnam had forced Johnson to renounce any ambition for reelection, and his "war on poverty" lay in tatters.

. . .

The fragile consensus blacks had managed in sustaining the Movement's broad goals, which had enabled their relative unity through the critical campaigns of the early 1960s, had also begun to fray following the achievement of voting rights. It is certainly possible that the "culture of poverty" thesis that Moynihan's report advanced might have drawn less attention had it not clashed with grievances already building among younger Movement activists and the restiveness of black communities in the urban North. Finding integration irrelevant to their own circumstances and nonviolence incomprehensible, many residents of black urban communities were drawn increasingly to the nationalist rhetoric of Malcolm X. Many of the younger southern activists, having reached an obvious turning point in the freedom struggle by the mid-1960s, were also attracted to Malcolm's powerful rhetoric and charismatic personality.

Born in Omaha, Nebraska, in 1925 and reared in rural Michigan, Malcolm Little had been rescued from a life of street hustling and petty crime by Elijah Muhammad's Nation of Islam, then just one among many religious sects spawned by northern black urban communities during the interwar years. Although largely apolitical and the object of derision by most blacks throughout its first three decades, Muhammad's group was growing rapidly by the mid-1950s, recruiting in prisons and pool halls and making astute use of the black radio stations that proliferated in the postwar era to broadcast its message of white deviltry and black redemption. Malcolm (now "Malcolm X") had emerged as the Nation's most charismatic and articulate spokesman by the late 1950s, although he was still relatively unknown among black Americans nationally. By 1963, however, he had largely eclipsed the titular leader, Elijah Muhammad, whose message and style struck most younger blacks as frankly irrelevant, if not somewhat comic. Malcolm, by contrast, had moved well beyond Muhammad's fantastic separatist myth about "white devils" created in test tubes by an evil genius. While referencing Muhammad in deferential asides, Malcolm began to frame the black condition and prospect for resistance as part of the rising tide of third world mobilizations. Conversion to Islam was as much a political as a religious act because it allied African Americans with others who contested white American and European hegemony. In that context, as he explained with biting sarcasm in his 1963 speech "Message to the Grass Roots," black Americans' nonviolent "revolution" for racial integration was not only exceptional but highly suspect. Drinking from the same water fountain or sitting on the same toilet were not exactly revolutionary goals, Malcolm sneered. Everywhere else in the world, revolutions were violent and intent on seizing power.

Malcolm's caricature of the Movement struck a chord not only among a northern black public that had largely been spectators to the dramas unfolding in the South but among some of its southern activists. Most northern blacks knew even less about the origins and real character of the southern protests than Malcolm. They knew the recent visual "sound bites" of black supplicants succumbing to white terror, not the protracted struggles against economic deprivation and political suppression that preceded them by many decades, and which were the demonstrators' ultimate targets. Distant northern black audiences seethed in anger at what they saw, but could not resist perhaps some feeling of contempt for the seemingly docile victims of that violence. King's flowing rhetoric gave the impression, moreover, that all Movement activists embraced the nonviolent discipline as a moral creed and imperative rather than simply a necessary and expedient tactic. Their only realistic choice had been either nonviolent action or no action at all. They chose to act.

In fact, armed self-defense of black communities and civil rights workers had long been a practice among southern black folk, despite censure from some northern-based civil rights organizations. These cautious leaders were right to fear that publicizing the quiet arming of SNCC and CORE "safe houses" and offices in Mississippi and Louisiana, or the mobilization of local folk to protect them, would not have been helpful to their larger campaign. Nonetheless, by the mid-1960s, many veteran activists, having embraced nonviolence earlier as a tactical expedient rather than a faith, now found their original hopeful optimism worn down by a growing list of martyrs and began looking to alternative models of popular liberation in Africa and Latin America. In February 1965, Malcolm X was added to their list of martyrs, notwithstanding strong suspicions that his assassination was actually at the hands of his former comrades in the Nation of Islam. Within a year of his death, two of the five principal civil rights organizations, SNCC and CORE, had repudiated integration as a goal. Black liberation could be achieved, they insisted, only through "black power."

Far more than either contemporaries or historians have recognized, the militants' embrace of separatism resonated with the emerging mainstream narrative of racial difference and separation. President Johnson's allusion to blacks constituting a nation apart was a metaphor that otherwise disparate voices could embrace and turn to radically different ends. Black Americans' social condition, cultural makeup, and worldview were different from those of white Americans, numerous social surveys, opinion polls, analysts, and activists seemed to attest. Moynihan's dissection of the deep historical dysfunction of the black family that allegedly fostered "a culture of poverty" provided an exclamation point to like-minded scholarship and underscored the foreboding image of "the ghetto" that proliferated in both academic and popular media. Movies, television dramas, and the evening news popularized the notion that Watts and other urban rebellions had confirmed a fundamental racial disjuncture in the national fabric. The core black nationalist message—that African Americans should seek to empower themselves as a "nation within the nation"—was not, then, so far-fetched conceptually, even if it proved politically naïve.

Certainly, the idea that black Americans suffered from the deprivation of mainstream cultural values (or were "culturally deprived") could be—was perhaps bound to be—flipped to invest cultural differences with more positive valences, especially given that mainstream culture was then being relentlessly discredited by the brutal war being waged in Vietnam. During the 1960s, many young civil rights workers had encountered the rural black culture of the Deep South for the first time, and like young Jean Toomer a half century earlier, they had emerged with a new frame of reference for their analysis of the dominant culture. During the Mississippi Summer Project of 1964, more than two thousand students in twenty communities had attended the "Freedom Schools" that SNCC and CORE set up to provide both compensatory education to children neglected by the state's segregated school system and to acquaint them with "a usable past" that might instill the racial pride that their parents seemed to lack. Eventually SNCC produced a black history primer, which like the readers missionaries taught from in the schools they set up for freedpeople after the Civil War, provided accessible texts festooned with heroes and heroines from black history, with the Haitian Revolution occupying a privileged space in some texts alongside domestic challenges to the racial order. Students were taught to appreciate black music and its relevance to contemporary struggles. They read the poetry of Langston Hughes and wrote and recited their own. Meanwhile, Gilbert Moses, John O'Neal, and Doris Derby founded the Free Southern Theater (FST) to bring similar cultural enrichment to adults in the larger community. Just weeks before the MFDP boarded buses for Atlantic City, the FST toured scores of Mississippi communities with its production of Martin Duberman's *In White America*, a virtual illuminated history of African Americans from the slave trade to the 1957 Little Rock crisis, the script drawn from actual documents and speeches. Described by a Freedom School teacher in Fannie Lou Hamer's Ruleville as "woven out of the very stuff of these people's lives," the play drove home the point that the cultural sphere was important to the Movement's larger political goals. Cultural self-awareness was a necessary first step to political action. African American culture could be "a counterhegemonic force."

Following the rebellion in Watts, Ron Karenga formed US, an organization that embraced black cultural revitalization as its principal political agenda. Having done graduate work in African studies at UCLA, Karenga urged blacks to think of themselves as an African people who just happened to be in America. The members of US (as opposed to "THEM," or alternatively parsed as "United Slaves") adopted Swahili names, wore African clothing, embraced an elaborate "African" value system, and substituted an African harvest festival, Kwanzaa, for Christmas. A year later, while Karenga was touting racial salvation through cultural nationalism in Los Angeles, Huey P. Newton was founding the Black Panther Party in Oakland on radically different principles. Incited by the police brutality that was endemic to black communities nationally, the Panthers were committed to a hard politics of armed self-defense, modeling themselves less on a mythic African past than a romantic vision of contemporary third world revolutions. Sporting black berets and bandoleers, the Panthers cut dashing figures, black Che Guevaras who won over fascinated (and intimidated) white and black middle-class romantics and black ghetto youth. Behind the theatrical facade, the organization—or at least its female members—developed an impressive array of grass-roots service programs, including free breakfasts and medical care for poor children, which won over more circumspect adult ghetto residents. The Panthers employed culture as a political weapon much like Karenga's US, but they were not separatists; they leavened their Garvey and Malcolm X with Mao and

Marx—or vice versa. Differences over turf as much as ideology eventually brought the Panthers into violent conflict with US: a shootout in a UCLA student cafeteria in January 1969 left two Panthers dead. The Panthers promoted decidedly different cultural politics than Karenga's. With bureaucratic pomp Garvey might have envied, they appointed a "minister of culture," Emory Douglas, whose illustrations and cartoons were published in the *Black Panther* newspaper with the intent of fashioning "a protest aesthetic." In Douglas's imagery, African Americans were sketched in the hard lines of black proletarian fantasy rather than the flowing robes of an African elsewhere; nonetheless, the idea of cultural otherness, a nation apart, was just as inescapable.

Ironically, the trope of black cultural deprivation and difference evolved at precisely the moment of a historic convergence of black and white cultural expression. Black culture burst onto the American cultural mainstream during the 1960s and '70s. Within a short time, African American popular music and dance had become for much of the rest of the world the face and signature of American culture. African American musicians opened the door to African and Caribbean infusions into the world music scene. Internationally, African American music soon became the veritable soundtrack of everyday life.

There were nineteenth- and early-twentieth-century roots of this integration of African American forms and themes into the national and international cultural mainstream: the touring gospel choirs formed immediately after emancipation, the black minstrel troupes of the 1890s, the triumph of ragtime at the turn of the century and of the Harlem Renaissance in the 1920s. More recently, however, black cultural recognition and distribution had been enhanced by an unlikely source: the federal government decided in the early 1950s to deploy jazz and the blues as its "secret weapon" in the cold war. Just a month before Rosa Parks's fateful encounter in Montgomery, the State Department approved a tour of the Middle East by Louis Armstrong's band. Angered by Eisenhower's handling of the school desegregation crisis in Little Rock, Arkansas, in 1957, Armstrong declined that first invitation but accepted subsequent tours. A stream of other jazz musicians would follow him over the coming decade, including most of the major black and white musical talent in America, such as John "Dizzy" Gillespie and Duke Ellington.

All these developments coincided with the rapid commercialization of musical performance more generally, which would prove crucial to the explosion of black cultural expression and creativity. Sports spectatorship, record sales, movies, radio, and television—all enjoyed technical innovations and audience growth that revolutionized the cultural landscape, and blacks were at the center of these developments. Jackie Robinson had integrated the ranks of Major League Baseball in 1947; by 1983, blacks constituted 30 percent of the major leagues and remained for the rest of the century at roughly one fifth of its players. The black presence in Major League Football and Basketball that year was even more impressive (61.5 and 72 percent, respectively). In most of the country in the mid-1950s, one needed to dial to a black radio station to find black music, and one rarely glimpsed black personalities on television—at least few who were not accused of having committed some crime. Except for the productions with all-black casts that flourished in the late 1940s and early '50s, black roles in movies seldom ventured beyond servants and comic stereotypes. Between 1968 and 1990, however, black musicians claimed an average of 20 percent of the annual number one singles recorded in America compared with just 8 percent during the previous thirteen years, 1955 through 1967. Their share of gold (and later platinum) record albums was even more impressive. By the early 1970s, the faces on American televisions had darkened, and black comedian Bill Cosby had the top-rated show. The revolution in music and popular culture paralleled developments in literature, the visual arts, and academic scholarship. Those who had come of age before the Second World War scarcely recognized the world that the Civil Rights Movement had wrought.

Given the depth and breadth of the changes in black America's cultural relation to white America, one can understand the failure of most observers to notice an equally profound cultural transformation that culminated in the 1960s: the integration of the two regional cultures of black America. For the first time since their arrival on the continent, black Americans inhabited a single cultural world with a common cultural repertoire. Just decades earlier, northern blacks sojourning in the South—such as Du Bois, Jean Toomer, or Zora Neale Hurston—would have found a black culture that was unfamiliar and exotic. The northward migration of southern talent, the now-common template of urban life, the technological diffusion of expressive instruments and forms, the blending of regional musical styles—all these developments created a common repertoire

across otherwise disparate spaces, for which older regional stylistic variations were now merely the spice. By the late twentieth century, then, African American cultural workers had achieved the dual task of melding
two regional cultures into one while at the same time making black culture the template for the nation's cultural identity.

Even as African Americans moved—oftentimes quite literally—out of the
cultural ghetto to conquer the world of music, the simultaneous cultural
turn in the world of politics was fostering a much narrower focus. In striking contrast with the strategic thrust of the mature Civil Rights Movement
in the early 1960s, black nationalists and Black Power advocates set their
sights on local goals, focusing on particular cities and sometimes even on
particular neighborhoods within those cities. Poverty programs and may-
oral campaigns may well have reinforced these tendencies. The key institutional embodiment of the poverty war were the community action
agencies, or CAPS, that formed in cities and rural districts to coordinate
and administer a diverse range of projects. During the 1950s, the Ford
Foundation had funded experimental projects to explore ways to address
the growing problem of juvenile delinquency. Although originally empha-
sizing research and interventions by social workers, some of the leading
programs—such as New York City's Mobilization for Youth—soon switched
to organizing the poor to confront the welfare, housing, and education
bureaucracies. This became the model for OEO's community action programs, which meant that they quickly found themselves at odds with
big-city mayors, who resented the challenges to their authority and the
competition for both federal funding and the political allegiance of local
communities.

The unequal contest for federal support sometimes overlapped with
electoral contests for control of city hall, which further reinforced the
characteristically local orientation of political movements during the late
1960s and '70s. Mass mobilizations of black voters to elect mayors and
other local officials and to seize control of schools and their curricula
erupted in several major cities. Some of the early movements were no
doubt encouraged by the voting rights victory of the mid-1960s. A less favorable climate for new legislative initiatives at the federal level also likely
pushed activists toward locally based initiatives. Certainly, given growing

black population pluralities and increased militancy, reform at the local level may simply have seemed a more plausible strategy.

In any case, the inward gaze gave renewed prominence to self-help initiatives more generally. Self-help had long been part of the repertoire of tools for uplift in black communities, of course, but the old ideas were now infused with themes of cultural revitalization. The fact that many such groups loudly disavowed outside "white" support or control neatly aligned them with the nationalist message. Contrary to their billing, such initiatives did in fact depend on external sources of funding, whether federal or private. After 1968, however, with the election of President Richard M. Nixon, self-help advocates gained a powerful supporter in the White House. Given a paper-thin victory over Hubert Humphrey, Nixon entered office to confront a Democratic-controlled Congress and liberal groups thoroughly mobilized to resist retrenchment of the Great Society. During his first term, therefore, Nixon's policy initiatives were crafted to preempt and redirect liberal policies, such as welfare reform, affirmative action, and social services. Nixon had campaigned on a promise of restoring "law and order," an ambiguous phrase that might reference sup-pression of civil rights demonstrations as well as urban rioting. Once in office, he sought to deflect suspicions of his hostility to the civil rights agenda, however, by advancing programs ostensibly aimed at fostering black capitalist enterprises. Although most Movement leaders kept their distance from Nixon's overtures, some nationalist-oriented black leaders embraced them. The president's program might have seemed consistent with their own, but his ultimate objective was to foster a new Republican coalition formed around suburban whites, white southerners, and disaf-fected members of the white working class. Rather than a straightforward battle between distinct camps, therefore, the Machiavellian politics of the Nixon years reinforced the ongoing fragmentation among black activists and underscored a complex interplay of themes and forces. The initially strong shift to self-help initiatives and nationalist themes ultimately faltered in this environment, as demonstrated by the heroic, but ultimately futile, efforts of Jesse Gray in Harlem and Leon Sullivan in Philadelphia.

Gray burst onto the national scene when he led a series of rent strikes in Harlem in the mid-1960s. By that time, like his sometime associate Malcolm X, he had rejected integration and grown skeptical of alliances with white middle-class reformers, notwithstanding the fact that the roots of his early political formation were in postwar leftist politics. A native of Louisiana who had served in the U.S. Merchant Marine during World War II, Gray had been an organizer for the National Maritime Union until the anticommunist purges of the McCarthy era. His work with the American Labor Party gave Gray experience during the early 1950s organizing a tenants' union in Harlem, which he put to use when he organized a rent strike protesting tenement living conditions that had contributed to a young boy's death in 1959. The strikers demanded enforcement of building codes, garbage pickups, and rat abatement programs. Their protests peaked in late 1963 and early 1964, when Gray and CORE organized two hundred buildings under the banner "No Heat, No Rent." Energized by demonstration tactics such as dumping dead rats in courtrooms, the Harlem strikers inspired imitators in Cleveland, Chicago, and other cities. Organizing poor, vulnerable, often transient tenants, however, proved every bit as difficult in some respects as mobilizing farm laborers in Mississippi. Victories were temporary and limited in scope; defeats were frequent. Substantial gains were made only after young lawyers from the new Legal Services Program funded by OEO entered the fray and mounted a sustained legal assault on landlord practices.

The political formation of West Virginia native Leon Sullivan tracks closer to Martin Luther King's trajectory than Malcolm X's, but he, too, ended up embracing a political orientation that shared some features of the economic and social conservatism that characterized nationalist thinking. While Jesse Gray was organizing tenants, Sullivan was assuming the pulpit of Zion Baptist in North Philadelphia, following a brief stint as Congressman Adam Clayton Powell, Jr.'s assistant pastor at Harlem's Abyssinian Baptist Church. Sullivan's political apprenticeship included work with A. Philip Randolph's March on Washington Movement in the 1940s, community work on juvenile delinquency, and protests against housing discrimination in the 1950s. In 1960, he had organized picketing of a local Woolworth in sympathy with the Greensboro sit-ins. In March 1960, Sullivan convened fifteen ministers to undertake a selective patronage campaign aimed at job discrimination in Philadelphia. His group won significant employment concessions from several major enterprises in Philadelphia, and by early 1963, groups had formed in several other cities seeking to emulate its model of quiet coercion and negotiation. Among them was King's SCLC, which consulted with Sullivan in the fall of 1962 before launching boycotts in several cities and eventually dispatching a young Jesse Jackson to organize "Operation Breadbasket" in Chicago.

Sullivan himself soon realized, however, that black unemployment could not be addressed solely through attacks on job discrimination. An inadequate public education system and exclusion from union apprenticeship programs left blacks structurally disadvantaged in a rapidly automating labor force. Early in 1964, Sullivan opened the first Opportunities Industrialization Center (OIC) to provide compensatory education and skills training for the unemployed. Funded initially by the Ford Foundation and later by OEO, the OIC worked closely with major businesses to design training programs and to place its graduates. With their emphasis on industrial training and the promotion of black business enterprises, OIC programs evolved to resemble a mid-twentieth-century echo of Booker T. Washington's agenda in the early 1900s. Indeed, by the early 1970s, Sullivan had been drawn into a tacit alliance with President Richard M. Nixon, who was then making support for black capitalism the core of his civil rights initiatives. Although Sullivan rejected the term "black capitalism," insisting that black businesses had to compete in the same economy as white businesses, he avidly embraced the idea of fostering black-owned enterprises as a solution to black unemployment. In 1972, Sullivan was appointed to the board of directors of General Motors, where he would later play a leading role in crafting a compromise allowing American companies to do business with the apartheid regime in South Africa. By that time the petty capitalist enterprises set up by Philadelphia's OIC had all failed.

Sullivan can hardly be faulted for the unhappy ending of the Philadelphia story. None of the alternative initiatives successfully addressed the broader structural issues underpinning black exclusion from the job market, either. Philadelphia was but one among many cities undergoing a racial reallocation of jobs and economic resources. In America's apartheid regime, the inner cities came to resemble mirror images of South African Bantustans, sites of deprivation encircled by outer suburban rings of racial privilege. Ironically, Philadelphia industries had been among the pioneers of such developments. Practically contemporaneous with the onset of apartheid in South Africa in 1948, US Steel decided in 1951 to locate a plant in Bucks

County and hired William Levitt to build one of his patented housing complexes for the company's workers. Given Levitt's racial policies, none of the twenty thousand homes he built was available to a prospective black employee. The pattern of jobs migrating to the suburbs was similar in other major cities during the postwar period and embraced retail and wholesale as well as industrial enterprises; as a result, "79 percent of [all] employment growth between 1959 and 1967 occurred outside city limits." By the early 1970s the central city's share of the total industrial jobs in the country's twelve largest metropolitan areas "dropped from 66.1 percent in 1947 to less than 40 percent in 1970." Residential apartheid and economic deprivation went hand in hand. The racial asymmetry of Philadelphia provides a graphic illustration: 85 percent of its black population increase since the 1940s had taken place in its inner city, while 96 percent of white population growth had been in its suburbs.

The federal government's role in housing policy—contradictory, weak, and complicit—had not been helpful in staying these trends. Although a Supreme Court decision in 1948 (*Shelley v. Kraemer*) had outlawed enforcement of racial covenants designed to keep black purchasers out of white neighborhoods, the Federal Housing Administration had continued its overt support of such practices until 1950. Recognizing the federal government's own substantial involvement in the housing market, on November 20, 1962, President Kennedy had issued an executive order barring such discrimination, only to see it languish because of lax enforcement. Meanwhile, the government's own decisions to authorize construction of public housing in black neighborhoods reinforced the trend toward segregated housing. Remedies for racial discrimination in housing badly lagged behind action on public accommodations; for example, programs of mortgage insurance were exempt from the Civil Rights Act of 1964.

Unlike in the southern Movement, racial discrimination in housing had long been one of the principal targets of northern civil rights protests. Jesse Gray was embroiled in open-housing protests, for example, long before he turned his attention to improving housing in the Harlem ghetto. In May 1961, there was a "Freedom Ride" in Chicago coinciding with the one in the South that month; twenty-five hundred blacks from the Woodlawn Organization boarded forty-six buses and headed to city hall to demand jobs and better housing. Black Chicagoans had also engaged in protests against unequal education since 1962, which peaked in the spring of 1965 with hundreds arrested at the city's Board of Education. It became increasingly apparent that housing discrimination was at the root of educational inequality and job discrimination, and the ensuing struggles for open housing made Chicago the site of some of the most intense and violent encounters in the country.

Given this history, when Martin Luther King, Jr., sought in 1966 to bring the southern-style Movement north, he was necessarily drawn onto the unfamiliar terrain of open-housing protests. After renting a small apartment on Chicago's West Side, King went about organizing protest marches and mass meetings like those that had sustained the southern mobilizations, but he met with only limited success. Rioting in July underlined the resistance of urban black youth to his pleas for nonviolence. A series of open-housing marches in white working-class neighborhoods from July through late August made it clear that urban whites were even less amenable to nonviolent appeals. The city administration stonewalled and offered only weak concessions, but these were accepted, allowing King to cover the project's failure with a strategic retreat.

Shortly thereafter, King shifted his attention to the broader problem of poverty, which culminated in the Poor People's Campaign he was in the process of mobilizing just before his assassination on April 4, 1968. In the wake of his death, Congress finally passed a Fair Housing Act, but without effective means of enforcement. The results were predictable. As one careful survey of racial housing patterns has concluded, "The only urban areas where significant desegregation occurred during the 1970s were those where the black population was so small that integration could take place without threatening white preferences for limited contact with blacks." In 1980, Chicago remained the most segregated city in America: "two societies, one black and one white—separate and unequal."

Suburbs, shopping malls, and highways hardened the spatial and institutional distances between black and white America. In popular and political discourse, black America became synonymous with "the inner city" or simply "the cities," supposed enclaves of poverty, crime, and welfare dependency. Although thoroughly routed in their battle against the equal rights campaigns of the 1960s, white racial reactionaries found in these developments new targets and a new voice. They would no longer oppose "equal rights" but simply "special rights," not government interventions to uphold the courts and the Constitution but government "giveaways" to an idle and criminal class. Among their principal targets were the income supports provided to poor women and their children through Aid to Families with Dependent Children. AFDC had been the part of the Social Security Act of 1935 that subsidized grants-in-aid by state and local authorities to support unemployed single parents. Although most recipients were white, the proportion of blacks receiving aid grew with their increased presence and immiseration in northern cities. By 1961, blacks made up 40 to 73 percent of the total welfare recipients in six northern cities. By that year, welfare had emerged as not simply a public policy issue but a racial one. Efforts were made to strengthen residency requirements to discourage the in-migration of the impoverished residents of other (mostly southern) states, to cut off unmarried child-bearing women recipients, and to deny aid when there was an able-bodied man in the house, all of which produced a web of administative rules and practices that humiliated recipients and made being "on welfare" a shameful social status.

Contrary to the image of welfare cheats and "queens" fostered by conservative politicians, many women became dependent on public assistance reluctantly, and all chafed at the indignities of the system. Some chose to fight that system. Among them was Johnnie Tillmon. Born into an Arkansas sharecropping family, Tillmon had left the farm for Little Rock when she was eighteen years old. There she held a series of menial service jobs, married, and had five children. After divorcing her husband, she moved to Los Angeles in 1960 and found work ironing shirts. She eventually became shop steward of her laundry workers' local, but an injury and hospitalization forced her to quit working. Being the sole supporter of six dependents (having borne another child out of wedlock), she swallowed her pride and accepted welfare. She felt shame upon cashing her first check, which was just half of what she had earned previously. Worse yet was the humiliation of enduring verbal abuse from social workers and having her bedroom searched for signs of "a man in the house." Finding other women who shared similar experiences, she organized with them a local support group and they began fashioning a collective response to their treatment, demanding that their ostensible welfare "benefactors" respect their rights under the law.

Johnnie Tillmon's organization was one of many local groups that formed in the mid-1960s. In 1966, aided by the crucial organizational skills of George Wiley, a former head of CORE in Syracuse, New York, they founded the National Welfare Rights Organization (NWRO) and began a struggle that revolutionized the system of public assistance. Running counter to the self-help, nationalist, and localist trends of the late 1960s and early '70s, the welfare rights mobilization was a biracial movement aimed at achieving national reform through local grass-roots action. Between June 1966 and June 1967, the NWRO launched demonstrations in at least thirty-four cities across the country, placing welfare issues more firmly on the anti-poverty/civil rights agenda than they ever had before.

As with Jesse Gray's tenants' rights campaign, the Legal Services Program funded by the federal poverty program (OEO) provided critical support to the NWRO's struggle for welfare rights, earning it the enmity of then-governor of California Ronald Reagan and many other conservative politicians. In one of its class-action suits, *Goldberg v. Kelly*, the U.S. Supreme Court ruled that welfare was not a gratuity but a right. Given that social policy analysts had long recognized transfer payments to the unemployed as one of the more efficient ways of alleviating poverty, the expansion of eligibility and levels of assistance payments was a legitimate and, some argued, more effective means of fighting poverty. And on those terms the NWRO enjoyed considerable success. By 1971, 90 percent of eligible families were receiving AFDC, and the total served reached 10.1 million by 1974. It was perhaps a concession to the strength of the welfare rights movement that during his first term, even President Richard Nixon embraced the idea of income maintenance for the unemployed and working poor. At the urging of Patrick Moynihan, now a key adviser to the Republican president, Nixon endorsed the liberal idea of a guaranteed annual income and proposed that a Family Assistance Program (FAP) replace AFDC, albeit with lower payments than under the current welfare system. Encountering resistance from both the left and the right in Congress, he abandoned the effort by 1970, setting the stage for his reelection campaign in 1972, which embraced a full-scale attack against welfare instead. Thereafter the issue became a principal item of the Republican platform until the program was radically revised in the spring of 1996, with new limitations on eligibility and a work requirement.

Thus, although NWRO achieved reforms that improved the lives and enhanced the dignity of millions of women demeaned by a brutal and racist system, the movement may, nonetheless, have inadvertently reinforced the seeming "otherness" of blacks as a people and a culture. More than forty years after they had stood before Lincoln's Memorial demanding simply "Jobs and Freedom," African Americans found themselves etched in the nation's political discourse as victims not of unprecedented economic transformations but of their own inner deficits—a separate class, a separate culture, a nation apart.

A New Economy, a New Politics

By 1980, the motif of two unequal nations was being applied as readily to the class divisions emerging among black Americans as to the divide between black and white. By almost every measure, the 1950s and '60s had witnessed the greatest expansion of the black middle class in American history. America transitioned from an industrial to a service economy just as black Americans moved out of agriculture and into urban industrial and white-collar employment, developments that were at once complementary and contradictory.

The third quarter of the "American century" witnessed phenomenal economic growth in corporate earnings and individual incomes, notwithstanding a recession and periodic slumps in the business cycle. The nation's economic growth rate averaged 4.1 percent during the 1960s, and its corporations earned an average annual real rate of return of 15.5 percent in the decade's early years. With the unemployment rate falling below 4 percent during the last four years of that decade, the average family had one third more real income in 1970 than in 1960.

Behind this overall prosperity, however, the American economy was undergoing a radical and historic transformation. In 1947, more than half the nation's labor force had worked to produce material goods for the market; by 1968, 64 percent were producing services instead. By 1960, almost one of every eight American workers held a government job; ten years later the ratio was closer to one of every six. Among black workers the shift was even more dramatic. Blacks entering the work force found themselves heavily concentrated in public services. For Mamie Bradley's and

Rosa Parks's generation, state and federal civil service employment had provided the great breakthrough to middle-class status, one begun well before the dramatic civil rights gains of the mid-1960s. The pattern accelerated thereafter, however, and would endure through the rest of the century. The job categories in which white-collar employment among blacks were distributed shifted dramatically: whereas teachers and the clergy had together made up almost half (46 percent) of such employees in 1940, they constituted just 28 percent in 1980, their former dominance shrunken by a rapidly expanding black managerial class. The sectoral sources of black income continued, nonetheless, to evolve in the same direction through the final decade of the century: by 1995 more than half of all black professionals were working in the public sector.

Black workers gradually gained a small share of the high-wage union jobs in the postwar economy, however. No doubt Simon Owens would have been surprised to find that by 1987, one of every four autoworkers was black and that the proportion of black workers belonging to unions (22.6 percent) was actually greater than that of whites (16.3 percent). Read differently, however, these figures reveal that unions' overall share of the American work force was declining. The nation's economic boom had petered out by the late 1960s, with corporate earnings averaging 12.7 percent for nonfinancial enterprises and falling further to 10.1 percent during the early 1970s; the oil crisis of 1974 would delay recovery for some time after that. The decline was uneven, of course, but many of the areas hit hardest were those to which blacks had migrated in the greatest numbers earlier in the century. Meatpacking had already disappeared from Chicago's West Side during the late 1950s, taking with it one quarter of the United Packinghouse Workers' national membership. Even with auto production breaking new records, Detroit had lost 140,000 workers between 1947 and 1963. Everywhere, large retail operations moved to suburban malls at roughly the same time as they began begrudgingly opening jobs to black clerical help. Between 1969 and 1976, northeastern states lost more jobs than they created; and although the Midwest figures were more positive overall, the region still lost more than ten million jobs.

The situation would grow worse during the decades that followed. In a stretch of time from January 1979 to December 1980, domestic automakers shut down 20 facilities employing 50,000 workers. The effects on their suppliers were even greater, with estimates of job losses ranging from

350,000 to 650,000. The accelerating automation of skilled labor and the relocation of entire factories to low-wage zones in the anti-union American Sun Belt or to foreign countries were the main culprits churning this regional upheaval. During the decade 1957–67, a third of U.S. transportation equipment plants moved abroad. Meanwhile, Philadelphia's largest employer, the Philco radio and television plant, which had long confined black men to menial jobs and refused to employ any blacks alongside white women, was finally forced to concede to fair employment practices— just as it was contemplating moving to suburban Bucks County. Sometime later, it sent the bulk of its operations out of the country entirely.

Whether in white-collar or union jobs, therefore, blacks found themselves the late-arriving guests as the feast for an expanding American middle class was ending. The rapid and impressive growth of the black middle class within a decade of the bloody clash on the Edmund Pettus Bridge in Selma had secured the fondest hopes of the Civil Rights Movement, but by the final decade of the century it had become clear how precarious that progress was. Even in the mid-1960s, a number of civil rights leaders were well aware that deeper structural changes were already under way that could rob the newfound freedom of its material substance. They had worried—as had Johnson and Moynihan, it must be conceded— that winning the immediate battle against racial prejudice would not ensure victory against a historic injury: their economic dispossession. They had placed their hopes on government intervention to right that history.

Indeed, if during the last quarter of the twentieth century blacks had received government support comparable to that given white Americans during the first twenty-five years after the Second World War, they might have been better positioned to weather the economic shocks and political backlash of that period. A relatively recent creation itself, the greatly expanded white middle class had gotten a head start from government subsidies to higher education and homeownership and had been sustained by an expanding postwar economy together with strong union protection of their income gains, health care, and pensions. The rapid creation and transmission of real and personal assets in these years was truly unprecedented— for whites. When the inevitable downturn came, rising home values cushioned both middle- and lower-middle-class white families from the diverse shocks of the economic cycle, while providing them the means to continue funding higher education for their children. Public policies, such as favorable tax treatment of homeownership, further underwrote what in retrospect became a massive racial bonus.

The vast majority of black Americans missed out on these subsidies to middle-class formation, and many of those who managed against the odds to achieve middle-class wages and social status confronted negative restraints on their capacity to keep them, or to create and transmit to their children the real assets that constitute wealth. Concurrent with the decline in black farm ownership, a segregated housing market shortchanged urban black homeowners, whose property was systematically devalued. The real returns they received were much less than those of white homeowners, and sometimes even negative because of falling property values in racially marked neighborhoods. All of this deprived them of the passive savings that might have underwritten higher education for their children or loans to those children for the purchase of their first homes. As a consequence, blacks would continue to be more dependent than whites on public subsidies for higher education and thus vulnerable to growing restrictions on their social mobility.

In sum, given the broad economic transformation under way during the mid-twentieth century—deindustrialization and global reallocations of labor—those black industrial workers fortunate enough to have made it into the middle class had a precarious hold on that status. The situation of those in white-collar occupations, which were heavily concentrated in the public sector, was also precarious because public jobs were vulnerable to political as well as economic retrenchment. The conservative political resurgence that began in the 1970s and triumphed with the election of Ronald Reagan in 1980 made government spending on social services and the public payroll special targets. Reagan's efforts to roll back the New Deal order and to undermine the interregional, biracial political coalition that had sustained it would dominate American politics for a generation.

By the 1980s and '90s, the bold hopes many black leaders had had for transforming the nation's racial regime through a more fundamental social-democratic reform had been blunted. The alliance with progressive labor of which Bayard Rustin had dreamed proved illusory. Instead, efforts to mount effective attacks on job discrimination had turned some of the major labor unions into avowed enemies of civil rights organizations during the late 1960s and '70s, an outcome that would not have surprised either Simon Owens or Rayfield Mooty. By the 1980s, declining union membership, the intensification of residential segregation, and the racial compartmentalization of institutional life generally fostered a society badly fractured along racial lines. As diverse public opinion polls made clear, black and white Americans saw and experienced the world very differently. Conservative-led tax revolts had undermined the possibility of expanding, or even sustaining in some instances, the public services, education, or income supports that working-class blacks desperately needed. Meanwhile, black adolescent boys faced unprecedented risks of incarceration in the world's largest prison system. Given this array of challenges, it is perhaps an index of the contraction of civil rights goals and the Movement's diminished prospects that the most heated controversies now arose over affirmative action, which had heretofore been practically an afterthought on the civil rights agenda.

Precedents for the idea of making special, "affirmative" efforts to reverse the effects of a long history of overt racial discrimination can be found in government policy documents that predated the modern Civil Rights Movement. The idea was at least implicit in Franklin D. Roosevelt's executive order to increase black employment in government service and the defense industries during World War II (Executive Order 8802), and it was made explicit in the policy language of President Harry Truman's Committee on Government Contract Compliance in 1953, which urged the Bureau of Employment Security "to act positively and affirmatively" to eliminate racial bias as it carried out its various functions. Similar language can be found in President John F. Kennedy's executive order in March 1961 (Executive Order 10925) creating the Equal Employment Opportunity Commission, which was charged with taking "affirmative action" (the term borrowed from labor law) to ensure nondiscriminatory hiring for government service and in defense contracts. In September 1965, President Lyndon B. Johnson ordered the Office of Federal Contract Compliance to demand that government contractors file plans detailing the "affirmative" steps they had taken to constitute a racially diverse work force (Executive Order 11246). In most of these early policy initiatives, the mandate to take affirmative action referred to direct, self-conscious efforts to ensure that normal, business-as-usual procedures not be biased against a historically excluded group. The way pools of potential recruits were constituted, selections were made, and promotions determined should not inadvertently disadvantage racial minorities or women. With the advent of job training and other social programs in the late 1960s, the term "affirmative action" took on a meaning consistent with the metaphor of the unshackled runner Johnson had invoked in his Howard University commencement speech—that is, compensatory education and training to prepare the historically disadvantaged to compete. Given this interpretation and an expanding economy, the policy aroused relatively little controversy through the early 1970s.

The reversal of that prosperity in the mid-1970s likely accounts for much of the subsequent violent reaction and political vilification of affirmative action. Given an economy that resembled a zero-sum game rather than an expanding pie, policies of racial preference became the scapegoat for a tightening labor market and contraction of educational opportunities, especially in the very few areas of real job growth, such as those requiring university or professional education. It is also true, however, that the original notion of affirmative action as merely designed to level the playing field had undergone a subtle reorientation by the mid-seventies. Ironically, the agent of this change was the conservative stalwart President Richard M. Nixon, whose administration altered affirmative action's implementation in ways that would make it a lightning rod for the conservative reaction of the 1980s. Consistent with his first-term policy initiatives aimed at building a conservative alternative to more radical social policies, Nixon toughened affirmative action requirements in skilled trades dependent on contracts awarded to government vendors. His "Philadelphia Plan" added specific numerical goals and timetables to the affirmative action plans Johnson had required of federal contractors, and he began the practice of setting aside a portion of the government's contractual work exclusively for minority bidders, an effort to create black capitalists—and presumably thereby at least a few black Republican voters.

The new policy enjoyed some success. For example, the proportion of minorities holding construction jobs jumped from 1 to 12 percent. Public institutions and private employers opened many jobs to women as well as minorities that had hitherto been reserved for white males by rules and qualifications irrelevant to the actual work they were required to do. Height and other physical requirements had been used to exclude women and Latinos/Latinas, for example, and blacks had historically been denied jobs because they did not have access to the union apprenticeship programs that were the jobs' prerequisites.

A policy of hard targets and set-asides opened the affirmative action policies to conservative counterattack and more skeptical judicial scrutiny, however. In a pattern resembling the defense of segregation in the 1950s, systems of recruitment and selection through standardized tests that were largely postwar innovations were touted as timeless means of ensuring democratic and meritocratic reward to the most qualified applicants. Conservatives shamelessly invoked Justice Harlan's ringing dissents from the decisions that underwrote the Jim Crow regime in the late nineteenth century, when he declared that the Constitution was "color-blind." The twist conservatives gave that phrase was, in fact, more consistent with the arguments of Harlan's opponents, Justices Bradley and Brown. Recall Justice Bradley's declaration in 1883 that having already benefited from "beneficent legislation" passed after the Civil War, the freedman had reached that "stage in the progress of his elevation when he takes the rank of a mere citizen" and thus thereafter "ceases to be the special favorite of the laws." Or Justice Brown's lecturing Homer Plessy in 1896 that any notion blacks had that current arrangements were stacked against them was "solely because the colored race chooses to put that construction upon it." The election of Ronald Reagan to the presidency meant that for the first time since the mid-1930s the national government would be openly hostile to affirmative efforts to remedy racial discrimination. Reagan's administration either reversed or severely curtailed earlier affirmative action initiatives, eliminating in 1985 the goals and timetables specified in Executive Order 11246, gutting sanctions for noncompliance, and even declining to press suits to enforce the *Brown* decision.

African Americans conscious of the earlier history might well have felt a sense of déjà vu. At times the bright promise of the second Reconstruction seemed doomed to the fate of the first. Although a few black conservatives demeaned affirmative action policies, most African Americans defended them, while others simply recognized them as at best rearguard actions to hold more devastating forces at bay. On the other hand, to varying degrees, the faces in America's boardrooms, newsrooms, and universities *did* change, and the fragile, politically vulnerable black middle class *did* survive the onslaught of hostile court decisions and a sustained propaganda war to undermine their legitimacy. And yet, for large numbers of black male youth, the argument was distant if not irrelevant. They were far more likely to find themselves in a prison yard than a college classroom, and the institution most likely "to act positively and affirmatively" toward them was the American military.

Citizens of the New World

However disappointing African Americans may have found the mix of progress and regression during the final decades of the twentieth century, it was an immensely different America than the one a twenty-three-year-old Kenyan, Barack Obama, encountered when he arrived in 1959 to begin his studies at the University of Hawaii. Supported by a project originated by African independence hero Tom Mboya and funded in part by the black American media stars Harry Belafonte and Sidney Poitier, the ambitious and immensely self-confident Obama managed, within just five years of his arrival, to complete his studies at Hawaii and Harvard universities before returning to his homeland. In the meantime, he married Ann Dunham, a white woman from Kansas, who bore him an American son. They divorced two years later, when Ann discovered that Barack already had an African wife, and she raised their son alone. As that soon-to-be famous son would phrase it later, his father was among "the first large wave of Africans to be sent forth to master Western technology and bring it back to forge a new, modern Africa." Only in retrospect perhaps would this future president of the United States realize that his own destiny would be shaped, at least in part, by those subsequent waves from third world shores.

Unlike his father, these foreigners would come as permanent settlers rather than sojourners. They had been set in motion by the same Congress that had approved the Voting Rights Act in 1965. In October of that year Congress had removed the half-century-old immigration barriers that had long held such peoples at bay. Now forming the equivalent of a twentieth-century Middle Passage, nonwhite peoples from Latin America, Asia, and Africa would in time change the face and politics of America. By the time Barack Obama, Sr.'s American-born son came of age in the 1980s, it was already apparent to most observers that the white nation celebrated in Chicago's "White City" almost a century earlier was approaching its end.

Even so, the America of the 1980s was still in the grip of a fierce conservative reaction, one opposed to all that the sixties liberation movements had sought to accomplish. Black America's undeniable political progress since the confrontation in Selma two decades earlier now seemed stalled. The number of black officeholders had grown dramatically. For the generation of African Americans coming of age in the mid-1980s, however, the struggles at Montgomery, Birmingham, and Selma were stories of a distant past, told to them perhaps by their parents, read in some cases in schoolbooks, recounted each year in celebrations of Martin Luther King's birthday. Some of them might have found it difficult to link those struggles to their own lived experience. Most had finished high school, and many more would finish college than ever had before. Like the elder and younger Obama, some of them matriculated at the nation's most elite educational institutions. And, indeed, many of the black students found on Ivy League campuses were either themselves recent black immigrants or the children of immigrants; in either case they were people not only distant from the struggles of the sixties but largely unburdened by America's peculiar racial history.

By the final decade of the twentieth century, it was unclear whether America's complex and changing racial-national demography would open radical new possibilities for the political integration of blacks into the American mainstream or set new limits on that integration. The explosive growth of black political representation over the two decades following Selma had occurred mostly in electoral districts that either had black majorities or large pluralities. The consistent political solidarity of black voters assuaged fears that the emerging class divisions among them might find political expression and division. Except for a handful of loud conservative spokesmen, blacks of all social classes were exceptional in their commitment to a progressive or social-democratic agenda. It became equally evident, however, that black power at the local level offered no clear path to realizing that agenda. Black mayors elected by black majority electorates found themselves in cities where white flight had robbed them of the tax base to fund the promised reforms. The conservative backlash constrained local and federal budgets, while Reagan's "new federalism" channeled what was left through state legislatures, further reducing the amounts reaching the desperate cities. Black mayors elected in white majority districts came to power by forging coalitions of black, Latino, and white liberal constituents, which sometimes proved difficult to sustain. In fact, there were serious outbreaks of violence in the 1990s in New York and Los Angeles that pitted blacks against Jews and Koreans. Moreover, while the nation's changing demographics meant that whites would soon be in the minority, it was equally clear that blacks would be displaced as the nation's largest minority group even sooner. The color line Du Bois had prophesized as the fate of the twentieth century seemed also destined to define the twenty-first, but with a different racial articulation.

If the American political environment at the dawn of the new millennium eerily resembled that of the previous century, however, it provided reasons for optimism and moments for creative engagement as well. In the teeth of the Reagan Revolution, Harold Washington had forged a powerful coalition of blacks, Latinos, and white liberals in two successful campaigns for mayor of Chicago. Meanwhile, the Reverend Jesse Jackson had mounted two campaigns for president, in 1984 and 1988, premised on the possibility of a similar cross-racial alliance of workers and the poor. Although his campaigns failed, Jackson won a respectable white vote nonetheless, with a message of economic populism that shook the Democratic Party to its core.

Indeed, the black political effervescence that followed in the 1990s and beyond may well have owed its enduring faith in the possibility of building cross-racial alliances to Jackson's campaign. The later campaigns were led, however, by men of a very different political formation. Political professionals nurtured within the party rather than Movement activists and outsiders, these men melded insurgent, social movement tactics with an insider's political knowledge to create new political coalitions in heavily white majority districts to elect blacks to office. Thus did America's two largest cities, New York City and Los Angeles, elect David Dinkins and Tom Bradley, respectively, as their mayors, with Bradley serving five terms between 1973 and 1993. (Dinkins was defeated after one term, 1990–93.) In 1990, Douglas Wilder won the governor's office in Virginia, becoming the first black governor of a southern state since Reconstruction, and Deval Patrick was elected governor of Massachusetts in 2006. All of these electoral successes depended on a powerful turnout of black and minority voters, but they also required a respectable share of the white vote. Perhaps, these victories suggested, the nation's stubborn social apartheid did not predict an absolute political schism.

Against this immediate historical backdrop, and certainly drawing on these political trends, Barack Obama won the Democratic Party's nomination for the presidency in 2008, and the subsequent general election. Obama's campaign seemed to unhinge the conventional racial-political dynamic; he won the votes of whites of all ages, genders, and class cohorts outside the South. With a margin of roughly two to one among voters of Latin and Asian descent and practically unanimous black support, Obama won an overwhelming victory nationally while making significant in-roads in areas previously hostile to Democratic presidential candidates. He did not win the majority of the nation's white voters, but then, neither had any other Democratic presidential candidate since Lyndon Johnson signed the Voting Rights Act in 1965—predicting as he did so that his party had lost the South. In the final analysis, Obama's political calculus resembled that of the urban insurgencies of the previous decade, and both could trace their roots to 1965, when America's political demographic prospects radically changed and its twenty-first-century transformation was set in motion.

Blacks were no better prepared for Obama's breathtaking electoral successes than other Americans. Many black leaders weaned on earlier conflicts remained skeptical of Obama's "post-racial" political stance and were slow to endorse him. His insistence on casting aside old grievances and thinking anew in the brave new world of the twenty-first century was an alien message for many. What the young candidate disparaged as "the old [racial] politics" was, after all, simply the product of the nation's stubborn racial history now deeply embedded in contemporary institutions and attitudes. At the height of the Democratic primaries, when the fiery, angry sermons of his longtime pastor, the Reverend Jeremiah Wright, were widely publicized, Obama was forced to address that history directly. In a brilliant, well-received speech delivered in Philadelphia's Constitution Center, the candidate acknowledged the reality and persistence of the racial tensions gnawing at the nation's soul, while insisting that the *dominant* theme of that history has been the never-ending search for "a more perfect union."

This progressive inflection of African Americans' long history on the North American continent is undoubtedly legitimate and plausible, especially given Obama's subsequent victory the following November. Given earlier moments of euphoria followed by disheartening defeats, however, the bitter skepticism of Reverend Wright was equally legitimate and plausible.

Wright, ironically, was himself the product of a biracial and inclusive educational and political environment: he had been part of the second wave of southern migrants moving North, had served in an integrated military service during the Vietnam War, and had built up a largely black congregation on the Chicago South Side that was part of a predominantly white national religious organization. His generation, which was Emmett Till's generation, knew the nation's deep racial scars all too well. They had known the euphoria of imminent change, and the sharp disappointment when the promised change faltered and retreated. Wright's sermons tapped into that deep well of resentment, into what the black poet Langston Hughes had once called "a dream deferred." Standing on the cusp of a historic American transformation, the new "New World" of Obama's amazing campaign, it is not surprising that Wright held back—if only as self-protection—from its embrace. He was not alone.

To his credit, President-elect Obama paid homage to African America's difficult past, even as he firmly counseled turning away from it and embracing the bright future. Thus even in his moment of triumph he encouraged reflection on that past. Organizing his inaugural festivities to provide occasions for revisiting African Americans' historic journey, he set his oath of office on the Capitol's western steps, within a physical frame that invited Lincoln's gaze from the memorial at the Mall's other end. Notwithstanding his limitations and vacillations in the face of that other historic moment of truth, President Lincoln and his memorial were both now thoroughly enmeshed with African Americans' continued struggle to realize the nation's "new birth of freedom" that "The Great Emancipator" had once proclaimed.

Missing from the symbolic repertoire that day were other heroes of that struggle: W.E.B. Du Bois, who had found language to express the complex duality of being both American and African; Frederick Douglass, Lincoln's antagonist, gadfly, and ally, who had forged the foundational narrative of the African American freedom fighter and kept faith in its darkest hours; Richard Allen, exemplary of those who fiercely insisted on an American identity, while remaining sympathetic to an African redemption; and Olaudah Equiano, whose uncertain biography, with its shadowy ambivalence about his literal place in the world, oddly prefigures the experience of generations of African Americans to come. Is it merely ironic or prophetic that

America's first black president would also have his origins and nationality similarly questioned? Born biracial and raised in international settings, Barack Obama experienced a personal formation that is the essence of cosmopolitanism. On the other hand, being the direct descendant of an African father, he lived a life that literally bridged the unarticulated hyphen between "African" and "American." At once cosmopolitan and yet deeply rooted in this nation's biracial heritage, Barack Obama is, in fact, the quintessential African American—itself an identity that is complex, multi-faceted, and hammered on the anvils of historical struggles.

The men who formed the Free African societies at the moment of the nation's founding would have recognized both the complexity and the manifold implications of their descendants' struggles. One such group, founded by Absalom Jones and Richard Allen, had declared in 1787 that "Every pious man is a citizen of the world." Being African American, they seemed to say, entailed consciousness of ones multinational identities and responsibilities. More than two centuries later, probably unwittingly, Barack Obama would paraphrase their words, introducing himself to a Berlin audience as "a proud citizen of the United States and a citizen of the world."

Even the most provincially oriented African Americans have known this complexity, what Du Bois once called the "two-ness" of being a part of and yet apart from the nation; and some have realized, like Du Bois, that there is creative space as well as pain that comes with that consciousness. To be a citizen of the world, then, was not necessarily to be a cosmopolite like Equiano or Obama, but simply to recognize one's kinship with all humankind. The corollary of that kinship is the insistent claim to one's own humanity, notwithstanding a history weighted against such claims. Prefiguring Obama's salutation at Berlin in 2008 and echoing the Free African Society's proclamation in 1787, then, was the quiet demand of a proud seamstress in Montgomery, Alabama, some twelve weeks after Emmett Till's murder and a half century before President Obama's inauguration— she sought to be known and to know herself, she said, "as a human being and a citizen." Rosa Parks's words could be the epigraph of a generation. And the promise of those yet to come.

NOTES

PREFACE

xiii *"[You] are the brothers of God's preparation . . .":* Children of God's Fire: A Documen-
      tary History of Black Slavery in Brazil, ed. Robert Edgar Conrad (University Park:
      Pennsylvania State University Press, 1984), 163–74, quote on p. 165.

xiii *"[E]verything shines by perishing . . .":* "Freedom in the Air: A Documentary on Albany,
      Georgia." Produced by Alan Lomax and Guy Carawan. Recorded by Student Nonvio-
      lent Coordinating Committee, Atlanta, Georgia.

xiv   *"the ideal of human brotherhood":* W.E.B. Du Bois, *Souls of Black Folk: Essays and
      Sketches* (Chicago: McClurg, 1903), quotes on pp. 3, 4, 11.

xiv   *"the harsh discipline of Negro life":* Ralph Ellison, *Shadow and Act* (New York: Vin-
      tage, 1964), 21.

xv   *"the arc of the moral universe . . .":* The speech, delivered on August 16, 1967, in At-
      lanta, was entitled "Where Do We Go from Here?" See Martin Luther King, Jr., *A
      Call to Conscience: The Landmark Speeches of Martin Luther King, Jr.*, eds. Clayborne
      Carson and Kris Shepard (New York: Grand Central Publishing, 2002), 199.

xvi   *generational units of time:* It should be noted that my use of "generations" references
      historical "cohorts" more than biological relationships and that "intergenerational trans-
      fers" necessarily invoke the theoretical question of history's relation to memory. For
      further explorations of these topics, see Jane Pilcher, "Mannheim's Sociology of Gen-
      erations: An Undervalued Legacy," *British Journal of Sociology* 45, no. 3 (Sept. 1940),
      481–95, and Gabrielle M. Spiegel, "Memory and History: Liturgical Time and Histori-
      cal Time," *History and Theory* 41, no. 2 (May 2002), 149–62. For the idea of framing
      history from a generational perspective, especially as applied to the African American
      experience, see Ira Berlin, *Generations of Captivity: A History of African American
      Slaves* (Cambridge, Mass.: Harvard University Press, 2003) and *The Making of African
      America: The Four Great Migrations* (New York: Viking, 2010). Also of interest on this
      point is David W. Blight's *Race and Reunion: The Civil War in American Memory*
      (Cambridge, Mass.: Harvard University Press, 2001).

1. MIDDLE PASSAGES, MIDDLEMEN

3   *"About the last of August . . .":* "The Generall Historie of Virginia by Captain John
      Smith, 1624. The Fourth Book," in Lyon Gardiner Tyler, ed. *Narratives of Early Vir-*
      ginia, 1606–1625 (New York: Barnes and Noble, 1907), 337.

3   *settlement in the Carolinas:* Peter H. Wood, *Black Majority: Negroes in Colonial*
      South Carolina from 1670 through the Stono Rebellion (New York: Alfred A. Knopf,
      1974), 3–5.

3   *muster roll for March 1619:* Engel Sluiter, "New Light on the '20. And Odd Negroes'
      Arriving in Virginia, August 1619," *William and Mary Quarterly* 3rd ser., 54, no. 2 (April
      1997): 395–98.

6   *the São João Bautista:* Ibid.; John Thornton, "The African Experience of the '20. And
      Odd Negroes' Arriving in Virginia in 1619," *William and Mary Quarterly* 3rd ser., 55
      no. 3 (July 1998), 421–34.

7   *captives seized in Portuguese-sponsored wafare:* Ibid., 422.

7   *Vasconçelos also sought revenge:* Vasconçelos may also have harbored dreams of pio-
      neering an overland link with the newly established Portuguese colony in East Af-
      rica, Mozambique, to complete his nation's centuries-old quest for a shorter route to
      India. Ibid., 424.

7   *they made a bad bargain:* Among others, see Walter Rodney, *A History of the Upper*
      Guinea Coast, 1545–1800 (Oxford, UK: Clarendon Press, 1970); Walter Rodney, *How*
      Europe Underdeveloped Africa (London: Bogle-L'Ouverture Publications, 1972); Basil
      Davidson, *Black Mother: Africa and the Atlantic Slave Trade* (New York: Penguin
      Books, 1961), 40–42.

8   *"Atlantic creoles":* Ira Berlin, "From Creole to African: Atlantic Creoles and the Ori-
      gins of African-American Society in Mainland North America," *William and Mary*
      Quarterly 3rd ser., 53, no. 2 (April 1996), 251–88; Ira Berlin, *Many Thousands Gone:*
      The First Two Centuries of Slavery in North America (Cambridge, Mass.: Harvard
      University Press, 1998), 17, 25.

8   *launching explorations of Africa:* John Thornton reports that Arab sailors made the
      journey but were forced to return by an overland route, while Janet Abu-Lughod sug-
      gests that Arabs possessed the navigational knowledge to circumnavigate Africa's
      southern cape, albeit in the reverse direction, east to west. See John Thornton, *Africa*
      and Africans in the Making of the Atlantic World, 1400–1680 (Cambridge, UK: Cam-
      bridge University Press, 1992), 15–16; Janet Abu-Lughod, "The World System in the
      Thirteenth Century: Dead-End or Precursor?," in Michael Adas, ed. *Islamic and Eu-*
      ropean Expansion (Philadelphia: Temple University Press, 1993), 19.

9   *Africans did . . . make such a journey:* Ivan van Sertima, *They Came Before Colum-*
      bus (New York: Random House, 1976).

9   *a thriving African inland commerce:* Robert W. Harms, *River of Wealth, River of Sor-*
      row: The Central Zaire Basin in the Era of the Slave and Ivory Trade, 1500–1891 (New
      Haven, Conn.: Yale University Press, 1981).

9   *Chinese sailors:* Janet L. Abu-Lughod suggests also that internal crises in China shifted
      attention inward. Abu-Lughod, "The World System in the Thirteenth Century,"
      343–47; Bailey W. Diffie and George D. Winius, *Foundations of the Portuguese Em-*
      pire, 1415–1580 (Minneapolis: University of Minnesota Press, 1977), 66–67.

11   *"Charlemagne, without Mahomet":* Lyle N. McAlister, *Spain and Portugal in the*
      New World, 1492–1700 (Minneapolis: University of Minnesota Press, 1984), 11.

12   *Orders such as the Knights Templar*: Robert Bartlett, *The Making of Europe: Conquest,
      Colonization, and Cultural Change, 950–1350* (Princeton, N.J.: Princeton University
      Press, 1993), 255–67.

13   *various dynastic and religious conflicts*: Beginning in the mid-fourteenth century, the
      Hundred Years' War continued to engulf France and England, and succession crises
      continued to distract England through large parts of the following century. From
      the thirteenth through the sixteenth century, peasant rebellions spilled over into
      northern Italy, coastal Flanders, France, and Germany.

13   *"all things considered, it was already halfway there"*: Fernand Braudel, *The Perspective
      of the World, Civilization and Capitalism, 15th–18th Century*, trans. Sian Reynolds,
      3 vols., vol. 3 (New York: Harper and Row, 1979), 140.

13   *Portugal's ruling House of Aviz*: McAlister, *Spain and Portugal in the New World*,
      46–47.

13   *The moniker "Navigator"*: Peter Russell, *Prince Henry "the Navigator": A Life* (New
      Haven, Conn.: Yale University Press, 2000).

14   *Henry was "Prince Henry"*: Ibid.

14   *Captain Lançarote*: Ibid., 201.

14   *As many as twenty thousand slaves*: A. C. de C. M. Saunders, *A Social History of Black
      Slaves and Freedmen in Portugal, 1441–1555*, Cambridge Iberian and Latin American
      Studies. (New York: Cambridge University Press, 1982), 47–61.

15   *required someone to go abroad*: Philip D. Curtin, *Cross-Cultural Trade in World His-
      tory* (Cambridge, UK: Cambridge University Press, 1984), 6.

15   *"weightless"*: Braudel, *Perspective of the World*, 162.

15   *new cultural-political linkages*: The most common form of these links—in Africa
      as well as Europe and America—was kinship ties, real or fictive, and the group
      allegiances of religious minorities. See Peter Mathias, "Risk, Credit, and Kinship
      in Early Modern Enterprise," in *The Early Modern Atlantic Economy*, ed. John J.
      McCusker and Kenneth Morgan (Cambridge, UK: Cambridge University Press,
      2000), 15–35.

15   *that a deal was indeed a deal*: For a fascinating discussion of the role of religious and
      national minorities in creating modern markets, see Braudel, *Perspective*, 165–67.

15   *The earliest of these merchant cohorts*: Steven A. Epstein, *Genoa and the Genoese,
      958–1528* (Chapel Hill: University of North Carolina Press, 1996), 273–74; Charles
      Verlinden, "Italian Influence in Iberian Colonization," *Hispanic American Historical
      Review* 33, no. 2 (May 1953): 200; Virginia Rau, "A Family of Italian Merchants in
      Portugal in the XVth Century: The Lomellini," in *Studi in Onore di Armando Sapori*
      (Milano: Istituto Editoriale Cisalpino, 1957).

15   *Thus Genoa was forced to look west*: Bartlett, *The Making of Europe*, 184–85; Imman-
      uel Wallerstein, *The Modern World System I: Capitalist Agriculture and the Origins of
      the European World Economy in the Sixteenth Century* (New York: Academic Press,
      1974); Braudel, *Perspective of the World*, 141, 162, 164.

16   *The Lomellini*: Verlinden, "Italian Influence in Iberian Colonization"; Rau, "A Fam-
      ily of Italian Merchants."

17   *Aided by such middlemen*: Berlin, *Many Thousands Gone*, 21–22.

18   *joint-stock companies*: Thornton, *Africa and Africans*, 21–24, 55.

18   *Africans spoke fifty different languages*: Ibid., 186.

18   *small decentralized societies*: Walter Hawthorne, "The Production of Slaves Where

There Was No State: The Guinea-Bissau Region, 1450–1815," *Slavery and Abolition* 20, no. 2 (August 1999): 97.

19 *peoples . . . were perforce either multilingual*: To the extent that language defines mutual cultural intelligibility, the vast human diversity found on the West African coast can be aggregated into three main cultural-linguistic zones: the Mande speakers living between the Senegal River and Cape Mount in Liberia, who supplied roughly a third of British North American slaves; the people embracing the Kwa family of languages (including Akan and Igbo), who inhabited the area of modern Ghana and eastern Nigeria; and the Bantu speakers from West Central Africa, of which there were two principal subgroups, Kikongo and Kimbundu. African historian John Thornton has likened the differences between Kikongo and Kimbundi to that between Spanish and Portuguese, suggesting both a cultural difference and the mutual intelligibility that could override it. Thornton, *Africa and Africans*, 188.

19 *numbers and overall patterns of the Atlantic slave trade*: Paul E. Lovejoy, "The Impact of the Atlantic Slave Trade on Africa: A Review of the Literature," *Journal of African History* 30, no. 3 (1989), 345–54.

20 *extant shipping records*: Data drawn from "The Trans Atlantic Slave Trade Database" at www.slavevoyages.org. Also see David Eltis, et al., *Atlas of the Slave Trade* (New Haven, Conn.: Yale University Press, forthcoming). For older data based on British shipping records, see Gomez's recalculation of Richardson's figures. Michael A. Gomez, *Exchanging Our Country Marks: The Transformation of African Identities in the Colonial and Antebellum South* (Chapel Hill: University of North Carolina Press, 1998), 29, table 2.7.

20 *"I was born, in the year 1745, situated in a charming vale, named Essaka"*: Literary historian Vincent Carretta has uncovered evidence suggesting that Equiano was American-born, thus casting doubt on his African narrative. However, the documents in question, a baptismal record and ship's crew registration, were made many years *after* his birth, thus must have been based on secondhand testimony rather than direct primary sources. Furthermore, Carretta concedes that even if Equiano's account were not based on his own experience, it had to have been cobbled from the stories told to him by others and as such can be taken as the collective memory of a generation's formative experience. Vincent Carretta, *Equiano, the African: Biography of a Self-Made Man* (Athens: University of Georgia Press, 2005). Quote is from *The Interesting Narrative of the Life of Olaudah Equiano Written by Himself*, ed. Robert J. Allison (Boston: Bedford Books, 1995), 34.

22 *Dom Miguel de Castro*: For more on diplomatic courtesies during this period, see William James Roosen, *The Age of Louis XIV: The Rise of Modern Diplomacy* (Cambridge, Mass.: Schenkman Publishing Co., 1976).

24 *Portuguese explorers had reached the Kongo*: Anne Hilton, *The Kingdom of the Kongo* (Oxford, UK: Clarendon Press, 1985).

24 *Even before Cão's party reached the capital*: Ibid.

24 *some form of sympathetic magic*: Ibid., 50–51.

24 *Mwene Puto, the Land of the Dead*: The term also referred to a group of cannibals. Ibid; Joseph Miller, *The Way of Death: Merchant Capital and the Angolan Slave Trade, 1730–1830* (Madison: University of Wisconsin Press, 1988), 4–6.

25 *a cultural "middle ground"*: Richard White, *The Middle Ground: Indians, Empires,*

and Republics in the Great Lakes Region, 1660–1815 (Cambridge, UK: Cambridge University Press, 1991), 50–52.

25   "[a] boundary to be maintained": James Clifford, The Predicament of Culture: Twentieth-Century Ethnography, Literature, and Art (Cambridge, Mass.: Harvard University Press, 1988), 344.

26   the Kongolese conversion to Catholicism: Hilton, The Kingdom of the Kongo, 90; John Thornton, "The Development of an African Catholic Church in the Kingdom of Kongo, 1491–1750," Journal of African History 25, no. 2 (1984), 147–67; Thornton, Africa and Africans, 235–71.

26   expelling those who offended them: Thornton, "The Development of an African Catholic Church in the Kingdom of Kongo," 153–55.

27   called the others his concubines: Ibid., 158.

27   Afonso, as the mani Kongo's son: Hilton, The Kingdom of the Kongo, 51–60.

27   Kongolese requests for "foreign aid": Ibid., 64.

27   Manuel Robrerdo: Ibid., 134.

27   Kongo an Episcopal see: John K. Thornton, The Kingdom of the Kongo: Civil War and Transition, 1641–1718 (Madison: University of Wisconsin Press, 1983), 65.

28   "a greater Kongo": Thornton, Africa and Africans, 104–105; Hilton, The Kingdom of the Kongo, 60.

29   traders distinguished those liable to sale . . . from those who were not: Harms, River of Wealth, River of Sorrow, 33. The Kongolese made similar distinctions among the degraded mbika and the infantilized nleke. Thornton, The Kingdom of the Kongo, 21–22.

29   fishing villages became trading posts: Harms, River of Wealth, River of Sorrow, 24, 48, 93.

30   an alliance with Dutch newcomers: Thornton, The Kingdom of the Kongo, 51.

30   Garcia II turned to the Pope: Hilton, The Kingdom of the Kongo, 142–51; and more generally, see Thornton, Africa and Africans, 253–62.

30   the political history of the Kongo: Thornton, The Kingdom of the Kongo.

31   Dona Beatrice Kimpa Vita: Ibid., 104–12.

34   "the saltwater people": Stephanie E. Smallwood, Saltwater Slavery: A Middle Passage from Africa to American Diaspora (Cambridge, Mass.: Harvard University Press, 2007).

34   "Igbo enwegh eze": Kenneth Onwuka Dike and Felicia Ekejiuba, The Aro of South-Eastern Nigeria, 1650–1980: A Study of Socio-Economic Formation and Transformation in Nigeria (Ibadan, Nigeria: University Press, 1990), 19; Elizabeth Isichei, A History of the Igbo People (New York: St. Martin's Press, 1976).

35   within the grasp of the slave trade: Equiano's recollection that his kidnapping reflected a relatively recent and growing problem conforms with what we know of the general temporal and spatial pattern of the slave trade. Since the Portuguese had focused their trading activities west of the Niger, and other European powers kept to the Upper Guinea Coast, the Bight of Biafra was practically ignored until the early eighteenth century and thus contributed only 4 percent of the slaves crossing the Atlantic in the seventeenth century. That number swelled to 14 percent by 1740, however, and would reach 28 percent by 1780, when 22,500 slaves per year embarked from its principal ports, Bonny and Old Calabar. Martin A Klein, "The Slave Trade and Decentralized Societies," Journal of African History 42, no. 1 (2001): 62–63.

35   In many ways, decentralized societies: Hawthorne, "The Production of Slaves Where

There Was No State," 107–8; Klein, "The Slave Trade and Decentralized Societies," 52.

36 *an intriguing hypothesis*: Dike and Ekejiuba, *The Aro of South-Eastern Nigeria*.

37 *The Aro cult . . . formal adoptions*: S.J.S. Cookey, *King Jaja of the Niger Delta: His Life and Times, 1821–1891* (New York: NOK, 1974; reprint, UGR, 2005), 7–9; F. I. Ekejiuba, "The Aro System of Trade in the Nineteenth Century," *Ikenga* (*Journal of African Studies*, University of Nigeria, Naukka) 1, no. 1: 11–26; Curtin, *Cross-Cultural Trade*, 47–49.

38 *a system of taxation*: Dike and Ekejiuba, *The Aro of South-Eastern Nigeria*, 98.

38 *"generational conflict . . . the market"*: Klein, "The Slave Trade and Decentralized Societies," 65.

39 *a prominent white southern historian*: Ulrich B. Phillips, *American Negro Slavery: A Survey of the Supply, Employment, and Control of Negro Labor, as Determined by the Plantation Regime* (New York: D. Appleton and Company, 1918).

39 *Patterson's exhaustive survey*: Orlando Patterson, *Slavery and Social Death: A Comparative Study* (Cambridge, Mass.: Harvard University Press, 1982).

40 *"His hair was shaven off . . . the household head"*: Dike and Ekejiuba, *The Aro of South-Eastern Nigeria*, 74.

40 *American-style slave plantations*: Robin Law, "Dahomey and the Slave Trade: Reflections on the Historiography of the Rise of Dahomey," *Journal of African History* 27, no. 2 (1986).

41 *culturally separate enclaves*: Bartlett, *The Making of Europe*; Rau, "A Family of Italian Merchants."

41 *"Permission was obtained . . . 'Portuguese'"*: Rodney, *History of the Upper Guinea Coast*, 202–20.

41 *"a trading diaspora"*: Boubacar Barry, *Senegambia and the Atlantic Slave Trade* (Cambridge, UK: Cambridge University Press, 1998).

42 *"a people apart"*: Dike and Ekejiuba, *The Aro of South-Eastern Nigeria*, 30.

43 *Captain Francisco Correia*: Rodney, *History of the Upper Guinea Coast*, 204.

43 *Among some English traders*: David Henige, "John Kabes of Komenda: An Early African Entrepreneur and State Builder," *Journal of African History* 18, no. 1 (1977); Berlin, *Many Thousands Gone*, 23–24.

43 *the Dutch once tried to assassinate him*: Henige, "John Kabes of Komenda."

43 *"It is not possible . . . without slaves"*: Johannes Menne Postma, *The Dutch in the Atlantic Slave Trade, 1600–1815* (Cambridge, UK: Cambridge University Press, 1990), 17. Also see Robin Blackburn, *The Making of New World Slavery: From the Baroque to the Modern, 1492–1800* (London: Verso, 1997), 195.

44 *A century after Columbus*: McAlister, *Spain and Portugal in the New World*, 131, table 1. See also P. J. Bakewell, *A History of Latin America: C. 1450 to the Present*, 2nd ed., *The Blackwell History of the World* (Malden, Mass.: Blackwell Pub., 2004).

44 *During the first fifty years*: Philip D. Curtin, *The Atlantic Slave Trade: A Census* (Madison: University of Wisconsin Press, 1969), table 34, p. 119.

44 *"without Negroes . . . no Negroes"*: Blackburn, *The Making of New World Slavery*, 205.

44 *The growth of sugar*: Cf. Richard Lee Turits, *Foundations of Despotism: Peasants, the Trujillo Regime, and Modernity in Dominican History* (Stanford, Calif.: Stanford University Press, 2003), 27–29.

45   *a baroque to a modern age*: Blackburn, *The Making of New World Slavery*, 20–23; José Antonio Maravall, *Culture of the Baroque: Analysis of a Historical Structure*, trans. Terry Cochran, *Theory and History of Literature*, vol. 25 (Minneapolis: University of Minnesota Press, 1986).

45   *Although religious conflicts*: The baroque movement was much stronger in Catholic than Protestant countries, perhaps because it was in many ways a reaction to the Protestant Reformation; the Catholic Church deliberately cultivated a sense of awe and mystery to counter the powerful rationality of Martin Luther's attack on their corruption and worldliness. Thus the Church sponsored architecture and works of art that embodied this sensibility. Maravall, *Culture of the Baroque*, 4–15, 157; Encyclopaedia Britannica Premium Service, "Baroque Period," Encyclopaedia Britannica, www.britannica.com/eb/article?eu=13605.

45   *The most striking examples*: Kenneth and William B. Taylor Mills, eds. *Colonial Spanish America: A Documentary History* (Wilmington, Del.: Scholarly Resources, 1998), 153–260; "Bresil/Baroque: Entre Ciel et Terre," (paper presented for the Catalogue de l'exposition, présentée au Petit Palais du 4 novembre 1999 au 6 fevrier 2000, Petit Palais, Musée des Beaux-arts de la Ville de Paris, 1999/2000).

46   *the Tupinambá*: Blackburn, *The Making of New World Slavery*, 164.

46   *mixed-blood peoples*: María Elena Martínez, "Space, Order, and Group Identities in a Spanish Colonial Town: Puebla De Los Angeles," in *The Collective and the Public in Latin America: Cultural Identities and Political Order*, eds. Luis Roninger and Tamara Herzog (2000). María Elena Martínez, "The Black Blood of New Spain: *Limpieza De Sangria*, Racial Violence and Gendered Power in Early Colonial Mexico," *William and Mary Quarterly* 61, no. 3 (July 2004), 479–520.

46   *The radical refashioning of America*: Blackburn, *The Making of New World Slavery*, 121–23; McAlister, *Spain and Portugal in the New World*, 66, 110.

47   *Leading the attack on Spain's hegemony*: Jonathan Israel, *The Dutch Republic and the Hispanic World, 1606–1661* (Oxford, UK: Clarendon Press, 1982).

47   *Pieter van der Haagen*: Blackburn, *The Making of New World Slavery*, 189; Postma, *The Dutch in the Atlantic Slave Trade*, 10.

47   *Aside from their moral proclivities*: Blackburn, *The Making of New World Slavery*, 189.

48   *It seems unlikely*: Ibid., 188–91; Postma, *The Dutch in the Atlantic Slave Trade*, 11.

48   *captured the entire Spanish silver fleet*: Blackburn, *The Making of New World Slavery*, 191.

48   *the 600 slaves on board*: Ibid., 189, 193; Postma, *The Dutch in the Atlantic Slave Trade*, 12.

48   *Once the company's mission shifted*: Postma, *The Dutch in the Atlantic Slave Trade*, 14, 17.

48   *They dispatched traders to Angola*: Blackburn, *The Making of New World Slavery*, 203.

49   *drove the Dutch out*: Ibid., 198–201; Postma, *The Dutch in the Atlantic Slave Trade*, 19.

49   *not very good at . . . slave trading*: Blackburn, *The Making of New World Slavery*, 211–12.

49   *integral to the commercial activities*: Ibid., 192; Postma, *The Dutch in the Atlantic Slave Trade*, 189.

49   *Rather, their crucial contributions*: Blackburn, *The Making of New World Slavery*, 213.

49 *After years of desultory growth*: Ibid., 166–74.
50 *Jewish involvement in the slave trade*: Seymour Drescher, "The Role of Jews in the Transatlantic Slave Trade," *Immigrants and Minorities* 12 (July 1993), 117–22.
50 *This debate, if one might call it that*: Blackburn, *The Making of New World Slavery*; Miriam Bodian, "'The Men of the Nation': The Shaping of Converso Identity in Early Modern Europe," *Past and Present* 143 (May 1994), 48–76; Jonathan Israel, "The Sephardim in the Netherlands," in *Spain and the Jews: Sephardi Experience, 1492 and After*, ed. Elie Kedouri (London: Thames and Hudson, 1992), 195–200.
51 *The Dutch Sephardic community*: Several moments of crucial inventions by or recruitment of New Christians are described in Blackburn, *The Making of New World Slavery*, 115, 170, 181, 200, 212–13, 314.
51 *The American sugar crop*: The 1720 figure is from ibid., 382. The figure for the mid-eighteenth century is from Richard B. Sheridan, *Sugar and Slavery: An Economic History of the British West Indies, 1623–1775* (Baltimore, Md.: Johns Hopkins University Press, 1974), 100. Sidney Mintz gives a mid-seventeenth-century figure of less than seven thousand tons of muscavado from Barbados, one of the principal early producers, which suggests an American total far less than the 1720 total given here. Sidney W. Mintz, *Sweetness and Power: The Place of Sugar in Modern History* (New York: Viking, 1985), 37.
52 *Importing 175 million tons of sugar each year*: Blackburn, *The Making of New World Slavery*, 382; see also Mintz, *Sweetness and Power*.

2. MANY THOUSANDS BORN

53 *about 1,200 whites in the Chesapeake*: Jack Greene, *Pursuits of Happiness: The Social Development of Early Modern British Colonies and the Formation of American Culture* (Chapel Hill: University of North Carolina Press, 1988), table 8.1, pp. 178–79.
53 *outnumbered Europeans three to two*: David Eltis, *The Rise of African Slavery in the Americas* (Cambridge, UK: Cambridge University Press, 2000), 9–11, Greene, *Pursuits of Happiness*, 178–79.
53 *roughly 2,600*: Peter H. Wood, "The Changing Population of the Colonial South: An Overview by Race and Region, 1685–1790," in *Powhatan's Mantle: Indians in the Colonial Southeast*, eds. Gregory A. Waselkov, Peter H. Wood, and M. Thomas Hatley (Lincoln: University of Nebraska Press, 1999). For other slightly higher estimates, see Ira Berlin, *Generations of Captivity: A History of African-American Slaves* (Cambridge, Mass.: Belknap Press of Harvard University Press, 2003), table 1, pp. 272–75. Over the first half century only 1,400 Africans were landed in British North America, or about 25 per year on average. David Eltis, "The Volume and Structure of the Transatlantic Slave Trade: A Reassessment," *William and Mary Quarterly*, 3rd ser., 58, no. 1 (Jan. 2001), table 3, p. 45.
54 *Johnson probably arrived*: Breen and Innes place him there in 1621. T. H. Breen and Stephen Innes, *"Myne Owne Ground": Race and Freedom on Virginia's Eastern Shore, 1640–1676* (New York: Oxford University Press, 1980), 8. See also Berlin, *Generations of Captivity*, 36–39.
54 *three hundred or so black inhabitants*: Population estimate is for 1649, from Anthony S. Parent, *Foul Means: The Formation of a Slave Society in Virginia, 1660–1740* (Chapel Hill: University of North Carolina Press, 2003), 109.

54   *contours of Johnson's world*: Douglas Deal, *Race and Class in Colonial Virginia: Indians, Englishmen, and Africans on the Eastern Shore During the Seventeenth Century* (New York: Garland Publishing, 1993). See also Douglas Deal, "A Constricted World: Free Blacks on Virginia's Eastern Shore, 1680–1750," in *Colonial Chesapeake Society*, eds. Lois Green Carr, Philip D. Morgan, and Jean B. Russo (Chapel Hill: University of North Carolina Press, 1988), 275–305.

55   *Anthony and Mary Johnson*: Preceding and following details on Johnson family are drawn from Deal, *Race and Class in Colonial Virginia*, 221.

56   *ominous threats*: Ibid., 221–23.

56   *When Anthony died*: Ibid., 228.

56   *Anthony Johnson's sons . . . an oath*: Ibid., 229.

57   *Seven years later . . . place name "Angola"*: Ibid., 231.

57   *Emanuel Driggus and his wife*: Ibid., 284–89.

58   *Emanuel's slave son . . . independent ways*: Ibid., 288–89.

58   *Sarah Driggus*: Ibid.

58   *"chicken or egg" question*: There is a long-standing debate on this issue, for which Ira Berlin has provided a very nuanced reframing. Berlin, *Many Thousands Gone*, 3–5. See also Winthrop D. Jordan, *White over Black: American Attitudes Toward the Negro, 1550–1812* (New York: Norton, 1977). James Campbell and James Oakes, "The Invention of Race: Rereading *White over Black*," *Reviews in American History* 21, no. 1 (March 1993): 172–83.

59   *liable for tithes*: For more discussion of this issue, see Kathleen M. Brown, *Goodwives, Nasty Wenches, and Anxious Patriarchs: Gender, Race, and Power in Colonial Virginia* (Chapel Hill: University of North Carolina Press, 1996).

60   *Elizabeth Key*: Warren M. Billings, "The Law of Servants and Slaves in Seventeenth-Century Virginia," *Virginia Magazine of History and Biography* 99, no. 1 (1991): 56; Warren Billings, "The Cases of Fernando and Elizabeth Key: A Note on the Status of Blacks in Seventeenth-Century Virginia," *William and Mary Quarterly* 3rd ser., 30, no. 2 (April 1973): 468–69.

61   *Key's suit*: Billings, "Law of Servants and Slaves," 57–58, quote on p. 57.

62   *"baptisme doth not . . ."*: Ibid., 58.

62   *One of Charles II's first acts*: For broader ideological and political background of these policies, see Steve Pincus, *1688: The First Modern Revolution* (New Haven, Conn.: Yale University Press, 2009), 372–81.

63   *between 240,000 and 295,000 people*: Greene, *Pursuits of Happiness*, 7.

64   *number reached just 1,400*: Eltis, "The Volume and Structure of the Transatlantic Slave Trade," table 3, p. 45.

64   *tobacco's secular trend*: John J. McCusker and Russell R. Menard, *The Economy of British America, 1607–1789*, Needs and Opportunities for Study Series (Chapel Hill: Published for the Institute of Early American History and Culture by the University of North Carolina Press, 1985), table 6.1, p. 121.

64   *80 to 90 percent of their labor force*: Parent, *Foul Means*, 74.

65   *white settlers of the Chesapeake*: Greene, *Pursuits of Happiness*, 10.

65   *lived short, brutish lives*: From 1625 to 1640, there was an average of about 1,000 newcomers per year. In 1635, there were 2,010, which was a high. A total of 1,800 people died that year. Also, of the 2,010, only 14 percent were women. In 1625, there were 325 men for every 100 women. Although there were 15,000 immigrants between 1625

and 1640, the population increased by only 7,000. Edmund Sears Morgan, *American Slavery, American Freedom: The Ordeal of Colonial Virginia* (New York: Norton, 1975), 158–63; Edmund Sears Morgan, "Slavery and Freedom: The American Paradox," *Journal of American History* 59, no. 1 (June 1972): 19. There was the possibility of a 30 percent death rate in any given year. See Greene, *Pursuit of Happiness*, 16. See also Russell R. Menard, "From Servant to Freeholder: Status Mobility and Property Accumulation in Seventeenth-Century Maryland," *William and Mary Quarterly*, 3rd ser., 30, no. 1 (Jan. 1973): 37–64.

65   *in Britain only during epidemics*: Greene, *Pursuits of Happiness*, 6–10.

66   *inflation of land prices*: Lois Green Carr, "Emigraton and the Standard of Living: The Seventeenth-Century Chesapeake," *Journal of Economic History* 52, no. 2 (June 1992): 271–91.

66   *civil status of landless whites*: Morgan, *American Slavery, American Freedom*, 338, 344–45.

67   *preadolescent Olaudah Equiano*: The dates here are as amended by Vincent Carretta, who questions Equiano's African birth, placing him in South Carolina instead, but then documents his sale to Lt. Pascal during the latter's stop in Virginia that year. Carretta, *Equiano, the African*, xv, 33–38.

68   *9,800 slaves entered*: David Eltis, "The Volume and Structure of the Transatlantic Slave Trade," *William and Mary Quarterly*, 3rd ser., 58, no. 1 (2001): 17–46.

68   *The pace would quicken*: Figures from Herbert S. Klein, *The Atlantic Slave Trade* (Cambridge, UK: Cambridge University Press, 1999), table A2, pp. 210–11. The black population in the Lower South increased by 3,000 during 1700–10, by 6,600 between 1710 and 1720, by 50,000 more by 1730, and by another 155,000 by 1770. Greene, *Pursuits of Happiness*, 143. For quarter-century estimates, see Eltis, "The Volume and Structure of the Transatlantic Slave Trade," table 3, p. 45.

68   *independent traders*: Independent traders sold 6,835 slaves between 1699 and 1710, compared with the Royal African Company's 679. Parent, *Foul Means*, 79, 86. For discussion of British political conflicts that encouraged the independent traders, see William A. Pettigrew, "Free to Enslave: Politics and the Escalation of Britain's Transatlantic Slave Trade, 1688–1714," *William and Mary Quarterly* 3rd ser., 64, no. 1 (Jan. 2007): 3–38.

68   *four of every ten slaves*: Eltis, "The Volume and Structure of the Transatlantic Slave Trade," table 1, p. 43.

68   *twice as many Africans*: Africans outnumbered Europeans three to one before the nineteenth century. David Richardson, "The British Empire and the Atlantic Slave Trade, 1660–1807," in *The Oxford History of the British Empire*, ed. P. J. Marshall (Oxford, UK: Oxford University Press, 1998): 462. Ratio of Africans to Europeans crossing the Atlantic is from Philip D. Morgan, *Slave Counterpoint: Black Culture in the Eighteenth-Century Chesapeake and Lowcountry* (Chapel Hill: University of North Carolina Press, 1998), xv.

69   *mainland's commodity exports*: McCusker and Menard, *The Economy of British America*, tables 5.2, 6.2, 8.2, pp. 108, 132, 174.

69   *125 great planters*: Parent, *Foul Means*, 96–97.

69   *25 percent of landholders*: Ibid., 36.

69   *Carter's Grove reveals*: Lorena S. Walsh, *From Calabar to Carter's Grove: The History of a Virginia Slave Community* (Charlottesville: University Press of Virginia, 1997), 26.

70   *to display the social power*: Rhys Isaac, *The Transformation of Virginia: 1740–1790* (Chapel Hill: Published for the Institute of Early American History and Culture, Williamsburg, Va., by University of North Carolina Press, 1982).

70   *defined slaves as real estate*: Walsh, *From Calabar to Carter's Grove*, 44.

71   *With the consolidation . . . importation of Africans*: Of course, the continued growth of the slave population suggests a limited impact of these measures. Parent, *Foul Means*, 94–95.

72   *exceeded three thousand*: Ibid., 87. The pressures exerted by the British government to expand the slave trade during these years explain the otherwise odd reference in Thomas Jefferson's draft of the Declaration of Independence blaming the king for forcing slaves upon American planters. Also see Robert Brenner, *Merchants and Revolution: Commercial Change, Political Conflict, and London's Overseas Traders, 1550–1653* (New York: Verso, 2003), 577–602.

72   *rhythms of the slave trade*: As Ira Berlin rightly warns us, Creolization never proceeded along straight unbroken lines but was subject to convoluted starts and stops in rhythm with the open slave trade. Berlin, "From Creole to African," 251–88.

72   *one historian estimates*: Morgan, *Slave Counterpoint*, 89.

72   *"a woman who brings a child . . ."*: Ibid., 81.

73   *survivors, such as Equiano*: For our purposes, the provocative questions raised by the literary historian Vincent Carretta as to whether we can take Equiano's account as literally true—while a legitimate caution—is even less an issue here than his description of his experiences in Africa. Whatever his origins, Equiano either had direct experience with the passage or would almost certainly have learned of it from older slaves. Carretta, *Equiano, the African*, xiv–xvii.

73   *mere boys and girls*: G. Ugo Nwokeji, "African Conceptions of Gender and the Slave Traffic," *William and Mary Quarterly* 3rd ser., 58, no. 1 (Jan. 2001): 47–68. Also see Klein, *Atlantic Slave Trade*, 168.

74   *"horrible looks . . ."*: Olaudah Equiano, *Interesting Narrative of the Life of Olaudah Equiano* (Oxford, UK: Heinemen, 1996), 65. On fear of European cannibalism, see John K. Thornton, *Africa and Africans in the Making of the Atlantic World, 1400–1680*, Studies in Comparative World History (Cambridge and New York: Cambridge University Press, 1992), 161.

74   *a six-week journey*: Sailing times from West Africa to the West Indian ports ranged between five and ten weeks, depending on ports of embarkation and debarkation and the seasons. Kenneth F. and Brian T. Higgins Kiple, "Mortality Caused by Dehydration During the Middle Passage," in *The Atlantic Slave Trade: Effects on Economics, Societies, and Peoples in Africa, the Americas, and Europe*, eds. Joseph E. Inikori and Stanley L. Engerman (Durham, N.C.: Duke University Press, 1992), 332n.

74   *enchantment and magic*: The turn to magical explanations was reinforced by other scenes of exceptional cruelty in the Atlantic world. Smallwood, *Saltwater Slavery*.

74   *600, tightly packed*: In the infamous case of the *Brookes*, a ship designed to hold 451 slaves was found carrying more than 600. Rawley, *The Transatlantic Slave Trade*, 283.

74   *"so crowded . . ."*: Equiano, *Interesting Narrative of the Life of Olaudah Equiano*, 66.

75   *"the necessary tubs"*: Ibid., 68. On descriptions of the Middle Passage, see Thornton, *Africa and Africans*, 153–62.

75   *the stench pervading slave ships*: Thornton, *Africa and Africans*, 161. Also see Richard Ross Watkins, *Slavery: Bondage Throughout History* (New York: Houghton Mifflin Harcourt, 2001), 46.

75   *a welcome death*: One source put the mortality rate at an estimated 10 to 20 percent, or between two and four million Africans. Toyin Falola and Amanda B. Warnock, *Encyclopedia of the Middle Passage* (Westport, Conn.: Greenwood Press, 2007), 99. See also Herbert S. Klein, *The Middle Passage: Comparative Studies in the Atlantic Slave Trade* (Princeton, N.J.: Princeton University Press, 1978), 229–38.

76   *Biafran ancestral origins like him*: Slaves from Biafra made up 41 percent of the trade to the Chesapeake. Michael Angelo Gomez, *Exchanging Our Country Marks: The Transformation of African Identities in the Colonial and Antebellum South* (Chapel Hill: University of North Carolina Press, 1998), 114–16.

76   *"wishing for death"*: Equiano, *Interesting Narrative of the Life of Olaudah Equiano*, 62.

76   *Virginia at mid-century*: Morgan, *Slave Counterpoint*, 84–85.

76   *they imported the bulk of their work force before 1740*: Walsh, *From Calabar to Carter's Grove*, 106.

77   *limited makeup of the slave cargoes*: This was less a matter of their own preferences than the timing of their purchases and the preferred trading patterns of merchant suppliers and creditors, all of which ultimately dictated the ethnic mix of Africans landed in America at any given time. It is for this reason that the overwhelming majority of those sold along the York River had been shipped, like Equiano, from West Africa's Niger Delta. See Lorena S. Walsh, "The Chesapeake Slave Trade: Regional Patterns, African Origins, and Some Implications," *William and Mary Quarterly* 3rd ser., 58, no. 1 (Jan. 2001): 139–70.

77   *the Africans' alien ways*: Walsh, *From Calabar to Carter's Grove*, 110–11; and Berlin, *Many Thousands Gone*, 129.

78   *tantamount to small villages*: By 1740, there were twice as many slaves as free whites in the Carolina colony: 39,155 slaves and 20,000 free whites. Berlin, *Many Thousands Gone*, 162–76; Wood, *Black Majority*, 152; Richard S. Dunn, *Sugar and Slaves: The Rise of the Planter Class in the English West Indies, 1624–1713* (Chapel Hill: University of North Carolina Press, 1972), 111–16.

78   *toward cultural Creolization*: For comparative discussion of the phenomenon, see Michael Mullin, *Africa in America: Slave Acculturation and Resistance in the American South and the British Caribbean, 1736–1831*, Blacks in the New World (Urbana: University of Illinois Press, 1992).

78   *by one historian's reckoning*: Morgan, *Slave Counterpoint*, table 29, p. 500.

79   *folktales*: Alan Dundes, "African Tales Among North American Indians," in *Mother Wit from the Laughing Barrel: Readings in the Interpretation of Afro-American Folklore*, ed. Alan Dundes (Jackson: University Press of Mississippi, 1990).

79   *"interpenetration of values" . . . "practical guides"*: Mechal Sobel, "'All Americans Are Part African': Slave Influence on 'White' Values," in *Slavery and Other Forms of Unfree Labour*, ed. Léonie J. Archer (London: Routledge, 1988), 181–83. Gary B. Nash, "New Light on Richard Allen: The Early Years of Freedom," *William and Mary Quarterly* 46, no. 2 (Apr. 1989), 332–40. Also see Mechal Sobel, *The World They Made Together: Black and White Values in Eighteenth-Century Virginia* (Princeton, N.J.: Princeton University Press, 1987), 128–203.

79   *a familiar cultural repertoire*: My approach to the Creolization process is indebted to

Sidney Wilfred Mintz and Richard Price, *The Birth of African-American Culture: An Anthropological Perspective* (Boston: Beacon Press, 1992). For an alternative perspective, see Sterling Stuckey, *Slave Culture: Nationalist Theory and the Foundations of Black America* (New York: Oxford University Press, 1987).

80 *"the off-beat"*: Robert Farris Thompson, National Gallery of Art (U.S.), and Frederick S. Wight Art Gallery, *African Art in Motion: Icon and Act in the Collection of Katherine Coryton White* (Los Angeles: University of California Press, 1974), 13; Maude Southwell Wahlman, "African Symbolism in Afro-American Quilts," *African Arts* 20, no. 1 (Nov. 1986).

80 *African American quilting*: Wahlman, "African Symbolism in Afro-American Quilts," 69.

81 *a culture at once . . . synthetic*: Berlin, "From Creole to African."

82 *"new man . . ."*: J. Hector St. John de Crevecoeur, *Letters from an American Farmer* (London: T. Davies, 1782), 63.

82 *Some Anglican clergymen*: Parent, *Foul Means*, 245–48.

82 *cohort of Christian slaves*: Ibid., 257, 258.

83 *St. Peter's Parish*: Ibid., 254.

83 *40 percent of all Methodists*: Sobel, *The World They Made Together*, 178–203.

84 *"Query: . . . misconduct"*: Ibid.

85 *religious disestablishment*: Monica Najar, "'Meddling with Emancipation': Baptists, Authority, and the Rift over Slavery in the Upper South," *Journal of the Early Republic* 25, no. 2 (2005), 182–86; Thomas E. Buckley, S. J., "After Disestablishment: Thomas Jefferson's Wall of Separation in Antebellum Virginia," *Journal of Southern History* 61, no. 3 (Aug. 1995), 445–80.

85 *"No person is entitled . . . servants"*: Sobel, *The World They Made Together*, 209.

85 *Richard Allen*: Nash, "New Light on Richard Allen."

86 *"a spiritual rebirth"*: Ibid., 338.

86 *His God was a present reality*: James T. Campbell, *Songs of Zion: The African Methodist Episcopal Church in the United States and South Africa* (New York: Oxford University Press, 1995), 168.

86 *the twenty-year-old Allen*: Carol V. R. George, *Segregated Sabbaths: Richard Allen and the Rise of Independent Black Churches, 1760–1840* (New York: Oxford University Press, 1973), 22ff.

86 *he lived a very different life*: Carretta, *Equiano, the African*, 171–74.

87 *his own life story*: Ibid. For more detail on how early abolitionists were ensnared in Sierra Leone colonization schemes, see Christopher Leslie Brown, *Moral Capital: Foundations of British Abolitionism* (Chapel Hill: Published for the Omohundro Institute of Early American History and Culture, Williamsburg, Virginia, by the University of North Carolina Press, 2006), and Deirdre Coleman, *Romantic Colonization and British Anti-Slavery*, Cambridge Studies in Romanticism 61 (New York: Cambridge University Press, 2005).

87 *Both Equiano and Richard Allen*: Cf. Campbell, *Songs of Zion*, 5.

88 *Philadelphia Free African Society*: Elizabeth Rauh Bethel, *The Roots of African-American Identity: Memory and History in Free Antebellum Communities* (New York: St. Martin's Press, 1997), 74–75. For more on the complex transformations of African identity during this era, see James Sidbury, *Becoming African in America: Race and Nation in the Early Black Atlantic* (New York: Oxford University Press, 2007).

88 *"Every pious man"*: Campbell, *Songs of Zion*, 67; Cf. Carretta, *Equiano, the African*, 368.

3. SLAVES AND CITIZENS

89 *slaves near Trois-Rivières*: Laurent Dubois, *A Colony of Citizens: Revolution and Slave Emancipation in the French Caribbean, 1787–1804* (Chapel Hill: University of North Carolina Press, 2003), 23–25.

89 *recollections of Victor Collot*: Ibid., 27–28.

91 *why or when Bréda chose his new name*: I use "Louverture" because it was how Toussaint signed himself. I am grateful to Laurent Dubois for a personal communication clarifying these matters (e-mail to author dated July 14, 2009). For a more extensive discussion of the intriguing possibilities, see Laurent Dubois, *Avengers of the New World: The Story of the Haitian Revolution* (Cambridge, Mass.: Belknap Press of Harvard University Press, 2004), 172–73.

93 *flocking to the advancing Redcoats*: Graham Russell Hodges, *Root and Branch: African Americans in New York and East Jersey, 1613–1863* (Chapel Hill: University of North Carolina Press, 1999), 140–46.

94 *in the South the slaves' choices*: Sylvia R. Frey, *Water from the Rock: Black Resistance in a Revolutionary Age* (Princeton, N.J.: Princeton University Press, 1991), 49, 51.

94 *house slave named Bacchus*: Ibid., 193.

95 *two women on a Georgia slave plantation*: Ibid., 54.

95 *House of Commons*: Ibid., 54–55.

95 *fears of slave uprisings*: Ibid., 57–58.

95 *Dunmore, declared martial law*: Sylvia R. Frey, "Between Slavery and Freedom: Virginia Blacks in the American Revolution," *Journal of Southern History* 49, no. 3 (Aug. 1983): 375–98.

96 *Thomas Jefferson's estimate*: Ibid., 378, 396. Jefferson's estimate and those of historians relying upon them have been challenged and corrected by Cassandra Pybus, "Jefferson's Faulty Math: The Question of Slave Defections in the American Revolution," *William and Mary Quarterly* 3rd ser., 62, no. 2 (Apr. 2005): 243.

96 *John Willoughby*: Ibid., 376, 378.

96 *Thomas Peters*: Ibid., 378–79.

97 *hit-and-run raids*: Gary B. Nash, *Race, Class, and Politics: Essays on American Colonial and Revolutionary Society* (Urbana: University of Illinois Press, 1986), 270–74.

97 *"Liberty to Slaves"*: Gerald Astor, *The Right to Fight: A History of African Americans in the Military* (Novato, Calif.: Presidio, 1998), 8–9.

97 *"on the most respectable Footing"*: Todd W. Braisted, "The Black Pioneers and Others: The Military Role of Black Loyalists in the American War of Independence," in *Moving On: Black Loyalists in the Afro-Atlantic World*, ed. John W. Pulis, *Crosscurrents in African American History* (New York: Garland Publishing, Inc., 1999), 4.

97 *the reorganized Black Pioneers*: Ibid., 11–12.

97 *a virtual civil war*: Nash, *Race, Class, and Politics*, 16.

97 *As in the North, . . . they were "liberating"*: Frey, *Water from the Rock*, 99; Hodges, *Root and Branch*, 152.

98 *dividing the spoils of war*: Frey, *Water from the Rock*, 113–14; Frey, "Between Slavery and Freedom," 389, 394–95.

98 *allocation of black servants*: Frey, "Between Slavery and Freedom," 389.

98 *expulsion of thousands of blacks*: Frey, *Water from the Rock*, 170.

99 *the precise number of evacuees*: Drawing on British Headquarters' papers and the records of Jamaica planter-historian Edward Long, John Pulis estimates that two hundred black Loyalists, two thousand white Loyalists along with five thousand of their slaves, and perhaps as many as sixty-five thousand blacks seized as contraband were evacuated or carried away. John W. Pulis, "Bridging Troubled Waters: Moses Baker, George Liele, and the African American Diaspora to Jamaica," in Pulis, ed. *Moving On*, 183. Cf. Pybus, "Jefferson's Faulty Math."

99 *2,775 leaving New York*: Nash, *Race, Class, and Politics*, 274.

99 *"Black Pioneers"*: Pulis, "Bridging Troubled Waters," 187.

99 *defend Britain's slave colonies*: Frey, "Between Slavery and Freedom," 395.

100 *Peter Salem*: Sidney Kaplan, *The Black Presence in the Era of the American Revolution* (Amherst: University of Massachusetts Press, 1989), 21.

100 *The fundamental difference*: Ira Berlin aptly describes the difference as one of slave societies versus societies with slaves. See Berlin, *Many Thousands Gone*, 8.

100 *an interracial struggle for freedom*: Ibid., 21–22.

101 *Most white enlistees . . . forty-two thousand men*: Graham Russell Hodges, "Black Revolt in New York and the Neutral Zone," in *New York in the Age of the Constitution, 1775–1780*, eds. Paul A. Gilje and William Pencak (Rutherford, N.J.: Fairleigh Dickinson University Press, 1992).

101 *Within two years . . . in place of their masters*: David N. Gellman and David Quigley, ed. *Jim Crow New York: A Documentary History of Race and Citizenship, 1777–1877* (New York: New York University Press, 2004), 19; Hodges, *Root and Branch*, 141.

102 *The military careers of Cato Howe*: Bethel, *The Roots of African-American Identity*, 30–34.

102 *"In Consideration . . . his Wages"*: Ibid., 31.

103 *Joining Colonel John Bailey's . . . Quomony Quash*: Ibid., 32–33.

103 *"the first large-scale rebellion . . ."*: Nash, *Race, Class, and Politics*, 280.

103 *Connecticut man who freed his slaves*: James and Lois Horton, *In Hope of Liberty: Culture, Community, and Protest Among Northern Free Blacks, 1700–1860* (New York: Oxford University Press, 1998), 64–76.

104 *"It always seemed . . . we have"*: Ibid., 56.

104 *"in every human Breast . . . lives in us"*: Gary B. Nash, *Forging Freedom: The Formation of Philadelphia's Black Community, 1720–1840* (Cambridge, Mass.: Harvard University Press, 1988), 39.

104 *"merely [coveted] . . . human being"*: See Madison to James Sr., Sept. 8, 1783, in William T. Hutchinson and William M. E. Rachel, eds., *The Papers of James Madison*, vol. 17 (Chicago: University of Chicago Press, 1962–), 304.

105 *Robert Carter III*: Gordon Bruce Turtle, "Slave Manumission in Virginia, 1782–1806: The Jeffersonian Dilemma in the Age of Liberty" (Ph.D. Thesis, University of Alberta, 1991), chapter 3. For another similar example of this phenomenon, see Melvin Patrick Ely, *Israel on the Appomattox: A Southern Experiment in Black Freedom from the 1790s through the Civil War*, 1st ed. (New York: Alfred A. Knopf, 2004).

105 *value of their current assets*: Donald L. Robinson, *Slavery in the Structure of American Politics, 1765–1820*, 1st ed., The Founding of the American Republic (New York: Harcourt Brace Jovanovich, 1970), 212, 216.

105   *Virginia's tobacco crop*: Allan Kulikoff, *Tobacco and Slaves: The Development of Southern Cultures in the Chesapeake, 1680–1800* (Chapel Hill: University of North Carolina Press, 1986), 157.

106   *advertisements for escaped slaves*: Graham Russell Hodges and Alan Edward Brown, eds. *"Pretends to Be Free": Runaway Slave Advertisements from Colonial and Revolutionary New York and New Jersey* (New York: Garland, 1994), app. 1, table 1, p. 305.

106   *one in four Connecticut households*: Rhode Island's slaves outnumbered its indentured servants eight to one in the early eighteenth century, and blacks were 12 percent of the colony's population by mid-century. Arthur Zilversmit, *The First Emancipation: The Abolition of Slavery in the North* (Chicago: University of Chicago Press, 1967), 4–5; Edgar J. McManus, *Black Bondage in the North* (New York: Syracuse University Press, 1973), 18–19.

107   *As late as 1790*: A total of 21,000 of 26,000 blacks in New York City were slaves in 1790. Zilversmit, *The First Emancipation*, 162.

107   *a bloody revolt in New York City*: Peter Charles Hoffer, *The Great New York Conspiracy of 1741: Slavery, Crime, and Colonial Law*, Landmark Law Cases and American Society (Lawrence: University Press of Kansas, 2003). Also see Jill Lepore, *New York Burning: Liberty, Slavery, and Conspiracy in Eighteenth-Century Manhattan*, 1st ed. (New York: Alfred A. Knopf, 2005).

107   *revenues from advertising slave sales*: Such ads appeared frequently in the *Gazette*. See notes in McManus, *Black Bondage in the North*, 24–27n.

107   *huge landed estates*: Zilversmit, *The First Emancipation*, 52–53; McManus, *Black Bondage in the North*, 42–45.

108   *Women of childbearing age . . . expensive nuisance*: McManus, *Black Bondage in the North*, 37–38, 39; Hodges, *Root and Branch*, 75.

108   *colonial household economy*: Joanne Pope Melish, *Disowning Slavery: Gradual Emancipation and "Race" in New England, 1780–1860* (Ithaca, N.Y.: Cornell University Press, 1998). Zilversmit, *The First Emancipation*, 15–24.

109   *indentured labor declined*: Shane White, *Somewhat More Independent: The End of Slavery in New York City, 1770–1810* (Athens: University of Georgia Press, 1991), 36.

109   *Philadelphia imported thirteen hundred slaves*: Nash, *Forging Freedom*, 9; Julie Winch, *A Gentleman of Color: The Life of James Forten* (New York: Oxford University Press, 2002), 9.

109   *turned increasingly to free wage workers*: White, *Somewhat More Independent*, 36.

110   *prohibit the importation of African*: Michael L. Nicholls, "'The Squint of Freedom': African-American Freedom Suits in Post-Revolutionary Virginia," *Slavery and Abolition* 20 (Aug. 1999), 47–62.

110   *Emancipation . . . progressed*: Horton, *In Hope of Liberty*, 56–57.

110   *the state's Quakers*: Nash, *Forging Freedom*, 59–63.

111   *On March 1, 1780 . . . French West Indies*: Zilversmit, *The First Emancipation*, 109–200 passim.

112   *These developments . . . such transactions*: White, *Somewhat More Independent*, 40.

112   *Left in limbo . . . children*: Ten thousand slaves were emancipated by New York's 1817 law, which left most of them under indentured contracts. The state's census reported 11,375 slaves in 1814. Zilversmit, *The First Emancipation*, 213–14, 214 n23; Winch, *A Gentleman of Color*, 129; Nash, *Forging Freedom*, 76.

113   *juridically free children*: Zilversmit, *The First Emancipation*, 181–84.

113 *the lifetime services of a slave*: Shane White, "'We Dwell in Safety and Pursue Our Honest Callings': Free Blacks in New York City, 1783–1810," *Journal of American History* 75, no. 2 (Sept. 1988): 451.

113 *live-in domestics*: Nash, *Forging Freedom*, 76; White, *Somewhat More Independent*, 451.

113 *negotiate private deals*: White, "'We Dwell in Safety and Pursue Our Honest Callings,'" 445–47.

113 *Philadelphia's dockworkers*: Ibid., 153–54.

113 *Occupational directories*: Ibid., 454.

114 *Among them was Richard Allen*: Nash, *Forging Freedom*, 97–98.

114 *free people of color elsewhere*: This was especially notable among free colored in the Caribbean and Brazil. See Thomas C. Holt, *The Problem of Freedom: Race, Labor, and Politics in Jamaica and Britain, 1832–1938*, Johns Hopkins Studies in Atlantic History and Culture (Baltimore, Md.: Johns Hopkins University Press, 1992), chap. 7.

114 *"holds the destiny of our people"*: Nash, *Forging Freedom*, 3.

114 *concentration of free people of color*: Nash, *Race, Class, and Politics*, table 1, p. 285; Nash, *Forging Freedom*, 3.

114 *Ballooning to two thousand*: Nash, *Forging Freedom*, 72.

115 *The lives and careers of James Forten and Richard Allen*: Winch, *A Gentleman of Color*, 17–25.

116 *parlayed his workshop*: Ibid., 73–76.

116 *a true ethnic melting pot*: See ibid., 74, 127, 289.

116 *ties with the French West Indies*: Ashli White, "'A Flood of Impure Lava': Saint Domingan Refugees in the United States, 1791–1820" (Ph.D. Thesis, Columbia University, 2003), 5–6.

116 *as many as 848 Haitians*: Susan Branson and Leslie Patrick, "Étrangers dans un Pays Étrange: Saint-Domingan Refugees of Color in Philadelphia," in *The Impact of the Haitian Revolution in the Atlantic World*, ed. David R. Geggus (Columbia: University of South Carolina Press, 2001), 196; White, "'A Flood of Impure Lava,'" 46; Winch, *A Gentleman of Color*, 133–35.

117 *Desiré . . . free man of color*: White, "'A Flood of Impure Lava,'" 34.

117 *Forten's friends and associates*: Winch, *A Gentleman of Color*, 118–20, 126–27.

117 *one of St. Thomas's strongest supporters*: Ibid., 108, 111, 139–43.

117 *Like Allen, . . . vowing never to return*: Carol V. R. George, *Segregated Sabbaths: Richard Allen and the Rise of Independent Black Churches, 1760–1840* (New York: Oxford University Press, 1973), 51–55.

118 *one third of the black adults in the city*: Nash, *Forging Freedom*, 132.

119 *(AME) . . . members in 1818*: George, *Segregated Sabbaths*, 92.

119 *pulpit in 1816*: See Nash, *Forging Freedom*, 197; George, *Segregated Sabbaths*, 84–85.

119 *"the same as if we were white people"*: George, *Segregated Sabbaths*, 74–75.

120 *Allen's crowded church*: Ibid., 105–107, 124–34.

120 *lodge of Freemasons*: Nash, *Forging Freedom*, 218.

120 *Prince Hall*: Bethel, *Roots of African-American Identity*, chapter 2.

120 *The Free African Society*: Nash, *Forging Freedom*, 123–25.

120 *such groups could be found*: Bethel, *Roots of African-American Identity*, 70–72.

121 *demanded self-respect . . . and moral uplift*: See Sterling Stuckey, *The Ideological Origins of Black Nationalism* (Boston: Beacon Press, 1972), 1–29.

121   *"a translocal moral community"*: Bethel, *Roots of African-American Identity*, 76.

121   *speak frequently of Haitian independence*: Winch, *A Gentleman of Color*, 135.

121   *Cuffee . . . Traveller*: Lamont D. Thomas, *Paul Cuffee: Black Entrepreneur and Pan-Africanist*, Illini books ed., Blacks in the New World (Urbana: University of Illinois Press, 1988).

122   *Robert Purvis*: Margaret Hope Bacon, *But One Race: The Life of Robert Purvis* (Albany: State University of New York Press, 2007), 135–36. See also Bruce Dorsey, *Reforming Men and Women: Gender in the Antebellum City* (Ithaca, N.Y.: Cornell University Press, 2002), 161.

122   *Forten petitioned Congress*: Nash, *Forging Freedom*, 186.

122   *Gale-force winds and rain . . . blacks as citizens*: Douglas R. Egerton, *Gabriel's Rebellion: The Virginia Slave Conspiracies* (Chapel Hill: University of North Carolina Press, 1993), 50–51.

123   *"benefit of clergy"*: An odd loophole in the law, not available to white defendants, ironically, allowed Gabriel to escape the gallows. Under the 1792 statute, if he could recite a verse from the Bible, a slave had the option of being "burnt in the left hand [by] the Jailor in Open Court" and thus winning his release from custody. Ibid, 32.

123   *the disposition of Gabriel's case*: Ibid., 32.

124   *Pointe Coupee*: Gwendolyn Midlo Hall, *Africans in Colonial Louisiana: The Development of Afro-Creole Culture in the Eighteenth Century* (Baton Rouge: Louisiana State University Press, 1992), 344–45.

124   *the rumored French allies*: Egerton, *Gabriel's Rebellion*, 32–33, Bert M. Mutersbaugh, "The Background of Gabriel's Insurrection," *Journal of Negro History* 68, no. 2 (Spring 1983), 209–11.

124   *Vesey and his co-conspirators*: See article and associated "Forum" in Michael P. Johnson, "Denmark Vesey and His Co-Conspirators," *William and Mary Quarterly* 3rd ser., 58, no. 4 (October 2001): 915.

125   *greater demand for slave labor*: John E. Baur, "The International Repercussions of the Haitian Revolution," *The Americas* 26 (April 1970): 401.

126   *slave population in the Carolinas*: Morgan, *Slave Counterpoint*, 481.

126   *Indian slaves*: Claudio Saunt, *A New Order of Things: Property, Power, and the Transformation of the Creek Indians, 1733–1816*, Cambridge Studies in North American Indian History (New York: Cambridge University Press, 1999), 54, 60.

126   *By and large, . . . swamplands well after that*: Ibid., 51, 164–85. Kenneth Wiggins Porter, *The Negro on the American Frontier: The American Negro, His History and Literature* (New York: Arno Press, 1971); Daniel F. Littlefield, *Africans and Seminoles: From Removal to Emancipation: Contributions in Afro-American and African Studies*, no. 32 (Westport, Conn.: Greenwood Press, 1977); Kenneth Wiggins Porter, "Relations in the South," *Journal of Negro History* 17, no. 3 (July 1922): 321–50.

126   *President James Monroe urged Congress*: Daniel Walker Howe, *What Hath God Wrought: The Transformation of America, 1815–1848*, The Oxford History of the United States (New York: Oxford University Press, 2007), 417–18.

127   *Charles Ball*: Charles Ball, *Fifty Years in Chains: Black Rediscovery* (New York: Dover Publications, 1970).

128   *the concentration of land and slaves*: Cotton production doubled every decade between 1800 and 1830, rising from 20,000 bales to 326,000 by the latter date. Joseph P. Reidy, *From Slavery to Agrarian Capitalism in the Cotton Plantation South:*

Central Georgia, 1800–1880, Fred W. Morrison Series in Southern Studies (Chapel Hill: University of North Carolina Press, 1992), 22.

128 *He offers acerbic sketches . . . resistance to be useless*: Ball, *Fifty Years in Chains*, 39–40, 45, 68, 71, 165. Also see Reidy, *From Slavery to Agrarian Capitalism*, 23.

129 *"died away within me"*: Ball, *Fifty Years in Chains*, 16, 330.

129 *James Forten wrote to William Lloyd Garrison*: James Forten to William Lloyd Garrison, Dec. 31, 1830, in C. Peter Ripley, *The Black Abolitionist Papers*, vol. 3 (Chapel Hill: University of North Carolina Press, 1985), 85–86.

130 *The revolt Nat Turner led*: Henry Irving Tragle, *The Southampton Slave Revolt of 1831: A Compilation of Source Material* (Amherst: University of Massachusetts Press, 1971).

130 *"Negro Conventions"*: Howard Holman Bell, *Minutes of the Proceedings of the National Negro Conventions, 1830–1864: American Negro, His History and Literature* (New York: Arno Press, 1969).

4. "A NEW BIRTH OF FREEDOM"

133 *Frederick Douglass*: Unless otherwise noted, all biographical information on Douglass has been gleaned from William S. McFeely, *Frederick Douglass*, 1st ed. (New York: Norton, 1991).

134 *deemed "irrepressible"*: William Henry Seward first used this phrase in a speech on October 15, 1858, referring to the irreconcilable economic interests of North and South, but institutional fissures over the preceding decade suggest that the sentiment long predated his apt turn of phrase.

135 *"a new birth of freedom"*: See "Gettysburg Address" in Abraham Lincoln, *Collected Works*, vol. 7, 22–23.

135 *Douglass's life in bondage*: McFeely, *Frederick Douglass*, 3–73.

137 *Covey's sadistic beatings*: Frederick Douglass, William L. Andrews, and William S. McFeely, *Narrative of the Life of Frederick Douglass: Authoritative Text, Contexts, Criticism*, 1st ed., A Norton Critical Edition (New York: W. W. Norton & Co., 1996), 47–50.

137 *more to this story of resistance*: McFeely, *Frederick Douglass*, 44–48.

139 *Free blacks found themselves*: James Oliver Horton and Lois E. Horton, *In Hope of Liberty: Culture, Community, and Protest Among Northern Free Blacks, 1700–1860* (New York: Oxford University Press, 1997), 221–23; Leon F. Litwack, *North of Slavery: The Negro in the Free States, 1790–1860* (Chicago: University of Chicago Press, 1961), 39; Nash, *Forging Freedom*, 247–48.

140 *Garnet imperiously declared*: Ripley, *The Black Abolitionist Papers*, vol. 3, 403–12.

141 *an intractable dilemma*: Blacks born free before the war sometimes taunted those freed by the war as merely "sot-free."

141 *On January 29, . . . "a wound on the head"*: Cincinnati *Daily Gazette*, January 29, 1856. The themes discussed owe much to Toni Morrison's evocative novel *Beloved*, which is based on this historical incident.

142 *"Slave Mother Murders Her Child"*: "The Late Tragedy in Cincinnati," *The American Baptist*, Feb. 14, 1856, 134, col. 3; ibid., March 13, 1856, p. 150, col. 2–3.

142 *"When I saw that poor fugitive . . ."*: *Reminiscences of Levi Coffin, the Reputed President of the Underground Railroad . . .*, 2nd ed. (Cincinnati: Robert Clarke and Co., 1880), 564–65. See also *Baltimore Sun*, February 18, 1856.

143 *"with my own teeth . . .":* Ibid. Some accounts suggested that the death of the subsequent child was an accident. *The American Baptist,* March 27, 1856, p. 158, col. 2.

144 *southern law disciplined not only the slave:* Eugene D. Genovese, *Roll, Jordan, Roll: The World the Slaves Made,* 1st ed. (New York: Pantheon Books, 1974), 25–49.

144 *as the twenty-first-century pensioners' interests:* For more on this comparison with contemporary stockholders, see Gavin Wright, *The Political Economy of the Cotton South: Households, Markets, and Wealth in the Nineteenth Century,* 1st ed. (New York: Norton, 1978), 4, 50, 55.

145 *By our best estimates:* Michael Tadman, *Speculators and Slaves: Masters, Traders, and Slaves in the Old South* (Madison: University of Wisconsin Press, 1989), 195–96.

145 *an Appalachian region:* Wilma A. Dunaway, *The African-American Family in Slavery and Emancipation: Studies in Modern Capitalism* (New York: Maison des sciences de l'homme/Cambridge University Press, 2003), 273.

145 *slave folklore suggests:* Lawrence W. Levine, *Black Culture and Black Consciousness: Afro-American Folk Thought from Slavery to Freedom* (New York: Oxford University Press, 1977), 90–121.

146 *Slaves cared about and for one another:* For more on how social relations built up during slavery revealed themselves in freedom, see Julie Saville, *The Work of Reconstruction: From Slave to Wage Laborer in South Carolina, 1860–1870* (Cambridge and New York: Cambridge University Press, 1994), 102–41 passim; and the volumes of the Freedom and Society Project: Ira Berlin et al., *Freedom: A Documentary History of Emancipation, 1861–1867* (Cambridge, UK: Cambridge University Press, 1982), inter alia.

146 *stable marital ties that endured for decades:* The literature documenting this point is voluminous. Among the seminal works along this line, see Herbert George Gutman, *The Black Family in Slavery and Freedom, 1750–1925,* 1st ed. (New York: Pantheon Books, 1976); John W. Blassingame, *The Slave Community: Plantation Life in the Antebellum South* (New York: Oxford University Press, 1972).

146 *two parents living with their children:* Dunaway, *African American Family,* 273.

147 *a mixture of hired slaves and free workers:* Barbara Jeanne Fields, *Slavery and Freedom on the Middle Ground: Maryland During the Nineteenth Century,* Yale Historical Publications, Miscellany 123 (New Haven, Conn.: Yale University Press, 1985), 1–22.

147 *two-parent families in Virginia:* Brenda E. Stevenson, *Life in Black and White: Family and Community in the Slave South* (New York: Oxford University Press, 1996), 160–61.

147 *"Send me a lock of the children's hair . . .":* Ira Berlin, Steven F. Miller, and Leslie S. Rowland, "Afro-American Families in the Transition from Slavery to Freedom," *Radical History Review* 42 (Fall 1988): 94, 105. Spotswood Rice to his children, Sept. 3, 1864, in Ira Berlin, Joseph P. Reidy, and Leslie S. Rowland, *The Black Military Experience,* Freedom, a Documentary History of Emancipation, 1861–1867, Ser. 2 (New York: Cambridge University Press, 1982), 689.

148 *slaves' reliance on kin relations:* Steven Hahn, *A Nation Under Our Feet: Black Political Struggles in the Rural South, from Slavery to the Great Migration* (Cambridge, Mass.: Belknap Press of Harvard University Press, 2003), 17–21.

149 *Nancy Johnson and her husband:* Ira Berlin, *The Destruction of Slavery,* Freedom, a Documentary History of Emancipation, 1861–1867, Ser. 1, vol. 1 (New York: Cambridge University Press, 1985), 150–54.

149 *Sheppard Mallory, Frank Baker, and James Townsend*: Robert Francis Engs, *Freedom's First Generation: Black Hampton, Virginia, 1861–1890* (Philadelphia: University of Pennsylvania Press, 1979), 14.

149 *moonlighting as slave catchers*: The troop served under General John Dix, who had been sympathetic to slaveholders. Berlin, *Destruction of Slavery*, 67. See also Gary W. Gallagher, *The Richmond Campaign of 1862: The Peninsula and the Seven Days: Military Campaigns of the Civil War* (Chapel Hill: University of North Carolina Press, 2000).

149 *General Benjamin Butler*: Chester G. Hearn, *When the Devil Came Down to Dixie: Ben Butler in New Orleans* (Baton Rouge: Louisiana State University Press, 1997), 18–20, 26, 29.

149–150 *Butler's convictions*: Berlin, *Destruction of Slavery*, 12, 15–16, 332.

151 *Butler was in New Orleans*: Ibid., 192–97.

151 *Meanwhile, the Lincoln administration . . . military laborers*: "First Confiscation Act," *Statutes at Large, Treaties, and Proclamations of the United States of America*, vol. 12 (Boston: Little, Brown, 1863), 319; and "Second Confiscation Act," *Statutes at Large, Treaties, and Proclamations of the United States of America*, vol. 12 (Boston: Little, Brown, 1863), 589–92.

152 *"mere friction and abrasion"*: Berlin, *Destruction of Slavery*, 61, 67. See also Abraham Lincoln, *Collected Works*, vol. 5 (New Brunswick, N.J.: Rutgers University Press, 1953–1990), 317–19.

153 *"a general strike"*: W.E.B. Du Bois, *Black Reconstruction: An Essay Toward a History of the Part Which Black Folk Played in the Attempt to Reconstruct Democracy in America, 1860–1880*, 1st ed. (New York: Harcourt, Brace and Co., 1935), 55, 64.

153 *"Fugitive Rebels"*: General David Hunter to Edwin M. Stanton, June 23, 1862, Berlin, Reidy, and Rowland, *Black Miliary Experience*, 51.

154 *"render him obedience and service"*: Berlin, *Destruction of Slavery*, 129–30.

154 *In the Sea Islands*: Willie Lee Nichols Rose, *Rehearsal for Reconstruction: The Port Royal Experiment* (New York: Oxford University Press, 1978).

155 *reframed the postwar labor problem*: Charlotte L. Forten, *The Journals of Charlotte Forten Grimké*, ed. Brenda E. Stevenson, The Schomburg Library of Nineteenth-Century Black Women Writers (New York: Oxford University Press, 1988). Willie Lee Nichols Rose, *Rehearsal for Reconstruction: The Port Royal Experiment* (Indianapolis: Bobbs-Merrill, 1964).

155 *Samuel Elliott's father*: Berlin, *Destruction of Slavery*, 146–50.

155 *150,000 slaves*: Ibid., 676.

155 *to private northern entrepreneurs*: Lawrence N. Powell, *New Masters: Northern Planters During the Civil War and Reconstruction*, Yale Historical Publications, Miscellany (New Haven, Conn.: Yale University Press, 1980), 124.

155 *Davis Bend*: Joseph Davis was forced to evacuate in April 1862, shortly after the capture of New Orleans by Union naval and military forces. Despite his earlier paternalistic treatment of them, most of the slaves refused to accompany the family into exile, but stayed on to raise crops in a collective. Steven J. Ross, "Freed Soil, Freed Labor, Freed Men: John Eaton and the Davis Bend Experiment," *Journal of Southern History* 44 (May 1978): 218–19; Janet Sharp Hermann, *The Pursuit of a Dream* (New York: Oxford University Press, 1981), 41–42.

156 *Octave Johnson*: "Deposition of Octave Johnson," in Berlin, *Destruction of Slavery*, 217.

156   *among slaves who stayed put*: Ibid., 193–94.

157   *the master-slave relationship dissolved*: Ibid., 42–43, 197, 264, 516, 666–78; Ira Berlin, *The Wartime Genesis of Free Labor: The Lower South*, Freedom: A Documentary History of Emancipation, 1861–1867, ser. 1, vol. 3 (New York: Cambridge University Press, 1990), 623.

157   *Mackley Woods . . . recruiters to take them*: Berlin, *Destruction of Slavery*, 263–65, 327.

157   *hardly a reassuring analogy*: Ibid., 668–69.

158   *"the rights of [a] freedman"*: General Order No. 14, March 23, 1865, in U.S. War Department, *The War of the Rebellion: A Compilation of the Official Records of the Union and Confederate Armies*, 128 vols. (Washington, D.C.: Government Printing Office, 1880–1901), ser. 4, vol. 3, pp. 1161–62.

158   *"fighting for the dead past, . . . among the whole people"*: The Frederick Douglass Papers, Series on Speeches, Debates, and Interviews, vol. 4, 1864–80, (New Haven, Conn: Yale University Press, 1991), 3–24, quotes 13–14.

159   *Lincoln adopted an approach*: David Herbert Donald, *Lincoln* (New York: Simon and Schuster, 1995), esp. 469–75, 483–88.

159   *little historical precedent*: For an extended discussion of the theoretical problem here, see Thomas C. Holt, "'The Essence of the Contract': The Articulation of Race, Gender, and Political Economy in British Emancipation Policy, 1838–1866," in *Beyond Slavery: Explorations of Race, Labor, and Citizenship in Post-emancipation Societies*, eds. Frederick Cooper, Thomas C. Holt, and Rebecca J. Scott (Chapel Hill: University of North Carolina Press, 2000), 33–59.

159   *post-emancipation social order in the British West Indies*: See Holt, *The Problem of Freedom*.

160   *the U.S. political order*: For an elaboration of this argument, see Eric Foner, *Nothing but Freedom: Emancipation and Its Legacy*, Walter Lynwood Fleming Lectures in Southern History (Baton Rouge: Louisiana State University Press, 1983).

160   *The Republican Party's stronghold lay*: For discussion of northern racial context and laws, see V. Jacque Voegeli, *Free but Not Equal: The Midwest and the Negro During the Civil War* (Chicago: University of Chicago Press, 1967); and Litwack, *North of Slavery: The Negro in the Free States, 1790–1860*.

160   *exclusionist sentiments*: For example, Illinois voted two to one to bar further black settlement. Voegeli, *Free but Not Equal*, 4, 17.

161   *ameliorative effect on racial prejudices*: Ibid.; Eric Foner, *Reconstruction: America's Unfinished Revolution, 1863–1877*, 1st ed., The New American Nation Series (New York: Harper and Row, 1988), 223.

161   *enthusiastic advocacy*: Black recruitment began to gain support from employers anxious to hold on to white skilled labor and from white males anxious to avoid the draft. Mary Francis Berry, *Military Necessity and Civil Rights Policy: Black Citizenship and the Constitution, 1861–1868* (Port Washington, N.Y.: Kennikat Press, 1977).

161   *General Order No. 100*: Ibid., 61–62.

162   *unequal rates of pay*: Berlin, Reidy, and Rowland, *Black Miliary Experience*, 20.

162   *blacks were repeatedly thrown into battle*: In quick succession during the spring and summer of 1863, three battles in which black troops displayed exceptional valor under fire—Port Hudson (May), Milliken's Bend (June), and Fort Wagner (July)—substantially reduced invidious judgments of their readiness for battle. Ibid., 518–19.

162 *efforts to fill manpower needs*: Lincoln's effort to call up three hundred thousand more troops on October 17, 1863, was unsuccessful, for example. Berry, *Military Necessity and Civil Rights*, 65, 73.

162 *Congress passed legislation*: To track legislation and specific citations, see Berlin, Reidy, and Rowland, *Black Miliary Experience*.

162 *black men's military service*: A total of 178,975 black soldiers and 9,596 sailors made up 10 percent of Union forces. Ibid., 14. Also see Berry, *Military Necessity and Civil Rights*, 84, 89.

162 *unique social circumstance of black soldiers*: Berry, *Military Necessity and Civil Rights*, 90, 91.

163 *In July 1865, there were 123,156*: Ibid.

163 *right to keep their sidearms*: Allowing soldiers to buy their weapons was then common practice. Ibid., 92.

163 *"He who fights the battles of America . . ."*: Ibid., 94 n21.

165 *Even northern Democrats invoked the linkage*: For example, in January 1866, Democrat John W. Chandler declared that it could be foreseen that demands for full citizenship would be the logical consequence of the decision to enlist blacks into military service. Ibid., 69, 96. On the broader history of the link between military service and citizenship, see Linda K. Kerber, *No Constitutional Right to Be Ladies: Women and the Obligations of Citizenship*, 1st ed. (New York: Hill and Wang, 1998).

165 *"Above all, . . . our hope"*: Berry, *Military Necessity and Civil Rights*, 95.

165 *a resolution urging citizenship*: Ibid., 96.

165 *violence swept Memphis and New Orleans*: Hannah Rosen, *Terror in the Heart of Freedom: Citizenship, Sexual Violence, and the Meaning of Race in the Postemancipation South*, Gender and American Culture (Chapel Hill: University of North Carolina Press, 2009); Gilles Vandal, *The New Orleans Riot of 1866: Anatomy of Tragedy* (Lafayette: Center for Louisiana Studies at Southwestern Louisiana University, 1983); and James G. Hollandsworth, Jr., *An Absolute Massacre: The New Orleans Race Riot of July 30, 1866* (Baton Rouge: Louisiana State University, 2001.)

166 *Congress passed four statutes . . . "male citizens" . . . as whites*: "Chap. CLIII—An Act to provide for the more efficient Government of the Rebel States." *Statutes at Large*, 39th Congress, 2nd session (March 2, 1867), pp. 428–30; "Chap. VI—An Act supplementary to an Act entitled 'An Act to provide for the more efficient Government of the Rebel States.'" *Statutes at Large*, 40th Congress, 1st session (March 23, 1867), pp. 2–5; "Chap. XXX—An Act supplementary to an Act entitled 'An Act to provide for the more efficient Government of the Rebel States.'" *Statutes at Large*, 40th Congress, 1st session (July 19, 1867), pp. 14–16; and "An Act to amend the act passed March 23, 1867, entitled 'An Act supplementary to an Act entitled 'An Act to provide for the more efficient Government of the Rebel States.'" *Statutes at Large* (March 11, 1868). Tennessee was excluded because, although nominally part of the Confederacy, large sections of the state had been substantially under Union control throughout the war, which facilitated an earlier start to the readmission process. It had already ratified the Fourteenth Amendment when the Reconstruction legislation was enacted.

166 *Black women and children joined them*: Elsa Barkley Brown, "Negotiating and Transforming the Public Sphere: African American Political Life in the Transition from Slavery to Freedom," *Public Culture* 7 (1994): 107–46; Thomas C. Holt, *Black over White: Negro Political Leadership in South Carolina During Reconstruction*, Blacks in the New World (Urbana: University of Illinois Press, 1977), 35.

167   *southern white males' rejection of blacks*: Rosen, *Terror in the Heart of Freedom*, 93–105.

167   *Efforts to build political community*: Holt, *Black over White*, 9–40; Elsa Barkley Brown, "Negotiating and Transforming the Public Sphere."

167   *the freedpeople's political sophistication*: Holt, *Black over White*, 43–71.

168   *Almost all of them were ministers*: The power of church discipline on broader community mores and leadership can be gleaned from discussions in Genovese, *Roll, Jordan, Roll*; Sobel, *The World They Made Together*.

168   *Reverend Garrison Frazier*: Berlin, *The Wartime Genesis of Free Labor: The Lower South*, 332–37.

168   *Special Field Order No. 15*: "Special Field Order, No. 15, Headquarters Military Division of the Mississippi, Jan. 16, 1865, in Berlin, *The Wartime Genesis of Free Labor: The Upper South*, Freedom: A Documentary History of Emancipation, 1861–1867, ser. 1, vol. 2 (New York: Cambridge University Press, 1993), 339–40.

169   *to clear the black settlers off the land*: William S. McFeely, *Yankee Stepfather: General O. O. Howard and the Freedmen*, Yale Publications in American Studies 15 (New Haven, Conn.: Yale University Press, 1968); Steven Hahn, Steven F. Miller, Susan E. O'Donovan, John C. Rodrigue, and Leslie S. Rowland, eds. *Land and Labor, 1865*, Freedom: A Documentary History of Emancipation, 1861–1867, ser. 3, vol. 1 (Chapel Hill: University of North Carolina Press, 2008), 430–93.

169   *"remain on them working . . ." "stripped and flogged"*: Hahn, ed. *Land and Labor, 1865*, 440–41.

169   *Bayley Wyatt . . . "my people is poor"*: *Philadelphia Freedmen's Bulletin*, March 1867, 15–16, quoted in Edward Magdol, *A Right to the Land: Essays on the Freedmen's Community*, Contributions in American History 61 (Westport, Conn.: Greenwood Press, 1977), 171–72.

170   *that no worker be hired*: Ibid.

170   *These "Black Codes"*: Foner, *Reconstruction*, 199–202. See also Rebecca Scott, "The Battle over the Child: Child Apprenticeship and the Freedmen's Bureau in North Carolina," *Prologue: Journal of the National Archives*, 10 (Summer 1978), 101–13.

170   *refused to sign contracts*: Hahn, *A Nation Under Our Feet*, 154–59.

171   *to make the laborers his creditors*: For detailed exposition of this complex transition, see Gerald David Jaynes, *Branches Without Roots: Genesis of the Black Working Class in the American South, 1862–1882* (New York: Oxford University Press, 1986). And the volumes of Ira Berlin et al., Freedom: A Documentary History of Emancipation, inter alia.

172   *political mobilization of black voters*: Holt, *Black over White*; Foner, *Reconstruction*.

172   *prolonged secular depression*: For the profound implications of the 1873 crash, see Foner, *Reconstruction*, 512–19.

172   *The planter's control of the crop's disposition*: Harold D. Woodman, *New South, New Law: The Legal Foundations of Credit and Labor Relations in the Postbellum Agricultural South*, Walter Lynwood Fleming Lectures in Southern History (Baton Rouge: Louisiana State University Press, 1995).

173   *They would draw on the world they knew*: Holt, *Black over White*; Saville, *The Work of Reconstruction*; Hahn, *A Nation Under Our Feet*.

173   *Recent historical studies suggest*: Hahn, *A Nation Under Our Feet*; Dylan C. Penningroth, *The Claims of Kinfolk: African American Property and Community in the*

Nineteenth-Century South (Chapel Hill: University of North Carolina Press, 2003), 163–86; Saville, *The Work of Reconstruction*, 102–42.

173 *work regimes and demographic patterns*: It is not clear, for example, whether property rights and task work developed outside the large plantation zones of the Lower South, in places such as the Virginia Piedmont, a state where a plurality of slaves still resided on the eve of the Civil War.

174 *public relief in Georgia . . . social safety net.*: Susan Eva O'Donovan, *Becoming Free in the Cotton South* (Cambridge, Mass.: Harvard University Press, 2007), 163–64, 172.

174 *The transition . . . heads of their households*: For an insightful exploration of the complex, sometimes contradictory impact that emancipation had on freedpeople's households and gender relations, see ibid., 199–200; Nancy D. Bercaw, *Gendered Freedoms: Race, Rights, and the Politics of Household in the Delta, 1861–1875* (Gainesville: University Press of Florida, 2003), 31–50, 124–28, 145–57; and Noralee Frankel, *Freedom's Women: Black Women and Families in Civil War Era Mississippi* (Bloomington: Indiana University Press, 1999), 79–122.

175 *flocked to army chaplains*: Over a seven-month period in Vicksburg alone, 1,456 marriages were registered. In Warrenton, North Carolina, there were 150 in two days. Laura F. Edwards, " 'The Marriage Covenant Is at the Foundation of All Our Rights': The Politics of Slave Marriages in North Carolina after Emancipation," *Law and History Review* 14, no. 1 (Spring 1996): 24.

175 *"The Marriage Covenant is at the foundation . . .":* Ibid., 14. Also see Berlin, Reidy, and Rowland, *Black Miliary Experience*, 672.

175 *encouraged ex-slaves to marry*: For example, see southwest Georgia as discussed in O'Donovan, *Becoming Free*, 194.

176 *women and children as full participants*: Barkley Brown, "Negotiating and Transforming the Public Sphere." On this point more generally, see Saville, *The Work of Reconstruction*.

176 *committee studying labor conditions*: See especially the testimony of Floyd Thornhill and Thomas Smith in *Report of the Committee of the Senate upon the Relations Between Labor and Capital, and Testimony Taken by the Committee*, vol. IV (Washington, D.C.: Government Printing Office, 1885), 3–12, 447–50.

177 *"Like a clap of thunder . . .":* Frederick Douglass, "The Return of the Democratic Party to Power," in *The Life and Writings of Frederick Douglass*, ed. Philip Foner (New York: International Publisher, 1950–1975), 4: 413–26, quote on p. 423.

178 *"a bright octoroon, almost white":* "The Color Prejudice," *New York Times*, Nov. 25, 1879, p. 8; John R. Howard, *The Shifting Wind: The Supreme Court and Civil Rights from Reconstruction to Brown* (Albany: State University of New York Press, 1999), 125–32.

178 *The fifth and final case*: Ibid.; Charles Fairman, *Reconstruction and Reunion, 1864–88*, History of the Supreme Court of the United States, vols. 6–7 (New York: Macmillan, 1971), 551–57.

178 *The burden of defending*: In *Supreme Court of the United States at October Term, 1882, No. 28, Richard A. Robinson and Sallie J., his wife, Plaintiffs in Error, vs. Memphis and Charleston Railroad Company*, Defendant in Error, Statement of Case, Assignment of Errors, and Brief of Wm. M. Randolph of Counsel for Plaintiffs in Error.

179 *When a man has emerged from slavery . . . :* Fairman, *Reconstruction and Reunion*, 561.

179 *Justice John Marshall Harlan*: Linda Przybyszewski, *The Republic According to John Marshall Harlan*, Studies in Legal History (Chapel Hill: University of North Carolina Press, 1999).
180 *"it decreed universal freedom throughout the United States"*: Howard, *Shifting Wind*, 130–31.
181 *"Nothing has hurt us so much . . ."*: Ibid., 132.
181 *a hopeful biracial political movement*: Jane Elizabeth Dailey, *Before Jim Crow: The Politics of Race in Post-emancipation Virginia*, Gender and American Culture (Chapel Hill: University of North Carolina Press, 2000), 103–31.
181 *"conditions are changed . . ."*: Frederick Douglass, "The Return of the Democratic Party to Power," in *The Life and Writings of Frederick Douglass*, 413–26, quote on p. 413.

5. RAGTIME
185 *"the famous colored statesman"*: Chicago *Daily News*, October 21, 1892.
185 *American interests*: McFeely, *Frederick Douglass*, 366–67.
186 *"many rounds of applause . . ."*: Christopher Robert Reed, *All the World Is Here!: The Black Presence at White City*, Blacks in the Diaspora (Bloomington: Indiana University Press, 2000), 35; *Chicago Tribune*, Oct. 22, 1892.
186 *Frank H. Stewart and Charles McD. Carter*: These soldiers are described in the following muster rolls during this period: Register of Enlistments, M233, Reel 43, Vol. 82, p. 275 (Frank H. Stewart); Reel 44, Vol. 84, p. 225 (Charles McD. Carter). Also see Frank H. Stewart pension file, May 19, 1915, [file no.] C-2,470,377.
186 *black troops' principal assignments*: Frank N. Schubert, *Buffalo Soldiers, Braves, and the Brass: The Story of Fort Robinson, Nebraska* (Shippensburg, Pa.: White Mane Pub. Co., 1993), 19–42.
186 *back to Fort Robinson, Nebraska*: Willard B. Gatewood, *Black Americans and the White Man's Burden, 1898–1903*, Blacks in the New World (Urbana: University of Illinois Press, 1975), 43.
187 *Private Henry Venable*: See muster rolls listing Henry Venable and Charles Lewis, respectively: Register of Enlistments, M233, Reel 43, Vol. 83, p. 92; Reel 45, Vol. 87, p. 245; Reel 42, Vol. 80, p. 310.
187 *David Fagen*: Michael C. Robinson and Frank N. Schubert, "David Fagen: An Afro-American Rebel in the Philippines, 1899–1901," *Pacific Historical Review* 44 (February 1975); Frank N. Schubert, "Seeking David Fagen: The Search for a Black Rebel's Florida Roots," *Tampa Bay History* 22 (2008).
187 *service to their country's imperial ambitions*: See generally, Rebecca J. Scott, *Degrees of Freedom: Louisiana and Cuba After Slavery* (Cambridge, Mass.: Belknap Press of Harvard University Press, 2005).
188 *tensions . . . played out across many domains*: Nell Irvin Painter, *Standing at Armageddon: United States, 1877–1919*, 1st ed. (New York: W. W. Norton, 1987).
189 *José Martí journeyed to Ybor City*: Susan D. Greenbaum, *More Than Black: Afro-Cubans in Tampa*, New World Diaspora Series (Gainesville: University Press of Florida, 2002), 65–67; Nancy Raquel Mirabel, "Telling Silences and Making Community: Afro-Cubans and African Americans in Ybor City and Tampa, 1899–1915," in *Between Race and Empire: African Americans and Cubans Before the Cuban Revolution*, eds. Lisa Brock and Bryne Contenata Fuertes (Philadelphia, Pa.: Temple University Press,

1998), 49–69. See also Ada Ferrer, *Insurgent Cuba: Race, Nation, and Revolution, 1868–1898* (Chapel Hill: University of North Carolina Press, 1999); Scott, *Degrees of Freedom*.

189   *the World's Columbian Exposition*: The literature on the fair is voluminous and in- terdisciplinary. I have drawn this narrative and some of the interpretations mostly from the following sources: Curtis M. Hensley, "The World as Marketplace: Com- modification of the Exotic at the World's Columbian Exposition Chicago, 1893," in *Exhibiting Cultures: The Poetics and Politics of Museum Display*, eds. Ivan Karp and Steve D. Lavine (Washington, D.C.: Smithsonian Institution Press, 1991), 344–65. Robert W. Rydell, *All the World's a Fair: Visions of Empire at American International Expositions, 1876–1916* (Chicago: University of Chicago Press, 1984). Neil Harris et al., *Grand Illusions: Chicago's World's Fair of 1893* (Chicago: Chicago Historical So- ciety, 1993); Robert Muccigrosso, *Celebrating the New World: Chicago's Columbian Exposition of 1893*, The American Ways Series (Chicago: I.R. Dee, 1993).

190   *"a consummation and a new beginning"*: Alan Trachtenberg, *The Incorporation of America: Culture and Society in the Gilded Age*, American Century Series (New York: Hill and Wang, 1982), 209.

190   *Frederick Jackson Turner*: Frederick Jackson Turner, "The Significance of the Frontier in American History," in *The Frontier in American History* (New York: Holt, Rinehart and Winston, 1950), 1–37, quotes pp. 2, 3, 4, 24, 37.

191   *"a new Mediterranean" city*: "As Gath Sees It," *Chicago Tribune*, Oct. 19, 1892.

192   *total world production of goods and services*: E. J. Hobsbawm, *The Age of Empire, 1875–1914*, History of Civilization (London: Weidenfeld and Nicolson, 1987), 34–55.

192   *"a ghost of old commitments"*: McFeely, *Frederick Douglass*, 363.

193   *politics of reunion and sectional reconciliation*: David W. Blight, *Race and Reunion: The Civil War in American Memory* (Cambridge, Mass.: Belknap Press of Harvard University Press, 2001).

193   *"carnivals of the industrial age"*: Hinsley, "The World as Marketplace," 344.

194   *"an illustrated encyclopedia of humanity"*: Ibid., 346. Trachtenberg, *The Incorporation of America*, 213–16. See also Rydell, *All the World's a Fair*.

194   *"no 'white American citizen's day'"*: Elliott M. Rudwick and August Meier, "Black Man in the 'White City': Negroes and the Columbian Exposition, 1893," *Phylon* 26, no. 4 (1965): 360.

195   *Thomas J. Bell*: Reed, *All the World Is Here!*, 111.

195   *"The Reason Why the Colored American . . ."*: Rudwick and Meier, "Black Man in the 'White City.'"

195   *Douglass arrived early*: McFeely, *Frederick Douglass*, 370–72.

196   *Douglass's speech . . . "we kill their souls"*: Frederick Douglass, *The Frederick Doug- lass Papers*, ed. John W. Blassingame (New Haven, Conn.: Yale University Press, 1979), 593.

197   *the Fon villagers*: Reed, *All the World Is Here!*, especially pp. 143–78.

198   *The world the Fon came from*: Robin Law, "The Politics of Commercial Transition: Factional Conflict in Dahomey in the Context of the Ending of the Atlantic Slave Trade," *Journal of African History* 38, no. 2 (1997); Patrick Manning, *Francophone Sub- Saharan Africa, 1880–1985* (Cambridge, UK: Cambridge University Press, 1988); Dov Ronen, "The Colonial Elite in Dahomey," *African Studies Review* 17 (April 1974).

198   *Douglass paid them a visit*: Reed, *All the World Is Here!*, 168.

200 *410 black Arkansans:* Edwin S. Redkey, *Black Exodus; Black Nationalist and Back-to-Africa Movements, 1890–1910,* Yale Publications in American Studies 17 (New Haven, Conn.: Yale University Press, 1969), 175.

200 *back-to-Africa emigration movements:* Ibid.; Kenneth C. Barnes, *Journey of Hope: The Back-to-Africa Movement in Arkansas in the Late 1800s,* John Hope Franklin Series in African American History and Culture (Chapel Hill: University of North Carolina Press, 2004); Claude Andrew Clegg, *The Price of Liberty: African Americans and the Making of Liberia* (Chapel Hill: University of North Carolina Press, 2004); James T. Campbell, *Middle Passages: African American Journeys to Africa, 1787–2005,* The Penguin History of American Life (New York: Penguin Press, 2006).

200 *African missionary projects:* James T. Campbell, *Songs of Zion: The African Methodist Episcopal Church in the United States and South Africa* (New York: Oxford University Press, 1995), 98.

201 *"African missions . . . Providence":* Ibid., 99.

201 *Henry McNeal Turner:* Ibid., 83–88.

201 *AME women's groups . . . out of Egyptian darkness:* Ibid., 95–97.

202 *black seamen:* W. Jeffrey Bolster, *Black Jacks: African American Seamen in the Age of Sail* (Cambridge, Mass.: Harvard University Press, 1997), 2, 6, 220–32.

202 *McAdoo's Jubilee Singers:* Campbell, *Songs of Zion,* 103, 126, 129, 131–37.

202 *"the nadir" . . . "efforts to improve it":* Rayford Whittingham Logan, *The Betrayal of the Negro, from Rutherford B. Hayes to Woodrow Wilson,* new expanded ed. (New York: Collier Books, 1965), 62.

203 *As historian Christopher Reed has shown:* Reed, *All the World Is Here!,* chap. 6.

203 *Anna Julia Cooper, Fannie Jackson Coppin:* Vivian M. May, *Anna Julia Cooper, Visionary Black Feminist: A Critical Introduction* (New York: Routledge, 2007); Linda Marie Perkins, *Fanny Jackson Coppin and the Institute for Colored Youth, 1865–1902, Educated Women* (New York: Garland, 1987).

203 *working as a "chairboy":* Reed, *All the World Is Here!,* 58, 76–77.

204 *"a history beyond memory":* David W. Blight, "'For Something Beyond the Battlefield': Frederick Douglass and the Struggle for the Memory of the Civil War," *Journal of American History* 75 no. 4 (March 1989): 1156–78, quote on p. 1158. See also Blight, *Race and Reunion.*

204 *Washington's story of self-making:* Booker T. Washington, *Up from Slavery* (New York: Doubleday, 1901).

204 *Charles W. Chesnutt:* Frances Richardson Keller, "Toward Human Understanding: The Life and Times of Charles Waddell Chesnutt" (Ph.D. Thesis, University of Chicago, Department of History, December 1973), 170–76; Charles Waddell Chesnutt *The Journals of Charles W. Chesnutt,* ed. Richard H. Brodhead (Durham, N.C.: Duke University Press, 1993), 57–58, 93, 141–43, 146–48.

205 *Anna J. Cooper:* May, *Anna Julia Cooper, Visionary Black Feminist.* Also see Anna J. Cooper, *A Voice from the South,* Schomburg Library of Nineteenth-Century Black Women Writers (New York: Oxford University Press, 1988).

205 *"I sit with Shakespeare . . .":* W.E.B. Du Bois, *The Souls of Black Folk,* 109.

206 *"uplift the race":* Stephanie J. Shaw, *What a Woman Ought to Be and to Do: Black Professional Women Workers During the Jim Crow Era,* Women in Culture and Society (Chicago: University of Chicago Press, 1996), 13–40; E. Franklin Frazier, *Black Bourgeoisie: The Rise of a New Middle Class in the United States* (New York: Collier Books, 1962), 113. Also see Evelyn Brooks Higginbotham, *Righteous Discontent:*

The Women's Movement in the Black Baptist Church, 1880–1920 (Cambridge, Mass.: Harvard University Press, 1993).

206 *The Chicago fair itself . . .* Oak and Ivy: Reed, *All the World Is Here!*, 45, 102, 104.

206 *a speaker was shouted down:* Ibid., 128.

206 *More often than not . . . "is passing away":* May Wright Sewall, *The World's Congress of Representative Women: A Historical Résumé for Popular Circulation of the World's Congress of Representative Women, Convened in Chicago on May 15, and Adjourned on May 22, 1893, under the Auspices of the Woman's Branch of the World's Congress Auxiliary* (Chicago Rand McNally, 1894), 704–17, quotes on pp. 704, 714, 717.

207 *"the threshold of a new women's era":* Frances Ellen Watkins Harper and Susan B. Anthony Collection (Library of Congress), *Iola Leroy* (Philadelphia, Pa.: Garrigues Brothers, 1892), 271; Reed, *All the World Is Here!*, 122, 125, 126.

208 *At the Congress on Labor:* Reed, *All the World Is Here!*, 10, 86, 129.

208 *ordinary black Americans at the fair:* Ibid., 104–6, 118.

208 *Scott Joplin:* Susan Curtis, *Dancing to a Black Man's Tune: A Life of Scott Joplin*, Missouri Biography Series (Columbia: University of Missouri Press, 1994), 45–48.

209 *"the zest of unexpectedness":* Reed, *All the World Is Here!*, 103. On ragtime piano technique, see James Weldon Johnson, *The Autobiography of an Ex-Colored Man* in *The Selected Writings of James Weldon Johnson*, ed. Sondra Kathryn Wilson, 2 vols. (New York: Oxford University Press, 1995), 2:314.

209 *Aunt Jemima pancakes:* Other items introduced at the Chicago fair were hamburgers and Juicy Fruit gum. For other examples of racial advertising in this period, see Raymond Bachollet, Jean-Barthélémi Debost, Anne-Claude Lelieur, and Marie-Christine Peyrière, *Négripub: L'image des Noirs dans la Publicité* (Paris: Somogy, 1982).

211 *the least segregated mode of transport:* Charles A. Lofgren, *The Plessy Case: A Legal-Historical Interpretation* (New York: Oxford University Press, 1987), 9–17.

211 *The resegregation process:* Ibid., 21–22.

212 *first-class prices for second-class accommodation:* Ibid., 21.

212 *"blacks commonly found themselves . . .":* Ibid., 15.

213 *"[when] a poorly dressed, slovenly white man . . .":* Ibid., 16.

213 *"Citizenship is national and has no color":* Ibid., 28.

213 *the African American community of New Orleans:* Ibid., 16–17; Rebecca J. Scott, "The Atlantic World and the Road to *Plessy v. Ferguson*," *Journal of American History* 94, no. 3 (Dec. 2007), 726–33; Scott, *Degrees of Freedom*, 35–52.

214 *the Roudanez family:* Joseph and Caryn Cosse Bell Logsdon, "The Americanization of Black New Orleans, 1850–1900," in *Creole New Orleans: Race and Americanization*, eds. Arnold R. Hirsch and Joseph Logsdon (Baton Rouge: Louisiana State University Press, 1992), 229.

214 *the "New Negro" generation:* Ibid.

214 *the Comité des Citoyens contacted Albion W. Tourgée:* Otto H. Olsen and American Institute for Marxist Studies, *The Thin Disguise: Turning Point in Negro History; Plessy v. Ferguson; a Documentary Presentation, 1864–1896* (New York: Published for A.I.M.S. by Humanities Press, 1967), 1–30.

214 *setting up a test case:* Lofgren, *The Plessy Case*, 16–17.; Barbara Welke, "'When All the Women Were White, and All the Blacks Were Men': Gender, Class, Race, and the Road to Plessy, 1855–1914," *Law and History Review* 13, no. 2 (Fall 1995), 261–316.

215 *Daniel F. Desdunes:* Lofgren, *The Plessy Case*, 39–41.

215 *Purchasing a ticket . . . three more years:* Ibid.

216 *Chesnutt quipped, "I presume . . ."*: Brook Thomas, *Plessy v. Ferguson: A Brief History with Documents*, Bedford Series in History and Culture (Boston: Bedford Books, 1997), 157.

216 *Only Justice John Marshall Harlan . . . the wrong this day done"*: (All quotes pertaining to *Plessy v. Ferguson* that follow are from Harlan's decision. See full text in ibid., 51–60, quotes on pp. 59–60.

218 *The southern press and national law reviews*: Thomas, *Plessy v. Ferguson*, 127–34; Lofgren, *The Plessy Case*, 208.

219 *"such an unjust law . . . is inflicted"*: Thomas, *Plessy v. Ferguson*, 135.

219 *"My daddy was a free man"*: Nate Shaw and Theodore Rosengarten, *All God's Dangers: The Life of Nate Shaw*, 1st Vintage Books ed. (New York: Vintage Books, 1984), 26–27.

220 *"I seed my daddy cleaned up . . ."*: Ibid., 27.

221 *"wasn't a slave but he lived like one"*: Ibid., 33.

221 *"he'd feed us just on his game"*: Ibid., 31.

221 *"made up his mind . . . when you got too high"*: Ibid., xxi, 13, 16, 27, 31.

222 *Robert Charles*: William Ivy Hair, *Carnival of Fury: Robert Charles and the New Orleans Race Riot of 1900*, updated ed. (Baton Rouge: Louisiana State University Press, 2008).

223 *Robert Charles grew up*: Ibid., 1–32; Dailey, *Before Jim Crow*, 103–31.

223 *after the riot in Copiah*: Hair, *Carnival of Fury*, 33–68.

224 *Charles was deeply angered*: Ibid., 107; W. Fitzhugh Brundage, *Lynching in the New South: Georgia and Virginia, 1880–1930*, Blacks in the New World (Urbana: University of Illinois Press, 1993), 34, 82–84.

225 *five hundred blacks to Liberia*: Hair, *Carnival of Fury*, 103.

225 *Hayes Cobb's son Ned*: Shaw and Rosengarten, *All God's Dangers*, 312.

226 *Thirty-three-year-old W.E.B. Du Bois*: Du Bois, *Souls of Black Folk*, 112 (original article in *The World's Work*, June 2, 1901, 848–66).

226 *"we scarce know which we preferred"*: Ibid., 128, 129.

226 *Du Bois's unnamed personae*: For more on folklore traditions on outlaws and bad niggers, see Schubert, "Seeking David Fagen"; Leon F. Litwack, *Trouble in Mind: Black Southerners in the Age of Jim Crow*, 1st ed. (New York: Alfred A. Knopf, 1998), 437–44, 447, 450, 455; Lawrence W. Levine, *Black Culture and Black Consciousness: Afro-American Folk Thought from Slavery to Freedom* (New York: Oxford University Press, 1977), 407–20; and especially "The Ballad of Joe Meek," in Sterling Allen Brown, *The Collected Poems of Sterling A. Brown* (New York: Harper & Row, 1980), 148–52.

227 *"a raised road, built" . . . "by their forced labor"*: Du Bois, *Souls of Black Folk*, 122, 126.

227 *"the animate machinery . . ."*: Hair, *Carnival of Fury*, 36.

228 *the Louisville, New Orleans and Texas Railroad*: *Louisville, New Orleans & c. Railway v. Mississippi*, 133U.S. 587, cited in Thomas, *Plessy v. Ferguson*, 46.

228 *leased convicts provided southern employers*: Alexander C. Lichtenstein, *Twice the Work of Free Labor: The Political Economy of Convict Labor in the New South*, The Haymarket Series (London; New York: Verso, 1996), 3, 18–19.

228 *Southern convict lease . . . twenty years later*: Ibid., 40, 73, 77; Mary Ellen Curtin, *Black Prisoners and Their World, Alabama, 1865–1900*, Carter G. Woodson Institute Series in Black Studies (Charlottesville: University Press of Virginia, 2000), 1, 67–71.

229 *Lichtenstein has astutely observed*: Lichtenstein, *Twice the Work of Free Labor*, 62, 72.

229 *Indeed, Georgia discovered . . . a strikebreaker*: Ibid., 82.

229 Convict leasing posed . . . a white prisoner: Curtin, Black Prisoners and Their World, 2, 7, 98, 131; Lichtenstein, Twice the Work of Free Labor, xv, 86.

230 The overwhelming majority of the crimes: Lichtenstein, Twice the Work of Free Labor, 70–71; Curtin, Black Prisoners and Their World, 51–54.

230 dragnets to ensnare not only croppers but black renters and owners: Curtin, Black Prisoners and Their World, 51–54.

230 county court systems . . . fines and costs: Ibid., 178–79.

230 inter- and intra-class conflicts: C. Vann Woodward, Origins of the New South, 1877–1913, History of the South (Baton Rouge: Louisiana State University Press, 1951).

231 the incubus: Glenda Elizabeth Gilmore, Gender and Jim Crow: Women and the Politics of White Supremacy in North Carolina, 1896–1920, Gender and American Culture (Chapel Hill: University of North Carolina Press, 1996), 85.

231 Thrust beyond the boundaries of human sympathy: Glenda E. Gilmore, "Murder, Memory, and the Flight of the Incubus," in Democracy Betrayed: The Wilmington Race Riot of 1898 and Its Legacy, eds. David S. Cecelski and Timothy B. Tyson (Chapel Hill: University of North Carolina Press, 1998), 86.

233 Booker T. Washington: Louis R. Harlan, Booker T. Washington: The Making of a Black Leader, 1856–1901 (New York: Oxford University Press, 1972), 204–28.

234 received warmly by many prominent black leaders: Booker T. Washington, Louis R. Harlan, and Raymond Smock, The Booker T. Washington Papers, 14 vols. (Urbana: University of Illinois Press, 1972), 24–26.

234 "Tuskegee was a revelation", . . . "their children for instruction": Charles W. Chesnutt, "A Visit to Tuskegee," Cleveland Leader, March 31, 1901.

235 Frank H. Stewart: See Stewart pension file, May 19, 1915, [file no.] C-2,470,377.

235 the dishonorable discharge of 167 men: Roosevelt's Brownsville decision was reviewed in 1972 and overturned, thanks largely to the historical investigations of John D. Weaver (The Brownsville Raid [New York: Norton, 1970]), whose work provided the evidentiary basis for this paragraph, together with a personal communication from Frank N. Schubert (e-mail message to author, April 30, 2009). For the earlier violent incident in Tampa involving black troops on their way to Cuba, see Gatewood, Black Americans and the White Man's Burden, 52–53.

6. "A SECOND EMANCIPATION"

237 "to kill every damned nigger in the town": Gregory Lamont Mixon, The Atlanta Riot: Race, Class, and Violence in a New South City (Gainesville: University Press of Florida, 2005), 87.

237 violence in Atlanta: In a contemporaneous examination of the reports, newsman Ray Stannard Baker concluded that no more than two of the rapes were credible, and three more may have been attempted. David Fort Godshalk, Veiled Visions: The 1906 Atlanta Race Riot and the Reshaping of American Race Relations (Chapel Hill: University of North Carolina Press, 2005), 38.

238 the mob began random attacks: This riot narrative is collated from accounts found in Mixon, The Atlanta Riot, 85–100; John Dittmer, Black Georgia in the Progressive Era, 1900–1920 (Urbana: University of Illinois Press, 1977), 123–30; Godshalk, Veiled Visions, 85–124.

238 *By three o'clock on Sunday morning*: Mixon, *The Atlanta Riot*, 101–15; Godshalk,
     Veiled Visions, 110–14; Dittmer, *Black Georgia in the Progressive Era*, 128.
240 *Victory was short-lived*: Mixon, *The Atlanta Riot*, 109–10.
241 *"They told him*: Work and Rise"*: W.E.B. Du Bois, "A Litany of Atlanta," *Independent*
     61, October 11, 1906. For Du Bois's description of work in Calhoun, see Du Bois to
     Mary Ovington, Oct. 6, 1906, W.E.B. Du Bois Papers, microfilm. For his analysis of
     Hoke Smith and the southern political style contributing to the riot, see Du Bois to
     Dewey W. Grantham, Jr., Sept. 3, 1952, ibid. For contemporaneous analysis of the
     Atlanta riot, see W.E.B. Du Bois, "From the Point of View of the Negroes," in *Writings
     by W.E.B. Du Bois in Periodicals Edited by Others*, ed. Herbert Aptheker, *The Com-
     plete Published Works of W.E.B. Du Bois* (Millwood, N.Y.: Kraus-Thomson Organiza-
     tion, 1982), I:339–42. For Du Bois's more general analysis of the "Negro Problem" just
     months before the Atlanta riot, see Du Bois, "The Economic Future of the Negro,"
     Publication of the American Economic Association, 3rd series 7, no. 1 (Feb. 1906). For
     more on this period in his life, see David L. Lewis, *W.E.B. Du Bois: Biography of a
     Race*, 1st ed., vol. 1 (New York: Henry Holt, 1993), 333–37, 354, 427.
241 *protests against lynching*: Thomas C. Holt, "The Lonely Warrior: Ida B. Wells Bar-
     nett and the Struggle for Black Leadership," in *Black Leaders of the Twentieth Cen-
     tury*, ed. John Hope Franklin and August Meier (Urbana: University of Illinois
     Press, 1982), 39–61.
242 *"migration of the talented tenth"*: Carter Godwin Woodson, *A Century of Negro Mi-
     gration* (New York: AMS Press, 1970), 147.
242 *"something beyond the watch and guard"*: Alain Locke, ed. *The New Negro* (New
     York: Albert and Charles Boni, 1925), 3.
242 *New York riot*: Gilbert Osofsky, "Race Riot, 1900: A Study of Ethnic Violence," *Jour-
     nal of Negro Education* 32 (Winter 1963). Marcy S. Sacks, *Before Harlem: The Black
     Experience in New York City Before World War I*, Politics and Culture in Modern
     America (Philadelphia: University of Pennsylvania Press, 2006), 39–42.
243 most *black . . . in cities and towns*: Don H. Doyle, *New Men, New Cities, New South:
     Atlanta, Nashville, Charleston, Mobile, 1860–1910* (Chapel Hill: University of North
     Carolina Press, 1990), 12; United States, Bureau of the Census, *Thirteenth Census
     of the United States, 1910, Population, Vol. 1, General Report and Analysis* (Wash-
     ington, D.C.: Government Printing Office, 1913), 175–224.
244 *inhabitants in 1880*: Doyle, *New Men, New Cities, New South*, 3–6, 9–14.
244 *twenty-four cities*: My calculations based on statistics in United States, Bureau of
     the Census, *Thirteenth Census of the United States, 1910*, 175–224.
244 *329,166 blacks*: Ibid.; Doyle, *New Men, New Cities, New South*, 3–14 passim.
245 *"a second emancipation"*: Chicago *Defender*, Oct. 18, 1916. Du Bois would say some-
     thing similar.
245 *fifth essay*: W.E.B. Du Bois, *The Souls of Black Folk*, 75–87.
246 *Atlanta's white leaders*: Godshalk, *Veiled Visions*, 135–62, 187–90.
247 *new commercial-industrial ethos*: For further discussion of this phenomenon, see
     C. Vann Woodward, *Origins of the New South, 1877–1913*, History of the South (Ba-
     ton Rouge: Louisiana State University Press, 1951).
247 *"the New South and the Old Negro"*: Nothing had symbolized their intent so well per-
     haps as the painting decorating Judges' Hall at Atlanta's 1881 World's Fair. Their "New
     South" was a brunette draped in an American flag, framed by "Uncle Sam" above her

in one corner and "Uncle Remus" and "Old Si" in the other, overlooking blacks in a field picking cotton. Doyle, *New Men, New Cities, New South*, 156–57, 260.

247 *Blacks were excluded from . . . rebuilding*: Godshalk, *Veiled Visions*, 133–62 passim. Karen Ferguson, *Black Politics in New Deal Atlanta* (Chapel Hill: Univeristy of North Carolina Press, 2002), 21, 24, 28–29.

247 *official neglect*: For example, see Earl Lewis, *In Their Own Interests: Race, Class, and Power in Twentieth-Century Norfolk* (Berkeley: University of California Press, 1991), 80–85.

247 *"[A]n Afro-American policy, . . . or death"*: Thomas W. Hanchett, *Sorting out the New South City: Race, Class, and Urban Development in Charlotte, 1875–1975* (Chapel Hill: University of North Carolina Press, 1998), 131.

248 *black community in Charlotte*: Janette Thomas Greenwood, *Bittersweet Legacy: The Black and White "Better Classes" in Charlotte, 1850–1910* (Chapel Hill: University of North Carolina Press, 1994), chaps. 1 and 4.

248 *"Use these things . . . be well"*: Ibid., 85.

248 *Norfolk during this period*: Lewis, *In Their Own Interests*, 90–92, 95, 109.

248 *"money will accomplish . . ."*: Greenwood, *Bittersweet Legacy*, 214.

248 *alliances with white Prohibitionist parties*: Ibid., chap. 3.

249 *"better classes"*: Ferguson, *Black Politics in New Deal Atlanta*, 138–45. For developments in North Carolina more generally, see Gilmore, *Gender and Jim Crow*.

249 *systematic, legalized, and distinctly urban*: Woodward, *Origins of the New South, 1877–1913*; John Cell, *The Highest Stage of White Supremacy: The Origins of Segregation in South Africa and the American South* (Cambridge, UK: Cambridge University Press, 1982).

249 *"rural face to white supremacy"*: Mark Schultz, *The Rural Face of White Supremacy: Beyond Jim Crow* (Urbana: University of Illinois Press, 2005), 4–11.

249 *"a sprawling thicket"*: Ibid., 67.

250 *Hancock County*: Ibid., 31–33. The district, no. 116, was one of fifteen in the county. The others had more smallholders.

251 *"That's my nigger"*: Ibid., 41, 42, 91.

251 *peculiar patron-clientage*: Ibid., 89, 90, 98–102, 111–12.

251 *interracial boundary crossing*: Ibid., 80–84, 106–109. Observation on asymmetric church visitations was made by James Weldon Johnson in *Negro Americans, What Now?*, 83. Shultz reports that his interviews were inconclusive on this point. Personal communication with author, e-mail, July 9, 2009.

252 *Hancock's black landowners*: Ibid., 46–49, 52, 91.

252 *substantial black landowners*: Ibid., 54–55, 61.

252 *underemployed young men and women*: A survey of New York City in 1917 showed that migrants were mostly skilled or semiskilled, including longshoremen, freight handlers, miners, packers, warehousemen, southern factory workers, and craftsmen, all of which suggests that they were from southern cities and towns, not the fields.

253 *For young Jean Toomer*: Nellie Y. McKay, *Jean Toomer, Artist: A Study of His Literary Life and Work, 1894–1936* (Chapel Hill: University of North Carolina Press, 1984), 3–6, 13–20, 31–33.

254 *"strong with the tang" . . . "whole new life"*: Ibid., 51.

254 *"'Cane,'" . . . "song of an end"*: See Darwin T. Turner's introduction in Jean Toomer, *Cane* (New York: Boni and Liveright, 1923), xxii.

254 *began to compose passages for* Cane: McKay, *Jean Toomer, Artist*, 33.
257 *"favorable conjunction"*: Arna Bontemps, "The Awakening: A Memoir," in *The Harlem Renaissance Remembered*, ed. Arna Bontemps (New York: Dodd, Mead and Company, 1972), quote on p. 1.
258 *Philip A. Payton*: James Weldon Johnson, *Black Manhattan* (New York, 1931), 147–49.
258 *"forced colonization"* . . . *"shiftless Negro"*: Statement of Wilford Smith in *Report of the Sixth Annual Convention of the National Negro Business League*, August 1905, 76–77. See Records of the National Negro Business League, Part 1: Annual Conference Proceedings and Organizational Records, 1900–1919, ed. Kenneth Hamilton (Bethesda, Md.: University Publications of America microfilm).
258 *recession of 1907–08*: Gilbert Osofsky, *Harlem, The Making of a Ghetto: Negro New York, 1890–1930*, 1st ed. (New York: Harper and Row, 1966), 98–103.
259 *the Harlem community*: Johnson, *Black Manhattan*, 146.
259 *black newcomers*: U.S. Bureau of Census, "Fifteenth Census of the United States: 1930, Vol II, General Report; Statistics by Subjects . . . table 21, "Native Populations of Each Division and State by Birth: 1930," ed. Bureau of Census (Washington, D.C.: Government Printing Office, 1930), table 6, p. 32.
259 *"the laboratory of a great race-welding"*: Locke, *The New Negro*, 7.
259 *Ella Josephine Baker*: Barbara Ransby, *Ella Baker and the Black Freedom Movement: A Radical Democratic Vision*, Gender and American Culture (Chapel Hill: University of North Carolina Press, 2003).
260 *negotiate . . . space with West Indians*: Winston James, *Holding Aloft the Banner of Ethiopia: Caribbean Radicalism in Early Twentieth-Century America* (London; New York: Verso, 1999).
260 *another imagined community*: Bontemps, "The Awakening," 8–9. For Garvey's strength in the South, see Mary G. Rolinson, *Grassroots Garveyism: The Universal Negro Improvement Association in the Rural South, 1920–1927*, The John Hope Franklin Series in African American History and Culture (Chapel Hill: University of North Carolina Press, 2007).
260 *racial revitalization*: Lawrence W. Levine, "Marcus Garvey and the Politics of Revitalization," in *Black Leaders in the Twentieth Century*, eds. John Hope Franklin and August Meier (Urbana: University of Illinois Press, 1982), 105–38.
261 *"to repair a damaged group psychology"*: Locke, "The New Negro," 10.
261 *"No people . . . inferior"*: James Weldon Johnson, *The Book of American Negro Poetry* (New York: Harcourt, 1931), vii.
261 *African Americans published*: Ann Douglas, *Terrible Honesty: Mongrel Manhattan in the 1920s*, 1st ed. (New York: Farrar, Straus, and Giroux, 1995), 84.
261 *There was no black theater*: See Harold Cruse, *The Crisis of the Negro Intellectual* (New York: Morrow, 1967), 520–43.
262 *"In ten years . . . culture to another"*: Locke, *The New Negro*, 3–18.
262 *"the shows that please Seventh Street"*: McKay, *Jean Toomer, Artist*, 53. See also Cynthia Earl Kerman and Richard Eldridge, *The Lives of Jean Toomer: A Hunger for Wholeness* (Baton Rouge: Louisiana State University Press, 1987), 98.
262 *communal ethos to an individualist one*: Levine, *Black Culture and Black Consciousness*, 156–58.
263 *five to six million blues records*: Ibid., 225.

263 *Mamie Smith*: Ibid., 225–38 passim. Cf. Adam Green, *Selling the Race* (Chicago: University of Chicago Press, 2006), 55.

263 *oral traditions*: Levine, *Black Culture and Black Consciousness*, 229–31.

263 *Thus call-and-response*: Ibid., 232–33.

263 *"the blues allowed . . . their roots"*: Ibid., 238.

264 *"the music and dance . . . amalgamated"*: Ibid., 201.

264 *their leisure time at the movies*: Ibid., 228–29.

264 *Simon P. Owens*: In 1952, under the pseudonym Charles Denby, Owens published *Indignant Heart: A Black Worker's Journal* (Detroit, Mich.: Wayne State University Press, 1989). An expanded version of the autobiography was published under his real name in 1978.

264 *"a row of trees . . . highway"*: Ibid., 27.

265 *Owens was born*: Ibid., 1–26.

266 *The Great War*: Ibid., 3–4, 16.

266 *Owens's prior industrial employment*: Robert J. Norrell, "Caste in Steel: Jim Crow Careers in Birmingham, Alabama," *Journal of American History* 73 (December 1986): 671.

266 *skilled positions were reserved*: Henry M. McKiven, Jr., *Iron and Steel: Class, Race, and Community in Birmingham, Alabama, 1875–1920* (Chapel Hill: University of North Carolina Press, 1995), 23–27, 41–47.

267 *48 percent of the positions*: Ibid., table 7.1, p. 122.

267 *cut by 40 percent*: Norrell, "Caste in Steel," 671.

267 *"AlabamaNorth"*: By 1930, blacks made up 7.7 percent of Detroit's population, and 84 percent of them were from other states. Black Alabamians such as Owens were 15.7 percent of all those arriving from other states. United States, Bureau of the Census, *Fifteenth Census of the United States, 1930, Population, Vol. 4, Occupations, by States* (Washington, D.C.: Government Printing Office, 1933), table 12, pp. 803–10, "Males and Females 10 Years Old and Over in Selected Occupations". Cf. Kimberley L. Phillips, *AlabamaNorth: African-American Migrants, Community, and Working-Class Activism in Cleveland, 1915–45*, The Working Class in American History (Urbana: University of Illinois Press, 1999).

267 *Detroit's industrial production*: Richard W. Thomas, *Life for Us Is What We Make It: Building Black Community in Detroit, 1915–1945* (Bloomington: Indiana University Press, 1992), 25.

267 *In 1916, only about fifty blacks*: Calculations based on United States, Bureau of the Census, *Fourteenth Census of the United States, 1920, Vol. 4, Occupations* (Washington, D.C.: Government Printing Office, 1923), table 2, pp. 732–38, 1101–04, "Total Males and Females 10 Years of Age and Over Engaged in Each Selected Occupation . . . for Cities of 100,000 Inhabitants or More," 1920; table 14, "Negro Women 15 years of Age and Over Engaged in Each Specified Occupation in 1920"; U.S. Bureau of the Census, *Fifteenth Census of the United States, 1930*, table 12, pp. 803–10.

268 *Pittsburgh, the other industrial anchor*: Ibid.; Peter Gottlieb, *Making Their Own Way: Southern Blacks' Migration to Pittsburgh, 1916–30* (Urbana: University of Illinois, 1987), 91.

268 *The few who gained jobs*: Ibid., 106; Thomas, *Life for Us Is What We Make It*, 32.

268 *employed in Ford plants*: August Meier and Elliott Rudwick, *Black Detroit and the Rise of the UAW* (New York: Oxford University Press, 1979), 6.

269 *"when every man . . . family life"*: Ibid, 13.

269 *racial opportunity at Ford*: Ibid., 16–18.

269 *Detroit Urban League*: Ibid., 18–20.

270 *Urban League chapters in Chicago*: Ibid., 18; James R. Barrett, *Work and Community in the Jungle: Chicago's Packinghouse Workers, 1894–1922* (Urbana: University of Illinois Press, 1987), 212.

270 *Black workers' distrust of unions*: For more on black workers' strained relationship with labor unions, see Sterling Denhard Spero and Abram Lincoln Harris, *The Black Worker: The Negro and the Labor Movement* (New York: Columbia University Press, 1931); Philip Sheldon Foner, *Organized Labor and the Black Worker, 1619–1973* (New York: Praeger, 1974).

271 *black workers did ally with unions*: Black packinghouse workers are an example of such labor alliances. Barrett, *Work and Community in the Jungle*, 215–16.

271 *a stalwart union man*: Denby, *Indignant Heart*, 151.

271 *"Nigger work"*: Gottlieb, *Making Their Own Way*, 98, 122; Barrett, *Work and Community in the Jungle*, 49. Ironically, black steelworkers enjoyed better job opportunity before the Great Migration. See Dennis C. Dickerson, *Out of the Crucible: Black Steelworkers in Western Pennsylvania, 1875–1980* (Albany: State University of New York Press, 1986), 19–27, 49–53.

271 *seasonality of the work*: Gottlieb, *Making Their Own Way*, 103, 123–29; Denby, *Indignant Heart*, 31, 34, 37.

272 *residential segregation*: Thomas, *Life for Us Is What We Make It*, 54, quote on 92.

272 *steel strike in 1919*: Gottlieb, *Making Their Own Way*, 155–60.

273 *wartime riots*: See Dominic J. Capeci, Jr., *Race Relations in Wartime Detroit: The Sojourner Truth Housing Controversy of 1942* (Philadelphia: Temple University Press, 1984).

274 *"in the lobby of the Peabody Hotel . . ."*: Attributed by James C. Cobb to David Cohn, quoted in James Cobb, *The Most Southern Place on Earth: The Mississippi Delta and the Roots of Regional Identity* (New York: Oxford University Press, 1992), vii.

274 *Henry Lowry*: Nan Elizabeth Woodruff, *American Congo: The African American Freedom Struggle in the Delta* (Cambridge, Mass.: Harvard University Press, 2003), 110–12.

274 *"most southern place on earth"*: The phrase is Cobb's. Cobb, *The Most Southern Place on Earth*.

274 *black, by a margin of ten to one*: Woodruff, *American Congo*, 30–31, 76.

274 *66 percent of their farm owners*: Ibid., 22.

275 *plantations familiar to the Old South*: Ibid., 26–29, 33.

275 *The First World War shook*: Ibid., 40, 48, 51, 59.

276 *As these figures show*: Ibid., 42–43.

276 *"will not be the same sort of negro . . ."*: Ibid., 67.

277 *Frank Moore*: Ibid., 81.

277 *"We Battle for . . ."*: Ibid., 83.

277 *". . . killing them as they came to them"*: Ibid., 84–103, quote p. 100.

277 *"cutting off the ears or toes . . ."*: Ibid., 87–88, 102–103, quote p. 87.

278 *". . . killing men, women and children"*: Ibid., 97.

278 *Frank's wife*: Ibid., 98, 99, 104.

278 *John E. Miller*: Ibid., 104. On Judge Miller, see Richard C. Cortner and National Association for the Advancement of Colored People, *A Mob Intent on Death: The*

NAACP and the Arkansas Riot Cases, 1st ed. (Middletown, Conn.: Wesleyan University Press, 1988), 198.

278 *Wright also migrated to Chicago*: Debbie Levy, *Richard Wright: A Biography* (Minneapolis, Minn.: Twenty-First Century Books, 2007).

279 *eight of every ten black Chicagoans*: The 1920 census shows that 19,485 of Illinois's black population was Mississippi-born and 22,995 were originally from Tennessee. There is no state breakdown for the city as such, but later censuses show an overwhelming concentration of new migrants in Chicago.

279 *impressive economic progress*: Barrett, *Work and Community in the Jungle*, 190.

279 *By 1920, meatpackers*: Ibid., 15–17, 28–29, 48.

280 *"a grass-roots social movement"*: James R. Grossman, *Land of Hope: Chicago, Black Southerners, and the Great Migration* (Chicago: University of Chicago Press, 1989), 66–67.

281 *Mississippi migrants differed*: Ibid., 67.

281 *their new surroundings . . . "full of life"*: Jacqueline Najuma Stewart, *Migrating to the Movies: Cinema and Black Urban Modernity* (Berkeley: University of California Press, 2005), 146.

281 *"the Stroll" . . . a virtual theater*: For diverse class dynamics of Chicago in this period, see St. Clair Drake and Horace R. Cayton, *Black Metropolis: A Study of Negro Life in a Northern City*, rev. and enl. ed. (Chicago: University of Chicago Press, 1993), 521–63, 600–715.

282 *Abbott's The Chicago Defender*: Grossman, *Land of Hope*, 77–79, 88.

282 *a center for African American cinema*: Stewart, *Migrating to the Movies*, especially 9–10, 155–86.

282 *vibrant and innovative music scene*: Green, *Selling the Race*, 51–91.

283 *"Somewhere in the unknown . . . again"*: Richard Wright, *Black Boy* (New York: Harper Perennial, 1993), 77, 87.

7. "A SECOND RECONSTRUCTION"

285 *"I told him" . . . "what they did to my boy"*: Christopher Metress, ed. *The Lynching of Emmett Till: A Documentary Narrative* (Charlottesville: University of Virginia Press, 2002), quote on p. 29; Mamie Till-Mobley and Chris Benson, *Death of Innocence: The Story of the Hate Crime That Changed America*, 1st ed. (New York: Random House, 2003), 19–20, 100–102, 129, 138–39.

285 *What had been done to young Emmett Till*: "Open Letter to U.S. Attorney General Herbert Brownell and FBI chief J. Edgar Hoover from James L. Hicks, *Washington Afro-American*, Nov. 19, 1955, Metress, ed. *The Lynching of Emmett Till*, 197.

286 *young boy's mangled body*: Devery S. Anderson, "A Wallet, a White Woman, and a Whistle: Fact and Fiction in Emmett Till's Encounter in Money, Mississippi," *Southern Quarterly* 45, no. 4 (Summer 2008): 10–21; Federal Bureau of Investigation, Prospective Report of Investigation Concerning Roy Bryant in www.foai.fbi.gov/foiaindex/till.htm (accessed March 13, 2009); Till-Mobley and Benson, *Death of Innocence*, 141–42; Adam Green, *Selling the Race: Culture, Community, and Black Chicago, 1940–1955*, Historical Studies of Urban America (Chicago: University of Chicago Press, 2007), 198–202.

287 *Mamie Bradley and her companions*: Mamie Fortune Osborne, "An Interview with David Jordan on Emmett Till," *Southern Quarterly* 45, no. 4 (Summer 2008): 136–51.

287 *John Wiley Nash Carthan*: "Emmett Till's Grandfather Dies," *Chicago Defender*, Jan. 23, 1969, p. 2, ProQuest Historical Newspapers.

288 *threefold increase in nonwhite employment*: F. Ray Marshall, *The Negro and Organized Labor* (New York: Wiley, 1965), 169.

288 *brash young Louis Till*: Till-Mobley and Benson, *Death of Innocence*, 4–17. I have also benefited from reading the unpublished work on Louis Till by Jane Dailey, "Fighting Hitler and Jim Crow," in *Sex and Civil Rights* (New York: Harcourt, forthcoming).

289 *Rayfield Mooty*: "Rayfield Mooty Oral History Interview," by James B. Stewart (circa 1990), Pennsylvania State University, University Libraries, Special Collections Library.

290 *black unionized industrial . . . workers*: Marshall, *The Negro and Organized Labor*, 52.

290 *William Dawson*: "Republican Oscar de Priest, the first African American elected to Congress in the twentieth century," Thaddeus Russell, "William Levi Dawson," www.anb.org/articles/07/07-00069.html, American National Biography Online, Feb. 2000; Steven J. Niven, "Arthur Wergs Mitchell." www.anb.org/articles/07/07-00660.html, and Kristie Miller, "Oscar Stanton de Priest." www.anb.org/articles/06/06-00147.html, American National Biography Online, Feb. 2000. Bruce A. Ragsdale and Joel D. Treese, *Black Americans in Congress 1870–1989* (Washington, D.C.: Library of Congress, 1990), and Maurine Christopher, *Black Americans in Congress* (1971; repr. 1976), 185–93.

290 *Charles Diggs, Jr.*: "Charles Coles Diggs, Jr." www.bioguide.congress.gov/scripts/biodisplay.pl?index=D000344, Biographical Directory of the United States Congress; Carolyn DuBose, *The Untold Story of Charles Diggs: The Public Figure, The Private Man* (Arlington, Va.: Barton Publishing House, Inc., 1988).

290 *Charles Diggs, Sr.*: Angela D. Dillard, *Faith in the City: Preaching Radical Social Change in Detroit* (Ann Arbor: University of Michigan Press, 2007), 48.

290 *shift in political allegiance*: In 1936, 76 percent of northern blacks voted for FDR, and in every major northern city except Chicago his vote share exceeded 60 percent (in Chicago it was 49 percent). The realignment would not be completed until later, however, since most blacks remained registered Republicans while voting Democratic. Simon Topping, "'Turning Their Pictures of Abraham Lincoln to the Wall': The Republican Party and Black America in the Election of 1936," *Irish Journal of American Studies* 8 (May 2000).

291 *now reputedly determine the presidential election*: Five of these states—Illinois, Michigan, New York, Ohio, Pennsylvania—all former Republican strongholds, had shifted 157 electoral votes into the Democratic column. Ibid., 44.

291 *new black voters . . . registered*: Steven F. Lawson, *Black Ballots: Voting Rights in the South, 1944–1969*, Contemporary American History Series (New York: Columbia University Press, 1976), table 1, p. 134; Margaret Price, *The Negro and the Ballot in the South* (Atlanta, Ga.: Southern Regional Council, 1959), table 5, p. 5.

291 *Medgar Evers, Amzie Moore, and Aaron Henry*: Charles M. Payne, *I've Got the Light of Freedom: The Organizing Tradition and the Mississippi Freedom Struggle* (Berkeley: University of California Press, 1995), 29–66 passim.

292 *Murray Kempton in a dispatch*: Murray Kempton, *New York Post*, Sept. 23, 1955, in Metress, ed. *The Lynching of Emmett Till*, 87.

293 *"[M]istreated" . . . "a human being and a citizen"*: Quotes from 1956 radio interview with Sydney Rogers in West Oakland, cited in Stewart Burns, ed. *Daybreak of Freedom: The Montgomery Bus Boycott* (Chapel Hill: University of North Carolina Press, 1997), 82–87, quotes pp. 83, 84, 86. See also Rosa Parks and James Haskins, *Rosa Parks: My Story*, 1st ed. (New York: Dial Books, 1992), 116; Charles Marsh, *The Beloved Community: How Faith Shapes Social Justice: From the Civil Rights Movement to Today* (New York: Basic Books, 2005), 21; J. Mills Thornton III, *Dividing Lines: Municipal Politics and the Struggle for Civil Rights in Montgomery, Birmingham, and Selma* (Tuscaloosa: University of Alabama Press, 2002), 58–91.

293 *Parks scarcely suspected*: See David T. Beito and Linda Royster Beito, *Black Maverick: T.R.M. Howard's Fight for Civil Rights and Economic Power*, The New Black Studies Series (Urbana: University of Illinois Press, 2009), xiii–xiv, 139.

293 *her own life story*: There were only 140 black clerk typists in the entire state in 1940. Thornton III, *Dividing Lines*, 58–59.

294 *Rosa's demur exterior*: Douglas Brinkley, *Rosa Parks*, Penguin Lives Series (New York: Viking, 2000), 28.

295 *cities such as Montgomery*: Thornton III, *Dividing Lines*, 23–25.

295 *By the mid-1950s*: Ibid., 36, 38.

295 *"most enlightened city"*: Ibid., 40.

295 *victory for Dave Birmingham*: Ibid., 28–29.

295 *pattern evident in other southern cities*: Karen Ferguson, *Black Politics in New Deal Atlanta* (Chapel Hill: University of North Carolina Press, 2002), 228–30. Laurie B. Green, *The Plantation Mentality: Memphis and the Black Freedom Struggle* (Chapel Hill: University of North Carolina Press, 2007), 47–80. Leslie Brown, *Upbuilding Black Durham: Gender, Class, and Black Community Development in the Jim Crow South*, John Hope Franklin Series in African American History and Culture (Chapel Hill: University of North Carolina Press, 2008), 91–96, 217–47.

296 *rape of Gertrude Perkins*: Thornton III, *Dividing Lines*, 34–35; Green, *The Plantation Mentality*, 81–111.

296 *fractures along class and gender lines*: Edgar D. Nixon was born outside Montgomery in 1899, had been employed as a sleeping car porter since 1923, came of age in the union movement, and had been deeply influenced by his hero, A. Philip Randolph. By contrast, his nemesis, Rufus Lewis, was a graduate of Fisk University who had acquired a profitable funeral business through an advantageous marriage, and represented Montgomery's small black professional and business elite. Robinson, a Georgia native with a master's degree from Du Bois's Atlanta University, had arrived in Montgomery much more recently (1949) to take a position at Alabama State College. Since 1952, she had been president of the Women's Political Council, which drew its principal support from college colleagues and professionals. Thornton III, *Dividing Lines*, 32–33.

297 *176 cases of racial conflict*: Robin D. G Kelley, "'We Are Not What We Seem': Rethinking Black Working-Class Opposition in the Jim Crow South," *Journal of American History* 80, no. 1 (Jan. 1993), 104; Ferguson, *Black Politics in New Deal Atlanta*, 231–32.

297 *member and officer in the NAACP*: In April 1931, following a fight with some white boys on a train, nine teenage black youth were charged with raping two white women.

The case attracted international attention and intervention by the Communist Party's International Labor Defense and later by the NAACP, which eventually won reversals of lower court convictions. James E. Goodman, *Stories of Scottsboro*, 1st ed. (New York: Pantheon Books, 1994), 386–87.

297 *lent her secretarial skills*: Thornton III, *Dividing Lines*, 58–59.

297 *Claudette Colvin*: Ibid., 53–54, 60.

298 *"more polite segregation"*: Ibid., 598 n72.

298 *Thornton's argument*: Council membership figures drawn from ibid., 73.

299 *Florida A&M began*: Ibid., 91.

299 *racially mixed "Freedom Riders"*: Raymond Arsenault, *Freedom Riders: 1961 and the Struggle for Racial Justice* (New York: Oxford University Press, 2006), 93–176.

302 *local to a geopolitical axis*: The literature on the structural changes in political economy that shaped and enabled the Civil Rights Movement is only beginning to emerge. A useful article on one important area where defense spending mattered greatly is James T. Sparrow, "A Nation in Motion: Norfolk, the Pentagon, and the Nationalization of the Metropolitan South, 1941–1953," in *The Myth of Southern Exceptionalism*, eds. Matthew Lassiter and Joseph Crespino (New York: Oxford University Press, 2009), 167–89.

303 *sparks of resistance*: August Meier and Elliott M. Rudwick, *CORE: A Study in the Civil Rights Movement, 1942–1968* (New York: Oxford University Press, 1973), 2–58; Clayborne Carson, *In Struggle: SNCC and the Black Awakening of the 1960s* (Cambridge, Mass.: Harvard University Press, 1981).

304 *Harry Truman*: Mary L. Dudziak, *Cold War Civil Rights: Face and the Image of American Democracy* (Princeton, N.J.: Princeton University Press, 2000), 79–100.

304 *independent African and Asian nations*: Ibid., 152–82.

305 *"business progressives"*: Thornton III, *Dividing Lines*, 164–65.

306 *Its rising upper middle class*: Ibid., 178.

306 *housing benefits*: Ibid., 159.

306 *a dozen bombings*: Ibid., 160.

306 *black steelworkers*: Hosea Hudson and Nell Irvin Painter, *The Narrative of Hosea Hudson: His Life as a Negro Communist in the South* (Cambridge, Mass.: Harvard University Press, 1979), 338.

307 *postwar voter registration*: By 1962, black voters totaled 8,246. Ibid., 255–68.

307 *an Interracial Committee*: Thornton III, *Dividing Lines*, 193–94.

307 *"a sink of corruption and racial prejudice"*: Ibid., 179.

307 *increasingly restive with Connor's*: The white elite's impatience with Connor grew after an unsavory incident with sexual overtones that election year. For details, see ibid., 183.

308 *shrank the window for action*: See ibid., chap. 3, esp. pp. 191–92.

308 *Birmingham's black militants*: Ibid., 196.

308 *Fred Shuttlesworth*: Ibid., 188–89.

309 *The Birmingham Movement*: These campaigns were further empowered in May 1963, by a Supreme Court decision invalidating the use of municipal trespass ordinances to suppress sit-in demonstrations. For the impact in Birmingham, see ibid., 204.

309 *ordering a Coke*: Lizabeth Cohen makes a persuasive case for the increased importance of consumption in shaping political conflicts and claims to citizenship in the first half of the twentieth century. Elsewhere I have made parallel arguments about the shifting terrain of black equal rights struggles. These structural arguments

should not be confused with the popular notion that civil rights goals are reducible to consumer *desires* as such, however. Consumption simply became the terrain of long-standing struggles for human dignity and respect. Lizabeth Cohen, *A Consumers' Republic: The Politics of Mass Consumption in Postwar America*, 1st ed. (New York: Knopf, 2003), 41–53, 174–91, 323–31. See also Thomas C. Holt, *The Problem of Race in the Twenty-first Century*, The Nathan I. Huggins Lectures (Cambridge, Mass.: Harvard University Press, 2000).

310   *settlement's actual implementation*: Thornton III, *Dividing Lines*, 333–79 passim.

313   *a small group from Mississippi*: The author witnessed this event as he led a second group of picketers at the Justice Department from Danville, Virginia.

313   *that their fathers never dreamed of*: For more discussion of this wartime transformation, see Pete Daniel, "Going Among Strangers: Southern Reactions to World War II," *Journal of American History* 77, no. 3 (December 1990), 886–911.

314   *As a field secretary for the NAACP*: Medgar Wiley Evers, *The Autobiography of Medgar Evers: A Hero's Life and Legacy Revealed Through His Writings, Letters, and Speeches* (New York: HarperCollins, 2005); Payne, *I've Got the Light of Freedom*, 49.

314   *registration increased tenfold*: Payne, *I've Got the Light of Freedom*, 25.

315   *The NAACP had lost 246*: Ibid., 35, 43.

315   *Amzie Moore urged him*: Bayard Rustin had sent Moses to Atlanta to work with the SCLC, but he soon gravitated to SNCC, which was located in the same offices. In turn, Ella Baker introduced Moses to Amzie Moore, who was then vice-president of the NAACP state conference of branches. Ibid., 104–106.

315   *Kennedy administration's anxious desire*: Ibid., 108.

315   *"full government cooperation"*: Carl M. Brauer, *John F. Kennedy and the Second Reconstruction*, Contemporary American History Series (New York: Columbia University Press, 1977), 112–17.

316   *Sam Block*: SNCC was assigned this territory through the umbrella COFO, which had been formed in 1961 to seek a meeting with Mississippi governor Ross Barnett. It was restarted in 1962 to oversee the voter registration campaign, which was administered by SNCC under Moses's leadership and CORE under David Dennis. Payne, *I've Got the Light of Freedom*, 104–106.

316   *objections from some SNCC veterans*: Ibid., 111.

316   *hit-and-run strategy*: Since the SCLC's strategy was focused on building momentum for national legislation, King avoided as much as possible getting bogged down in long-term engagements in any one community.

317   *communities . . . transformed*: Barbara Ransby, *Ella Baker and the Black Freedom Movement: A Radical Democratic Vision*, Gender and American Culture (Chapel Hill: University of North Carolina Press, 2003).

317   *SNCC would have two branches*: Moses actually began operations in the southwestern hill counties of Amite, Pike, and Walthall, not far from the birthplaces of Robert Charles and Richard Wright.

317   *Greenwood's most relevant distinction*: Block discussed the personal impact of Till's murder. Payne, *I've Got the Light of Freedom*, 144–51.

317   *Block focused his efforts*: Ibid., 145–52.

317   *intergenerational networks of kinship*: Ibid., 64–65.

318   *situation for the Delta's blacks*: Chana Kai Lee, *For Freedom's Sake: The Life of Fannie Lou Hamer*, Women in American History (Urbana: University of Illinois Press, 1999).

319 *even Bob Moses*: John Dittmer, *Local People: The Struggle for Civil Rights in Missis-sippi* (Urbana: University of Illinois Press, 1994), 199, 212–13.

319 *Fannie Lou Hamer's story*: Lee, *For Freedom's Sake*, 15–18.

319 *Hamer was among those recruits*: Ibid., 27–29, 32–33, 39–40, 53.

320 *Aaron Henry heading the ticket . . . Eastland's party*: Ibid., 85–87, 107–11. For the legislative history of the Civil Rights Act, see Ted Gittinger and Allen Fisher, "LBJ Champions the Civil Rights Act of 1964, Part 2," *Prologue* 36, no. 2 (Summer 2004).

321 *Black and white supporters . . . embracing realpolitik*: Note the case of Verna Carson, who initially supported the Mississippi challenge but then withdrew under pressure that her husband would be denied a federal judgeship. Lee, *For Freedom's Sake*, 87–96. See Bayard Rustin, "From Protest to Politics: The Future of the Civil Rights Movement," *Commentary* 39:1 (Feb. 1965), 25–36. *Commentary* is a journal that soon became a bastion of neoconservatism.

322 *Events in Atlantic City . . . expelled its white staff*: This decision was taken in De-cember 1966 at a retreat in upstate New York on the estate of black entertainer Peg Leg Bates. The motion to expel whites from SNCC was carried by a single vote, but with twenty-four abstentions. Carson, *In Struggle: SNCC and the Black Awakening of the 1960s*, 142–52, 191–204, 239–41. Lee, *For Freedom's Sake*, 136, 138.

322 *tensions between MFDP and SNCC*: Lee, *For Freedom's Sake*, 119, 121–22, 125.

323 *senator James Eastland*: Ibid., 128.

324 *historical symmetry in the fact that Dallas County*: Thornton III, *Dividing Lines*, 384–417, quote on 417.

324 *Selma saw a rapid, steep decline*: The number of black tenants had declined to fifty-eight by 1974. Ibid., 385, 414.

325 *Craig Air Force Base*: During the Movement there was pressure to make the city off-limits to airmen. Ibid., 420. On the broader impact of postwar defense spending in the South, see Sparrow, "A Nation in Motion."

325 *Black voters . . . Cloverleaf Creamery*: Thornton III, *Dividing Lines*, 396.

325 *250 blacks registered*: Ibid., 382–83.

327 *Johnson's speech*: United States, President, *Public Papers of the Presidents of the United States* (Washington, D.C.: Federal Register Division, National Archives and Records Service for Sale by the Superintendent of Documents). In his speech, Johnson changed the Movement's anthem, "We *Shall* Overcome," to "We *Will* Overcome." Italics added by author.

327 *black elected officials*: For figures on black mayors, see David R. Colburn, "Running for Office: African-American Mayors, 1967–96," in *African-American Mayors: Race, Politics, and the American City*, eds. David R. Colburn and Jeffrey S. Adler (Urbana: University of Illinois Press, 2001), table 1.1, pp. 25–26. For southern officeholders, see Steven F. Lawson, "From Boycotts to Ballots: The Reshaping of National Poli-tics," in *New Directions in Civil Rights Studies*, eds. Armstead L. Robinson and Pa-tricia Sullivan (Charlottesville: University of Virginia Press, 1991), 184–210.

328 *on their picket signs*: For more on the Movement roots of the strike, see Green, *The Plantation Mentality*.

328 *Rosa Parks observed . . . extorting fifty-three dollars*: Parks and Haskins, *Rosa Parks*, 186–87. In a subsequent interview, Parks states that the amount was $103. Rosa Parks and Gregory J. Reed, *Quiet Strength: The Faith, the Hope, and the Heart of a Woman*

Who Changed a Nation (Grand Rapids, Mich.: Zondervan Publishing House, 1994), 103. For other accounts of this incident, see "Assailant Recognized Rosa Parks," *Detroit Free Press*, September 3, 1994; "Man Gets Prison Term for Attack on Rosa Parks," *San Francisco Chronicle*, August 8, 1995; and *New York Times*, March 20, 2006.

329 *Mamie Till Bradley*: Till-Mobley and Benson, *Death of Innocence*, 248–59.

8. CITIZENS OF THE NATION, CITIZENS OF THE WORLD

331 *Roughly three months*: Lyndon B. Johnson, "Commencement Address at Howard University: 'To Fulfill These Rights,'" in *The Public Papers of the Presidents of the United States* (Washington, D.C.: Government Printing Office, 1966), 635–40, quotes on p. 636.

332 *Except for a few demonstrators*: Based on personal observation; I was one of the graduates protesting, while my parents applauded.

332 *Their warm reception*: Lee Rainwater and William L. Yancey, *The Moynihan Report and the Politics of Controversy: A Trans-Action Social Science and Public Policy Report* (Cambridge, Mass.: M.I.T. Press, 1967), 4.

332 *The idea for the march*: Thomas F. Jackson, *From Civil Rights to Human Rights: Martin Luther King, Jr., and the Struggle for Economic Justice*, Politics and Culture in Modern America (Philadelphia: University of Pennsylvania Press, 2007), 166–82. For an eloquent and incisive discussion of how economic justice emerged along with "civil rights" by the mid-sixties, see Nancy MacLean, *Freedom Is Not Enough: The Opening of the American Workplace* (New York and Cambridge, Mass.: Russell Sage Foundation; Harvard University Press, 2006), esp. 6–7.

332 *"a mouthful of rights"*: Quoted in Jackson, *From Civil Rights to Human Rights*, 137.

333 *King's complex ideological formation*: See Martin Luther King, Jr., et al., *The Papers of Martin Luther King, Jr.* (Berkeley: University of California Press, 1992).

333 *In 1962, Harrington . . . Already, in his testimony . . . Finally, that July*: Jackson, *From Civil Rights to Human Rights*, 139, 170, 189.

333 *Although the grim statistical portrait*: See Robert Clifton Weaver, *The Urban Complex: Human Values in Urban Life*, 1st ed. (Garden City, N.Y.: Doubleday, 1964), 29–30, 228–77; Robert Clifton Weaver, *Dilemmas of Urban America*, The Godkin Lectures at Harvard University, 1965 (Cambridge, Mass.: Harvard University Press, 1965); Kenneth Bancroft Clark, *Dark Ghetto: Dilemmas of Social Power*, 1st ed. (New York: Harper and Row, 1965), 47–50. Of course, Frazier's work in the 1930s provided the template for such analyses. See Edward Franklin Frazier, *The Negro Family in Chicago* (Chicago: University of Chicago Press, 1932), and Edward Franklin Frazier, *The Negro Family in the United States*, The University of Chicago Sociological Series (Chicago: The University of Chicago Press, 1939).

334 *"moving toward two societies . . ."*: United States, National Advisory Commission on Civil Disorders, *Report of the National Advisory Commission on Civil Disorders* (Washington, D.C.: The Superintendent of Documents, U.S. Government Printing Office, 1968), 1.

334 *Born in Oklahoma*: Godfrey Hodgson, *The Gentleman from New York: Daniel Patrick Moynihan: A Biography* (Boston: Houghton Mifflin, 2000), 25–32.

335 *After President Johnson*: The so-called Urban Problem or Urban Crisis might be thought of as a discursive variant on the older "Negro Problem," with black urban

dwellers coming to represent the race as a whole. It is true that the problem of non-nuclear households was concentrated in the cities, for whites as well as blacks: the percent of "ever-married females with husbands absent" was 17.3 percent among nonwhites and 3.9 percent for white urban families, but just 8.6 percent and 2.0 percent, respectively, among rural families. Moynihan's collaborators were Paul Barton and Ellen Broderick. Rainwater and Yancey, *The Moynihan Report and the Politics of Controversy*, 4, 52.

335 *Using the work of the preeminent African American sociologist*: In addition to Frazier, the report is larded with quotes from black academics and social activists, including Kenneth Clark, Whitney Young, and Dorothy Height. United States, Dept. of Labor, Office of Policy Planning and Research, *The Negro Family: The Case for National Action* (Washington, D.C.: The Superintendent of Documents, 1965), 17, 34.

335 *Completed in March, the report*: Ibid., 43.

335 *It reached Johnson's desk*: It remains unclear whether the president actually read Moynihan's report, however. Rainwater and Yancey, *The Moynihan Report and the Politics of Controversy*, 4, 19, 27, 32.

336 *While certainly recognizing the broad social*: This interpretation is based in part on my personal experience as an OEO field agent from 1966 to 1968, but clearly the topic is controversial and there are (and were) many divergent viewpoints. A sampling of the range of views, some by people who were participants in the process, would include Daniel P. Moynihan, *Maximum Feasible Misunderstanding: Community Action in the War on Poverty*, The Clarke A. Sanford Lectures on Local Government and Community Life, 1967 (New York: Free Press, 1969); and Samuel F. Yette, *The Choice: The Issue of Black Survival in America* (New York: Putnam, 1971); also see David Zarefsky, *President Johnson's War on Poverty: Rhetoric and History* (Tuscaloosa: University of Alabama Press, 1986).

336 *"At the heart of the deterioration . . ."*: United States, Dept. of Labor, Office of Policy Planning and Research, *The Negro Family*, 5. Also see Rainwater and Yancey, *The Moynihan Report and the Politics of Controversy*, 51.

336 *"The family is the basic social unit . . ."*: United States, Dept. of Labor, Office of Policy Planning and Research, *The Negro Family*, 5.

336 *Whatever Moynihan's intentions*: It didn't help matters that this was precisely the interpretation to which the press gravitated. For example, Mary McGrory wrote in the *Washington Star* that the White House thought that black leaders must "come to grips with their own worst problem" and focus on "self-improvement" rather than "new demands." There was also an inflammatory piece by Richard Evans and Robert Novak purportedly exposing "the ugly truth about the big city Negro's plight." Rainwater and Yancey, *The Moynihan Report and the Politics of Controversy*, 133–54, quotes on pp. 135, 141.

336 *Given this public reception*: Jackson, *From Civil Rights to Human Rights*, 251–58; Nick Kotz, *Judgment Days: Lyndon Baines Johnson, Martin Luther King, Jr., and the Laws That Changed America* (Boston: Houghton Mifflin, 2005), 403–409.

336 *By late August*: Jackson, *From Civil Rights to Human Rights*, 239. Also see Rainwater and Yancey, *The Moynihan Report and the Politics of Controversy*.

337 *Those charges*: It is often forgotten that the initial propaganda campaign for the war on poverty was launched in and focused on white Appalachia.

337 *Although present at these meetings*: Rainwater and Yancey, *The Moynihan Report and the Politics of Controversy*, 248–56, 271–81; Kotz, *Judgment Days*, 358–60; Kevin L.

Yuill, "The 1966 White House Conference on Civil Rights," *The Historical Journal* 41, no. 1 (March 1998): 259–82.

337 *By August, the nation*: David E. Kaiser, *American Tragedy: Kennedy, Johnson, and the Origins of the Vietnam War* (Cambridge, Mass.: Belknap Press of Harvard University Press, 2000), 291–95, 304–85. Michael H. Hunt, *Lyndon Johnson's War: America's Cold War Crusade in Vietnam, 1945–1968*, 1st ed., A Critical Issue (New York: Hill and Wang, 1996), 84–85.

337 *That month, Johnson asked Congress*: Maurice Isserman and Michael Kazin, *America Divided: The Civil War of the 1960s*, 3rd ed. (New York: Oxford University Press, 2008), 189. Also see Robert Dallek, *Flawed Giant: Lyndon Johnson and His Times, 1961–1973* (New York: Oxford University Press, 1998), 308–11, 404–405.

338 *Although largely apolitical*: C. Eric Lincoln, *The Black Muslims in America* (Boston: Beacon Press, 1961), 106, 109, 128. Martha F. Lee, *The Nation of Islam: An American Millenarian Movement* (Syracuse, N.Y.: Syracuse University Press, 1996), 37.

338 *Malcolm (now "Malcolm X")*: According to a *Newsweek* poll in 1963, blacks had a very low opinion of the Black Muslims generally and of Elijah Muhammad in particular; few even knew Malcolm at that time. Thomas J. Sugrue, *Sweet Land of Liberty: The Forgotten Struggle for Civil Rights in the North*, 1st ed. (New York: Random House, 2008), 309–10.

338 *In that context*: Malcolm X and George Breitman, *Malcolm X Speaks: Selected Speeches and Statements* (New York: Grove Press, 1965), 3–17.

339 *Their only realistic choice*: In her memoir, Rosa Parks makes the distinction clear: she rejected the "philosophical" in favor of the "practical" version of nonviolence. Rosa Parks, *Rosa Parks: My Story* (New York: Dial Books, 1992), 174–75.

339 *In fact, armed self-defense*: The most famous instance of this was the long-running battle between Robert Williams, head of the NAACP branch in Monroe, North Carolina, and its national office, which led to Williams's dismissal and ended with his exile in Cuba. See Timothy B. Tyson, *Radio Free Dixie: Robert F. Williams and the Roots of Black Power* (Chapel Hill: University of North Carolina Press, 1999), 150–55.

339 *These cautious leaders*: Simon Wendt, *The Spirit and the Shotgun: Armed Resistance and the Struggle for Civil Rights*, New Perspectives on the History of the South (Gainesville: University Press of Florida, 2007), chap 6.

340 *During the Mississippi Summer Project of 1964*: Joe Street, *The Culture War in the Civil Rights Movement* (Gainesville: University Press of Florida, 2007), 81–94.

341 *Meanwhile, Gilbert Moses, John O'Neal, and Doris Derby*: Ibid., 94–98. quote on p. 97.

341 *Following the rebellion in Watts*: After serving time in jail in May 1975, however, Karenga renounced cultural nationalism for Marxist-Leninism. Thomas Lucien Vincent Blair, *Retreat to the Ghetto: The End of a Dream?* (New York: Hill and Wang, 1977), 149–53.

341 *A year later, while Karenga was touting*: Ibid.; Also see Street, *The Culture War in the Civil Rights Movement*; For more on the Black Panther Party, see Waldo E. Martin, *No Coward Soldiers: Black Cultural Politics and Postwar America*, The Nathan I. Huggins Lectures (Cambridge, Mass.: Harvard University Press, 2005); Elaine Brown, *A Taste of Power: A Black Woman's Story*, 1st ed. (New York: Pantheon Books, 1992); Andrew Witt, *The Black Panthers in the Midwest: The Community Programs and Services of the Black Panther Party in Milwaukee, 1966–1977*, Studies in African American History and Culture (New York: Routledge, 2007); Paul Alkebulan, *Survival Pending Revolution: The History of the Black Panther Party* (Tuscaloosa: University of Alabama Press, 2007); and David Hilliard and Dr. Huey P. Newton Foundation,

The Black Panther Party: Service to the People Programs (Albuquerque: University of
New Mexico Press, 2008).

341 *The Panthers . . . cultural politics*: Street, *The Culture War in the Civil Rights Movement*, 144; Davarian L. Baldwin, "'Culture Is a Weapon in Our Struggle for Liberation': The Black Panther Party and the Cultural Politics of Decolonization," in *In
Search of the Black Panther Party: New Perspectives on a Revolutionary Movement*,
ed. Jama Lazerow and Yohuru R. Williams (Durham, N.C.: Duke University Press,
2006), 289–305, quote p. 300.

342 *black cultural recognition and distribution*: Penny M. Von Eschen, *Satchmo Blows up
the World: Jazz Ambassadors Play the Cold War* (Cambridge, Mass.: Harvard University Press, 2004), 1, 22, 58. There were similar federal initiatives during and immediately after the the war, preceding the cold war efforts. See Laurie Boush Green,
Battling the Plantation Mentality: Memphis and the Black Freedom Struggle, The
John Hope Franklin Series in African American History and Culture (Chapel Hill:
University of North Carolina Press, 2007), 112–41.

343 *Their share of gold*: Black recording artists had ten gold albums in 1968, nineteen in
1972, and twenty-six gold and twenty platinum in 1978. Richard M. Merelman,
*Representing Black Culture: Racial Conflict and Cultural Politics in the United
States* (New York: Routledge, 1995), tables 1.6 and 1.7, pp. 13, 16–17; also see Donald
Bogle, *Blacks in American Films and Television: An Encyclopedia* (New York: Simon
and Schuster, 1989).

343 *inhabited a single cultural world*: Adam Green sheds light on the beginnings of this
process in the 1940s and '50s. Adam Green, *Selling the Race: Culture, Community,
and Black Chicago, 1940–1955*, Historical Studies of Urban America (Chicago: University of Chicago Press, 2007), 19–48, 207–10.

344 *Even as African Americans moved*: The idea of a retreat to localism in social justice
struggles has also been suggested by Tom Sugrue. See Sugrue, *Sweet Land of Liberty*, 399.

344 *This became the model for OEO's community action programs*: Jackson, *From Civil
Rights to Human Rights*, 194–95, 242. Also see George Lipsitz, *A Life in the Struggle:
Ivory Perry and the Culture of Opposition*, Critical Perspectives on the Past (Phila-
delphia: Temple University Press, 1988).

344 *schools and their curricula*: Alvin F. Poussaint, "School Desegregation: A Synonym
for Racial Equality," *The School Review* 84, no. 3 (1976). See also Jerald E. Podair,
*The Strike That Changed New York: Blacks, Whites, and the Ocean Hill–Brownsville
Crisis* (New Haven, Conn.: Yale University Press, 2002); Fabio Rojas, *From Black
Power to Black Studies: How a Radical Social Movement Became an Academic Dis-
cipline* (Baltimore, Md.: Johns Hopkins University Press, 2007), 40–42.

345 *Self-help had long been*: Despite a long history among people of diverse political
orientations, including Douglass and Du Bois, some scholars in this period began to
define the self-help idea as an exclusively nationalist idea.

345 *After 1968*: Michael K. Brown, *Race, Money, and the American Welfare State* (Ithaca,
N.Y.: Cornell University Press, 1999), 295–322; John David Skrentny, *The Ironies of
Affirmative Action: Politics, Culture, and Justice in America*, Morality and Society
(Chicago: University of Chicago Press, 1996), 178–82. Also see Kevin L. Yuill, *Richard
Nixon and the Rise of Affirmative Action: The Pursuit of Racial Equality in an Era of
Limits*, American Intellectual Culture (Lanham, Md.: Rowman and Littlefield Pub-

lishers, Inc., 2006); and Dean J. Kotlowski, *Nixon's Civil Rights: Politics, Principle, and Policy* (Cambridge, Mass.: Harvard University Press, 2001).

345 *Gray burst*: Jackson, *From Civil Rights to Human Rights*, 214–17. Also see "'I Never Met a Black Person Who Was in the Communist Party Because of the Soviet Union': Jack O'Dell on Fighting Racism in the 1940s," interviewed by Sam Sills, August 5, 1993, www.historymatters.gmu.edu/d/6927/, retrieved July 6, 2009.

346 *legal assault on landlord practices*: Sugrue, *Sweet Land of Liberty*, 402–10.

346 *In March 1960, Sullivan convened*: Matthew Countryman, *Up South: Civil Rights and Black Power in Philadelphia*, Politics and Culture in Modern America (Philadelphia: University of Pennsylvania Press, 2006), 101–108; Sugrue, *Sweet Land of Liberty*, 126–29.

346 *Among them was King's SCLC*: Sugrue, *Sweet Land of Liberty*, 129.

347 *With their emphasis on industrial training*: See Leon Howard Sullivan, *Alternatives to Despair* (Valley Forge, Pa.: Judson Press, 1972), 88.

347 *by the early 1970s, Sullivan*: Countryman, *Up South*, 112–17.

347 *Ironically, Philadelphia industries*: Ibid., 56.

348 *jobs migrating to the suburbs*: William J. Wilson, *The Declining Significance of Race: Blacks and Changing American Institutions*, 2nd ed. (Chicago: University of Chicago Press, 1980), 93.

348 *The racial asymmetry of Philadelphia*: Countryman, *Up South*, 53. For documentation of the rise of inner black cores and white outer rings in other major cities, see Douglas S. Massey and Nancy A. Denton, *American Apartheid: Segregation and the Making of the Underclass* (Cambridge, Mass.: Harvard University Press, 1993), 42–49, 67. Also see William H. Frey, "Black In-Migration, White Flight, and the Changing Economic Base of the Central City," *American Sociological Review* 85 (1980): 1396–417; and Frey, "Central City White Flight: Racial and Nonracial Causes," *American Sociological Review* 44 (1979): 425–48.

348 *Recognizing the federal government's*: This was Executive Order No. 11063. Massey and Denton, *American Apartheid*, 189–90. For a detailed description of federal policies that promoted housing discrimination, see David M. P. Freund, *Colored Property: State Policy and White Racial Politics in Suburban America*, Historical Studies of Urban America (Chicago: University of Chicago Press, 2007), 99–134, 158–63, 179–97. For a contemporary analysis, see Weaver, *The Urban Complex*, 61.

348 *the government's own decisions*: For an example of challenges to public housing built in Chicago ghettos in August 1966, see Brian Joe Lobley Berry, *The Open Housing Question: Race and Housing in Chicago, 1966–1976* (Cambridge, Mass.: Ballinger Publishing Co., 1979).

348 *Remedies for racial discrimination in housing*: Massey and Denton, *American Apartheid*, 191–92.

348 *In May 1961, there was a "Freedom Ride"*: Jackson, *From Civil Rights to Human Rights*, 136–37.

348 *Chicagoans had also engaged in protests*: Chicago's previous battles over open housing took place in Cicero, Deerfield, and Trumbull Park in the mid-1950s. See Green, *Selling the Race*, 184–90; Arnold R. Hirsch, *Making the Second Ghetto: Race and Housing in Chicago, 1940–1960*, Historical Studies of Urban America (Chicago: The University of Chicago Press, 1998), 212–58; Sugrue, *Sweet Land of Liberty*.

349 *After renting a small apartment*: Sugrue, *Sweet Land of Liberty*, 419.

349 *In the wake of his death*: Massey and Denton, *American Apartheid*, 195–96.
349 *As one careful survey*: Quote in ibid., 11. There were, however, a number of con-
     trolled integration projects that prescribed the neighborhood's careful selection of a
     limited number of black settlers with similar class profiles as their white neighbors.
     Sugrue, *Sweet Land of Liberty*, 421–22; Camille Henderson Zorich, "Black vs. White?
     Reexamining Residential Transition in the Chicago Metropolitan Area: Oak Park,
     1960–1979" (Ph.D. Thesis, University of Chicago, 2005).
349 *In 1980, Chicago remained the most segregated city in America*: It was followed, in
     descending order, by Cleveland, Detroit, Milwaukee, and New York. See Massey and
     Denton, *American Apartheid*, table 7.1, p. 203. For an astute account of developments
     in Detroit, see Thomas J. Sugrue, *The Origins of the Urban Crisis: Race and Inequal-
     ity in Postwar Detroit* (Princeton, N.J.: Princeton University Press, 1996), 231–71.
349 *Suburbs, shopping malls, and highways*: For the federal role in initiating these devel-
     opments, see Freund, *Colored Property*, 99–139.
349 *white racial reactionaries . . . a new voice*: For details on how conservatives re-
     grouped, see MacLean, *Freedom Is Not Enough*, 225–61.
350 *By 1961, blacks made up 40 to 73 percent*: Sugrue, *Sweet Land of Liberty*, 383.
350 *Born into an Arkansas sharecropping family*: Nick Kotz and Mary Lynn Kotz, *A Pas-
     sion for Equality: George A. Wiley and the Movement*, 1st ed. (New York: Norton,
     1977), 219–21; and Felicia Kornbluh, *The Battle for Welfare Rights: Politics and Pov-
     erty in Modern America* (Philadelphia: University of Pennsylvania Press, 2007), 28–38.
     See also obituary at www.nytimes.com/1995/11/27/us/johnnie-tillmon-blackston
     -welfare-reformer-dies-at-69.html, accessed July 7, 2009.
351 *Johnnie Tillmon's organization*: Sugrue, *Sweet Land of Liberty*, 386–90; Kotz and Kotz,
     A Passion for Equality, 221–37, 307–10. Kornbluh, *The Battle for Welfare Rights*,
     58–62.
351 *Goldberg v. Kelly*: Sugrue, *Sweet Land of Liberty*, 393.
351 *a full-scale attack against welfare*: Skrentny, *The Ironies of Affirmative Action*, chap.
     7; Jill S. Quadagno, *The Color of Welfare: How Racism Undermined the War on
     Poverty* (New York: Oxford University Press, 1994), 117–27; Sugrue, *Sweet Land of
     Liberty*, 396–97.
352 *Thus, although NWRO achieved reforms*: Brown, *Race, Money, and the American Wel-
     fare State*, 295–354.
352 *By almost every measure*: 16.4 percent of black males held middle-class jobs in 1950;
     35.3 percent did in 1970. Wilson, *The Declining Significance of Race*, 129.
352 *The nation's economic growth rate*: Barry Bluestone and Bennett Harrison, *The Dein-
     dustrialization of America: Plant Closings, Community Abandonment, and the Dis-
     mantling of Basic Industry* (New York: Basic Books, 1982), 17; Bluestone, foreword in
     Cowie, *Beyond the Ruins*, vii–viii.
352 *In 1947, more than half the nation's labor force*: Wilson, *The Declining Significance of
     Race*, 93–94.
352 *By 1960, almost one of every eight American workers*: Ibid., table 9, p. 103; 12.1 percent
     of all workers were employed by the government in 1960, and 16.1 percent in 1970.
     While 13.3 percent of all employed blacks held government jobs in 1960, 21.4 percent
     did so by 1970.
353 *The pattern accelerated thereafter*: In some cities, much of the early postwar growth
     may have been in the postal service, which had been a source of federal employ-

ment for blacks since the nineteenth century. In 1949, the postal service was the largest single employer of blacks in New York City, for example. Martha Biondi, *To Stand and Fight: The Struggle for Civil Rights in Postwar New York City* (Cambridge, Mass.: Harvard University Press, 2003), 140.

353 *The job categories*: Gerald David Jaynes, Robin Murphy Williams, and the National Research Council, Committee on the Status of Black Americans, *A Common Destiny: Blacks and American Society* (Washington, D.C.: National Academy Press, 1989), 165, 169, 170, table 4.1, p. 165; Clergy were just 1 percent in 1980; but had been 10 percent in 1940.

353 *sources of black income*: Sugrue, *Sweet Land of Liberty*, 505.

353 *No doubt Simon Owens*: Note that 14.4 percent of all employed union members were black as compared with just 10.0 percent of all employed workers, and 27.2 percent and 19.3 percent in 1983 of blacks and whites, respectively, were members of unions. Jaynes, Williams, and the National Research Council, Committee on the Status of Black Americans, *A Common Destiny*, 88.

353 *The nation's economic boom*: Bluestone and Harrison, *The Deindustrialization of America*, 17; GDP growth in the 1970s averaged 2.9 percent per year, and typically a family's income increased by just 7 percent. Barry Bluestone, foreword in *Beyond the Ruins: The Meanings of Deindustrialization*, eds. Jefferson R. Cowie and Joseph Heathcott (Ithaca, N.Y.: ILR Press, 2003), viii. See also Frank B. Woodford and Arthur M. Woodford, *All Our Yesterdays: A Brief History of Detroit*, A Savoyard Book (Detroit: Wayne State University Press, 1969), 356.

353 *Detroit had lost 140,000 workers*: Sugrue, *Sweet Land of Liberty*, 307.

353 *retail operations moved*: Bluestone and Harrison, *The Deindustrialization of America*, 33.

353 *Between 1969 and 1976*: By contrast, the Sunbelt gained 5.5 million jobs during this period. Ibid., table 2.1, p. 30. Barry Bluestone and Bennett Harrison, *Capital and Communities: The Causes and Consequences of Private Disinvestment* (Washington, D.C.: Progressive Alliance, 1980), tables 4 and 5, pp. 38, 40. J. W. Harrington and Barney Warf, *Industrial Location: Principles, Practice, and Policy* (London; New York: Routledge, 1995), 137.

353 *In a single year, between January 1979 and December 1980*: Bluestone and Harrison, *The Deindustrialization of America*, 36.

354 *During the decade 1957–67, a third*: Ibid., 42.

354 *Meanwhile, Philadelphia's largest employer*: Countryman, *Up South*, 62–63.

354 *A relatively recent creation itself*: Dalton Conley, *Being Black, Living in the Red: Race, Wealth, and Social Policy in America* (Berkeley: University of California Press, 1999), 25–27.

355 *The vast majority of black Americans missed out*: Ibid.

355 *The situation of those in white-collar occupations*: Ibid., 57–63, 138–52.

356 *As diverse public opinion polls made clear*: Michael C. Dawson, *Black Visions: The Roots of Contemporary African-American Political Ideologies* (Chicago: University of Chicago Press, 2001), esp. 255–80. Also see 2008 pre-election poll for more on racial differences in worldview. "Poll: October 25–29, 2008," *New York Times*.

356 *Precedents for the idea of making special*: Manning Marable, "Staying on the Path to Racial Equality," in *The Affirmative Action Debate*, eds. George E. Curry and Cornel West (Reading, Mass.: Addison-Wesley, 1996), 4–5; also the Philadelphia Commis-

sion on Human Relations (CHR) demanded affirmative action of employers. Countryman, *Up South* , 67–68.

356 *Similar language can be found*: Jackson, *From Civil Rights to Human Rights*, 126.

356 *In September 1965, President Lyndon B. Johnson*: Linda Faye Williams, "Tracing the Politics of Affirmative Action," in Curry and West, eds., *The Affirmative Action Debate*, 214–57.

357 *With the advent of . . . social programs*: The idea of addressing structural roots is also found in speeches in 1962 by Whitney Young and Martin Luther King, Jr., for example. Jackson, *From Civil Rights to Human Rights*, 136–37.

357 *Given this interpretation*: Williams, "Politics of Affirmative Action," 246.

357 *Given an economy that resembled a zero-sum game*: Ibid., 246–48. Affirmative action was extended to colleges and universities in 1972.

357 *Ironically, the agent*: For a discussion of Nixon's policy that emphasizes electoral and policy motivations, see Skrentny, *The Ironies of Affirmative Action*.

357 *His "Philadelphia Plan"*: For a detailed exposition of the formation of Nixon's policy, see MacLean, *Freedom Is Not Enough*, 96–103. Also see Williams, "Politics of Affirmative Action"; Marable, "Staying on the Path to Racial Equality," 7; Sugrue, *Sweet Land of Liberty*, 506; Skrentny, *The Ironies of Affirmative Action*.

357 *Height and other physical requirements*: A survey in 1964, for example, found that only 1.3 percent of blacks held apprenticeships in firms with government contracts. Jaynes, Williams, and the National Research Council, Committee on the Status of Black Americans, *A Common Destiny*, 87.

358 *Constitution was "color-blind"*: For a masterful dissection of this argument and a description of its evolution, see MacLean, *Freedom Is Not Enough*, 225–61.

358 *Reagan's administration*: Williams, "Politics of Affirmative Action," 249, 250.

359 *They were far more likely to find themselves in a prison yard*: On the growth of the black prison population, and equal opportunities in the military, see Jaynes, Williams, and the National Research Council, Committee on the Status of Black Americans, *A Common Destiny*, 460–64. In the long, post-emancipation history of the criminalization of black males, see Khalil Gibran Muhammad, *The Condemnation of Blackness: Race, Crime, and the Making of Modern Urban America* (Cambridge, Mass.: Harvard University Press, 2010). On the late twentieth-century growth of prisons, see Eric Schlosser, "The Prison-Industrial Complex," *Atlantic Monthly* (Dec. 1998); Marc Mauer, *Race to Incarcerate* (New York: New Press, 1999), 118–61; and Marie Gottschalk, *The Prison and the Gallows: The Politics of Mass Incarceration in America* (Cambridge, Mass.: Cambridge University Press, 2006), 197–215.

359 *"the first large wave of Africans . . ."*: Quote in Barack Obama, *Dreams from My Father: A Story of Race and Inheritance* (New York: Three Rivers Press, 2004), 9.

360 *Black America's undeniable political progress*: Sugrue, *Sweet Land of Liberty*, 501; cf. Jaynes, Williams, and the National Research Council, Committee on the Status of Black Americans, *A Common Destiny*, 15. By 1988 there were 6,800 black elected officials nationally, but this still constituted just 1.5 percent of the national total. The growth in black political participation (as measured by voting, party conventions, etc.) was roughly comparable, plus or minus 60 percent, respectively.

360 *black students found on Ivy League*: Douglas S. Massey, "Black Immigrants and Black Natives Attending Selective Colleges and Universities in the United States," *American Journal of Education* 113, no. 2 (Feb. 2007), 243–71.

360 *The explosive growth of black political representation*: David R. Colburn, "Running for Office: African-American Mayors from 1967 to 1996," in *African-American Mayors: Race, Politics, and the American City*, eds. David R. Colburn and Jeffrey S. Adler (Urbana: University of Illinois Press, 2001), 23–56.

361 *Although his campaigns failed*: There had been earlier presidential efforts, by Julian Bond in 1968 and Shirley Chisolm in 1972, but these were generally symbolic gestures with little expectation of success. Jackson's campaigns began as protests but became serious after good showings in early primaries. In 1998, General Colin Powell gained substantial support for the Republican nomination, before declining to run.

361 *All of these electoral successes*: Euphoria was dampened by the fact that each candidate lost a majority of the white vote.

362 *he won the votes of whites*: Most striking was Obama's clear victory over McCain in Levittown, Pennsylvania. See Michael Sokolove, "The Transformation of Levittown," *New York Times*, Nov. 9, 2008, www.nytimes.com/2008/11/09/weekinreview/09sokolove.html/, retrieved Nov. 9, 2008.

362 *Obama won*: For a vote breakdown, see "Election Results, 2008," *New York Times*, November 5, 2008, www.elections.nytimes.com/2008/results/president/exit-polls.html/.

364 *there is creative space*: Thomas C. Holt, "The Political Uses of Alienation: W.E.B. Du Bois on Politics, Race and Culture, 1903–1940," *American Quarterly* 42 (June 1990), 100–15.

ACKNOWLEDGMENTS

Undertaking a project of this scope and duration means that one necessarily incurs an immense debt to friends and strangers, to persons and
institutions that one can probably never fully repay. Hopefully the book
itself will be accepted as a small installment. As with most debts, the
most recent generally loom larger in one's memory than the earliest. The
gracious efficiency of staff at various archives and libraries has greatly
eased the final preparations of this book, especially as I sought to locate
and secure permission to publish illustrations. I am grateful to Kenneth
Johnson in the photoduplication department at the Library of Congress
and to Glenn Humphries in Special Collections at the Chicago Public
Library. Fellow historians Christopher R. Reed, emeritus professor at
Roosevelt University, and Ted Rosengarten at South Carolina have been
extraordinarily generous with their time and resources, loaning me images out of their personal files. Similarly, during these hectic final weeks,
I have benefited enormously from the generosity of Chris Winters, of the
University of Chicago Library's Map Collection, and Dale Mertes, of the
university's Digital Laboratory. Chris guided me through the intricacies of
ArcGIS map production, and Dale refined and polished my crude results
for publication. Their respective interventions came at a moment of despair upon finding that suitable historical maps simply didn't exist.

First among my longtime creditors are my many students, present and
past, undergraduate and graduate, including those now well launched on
careers of their own. The ideas and formulations in this book were first
tested in graduate and undergraduate classes at the University of Chicago. After that came the task of searching out and marshaling the sources
that documented those intellectual formulations and insights—all of which

would have taken a lot longer had I not enjoyed the assistance of numerous wonderful student researchers over the past decade. Among them was Jon White, a University of Maryland student recommended to me by Ira Berlin; I had never met Jon, but he undertook for me a timely preliminary search of the military service and pension files at the National Archives. Among those I know very well, there are no doubt some who will be surprised to see their names listed here, since in some cases their labors predated the inception of this particular book project. Nonetheless, A. J. Aiséirithe, Elizabeth Dale, Steve Essig, Laurie Green, and Hannah Rosen all did some of the crucial preliminary research that made taking on this project seem plausible. In a few cases the influence that their subsequent intellectual labors have had on me are evident in the endnotes of this volume.

My intellectual debt to Molly Hudgens and Elizabeth Wood will not be found in those endnotes, but the extraordinary research skills and diligence of each of them have greatly enriched this text. Indeed, there are paths I might not have explored to the depths that I did without Molly's persistence and "nose for sources," and it is impossible to imagine what bringing this project to a close would have been like without the absolute determination and reliability of Betsy Wood chasing down every last footnote and source.

Friends and colleagues have sustained me in this work throughout. As usual, my first reader was Leora Auslander, whose interventions emerged not only from reading various drafts as they flew off the printer but in long, sometimes tangential conversations that subtly shaped my prose as well as my thinking. Rebecca Scott has been a friend and intellectual comrade for more years than either of us wishes to count, and she never fails to be equally generous with her time and astute in her commentary. Ira Berlin, Fred Cooper, Laurent Dubois, Jim Grossman, William McFeely, Julie Saville, Frank "Mickey" Schubert, Mark Schultz, Jim Sparrow, J. Mills Thornton, Nan Woodruff, and Jean-Claude Zancarini have all generously taken time to read one or more of these chapters. Their expertise has not only saved me from many errors of fact and judgment but provided encouragement that my efforts were worthwhile. Needless to say, I alone am responsible for any errors or infelicities that remain. Or almost alone. Dan Crissman, my editor at Hill and Wang, and Jenna Dolan, my book's copy editor, have admirably formed the final line of defense against error and awkwardness.

Like the army, book writers travel on their stomachs. This book, too, owes its existence to the institutions that enabled its author to keep body and soul together long enough to finish it. The MacArthur Foundation enabled me to take a number of research leaves that facilitated the early stages of my research. The University of Chicago has been generous in its leave policy at crucial moments in this project, for which I thank my former and current deans, Richard Saller and Mark Hansen, respectively, and my former and current department chairs, Kathy Conzen, Prasenjit Duara, and Bruce Cummings. I stole time from a National Endowment for the Humanities fellowship intended to support a study of race-mixture to finish this history. I trust that repayment in a somewhat foreign coin is at least partially acceptable. In any event, I am confident that my deferred study of the broader problem of race in the modern world will benefit from this one having been written first. I must offer a similar I.O.U. to the American Academy in Berlin, which provided intellectual company and financial support during the critical final year of writing. Another institution that is no doubt oblivious to the support it has given this project is the John F. Kennedy Bibliotek of the Freie Universität in Berlin. During extended stays in that wonderful city, the open stack access to English-language resources that the FU has provided me has been an intellectual lifeline.

Finally, I have taken the unusual step of dedicating this book to three people, each of whom has been instrumental in its conception. The late John Hope Franklin was an inspiration and unofficial mentor to me, as he was to generations of students of the African American experience. Some years ago I read a paper celebrating the fiftieth anniversary of his influential historical survey of that experience. In the process I was reintroduced to the power of the first (1947) edition of that text and drawn to its singular vision, at once politically committed and intellectually honest. Few history texts, before or since, have equaled it, but it is a model to which his successors can aspire. Many years ago, I was privileged to hear his eloquent summation of the citizen-scholar's creed, and flatter myself that this effort is at least partly indebted to it: "If one believes in the power of his own words and in the words of others, one must also hope and believe that the world will be a better place by our having spoken or written those words."

I have also dedicated this book to the memory of my late father. Something of the reason for that acknowledgment is discussed in the preface.

Certainly reflections on my father's life have stimulated and shaped both the intellectual content and the sensibilities of this work.

Finally, I dedicate this book to my wife, Leora Auslander. After sharing more than twenty years of both triumph and heartbreak, it seemed about time. But, of course, it is much more than that. From the first, ours has been an intellectual as well as an emotional bond. This dedication acknowledges to the world how much that bond has energized and sustained me. In my darkest moments of self-doubt, it has been *my* fire.

Thomas C. Holt
Chicago

INDEX

Page numbers in *italics* refer to illustrations.